THE
EARTH
CHANGES
SURVIVAL
HANDBOOK

BY
PAGE BRYANT

CORRELATED BY
EVA PRANG

SUN BOOKS
Sun Publishing Company
Santa Fe, N.M.

First Sun Books Publishing.....1983 Oct
Second Sun Books Publishing....1984 Oct
Third Sun Books Publishing.....1986 Aug
Fourth Sun Books Publishing....1987 Mar
Fifth Sun Books Publishing.....1987 Sep
Sixth Sun Books Publishing.....1988 Jul
Seventh Sun Books Publishing...1989 Nov
Eighth Sun Books Publishing....1990 Oct
Ninth Sun Books Publishing.....1992 Aug
Tenth Sun Books Publishing.....1993 Aug
Eleventh Sun Books Publishing..1994 Jun

ILLUSTRATIONS BY SCOTT GUYNAP

SUN BOOKS
Are Published By

Sun Books
Sun Publishing Company
P.O. Box 5588, Santa Fe, N.M. 87502-5588
U.S.A.

ISBN: 0-89540-150-9

TABLE OF CONTENTS

ILLUSTRATIONS

Illustrations by Scott Guynap

—PUBLISHERS STATEMENT—

Not since the publication of J.R. Jochman's "Rolling Thunder: The Coming Earth Changes" has there appeared a book of such magnitude and importance as the "Earth Changes Survival Handbook" by Page Bryant and Albion.

The message is clear: the earth changes are coming, soon, and we had best delay no longer in preparing for them. In fact, as indicated in the book, and apparent in daily news broadcasts, the changes have already begun!

Although this is a lengthy book, and by the author's own admission a sometimes redundant one, it still carries a message and information vital to every man, woman, and child on this planet who wishes to pass thru the Earth Changes relatively unharmed.

If a particular chapter or section begins to feel tedious you may wish to jump to the next chapter and then go back to the section you missed after finishing the rest of the book.

This book is intended as a general information guide and knowledge foundation upon which you may wish to add other material more suitable to your own situation.

Please pass word of this book on to your friends; it may mean a great deal to them, some day soon.

Any comments or suggestions would be appreciated.

Skip Whitson, Publisher

DEDICATION

For Scott, my husband, friend,
and spiritual colleague . . . for his help.

ACKNOWLEDGEMENTS

Many people have been of assistance to me with this work in many different ways. My thanks must go to Helaine McLain for her devotion to both myself and Albion and for her typing of the manuscript. Special thanks goes to Eva Prang and Fred Spinks for their many contributions of time and effort. Thanks also to Lorraine Walton, Ron McLain, Mary Page Bryant, Brad Steiger, Sun Bear, Wabun and the Bear Tribe, Larry Bearson, Alan Holt, Gary Lange, Billie Keropian, and a special thanks to Reverend LeRoy Zemke whose encouragement has been most rewarding throughout my career, and to my husband, Scott Guynup for his love and patience.

9

FOREWORD

This book is a book about the Earth, its beginnings, its evolution, its problems and its karmic responsibilities. The writing had its birth at the urging of my spiritual Teacher, whom I call Albion. I have been an "Instrument" for Albion for twelve years, during which time lessons and information on a wide variety of subjects have been channeled. Also, Albion has worked through me to do spiritual "readings" known as Depth Studies, as well as being a constant source of guidance and strength on a purely personal level to myself and my loved ones.

Albion has never talked much about himself, he seems more interested in sharing what he feels is more important information. But when asked in the past, he has stated that he has lived on the Earth twice, once on Atlantis, as an astronomer, and once on the Isle of Crete, as a Teacher in a "Mystery School". Myself and others "see" him as a tall, thin, male "Being" who is bearded and who speaks in a rather loud British accent.

Much of this information is channeled material. As often as possible, the Teacher's words have been repeated exactly as they were stated, the only changes being to make complete sentences, punctuate properly and just to generally make the work more readable. The story of Albion's appearance in my life is shared, along with my attempt to preserve "his" way of saying things and "his" own unique personality and identity. I have only filled in the gaps with research.

You will find that two of Albion's students, referred

to simply as A. S. (female) and D. (male) are mentioned throughout the writing and their help was most appreciated.

This book is designed to serve four major purposes:
1. To acquaint you, the Reader, with the planet Earth so that you might become greater allies and friends to one another.
2. To show that the Earth is a living, evolving organism.
3. To show that the "Earth Changes" are a natural part of the planet's growth and how we might take a realistic approach to this truth.
4. To promote survival, on all levels, for we are multi-leveled Beings. Thus, it becomes truly a handbook for this important cycle leading up to the New Age.

Page Bryant
July 16, 1982
Sedona, Arizona

INTRODUCTION
By Brad Steiger

This is an exceedingly fascinating book!

I have known Page Bryant as a friend and as a colleague in the metaphysical field for many years now. When she asked me if I would review her book with the suggestion that I might write an introduction to the contents, I willingly acquiesced as one would for a friend. I knew that she was a serious and gifted psychic-sensitive, so why not see what she had to say.

Let me tell you that Page has a great deal to say about the coming Earth changes and humankind's transformative steps into the future. Although I had anticipated dutifully skimming the book so that I might say something nice about the volume, I found myself carefully reading and re-reading section after section.

You see, Page is not merely giving us her psychic impressions; she is not simply recording the channelled messages from her spiritual contact, Albion; she is also documenting the aforementioned subjective material with objective data from hardnosed scientists. *THE EARTH CHANGES SURVIVAL HANDBOOK* is not a book to be taken lightly. There is so much information of a sobering and provocative nature that one must truly seek his or her own heart-mind-guidance to check out how much relates-vibrates with his or her own inner truths.

Francie and I have traveled to so many of the Earth Mother's chakra points that Page discusses, and we have

12

sensed those same powerful emanations which she describes so well. As a guidebook for those who wish to accomplish similar spiritual odysseys to these holy places, the careful charting recorded by Page will serve as an invaluable guide and reference volume.

Practical advice on survival in the troubled times which lie ahead is carefully delineated, and here the author quotes a great deal from the wise Medicine person, Sun Bear, and other members of the Bear Tribe.

This is a valuable book. We are fortunate, indeed, that Page Bryant has seen fit to share it with us.

Brad Steiger
Scottsdale, Arizona

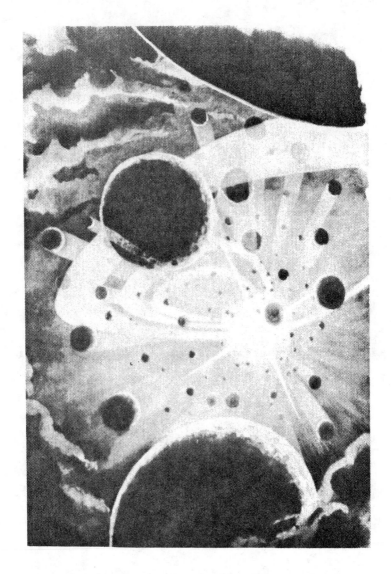

Creative Explosion

CHAPTER ONE

IN THE BEGINNING . . .

"The Earth was created by the assistance of the Sun and it should be left as it was . . . it is no man's business to divide it."   *-Chief Joseph*

The Earth is a "Pilgrim", weaving its way through time and space in what far too many of us believe is but a mute and aimless existence. You are a "pilgrim", living your life upon this small speck in the Cosmos, perhaps sometimes feeling your purpose and place in the Cosmic scheme of things is just as aimless, yet "knowing" somehow that it is not. At this very moment, with the Earth as your spacecraft, you are being propelled through space at the incredible speed of 20 kilometers per second! The galaxy in which the Earth resides is moving at 871,000 kilometers per hour! Man and his planet, the planet and its galaxy, rushing towards destiny, a destiny that is assured.

Since the dawn of prehistory man has wondered about the world upon which we live; its origin, its destiny..

. . his origin, his destiny. Both ancient and modern man have pondered questions concerning the nature of creation, the source of life, the structure of matter, his relationship with the other kingdoms, life on other planets and the destiny of all forms. Time has seen man rise from a primitive state to his present status as a technological giant, and all of this has occurred in a relatively short span of time. According to myths and legends of the past, this cycle of physical and intellectual evolution has been repeated many times as humanity has carved out a "parasitical" existence on planet Earth. He has inched his way across the vast oceans and scaled the highest peaks so that he could familiarize himself with this piece of rock he calls Home. History reminds us of our accomplishments and failures in a dim past while NASA's planetary probes are racing through the Solar System to examine alien worlds. Space shuttles are now marking the beginning of a freedom we have never known before. All of these are giant steps toward a future that promises to be richer in hopes and mysteries far beyond our wildest dreams. Man and his planet seem to be intertwined in a "cosmic dance" of celestial and human powers that are shaping the destiny of both.

"Intertwined" is a revealing term. As we stand on the Earth and look out into the night sky, we become aware that amidst all of our material securities, of which the planet itself is often the least considered as being a part, that we are a minute part of a huge galaxy of suns approximately 250 billion strong! That in itself is mind-boggling, until we stop to think that we are part of only one galaxy and that it is estimated by modern astronomers that there are 100 billion other galaxies in the universe!

How did it all begin? How did this ball of rocks and dirt come to revolve around an ordinary star in an ordinary galaxy located in the suburbs of the cosmos? What is the Earth made of? Could it be that the appearance of life on the planet was an act of Divine Will or was it an accident of Cosmic proportions?

Modern scientists have now taken on the task that once belonged to the philosophers and mystics alone. Since the days when the "star" pupil of Plato's Academy set a pattern of thinking that lasted 2,000 years, things have changed. That pupil was Aristotle. Aristotle's reasoning placed the Earth at the center of the universe and our position and existence was one of greater importance to the vast scheme of things as a result. However, physicists have now developed a much different model of the universe and one that surely would have frustrated Aristotle, but it might have taught him a thing or two! One might quickly jump to defend Aristotle's theories, considering the fact that he was at a disadvantage, living before technology was born. He did all right as a "thinker," all things considered. His thoughts were born under the "truths" of his observations, which he coupled with his reasoning powers. He must have stretched his intellect to the limit! Though such a response of defense might be valid to a point, I think it is more important that we look at the position Aristotle, and other philosophers like him, held over the masses. They considered him to be a qualified source of information and truth and his theories were not challenged for a long time. This serves to point out that we have a need not to be too quick to draw our conclusions or to accept, unconditionally, the conclusions of others. But can we afford to question theories and their effect on our lives? Certainly non-truth can survive a long time and can delay our progress towards a continued and truer understanding of the universe in which we live.

The masses have not changed. Collectively, we are perhaps as vulnerable to a higher "authority" for our truth, just as were the people of Aristotle's day, and we are just as afraid or apathetic about theories of the universe's behavior as the general public of any time in history. Only the methodology has changed. The way in which we gather our knowledge has advanced. It is no longer dependent on the eyes only for observation.

We have developed sophisticated equipment that can "see" out into deep space, farther than any eyes or mind on the Earth have previously imagined. The birth of modern radio astronomy, for example, has given man "ears" to listen to the Universe, at least in our own general vicinity. We now have computers that can reduce photographs of entire galaxies far distant from us, which were not even known to exist until this century, into color codes which reveal their physical make-up. All this, coupled with the interplanetary travel of recent times, has served to broaden our view of the Cosmos and the Solar System of which we are a part. Although it is not the task of science to go beyond a physical examination and interpretation of nature, the theories that have come to us through the minds of scientists cannot help but make us more curious, if nothing else. In order to gain a better knowledge of these up-to-date scientific "wisdoms" that attempt to explain the origins of Nature and matter, let us first go back in our thoughts to some of the more ancient ideas on the subject.

The archaic Egyptians believed that creation began when the lotus flower gave birth to the Sun-God, Amon-Ra, on the surface of a primordial ocean. Amon-Ra had three children: two boys, Shu and Keb and a girl, Nut. Shu found his brother and sister confined and tangled in a web of Chaos and tried to conceive of a way to correct this unfortunate situation. He soon decided to lift the body of Nut high up, leaving Keb stretched far below. Thus, Nut became the sky, Keb, the Earth, and Shu, the air that separated them.

We also have the biblical account of Creation, which is familiar to most of us, especially in the western world. Genesis describes a sort of "anthropomorphic" God, who fashioned the firmament in seven days. The heavens and the Earth, all of the various kingdoms of life, including man, were made by the Supreme Being. Many of us have come to accept and understand this allegory given to explain the creation, while still others accept the Genesis account quite literally!

There are many other ancient sources that speak of how it all began, some that use abstract terminology, such as with the East Indian Vedas, and others that indicate a more mythological theme, as with the ancient Greeks. Such stories of the beginning of time and matter have had both religious and philosophical value, right through to the present day.

Let us take a look at our beginning through the eyes and intellects of a more modern perspective: present day science. Since the views of Aristotle, which placed the Earth at the center of everything, science has progressed man into many changes of belief. Maybe the whole process of mental evolution has moved to a point where man now has a greater need to know. His questions have become more complex. He groped for answers. Up until the late 1940's, a theory that represented a "perfect cosmological model", was heralded as *the* big advancement in science. It involved an assumption, as most theories must, that underlies the model of the Universe we accept even now. It states that no universal model could be prescribed without assumptions, as they are the starting point for any hypothesis. We must assume then, based on observation and data, that the observed phenomenon is true. Then, we base our theories on these "assumptions" to describe the appearance of the Universe and its behavior. We must also assume that observations made by science apply to the entire Cosmos and not just the part of it we can see. The observable universe must represent the same or similar view to observers anywhere in space. There is no evidence to support any different idea. So, one part is akin to all other parts. This is the "Cosmological Principle".

One of the first cohesive theories to come on the scene and make a definite statement about the actual birth of matter was authored by three men in the 1940's, all of whom were well-respected in the fields of Cosmology and Astrophysics: Hermann Bondi, Thomas Gold and Fred Hoyle. Their "Steady-State" theory required only one assumption, the "Cosmological Principle". With the Universe assumed to be the same everywhere, then it must be realized that this would imply that if you could become a traveler into the future or the past, you would find that everything would have the same general appearance in the Universe. Nothing has changed with time. In order to insure the validity of their Steady-State hypothesis, Bondi, Gold, and Hoyle responded to the principle by expounding upon the continuity of matter in this perpetual state. New matter was described as springing into existence spontaneously, thus filling the gaps left by a constantly expanding Universe. This description led to their theory being referred to as the "Continuous Creation" theory as well. Even though their thoughts gained in favor with many scientists and its authors became famous, there were still those who felt that matter could not be created out of "nothing". They felt that the Steady-State strongly suggested some "unspoken" Diety to account for the spontaneous appearance of new matter or it led scientists into the field of miracles. Neither is a part of the scientific procedure. One of the men got wind of the criticism which caused him to point out that it shouldn't be difficult to accept the trio's answer for matter's birth, for the fact that matter exists to begin with is miraculous! The Steady-State did have two very important things going for it. It took a stand which gave all thinking people a new "mental rack" for them to hang their hats on in considering its predictions about the behaviour of the Universe. Secondly, it appealed to the philosophically-minded, for it spoke of the "eternal" nature of things and it was also easy to understand. Perhaps that appealed to the layman more than anything. It suggested that matter came out of nothing. It said that fresh hydrogen, the most abundant element in the Universe, would continuously provide the ingredients for new suns to replace the old. Such a hypothesis could easily have been called the Alpha-Omega Theory.

In the early 1900's, a man came along that stands

alone thus far, as the most brilliant scientist of our century. His thoughts and subsequent theories changed our views of the Universe drastically. His theory of Special Relativity, proposed in 1905, deals with high-speed motion or relativistic speeds (speed of light) and General Relativity, proposed in 1915, that deals with gravity. It is said that Einstein "rewrote" the laws of gravity entirely!

For a long time after their appearance on the scene, the German scientist's views were considered too abstract and difficult to comprehend. But time, experiments and technological discoveries have changed all of that, and Einstein and his work have become "monuments" in the scientific fields of physics and astronomy. Mankind is truly indebted to Einstein for advancement far beyond the call of duty for any mind. He made the Cosmos make sense.

Einstein's work gave rise to a theory that has all but taken the place of the Steady-State. It is known as the"Big Bang". It suggests that all matter "exploded" into being which began the expansion of the Universe some 18 billion years ago. Aside from suggesting that the Cosmos has a finite age, it also indicates that all galaxies are rushing away from each other at enormous speeds; relativistic speed! Relativistic speed, the speed of light (186,000 miles per second), was also brought to the world's attention by Albert Einstein, and it turned the world of physics up on its head! Such movement also provides the assertion that all galaxies are aging and evolving together. It allows the total mass of the Universe to be constant and that no new matter is being formed at all. The Big Bang suggests that all matter must have been "lumped" together at some time, since it is now seen as expanding. When this exploded matter cooled and condensed, it formed the planets, stars and galaxies. The Big Bang, originally authorized by physicist George Gamow and a Catholic priest, L'maite, proved by Einstein, purports that the Universe began its existence at an extremely high density and temperature as a single droplet of matter. It could be compared to a sort of "Primordial Egg". Various internal pressures inside the hot droplet, containing all ingredients of matter and radiation, caused it to expand extremely rapidly. This rapid expansion caused the temperature to drop, along with the pressure. The components of matter: protons, electrons, and neutrons, had their birth in this manner. The expansion caused by the initial explosion continued, cooling took place and the particles fused into form. All of the 92 known elements formed in this way in the first half-hour in the life of the infant Universe.

The Big Bang has gained a lot of followers and is the primary hypothesis for the birth of the universe amongst scientists today. Although there are still some serious questions regarding the theory, it has yet to be challenged to the point of proving it wrong. When the Big Bang was first purported as an explanation for the birth of matter, Gamow suggested that there should be remnants of the explosion, if it did indeed occur. That evidence should, in fact, be floating about in space in the form of wavelengths, and it would have to be far out in space due to the continual expansion. Also, an important fact presented by Einstein that is wise to bear in mind when viewing the Universe, is that when we look into space, we are looking back into time. This again is due to the expansion that goes on even now.

In 1965, two Bell Telephone scientists, A. A. Penzias and R. R. Wilson, were trying desperately to determine the source of some noise in their radio antenna. They were disturbed over these signals which were causing interfering "background" noise on long distance telephone calls. The strange cloud seemed to be coming from all directions. It was soon determined that the noise must be coming from outer space, since no other cause could be found. The world of science was excited about the discovery, and it was interpreted to be the "background radiation" from the original Big Bang! This made a major contribution to the credibility of the

Big Bang theory and has caused the virtual dismissal of the Steady-State theory of Hoyle, Bondi and Gold.

The Big Bang may or may not be correct. But it does enjoy the "limelight" at this time. Let's review. It says that the Universe had a violent birth, will have a continual life of expansion, and will suffer a violent death of some sort of the celestial matter within it. Science, at least for the time being, seems satisfied with this script. The only major question that still remains unanswered is the end of the "Cosmic drama". If the Universe exploded into being, when and how will it all end? Will it end? These may turn out to be the most perplexing questions of all.

As with many questions that science attempts to answer, there is a controversy that has yet to be resolved. It has only been in the last year or so that any real evidence has come in that may prove to eventually solve the problem of the "death" of the Universe. When we ask questions about the birth, we must question the death, and often they prove to be the same. Ideas ranging from the eternal Universe of the Steady-State, to the infinite expansion of the Big Bang, have been offered by various thinkers in the field of Cosmology.

The only real theory that has evolved, and it is proven fact, is that we know the Universe is growing. It is expanding. Spatial bodies are moving away from each other. But will this always be the case? If so, we live in an "open" Universe and it will never die! It isn't quite that clear cut in the minds of some, however. Many favor the opposite view, which would have the Universe lose its state of immortality. The "Oscillating" theory "closes" the Cosmos into an endlessly repeated phenomenon of expansion and contraction. You see, of the known forces, gravity is the weakest. But, in an oscillating Universe, gravity becomes the strongest. As the expansion continues, matter will slow down all the time, due to a loss of thrust gained during the initial explosion. It is theorized that as the slowing down occurs, it will reach a point that the pressure of gravity will overcome the racing galaxies and cause them to eventually draw back together! The Big Bang reversed! The implications of either an open or closed Cosmos are many.

In Walter Sullivan's book, entitled *Black Holes*, he speculates about the various implications of the expansion being reversed. He speaks of the possible phenomenon of time reversing, for time is a part of the question. The picture that is painted is one that almost seems more humorous than one we can readily imagine. With time moving backwards, he suggests that we might stand in front of a fire to cool ourselves. Stars might be heated from "infalling" radiation as opposed to their own internal heat! While such concepts are mere speculation, and do seem highly unlikely at least to our imaginations, the questions of what an imploding Universe would really be like still remain. The only real agreement that has been reached thus far is that the results of a closed Universe is one of the real puzzles of science.

One source of reference that may shed some light on this subject of the general behavior of the Cosmos, as well as its birth and death, lies in the pages of *The Secret Doctrine* of Madame Helena P. Blavatsky. H. P. B., as she was known to her friends and colleagues, was a Russian-born occultist whose controversial life was well-publicized. Blavatsky spent her life travelling all over the world seeking knowledge of the Universe, how it came into existence, and what has transpired since. She was also very interested in how it will all end as well. Her monumental work, *The Secret Doctrine*, published in London in 1888, is considered by her followers to be her greatest literary achievement. H. P. B. engaged in many adventurous travels, coming to America in 1873. It was in New York that she met Colonel William Steele Olcott, an American Lawyer, who was also interested in the Occult. Blavatsky and Olcott, along with others also interested in the laws of Nature, founded the Theosophical Society in 1875, which still exists today. It was designed to unite both eastern and western teachings of the Ancient Wisdoms. Madame Blavatsky had a great desire to enter Tibet, in hopes of gaining access to ancient knowledge of the Universe and its laws, to add to her already incredible occult understandings. Failing in her initial attempt to enter that country, she kept trying, and was finally successful around 1854. She was again in Tibet from 1867 through 1870. During her visits she claims to have seen a collection of archaic manuscripts in the form of palm leaves that had been preserved by a long-forgotten process. H. P. B. realized that the information contained on these unusual pages represented the Cosmos before and after its birth. Although all of the scripts were not interpreted by their curious Russian observer, Blavatsky's partial translation of the available material became her last volumes of work.

The Secret Doctrine of H. P. B. presents a version of Creation that is not unlike the Big Bang of modern science! Terms such as "Fiery whirlwind", "lightning through fiery clouds", and "balls of fire", all suggest a violent or explosive "beginning". However, the real point of interest lies in the fact that Blavatsky's doctrine clearly states that it has all happened before and that the universal "sparks" are but reawakened once again, a reincarnating Cosmos! Light born out of darkness, energies that lay asleep springing once again into activity! *The Secret Doctrine* goes on to explain how such "creation" has occurred before and will occur again, a total of seven times. Periods of manifestation are called "Manvantaras", whereas the period in which all is reabsorbed into non-being are called "Pralaya". Could it be that the Manvantaras and Pralayas of Blavatsky's translation of ancient writings are correct? If so, is it possible that Tibetan mystics who lived thousands of years ago, already knew the answer to the most perplexing and unanswered questions of present-day science? The answer must remain mute until a time that evidence is discovered that will prove *The Secret Doctrine* and all of the proponents of the Oscillating

Universe theory right or wrong.

We may not have to wait as long as we might think. Fairly recently articles began to appear in various scientific publications suggesting that sub-atomic particles, which are the components of matter, do indeed have mass. Since mass signifies both weight and density, it declares their very existence in reality, instead of in our minds and theories of their existence having to go unproven. This might not make much sense to the layman, until one considers that the major argument against the Oscillating Universe theory is that there is not enough matter in the entire Cosmos to cause gravity to take over as the process of expansion gradually slows down. The newest information about the properties of sub-atomic particles and the continued understandings coming from Quantum mechanics, which is the study of the laws of the microscopic worlds where these particles reside, could indicate that the Universe may indeed be like a yo-yo! Only time will tell. It won't be the first time that controversy has been the motivator for finding answers. Nor will it be the first time that the Ancients may not have been as primitive in their understandings of the world in which we live as we might have thought and that they may have had monumental knowledge of that which lies far beyond our world and dimension of reality. Given their lack of technology and the greater ease for research that it provides, that would be quite a mental and spiritual accomplishment! It seems almost ironic that the Ancients may have known what all of our advancements and computers still have yet to reveal.

In our consideration of how creation began, the mind can really be stretched to the limit! We've come a long way toward grasping ideas that contribute to filling the gaps left by time. More than once we have had to turn to legends of the past for hidden clues as to how early man viewed the questions science still struggles over.

While we can pour endlessly over various sources of old and new religious literature for indications, there is little contribution that surpasses the stories of the

Hopi Indians of North America. Contrary to many religions and cultures, the Hopi seemed to have a rather simple approach to it all. Attunement to the Universe can tend to bounce our thoughts back and forth between seeing ourselves, as man, as part of it all, and our role in the ongoing process of evolution. We have become so accustomed to wading through the difficult reading material of both scientific and occult teachings, that many of us simply don't choose to involve ourselves with it. So we tend to go ahead and accept the eastern or western religious versions of Creation and man's subsequent development. The Hopi's account of the beginning of the Universe and life as we know it is beautifully written in story form, simple to read and to understand. It becomes even more useful and exciting to refer to the Hopi legends when we consider that there is more and more concrete evidence to support the antiquity of this tribe of people and their knowledge. The further back we go the more primitive the knowledge becomes, which may well add to the value of the accounts themselves.

The Hopi differ in many ways from other American Indians. The word "Hopi" means peaceful people. They are the western-most of the Pueblo Indians. Pueblo ruins are visible throughout the Southwest, some perched atop flat mesas and others nestled in massive cliffs of rock. The Hopi built their present dwellings on three large mesa tops, situated in the center of what is now the great Navajo Nation. When one stands on the mesas it seems as if one is viewing an alien planet. Vast stretches of desert and volcanic domes dot the barren landscape that spreads out for miles in every direction. One is amazed immediately that these people have somehow managed to eke out a living and grow food in this terrain that seems to defy all limits of fertility.

The Hopi also defy the stereotyped picture we have of Indians in general. While we usually think of tall, red men with feathered war bonnets and painted faces, we encounter something quite different upon meeting

29

a Hopi. They are often short and slight of build, mild-mannered and simple in their dress. Although white man's culture has inched its way into Hopi life, it has done little to disturb the traditional Hopi way. When one gets familiar with these people, the only real evidence of major change is visible in the politics that exist through the activities of the Tribal Council. There is an on-going struggle between the forces of "traditionalism" and "non-traditionalism". Although this struggle is unimportant to most outsiders, it is of paramount importance to the Hopi and others who feel that their religion and age-old lifestyle should be preserved. That becomes more apparent as their legends are studied closely, for they may very well be legends that go far beyond the boundaries of superstition and primitive behavior.

Amongst Indians and non-Indians alike, the Hopi are best known for their elaborate religious ceremonies. Personifications of their gods, known as "kachinas", offer a dramatic idea of the principles of man and the Universe they represent. The Federal Government has attempted to label many of their rituals as "heathen", and still others as dangerous. An example of this is the Snake Dance, a rain invocation that is performed with live reptiles, mostly rattlesnakes. The serpents are gathered ceremoniously and held in the mouth of the Snake Priests, who then turn them loose to carry their messages to the Great Spirit so that precious rain might come down on the dry, cracked land. The feelings of the Hopi regarding their ceremonies run deep. Their determination to keep their way of life has made most attempts by the government and missionaries from various orthodox religions, mostly the Mormons, quite futile. Failures such as this have helped preserve a tradition that may yet prove to be one of the most valuable accounts we have of the past, but the situation is fragile to say the least.

The Hopi myths of the Creation of the Universe and events that have occurred since are rich in content. They couple the beginnings of the Cosmos with their own sequence of events as man has experienced the "growing pains" of the infant Universe and the planet on which he lives.

These legends are commonly known as the Four Worlds of the Hopi. The accounts were exposed for the first time to the world audience through the Book of the Hopi by Frank Waters. The illustrator of the work, White Bear, a Hopi Artist, filled the book with many symbols that show accurate representations of reality as well as the ancestry of these ancient people. A recount of the Four World legends is necessary to demonstrate how detailed and valuable the Hopi version of Creation and the subsequent events just may be to our understanding.

The First World of the Hopi, Tokpela, was created by Tiowa, an obvious aspect of a "Supreme Being". Creation took place in three stages. The first phase, the "time of the dark purple light" speaks of a time that contains no life. The vehicles or forms of life were part of the world but were without the "breath of life" until the second phase, known as the "time of the yellow light". By the third phase or "time of the red light", life forms were completed and began to evolve. The origin of these bodies who dwelled in the "endless space" came from Spider Woman, who fashioned man out of the various colored clays of the Earth. So were created men who were red, yellow, brown and white.

Then we find the first mention of the Earth, as the Hopi related Creation and man to the Earth. North and South poles and Spider Woman were all created by Tiowa. The newly created people began to grow and eventually lost sight of their origin. It is said that they lost the use of the "soft spot on the top of their heads" as a connection to their Source. The spot hardened. This seems to indicate a telepathic type of communication process that was employed by these early people. The loss of a sense of spiritual values caused disagreements and contributed to the destruction of this world. Only a few

31

"good" Hopis were saved, those who adhered to the true ways. Salvation came for the traditional Hopi who were led to the center of the Earth to live with the Ant People. The First World was destroyed by fire.

Topka, the Second World, was a big land that is said to have spread out to the other side of the world. A re-emergence of the underground survivors occurred and the Hopi once again spread all over the globe. They built houses and were separated from the animals. But alas, this new paradise did not last for the people became greedy. A Second World destruction ensued. The Great Spirit, Tiowa, called on the sons of Spider Woman, the North and South Poles to exchange places. This caused the planet to lose its orbital balance and spin wildly out of control, rolling over twice! The world then froze into solid ice. Once again, only the Hopi dedicated to the True Way were spared.

A Third World blossomed into being and was named Kuskura. The people began again. They became city builders. Technology may have had its birth during this time although we think of technology as modern. These ancient people were said to have constructed "shields of hide" and flew them in the air during times of warfare. Perhaps this was the reason that Tiowa once again called for destruction to take place. The Hopi that had not fought with each other and had maintained the true path were placed in hollow reeds that would float, for the Third World was destroyed by water. It is interesting to note here that virtually every qualified source of myths and legend contain an account of an ancient flood. The Navajo, a large tribe of Native Americans that live in the same area as the Hopi in Northeastern Arizona, have a similar flood story. They say that it carved out the Grand Canyon. They believe their people turned into fishes in order to survive. To this day, the elder Navajos will not eat fish for fear that they are eating the spirits of their ancestors.

The Fourth World of the Hopi, our present world, is called Tuwaquachi. The last emergence of the surviving Hopi took place and a spirit known as Masaw was appointed as a "guardian" to this world. Migrations have led the Hopi to settle on First, Second and Third Mesas, where they live to this day. But all may not be well. Hopi prophecy contains repeated warnings to the people as to the necessity of continuing to live the traditional life or further destruction will take place. A close look at the prophecies will be dealt with later in this work.

The Four Worlds of the peaceful people gives a vivid account of Creation and the changes that our planet has endured since time began. This brings our thoughts to the Earth in a very real manner. It would seem that regardless of how the Universe as a whole came into beging, the Earth is the place of our most major concern.

So that we might gain a greater perspective of our planet's place in the Universe, it might be wise to investigate the Earth, its beginnings and development, scientifically. Perhaps this will give us a clue to the validity of the Hopi accounts, as well as other literary documents that refer to the quest.

The most accepted view of the origin of the Earth is that it was formed out of the solar nebula, which was born of interstellar gas and dust and pulled together by the forces of gravity, and grew into our Sun. This slowly rotating gaseous, cloud-like nebula probably began to spin faster, increasing in speed over a long period of time. Spinning caused the gases to condense into a smaller ball which caused the nebular mass to move around the created center. That whirling disk eventually formed the planets, leaving the largest and hottest globule of gas at the center to form the Sun. Other theories have been proposed to explain planetary beginnings, but none has overridden the nebular theory. It is believed that the heat within the inner area of the young Sun would have resulted in evaporation of those particles that were vaporous, leaving the rocky and metallic. These heavier particles constantly being spun around the solar disk collided with each other and bound

33

together forming larger masses. These clumps of matter continued to grow until their size caused them to win out and become bodies in their own right. The young planets continued to suck up the remaining solid chunks in the solar wheel. The grouping of bodies, the "planetary nursery", became our Solar System.

All of the planets that are part of the inner solar system are terrestrial or rocky and metallic, and they include Mercury, Venus, Mars and the Earth. The outer edges of the nebula were much cooler, allowing for the existence of ice particles in addition to terrestrial material. This condensed to form the so-called Jovian group of planets that include Jupiter, Saturn, Uranus and Neptune. These gas giants, especially Jupiter, due to their size and composition, are more like the Sun than a terrestrial planet. There is much speculation about tiny Pluto, most likely a frozen ball at the outer reaches of the known Solar System. A decision has not really been made whether to call Pluto a planet or merely one of the "escaped" moons of Neptune. Also, there may be planets beyond Pluto. Much of the remaining gas and dust inside the solar nebula that did not become part of a planet has been swept by the pressure of light and the solar wind. We have good reason to believe that the Solar System has undergone many changes since its birth, some of which may well have been catastrophic!

Our planet Earth was formed of the secretions from the solar nebula and has continued to grow until it has reached its present size. It is believed that the compression caused during the formation has made the center core of the Earth a molten mass. The Earth's age, based on radiation readings from decaying elements, is assumed to be approximately 4½ billion years old.

Geologists paint us a picture of a core of iron covered by a rocky mantle, and an atmosphere that has been created by the rocks beneath its surface. Heat produced by decay, volcanic activity, and the escape of water, formed the oceans, while the presence of other gasses such as carbon dioxide, nitrogen, oxygen, argon and others combined to form the so-called "greenhouse effect".

Extending far beyond the Earth itself is the planet's magnetic field. Its strength is strongest near the surface and grows weaker as it extends toward the Sun. This magnetic field attracts charged particles which surround the planet as two broad belts, known as the Van Allen Belts. The particles that comprise these belts are believed to come from the solar wind and from upper atmospheric cosmic ray collisions. This magnetically charged field is forever changing, and it is said to have reversed its polarity as many as 171 times in the past 76 million years! This discovery has been found through study of the magnetized iron that leaves a history of the magnetic influences as a permanent record.

The appearance of dry land on the Earth is still a matter of ongoing study. Actually, very little is known of how the Earth arrived at its present state. There is one school of thought that suggests that the young Earth probably melted during its infant stages due to the bombardment it suffered in the last phases of its formation. Another explanation stated that such a melting may have occured because of radiation and heat from decaying substances. Whether the entire planet melted or not still remains a point of disagreement. We do know that parts of it did melt at some point, for were there no melting, the iron contained in rocks would be distributed at random throughout the Earth's interior instead of together in a molten core. Melting would have caused the iron to "fall" to the center, creating a molten core, while lighter rocks "floated" to the surface and formed the continents. The areas between the dry land provided giant valleys which became the oceans. Some believe there was a time of one continent, where all the present land masses fitted together. In time they broke apart and drifted, slamming together causing mountain chains to form. We have no reason to presume that this continental drift occured all at once, but in millions to billions of years. These shifting land masses are called tectonic plates. The movement of these plates creates space for new plates to be formed. Both legend and science offer indications that large land masses once in existence have sunk beneath the sea. Atlantis and Lemuria may be among these.

Once we gain a basic understanding of our Earth's history, as given by the science of geology, we can see how unstable and changeable this planet has been and still is even today. It makes us wonder how the violent beginnings of the Universe could have possibly allowed individual suns to be born, much less tiny planets to revolve around them. The next miracle and perhaps the greatest one of all is how life itself appeared! The mental muscles would welcome a rest and just accept religion's "Supreme Being" as the Creator of life and thus avoid a lot of questions. But in our quest for knowledge we must not leave a stone unturned -- even though that final stone may lead us to Theology's door.

As science seeks to unravel the mystery of life, it may have taken on the most complicated mystery of all. Many pieces of the puzzle are known and time helps to slowly pull them all together.

Perhaps the simplest way to pull them together is with the assistance of Dr. Robert Jastrow'a book, *Red Giants and White Dwarfs.* Jastrow states that "life can appear spontaneously in any favorable planetary environment and evolve into complex beings, provided vast amounts of time are available". Assuming that the Earth is indeed 4½ billion years old, then we can see what Jastrow means by "vast amounts of time". Scientists have to go to many different fields of study in order to gather data that helps to piece together the "life appearance puzzle". We know that no form of life as we know it could have existed on the early Earth, for the "Earth building" processes described earlier are clear indications of this fact.

Theory has it that most primitive life forms would have been fashioned when massive lightning flashes reacted with amino acids and nucleotides to form the most primitive molecules. Attraction would have caused them to stick together forming molecular structures, which became more and more sophisticated. All of this would have taken millions of years. Once the molecules became sufficiently complex, they ceased being mere inorganic matter into being organic life. This process required another long time span. Only now can we really begin to see the role time plays in the process of life. Complex molecules lead to intelligent man as the march of evolution proceeds. The countless myriad forms of life in between only serve to boggle our minds further.

Leaving the confines of the Earth for a moment, let us consider the possibilities of life existing in other parts of the Cosmos. We live on a planet in one of many solar systems in one of the many galaxies. In the multitude of stars that exist in our own Milky Way galaxy alone, it would be unfair to assume that there are no planets rotating around other stars in other solar systems, some larger than our own. Many of these planets could be similar to this Earth. Even being extremely conservative in counting, there could be thousands of planets in this galaxy alone capable of supporting life. Many astronomers consider it to be a "chauvinistic" attitude that life does not exist anywhere else in the Universe. Whether we are alone in this vast expanse of heavenly bodies or merely one of many, either thought is mind-boggling! Many in our present society approach the question of presence of life forms on other planets to be more likely than not. Exobiologists are beginning to gain ground towards establishing the study of such possibilities as a science. Well-known scientist, Carl Sagan, is a leading proponent of this new branch of science. Some groups take another more unconventional approach to this question. Organizations such as Aerial Phenomenon Research Organization and Mutual U.F.O. Network are set up for the purpose of researching reports of "unidentified flying objects". These reports, flourishing worldwide since 1947 have excited thoughts of other worlds, other peoples. A closer look at various types of literature seems to suggest that other cultures have believed that aliens from other planets have visited the Earth. While science does not go that far, it does favor the extra-terrestrial theory. If life has indeed developed elsewhere, it is fair to assume that some of it would be intelligent, to a greater or lesser degree than our own. The age of this galaxy and solar system is not identical to others in the Universe. If intelligent life does thrive in other places, the age differences could definitely account for both infant and advanced extra-terrestrial societies.

Going back to life on its early molecular level, we find that the life-building process is a chemical one. Life appeared on Earth during the first billion years of existence. Simple organisms became the foundation of each kingdom from mineral to man.

There is another theory about how the Earth's population of basic life forms appeared for us to consider, which contradicts the scientific supposition that life evolved from a "primordial soup". In January, 1982, astrophysicist Dr. Armand Delsemme, professor at the University of Toledo in Ohio, proclaimed a growing acceptance of the theory that life was "seeded" by comets hitting the barren Earth billions of years ago! These comets contained the ingredients for life. At the annual meeting of the National Aeronautics and Space Administration's Ames Research Laboratory, Delsemme said that the hypothesis was growing in popularity because much has been learned about the "richness" of life-building amino acids found in space. Scientists at the meeting argued the "how" of the seeding as opposed to the actual validity of the theory itself. Dr. Delsemme explained to the press in an article that appeared in the January 16, 1982, issue of the Phoenix Arizona Republic, that the elements that comprise our bodies are 99.9% of the "life" group, including hydrogen, nitrogen, oxygen and carbon. He explained that these same elements are found in the oceans but not within the planet's interior. He goes on to question how these elements got to the Earth and pointed out that all of these same components are also found in outer space! He explained that huge concentrations of water are found in space, as well as two other precursors of life, formaldehyde and hydrogen cyanide. One of the unanswered questions with the theory is the possibility of linking the molecules to the development of life on Earth and other planets. The question is addressed by comets.

During its various stages of growth it was periodically swept by comet tails which left behind cosmic dust that many believe carried the original basic elements of life. Speculation has it that the dust accounts for the Earth's crust, rich in nitrogen, hydrogen and the other essentials for life. This too would have required vast amounts of time, conceivably accomplished by 100 billion comets in a vast cloud surrounding our Solar System. Delsemme further asks that we consider that the Earth has been in existence for more than 4½ billion years. So life has happened quickly in relationship to the whole span of time involved! Something almost automatic happened but scientists don't know exactly how. Further exploration continues to determine whether or not amino acids, the building blocks of protein, and therefore life, exist in outer space. So far the smaller of these have been found. The continuing advancement of radio astronomy will likely yield more of the amino acid discoveries. Among others, Dr. Delsemme believes that the crucial question concerning the comet seeding theory will be determined within the next twenty years.

Another scientist who is at the cutting edge of the "comet theory" is Sir Fred Hoyle. Hoyle, along with Professor Chandra Wickramsinghe of University College in Cardiff, England, published a book entitled *Lifecloud* in 1978. *Lifecloud* marks a new era in the understanding of the Universe through the theories presented in the work. Both Hoyle and Wickramsinghe accept the knowledge that the basic ingredients of life have existed in spatial dust clouds and that they congregated into ancient comet-sized planetesimal bodies. These bodies struck the Earth and the planet received all the active components that comprise the atmosphere, the oceans and life itself. Life is said to have showered upon the terrestrial surface as living cells!

Although the research goes on, the comet theory continues to gain strength. It is not the first time that comets have captured the spotlight in both scientific and non-scientific literature. Reports about these celestial visitors are to be found in the works of Madame Blavatsky and others. Whether there is any significant relationship to be found in these various references or not, we will be hearing much more about comets as time goes on.

Until the question of how life first began is settled, assuming that some day it will be, we can rely on what is known about the course that evolution on this planet has taken. About 600 million years ago the pace of evolution seemed to quicken and the first hard-bodied corals, starfish, and snails began to appear. Another 200 million years passed as life differentiated into countless forms. By 400,000,000 B.C. the animal kingdom had developed, though still confined to the oceans of the world. Land was still barren of animal life. Eventually, life crawled onto dry land and the amphibians began to appear. Eventually mammals evolved and man appeared.

Whether we approach the origins of life from one-cellular life through to intelligent man or from a solar nebula to the Earth or from the Big Bang to the basic ingredients of all these, the subject of Creation and evolution is complicated indeed.

If we narrow our view to just the Earth, we can at least rely on science for some reasonable explanation of how it began and its past history up to the present time. This will give us a good yet objective understanding. Perhaps it is time to go beyond physical data. Maybe to gain a truer and more complete understanding, we must go into a study of the esoteric processes that are involved with

Creation itself. This is a step toward more of an understanding and at-one-ment with the Universe.

We can begin with the Earth, a good starting point to relate to abstract thought. Once we are armed with the scientific and general metaphysical foundation, we can proceed.

Assuming that our planet was indeed born as a remnant of the solar nebula, then it can be said that the Sun is the "Progenitor" of the primordial Earth, Father Sun. This is in keeping with the Theosophical model of thinking as well as the Native American Indian philosophy. Even the ancient Egyptians, among many other cultures, had as their one diety, Ra, the Sun God. The Earth was not alone in its birth, it has planetary brothers and sisters and they collectively make up the Solar Family. Most serious students of esoterism will have reached this conclusion and will therefore, view the Sun, Earth and planets in a personified way. But this does not go quite far enough. We cannot leave the personification on the intellectual level only. We must bring it into other levels of reality.

I must say that I had not done so until I had spent many years studying both science and metaphysics, during which I sought to grasp the wisdom in each mode. Those years of study yielded two very important perspectives that aided me in reaching a proper mental and emotional attitude so that I might apply the knowledge in a logical and useful way. The first point was the "blending" of studies scientific and metaphysic as mentioned, while the second was what I like to think of as the "Mediator" that merged with and into my consciousness along the way.

In 1971, while teaching an introductory Kaballah class at my home in Tampa, Florida, I was asked a question pertaining to the Law of Karma. As the answer began to formulate from my thoughts, my voice slowly began to change, my own replaced by a deep throaty tone. My southern accent became a distinctly British one. The change was apparent to me at once and to everyone in the room! My own understanding of the Law of Karma gave way to thoughts and concepts beyond what I consciously knew. Thirty minutes later, my normal consciousness returned, and I settled back into my own "reality". I learned that during that time a dissertation on Karma had been given. It was an experience unlike any I'd known and was both exciting and frightening at the same time. I was aware that a "consciousness" other than my own had created that experience. I remembered the feeling that it had given me and began to analyze, as all Virgos do, the situation very carefully. Luckily, one of the class members had a tape recorder operating during the class so that I had access to the information that had come through. I was aware that it was not an experience of mediumship. There was no trance state, nor an identifying entity. There was just the voice change and the information given beyond my conscious knowledge.

This was the first experience, but it turned out not to be an isolated event. Over the next two weeks, there were several occasions when a "feeling" impressed me that there would be information that would be given. After several experiments with what felt comfortable for me, I discovered some clues to what was occuring.

I soon learned that to sit down in a darkened room and "allow" the information to come through was the most productive manner to deal with the phenomenon. Within a few weeks there were several recordings of the sessions in which various subjects were discussed, but no identity was offered. It seemed that my willingness to allow the information to be channeled through me was the key to the success of the manifestation.

I collected a half-dozen tapes that had been made with the help of the class members to share with a woman living in St. Petersburg, Florida, whom I respected a great deal as a teacher of the Ancient Wisdoms. I took the recordings to her and asked for an opinion of what was happening. Ann Manser, author of the wisdom teachings known as Shustah, quickly identified the voice as one of the Teachers she was familiar with in her own work. She called the voice Albion.

The explanation she offered felt right. She advised that I not hinder the channeling, for it would surely prove beneficial in time to come. Manser explained that the "Inner Plane" Teachers select "channels" from those of us who are incarnate to share various types of information, all of which is designed to further the work of the Spiritual Hierarchy in its unfoldment of the Divine Plan.

I accepted the name of Albion; it stuck. I think that having the name helped me feel more in touch with the Teacher. It was more real to me. It seemed to help cultivate a "personality" that became more independent as the years went by. I became more in balance with the times of working, in terms of my own physical and emotional energies, although I never have been able to channel except in a darkened room which has posed minor problems from time to time.

A class was formed around Albion's teachings. Hundreds of lessons on a vast assortment of metaphysical subjects have been presented, all from the Teacher's own unique and objective point of view. These lessons, collected during the twelve years of work, are currently being prepared for public access and study groups.

It was Albion who directed that this book be written. A. S., who had been a student of Albion's for 10 years and had moved to Sedona, Arizona in 1980 was asked to help to correlate the information that Albion would give for the book. The channeling sessions were to take a year and a half to come through. To gain a greater understanding and relationship with the Earth was undoubtedly the purpose of this work.

On November 4, Election Day of 1980, my husband, Scott, along with A. S. and her future husband, D., were gathered in my home in Sedona, Arizona. Scott and I had been residents of Arizona a little over a year, but had only recently moved to Sedona from Phoenix. A. S. and D. had been in Sedona almost a year. All of us had come from long-time Florida roots.

Sedona is an amazingly beautiful town nestled in the "red rocks" of north central Arizona. Magnificent spires dot the landscape, breathtaking scenes that attract thousands of tourists each year from all over the globe. We all considered ourselves blessed to live in and be a part of this very special place.

How we had all come to be here must be attributed to my having "discovered" Sedona while on a trip to Arizona in 1975, to lecture on my recently published book on the Bermuda Triangle. On a side trip to Sedona, I was strongly impressed by Albion that I must move there. I knew that someday I would do just that. That "knowing" seemed clear and sound to me. Six years and many changes later, it finally became reality. During the time between that first visit and my eventual move, I shared my enthusiasm for Sedona with many friends, including A.S. A.S. was scheduled to speak in Phoenix in April of 1979. Her trip coincided with plans that Scott and I had to be in Phoenix at the same time, so a side trip to Sedona was quickly planned. A. S. was so impressed with the area that she gave up her lifelong Florida home and moved here with her husband-to-be less than a year later. Scott and I also moved from Phoenix to Sedona in the fall of 1980.

The evening of November 4th was no different, or so we thought, than any other. We had shared a lot of evenings conducting personal channeling sessions with Albion. We were hoping to learn more aspects of metaphysics and the Ancient Wisdoms to apply to modern times, as had occurred in the past sessions. Albion had been offering this caliber of information through classes for twelve years. A. S. had been a member of the group in Tampa, along with my husband, Scott.

The session began with Albion making some general comments about the chain of events that had occurred on this day of Ronald Reagan's "landslide" victory as the new United States President. He said:

44

"We would bring these thoughts to yourself and as the next several months unfold, it would be very much to your advantage to give them careful consideration, as well as sharing them with others. This country (U.S.A.) as well as other countries throughout the world, is a 'living entity' unto itself. It has its own social karma, racial karma and its own national and spiritual destiny. There has never been a more critical time in your country's history, my friends, critical to its survival. We are not speaking of the survival of the government or the presidency but of the people being unified in order to keep things going. During the period since 1963, you have experienced a great deal of national trauma and insecurity. There is not one single individual who could sit in the office of the Presidency of the United States that can change this situation entirely. But unity of the people can and it must be maintained. There will be three different individuals that will sit in the presidential seat during this decade (1980's). Each will seek to bring forth a greater sense of unity and progress, while all the time trying to eliminate this sense of national fear. The future of the planet will depend on the activities of the countries of Iran, of the Soviet Union, of the United States as well as the countries of Saudi Arabia, Egypt and Israel."

The words came out in the clipped British sort of accent familiar to us all.

"Remember this. These lands are to be the decisive factors in the process of the evolution of the Divine Plan in regard to international affairs."

It was not unlike Albion to be brief and to the point with his information, but these words seemed to make a special and lingering impression on us all. We felt as if we had been privy to some prophetic information, as Albion's words were. But that night, perhaps due to the election, they seemed to leave a particular sense of importance in our thoughts.

The Teacher's words about the future of the world had barely been completed when the tide of the information changed. It was during the second phase of the session that Albion began to speak of a "project" that he intended to instigate, a project that would involve all of us present, but primarily myself.

"There is work to be done and much information that we wish to share, information we are not interested in having fall on deaf ears. We will carry on this work. We have said time and time again, my friends, that humanity as a whole, as well as the Earth, is moving rapidly toward a point in time that is critical in nature. This time will be of the utmost importance to the spiritual evolution of the planet, of mankind, and of life itself."

The tiny red light on the tape recorder blinked silently in the darkened room as the words continued.

"There is work to be done in order to help insure that the information that I, Albion, will share through this 'Instrument', as well as the same information which will be and is being channeled through others is acted upon. Is that clear?"

The Teacher began to unfold his plan. We were told of a book that he would channel that would concern itself with the "beginnings" of the Universe, its process of development, the Earth, and in particular, the periods of great changes that the planet has undergone. He stressed that he would let us know how these period of "Earth changes" had affected man in the past and how they would affect him in the future. As if that was not enough to capture our interest and imagination, he went on to describe the planet as a "living organism" and that it was time that this concept was made clear. He spoke of educating the readers of his work about the planet from both a physical and scientific point of view, as well as a spiritual one.

When he finished his initial statements, he paused to ask for questions. Thoughts were running free for Scott, D., and A. S., but it was A. S. who finally broke the silence. "I have a question regarding the procedure to be taken with this book." Albion responded with his usual, "Very well". "Am I to understand that you will

46

channel the information for this book through Page?" Albion replied, "Yes". A. S. went on, "And we are all going to be involved with helping to create a book around your words?" Again the reply was, "Yes".

The session ended with Albion's assurance that he would speak more about this matter in the near future, leaving us all in a state of suspense and anticipation. Although we were not too sure of the degree of the task and what each of the personal contributions would be, except for myself. We were ready.

After the material for the book began to come through, we began to realize the truly broad scope of the information being given. The Teacher took us from a view of the Earth as a living being through its great periods of change and on into the prophecies concerning such upcoming cycles. He went into how we might survive those changes on all levels of consciousness. Most of his information from those sessions is reprinted in this work. While there are places in the material where his words have been edited or rearranged in order to be more readable, most of his words are as they were spoken. Albion's identity has been established by the unique manner of his expression. He is rather lengthy at times and somewhat redundant, but I think a closer connection can be experienced between you, the reader, and the "Source" of the words, if they are reprinted as closely as possible to the way he expressed them. Albion himself often stressed to us during the sessions that he wanted such and such a thing "written just as we have said it".

You will notice that when making reference to himself, he rarely speaks of "himself" in the singular. The use of the word "we" appears throughout the work. He has, from the very beginning, expressed himself that way. I feel that his choice of words must indicate that he is a "collection" of entities or minds or that he is including myself in his collective reference. This began to clear up a bit when once during a session, after the usual invocational remarks, Albion spoke of giving information through a physical channel:

"Efforts in this manner are used primarily to give instruction or information that is intended to have an effect on certain groups of people or the masses as a whole." I, Albion, and other entities like myself, make a choice of an individual that has the physical, emotional, mental and karmic conditions that balance best with our own. One is also chosen due to one's specific point in evolution, as well as their intellectual capacity. It is not a matter of what is already known but rather how much knowledge is capable of being filtered through the mind of the chosen Instrument."

He became a bit more personal as he related, "another important point to be noted is that, in the case of our Instrument, the choice had to do with a past life experience". He said that I had been watched and monitored over a period of over a hundred years. This obviously covered all of my present life, maybe a period of time in between, and the previous life he referred to.

"This was to test, to monitor, and to watch, so that we could be sure that the dedication and energy required were within her potential."

One of the few references that the Teacher has ever made to himself was given next.

"I, Albion, am a Ray One Entity, an Entity that works with the energies and use of will and power, for the purpose of spiritual growth. Knowledge is power, power is movement, movement is progress and action, action is karma. Karma is the 'grist' for the mill of evolution."

Further reference was then made to the past life I had experienced, which Albion said had played a role in our present relationship.

"There were many personality traits that the Instrument demonstrated, such as aggressiveness and destructive attitudes during that time that were the result of the 'Ray One' force. In that life, our words were channelled through her hands rather than with her voice."

This was taken to mean that I had been a writer.

"Thousands of words were shared. The name of this individual is unimportant, for a name is only a label.

In this life, we intend to continue giving the same type of information, along with accomplishing the purpose of simplifying a vast amount of ancient occult knowledge."

Albion indicated that the New Age was the time for the masses to be exposed to ancient teachings and to insure their interest, it must be able to be understood. Any of us who have tried to read some of the available occult literature can readily appreciate this consideration.

"You are all 'seekers of Truth'. There is no organization or individual higher than Truth and it is imperative that Truth be shared."

Albion began the information for the book by giving a perspective of the Earth that was to open many new doors of thought to myself and the others involved with the sessions.

"As we come forward here now, we come into this vibration in order that we might share information that will help you to gain a greater understanding of the planet upon which you reside. You are all obviously aware of the physical body of the Earth, but there is much more to it than that. The Earth is alive. It has a Soul. It has an emotional body, an etheric body, an aura, and the potential for all other subtler bodies that are within your own human consciousness. The Earth's 'Being' is Divine in its nature. Its 'Being' is immortal.

In order to get a clearer picture of the planet's birth from our point of view, we must go back to a time when your planet was but a concept within the framework of Divine Thought. At the time of 'Creation', all within the Cosmos, all suns, all galaxies, all the many life forms, and each terrestrial and gaseous planetary body, existed in Divine Thought before they became a part of physical reality. The Earth had its own birth after going through its 'prenatal' stages within the womb. This 'womb' was a mass of gas, cosmic particles and specks of interstellar dust that through a whirling motion gave rises to the Sun. From the Sun 'womb' came the offspring you call the Solar System. There were only seven such offspr-

49

ings. All the other bodies that now reside in this Solar Family are not natives. They have joined the Family through the force of gravity and the Law of Attraction and Repulsion. We say 'repulsion' for there are bodies that are no longer a part of the Solar System but have been pulled away or destroyed. These original planets and their satellites, also attracted to them at later times, have a special esoteric relationship with the Sun. It is a telepathic, psychic link. This link monitors their growth. Mercury, Saturn, Earth, Mars, Vulcan (believed to be a planet that was destroyed creating the present asteriod belt), Jupiter and Venus are the original planet bodies. They are the children and the Sun is the Father. In the end, just as the Sun gave birth to the planets, it will also reclaim them in death."

Albion's words were not totally esoteric. His description of the Sun's being the "parent" of the planets is very close to the Nebula Theory described earlier in this chapter. The reference to the Sun "reclaiming" the planets is also a feasible statement, for our Sun will, in its dying stages, swell into the "red giant" stage, causing its heat and gases to extend beyond the orbit of Mars. This would evaporate the planets, including the Earth.

Until recently, the Teacher's information about the Earth being a "living organism" would have drawn frowns from the scientific community. However, evidence now suggests that science may be reaching the same conclusion. More about this later. Albion continued.

"Each planet in the Solar System evolves at its own pace. Each is alive. Each has a consciousness. Each has its own Karmic conditions to deal with. For example, Jupiter will someday become a sun. Its existence is to train for this purpose. Planetary karma is specified or chosen before and begins at the very onset of their physical life. Each of these planets has been designed by the Solar Mother-Father energy to serve a special purpose within the Solar Group. The Earth's purpose is to support life in the myriad forms that exist here now."

More about the Earth's process of development came through.

"At the time of his birth when the Earth was still very chaotic, it went through a period of having all of the particles that composed the atoms that composed its physical body to come together. Then the Spirit became implanted. Through various stages of growth, it hardened into its present state. This took millions of years. During this physical process, another invisible process was taking place. Layer upon layer of bodies and consciousness was formed. This captured the Spirit inside the fibers of the Earth's being and formed its Soul.

In these early stages of evolution, the Sun also gave life to invisible Forces which take the form of gigantic Devas who are concerned with the evolution of each planetary sphere. They could be considered as the 'personified consciousness' of the planets. They conceive of the life forms, through thought, that appear on the Earth, as well as the life force that motivates the physical orbs. These Devas are the "Watchers' or 'Seed Manus'. A Manu is an 'overseer'. These beings have no form except the body of the planet itself. They hovered over and engulfed the infant sphere, planning and designing within their Being all that would become the kingdoms of life. Therefore it is correct to say that *all* life that exists on the Earth had its seed in the mind of the Planetary Deva or Spirit."

Albion's next words were filled with foreboding.

"This is why there is much concern within the Hierarchy about the genetic engineering that is going on today. It is not 'natural'. It is not 'life' in the truest sense. It cannot ever hope to have a soul. Karmic conditions are being created by the supporters and experimenters of such genetic tampering. True life forms must be fertilized and given birth through natural channels, not forms that are artificially conceived. This includes a clone or any future physical life form that would be transplanted here from any other planet. They cannot be interwoven into the Karmic fabric of the Earth. On

51

the other hand, all of the life forms that have been conceived by the Planetary Devas have not yet appeared
on Earth. From time to time there will be new forms
that will emerge through the on-going process of
evolution."

The session was a long one, filed with information. The
Teacher continued.

"Because the Earth is still growing as planets go, it
has not yet evolved to the point that it is aware of its
own Divinity. Neither is it totally conscious of its reason
for existence, spiritually speaking. But this will soon
change. The planet Earth is approaching a period of
great change. It is a time of Initiation. There have
already been two such major periods in the past. These
Initiations are recorded in geological and cultural
history. The next Initiation will be soon. You should pay
attention to the prophecies that you have heard, for
many of them are true. The coming Initiation is for the
purpose of awakening the Earth's Ego, thus to give it
its first taste of having a mind. It will develop its mental body. The last two Initiations made its physical body
and the adjustment to it, along with its astral or emotional body. The etheric body is a natural counterpart
of the physical. So, the planet after the third initiatory
experience will have four of the seven possible bodies.
We will stop now and allow yourselves to digest what
we have said. God bless yourselves."

With that the session ended. I had never heard things
put quite this way before. We were all excited and pleased with Albion's perspective of the creation of the Earth
and its subsequent evolution. Little did I realize that
that might have been the beginning of what the Teacher
later described as his primary reason for channeling the
information. It was to become the thrust of my life's work
and would change and expand the course of my thinking and the direction of my work.

It was a week before we could work again. In the mean-
time, I had done some research and some thinking about
the process of Initiation. I remembered that the word

itself is a making of a beginning, a new step towards spirituality. Each initiation marks the passing of the "student of life" into a higher level of consciousness. The understanding I had gathered from past study and experience had led me to believe that Initiation makes way, step by step, for the Inner Light to be revealed. It is a transition from one point to another along the spiritual path and results in an increasing and more conscious sense of unity with all living things. It eventually leads the Soul of whatever life form is concerned into an awareness of the Divine Plan and a greater ability to enter into an active participation with the Plan.

By the next session we were ready for more information. The Teacher began by reminding us of the period of great changes the Earth is approaching.

"This will mark the beginning of the Earth becoming more self-aware. As time goes on the Earth will move more into this state of awareness. That time shall arrive."

This added a whole new perspective to Earth changes for myself and the others. We sat around for a long while after the session talking about some of the prophecies we were familiar with, such as the ones of Edgar Cayce. We were beginning to see some reason and purpose in the disasters predicted for the future. That made a difference somehow at that time, but it was to make much more as time went on.

"During the planet's infant stages, when the Spirit lay asleep, the Kundalini was still coiled. The land masses did not exist. The Earth was totally covered by a shallow ocean. Then the continents gradually appeared as a result of volcanic activity caused by the heating of the core. Through time there have been many continents. As the planet approached the time when the land masses were to become as you know them now and the present races of humans came into being, the White Brotherhood began to set up ashrams all over the globe. Prior to this the seven major vortices, or chakras, of the planet had already been established during the forma-

53

tion of its etheric body. The Spirit, the immortal part, has its roots in the center of the Gobi Desert. It is sometimes called Shamballa or "White Island'. These chakras and vortices are located all over the planet and are stimulated into action through the processes of planetary formation and change, one by one. You call it geological history. We call it planetary evolution. These chakras sustain the Earth and perpetuate its life. These centers are the links that permit energy from the Sun to penetrate the planet and provide life-giving energy. The Earth continues to evolve. The Cosmic 'umbilical cords' have long been removed. The Great Devas have done their tasks."

The Teacher progressed our thoughts far into the Earth's history.

"When man appeared, the Earth was well into its late adolescence, and the rise and fall of many civilizations have taken place since that time."

Albion's next words were quite abstract but attempted to share with us a very deep esoteric understanding.

"It would be incorrect for you to think of the Earth as being younger than the Universe as a whole, or indeed to think of any sphere or atom of matter as has not been in its present state since the presumed birth of the Cosmos twenty billion years ago, you can be sure that the particles that constitute the atoms that collectively compose it, have existed since it all began. Particles form atoms; atoms form the molecular structure of all bodies of matter. These atoms all come together through the Law of Attraction. They are held together through the Law of Cohesion. This precipitates 'group consciousness'.

Let us think together for a moment. If we consider empty space/time as the vehicle for matter, we must realize that it is empty only in the sense that particles have not yet coagulated. Thoughts of Divine Will, along with gravity, brings these atoms through their evolutionary processes to their present state. These are the building blocks of creation. The 'groups' of atoms form every single body of matter, no matter what shape or form it takes, be it a human, a tree, a star or a galaxy.

As the atoms that make up the Earth came into group consciousness, this was the Initiation by fire, of which we spoke. That is creation."

There is no way to prove the validity of Albion's next concepts. I will repeat them here in his exact words.

"Now we will make a statement that will be one of the most questioned and cause the most chatter indeed. It is a comment that will be rather controversial. We are choosing to equate the Earth to your knowledge of astrology. As the Sun gave birth to the planets, each at varying times, the new solar body moved, as it still does, through the stars in its elliptical path. The Earth was born while the Sun was in the sign of what you now call Aries. The time it took to spin the Earth particles off from the Sun, gave the Sun time to move to the sign of Sagittarius. This was during the time of its initial, fiery stage of growing into a full-fledged planet. Now the point we wish to make is that the Sun sign of the Earth is Sagittarius. This would make for a special esoteric relationship with its 'brother', the planet Jupiter, for Jupiter now has a position as the ruler of this astrological sign. In many of the Wisdom Teachings, it is said that there will be another planet that will someday become inhabited and thus be the next one to accept the karmic responsibility of supporting life in this Solar System.

Consider the symbol that astrologers use for the sign of Sagittarius. It is the centaur, half man, half animal. The archer and the bow. The arrow goes out into space. The arrow is evolution. As you look out into the night sky, Sagittarius is in the direction of the center of the Milky Way galaxy, and the center is the most important part of the whole galactic structure."

Certainly there is no way to confirm the Teacher's thoughts scientifically. But there is one interesting piece of scientific data that has come to light in the last couple years concerning the galactic center. There has always been considerable interest in the study of galaxies, which has led scientists into realizing that galaxies come in "groups" or "clusters" as they are called rather than being distributed at random through space. Our own Milky Way belongs to what has been named the Local Group, of which there are at least twenty-one accepted members. Some researchers say there are as many as thirty-seven. The Universe is populated with many such groups.

Additional research has shown that galaxies come in basically four different types. The center of each is an area of high density and energy, a whirling mass of suns. Opinion as to the activity going on in our own galactic center and possible in every galactic core has taken a turn towards thinking that there may be a black hole that resides there. The implications of this are astounding! The black hole behaves like a "cosmic vacuum cleaner", slowly sucking up every bit of matter close to it into itself. The destiny of the matter that has been digested continues to be a major puzzle. We can indeed peer towards the center of our own galaxy by looking towards the constellation of Sagittarius. In doing so we could be seeing the area that all of the stars are being pulled by a cosmic monster that will eventually devour it all. It could be the reverse of the Big Bang in action!

Many "thinkers" have tried to imagine what happens to matter that falls into a black hole. One theory has it that the matter "pops" out in another area of the Universe. The recent discovery of quasars, the most distant objects that have been found in the Universe, caused a lot of excitement. These relatively small objects were soon recognized as phenomenal sources of energy for their size, which puzzled astronomers and led them to theorize that they may be galaxies being born, possibly from matter that had been drawn into a black hole. Cosmic recycling? It would account for tunnels in the universal fabric which Einstein believed existed, that would serve as transport systems throughout space.

Whether this is the answer to the black hole's treatment of the victims of its insatiable appetite or whether the matter simply ceases to exist or remains forever "trapped" is debateable. The questions continue and I trust that someday the answers will be known. The past few decades have seen remarkable strides in our understanding, scientifically, of the physical Universe and cosmology is one of the few areas that the material data and Esotericism can join forces for the answers. Whatever truths are revealed both individually and together are bound to be exciting to say the least.

The questions concerning the origin of the Universe and all that is within it are big ones. The answers comprise the foundation of both science and Theology. When we look up into the starry night skies, we cannot help but wonder about the beginning and end of things. We wonder about space and time and creation. But perhaps it is the period in between the beginning and end that challenges us ever more. We can relate to it more quickly, for it has to do with our own appearance on the scene and our own growth.

This became the next focus of Albion's work. The changes that our home planet has undergone and how those changes have affected humans and other life forms in the past. We were ready.

"Time does not become sacred to us until we have lived it."
—John Burroughs

CHAPTER TWO
A STEP TOWARDS
AT-ONE-MENT

"WHEN WE TRY TO PICK OUT ANYTHING
BY ITSELF, WE FIND IT HITCHED TO
EVERYTHING ELSE IN THE UNIVERSE."
Muir

The process involved with the Creation has become
one that is obviously quite complicated, as we have seen.
One cannot approach the scientific data, at least, without
seeing how little is really known and how much is still
in the realms of speculation. But the world of science
is a different one from the world of metaphysics, both
in methodology and in scope. But someday we may see
the two joined together, being of benefit to each other
toward providing a more toal understanding of Nature.
It is already starting. Such indications are seen in the
work of Fritjof Capra in his book *Tao of Physics* and in
Gary Zukov's *The Dancing Wu Li Masters*. Each of these
writings deals with the point of unification that is reached once we come to the dimension in which quantum
mechanics applies, which is the world of sub-atomic particles. Newtonian laws that apply only to the visible
Universe, must go right out the window when we approach this "invisible" world of the particles. We have
to have laws that go beyond our three-dimensional level
of existence. A whole new set of laws was found and
there is a revolution going on in the science of Physics
which seems to speak the same language as Tao or Zen,
as well as other branches of Eastern philosophy. This
could very well signify the beginning of the eventual

union of these two opposing fields of study.

We have seen in Chapter One, there are both scientific and non-scientific explanations as to the origins of the Universe, the Sun and the Earth, and life as we have come to know it. However, this book is not intended to be a scientific text. It is to be a guide in which we can explore these magnificent processes through a practical application of these processes towards gaining a greater understanding of the Universe and the planet upon which we live.

In order to do this, let us take the previous information concerning the Creation and subsequent planetary evolution and apply it to metaphysical teachings. In doing so, hopefully we will gain greater perspective.

One of the most thorough of all metaphysical writings was channeled through Alice Bailey in the early part of this century. Spurned by the works of H. P. Blavatsky, Alice Bailey became the "Instrument" for a Teacher who gave many volumes of information, enlarging upon the precepts laid out in *The Secret Doctrine*. An Entity, identifying himself only as "The Tibetan", claimed only to be a disciple of a certain degree, living in a physical body and residing on the borders of Tibet. He spoke of himself as a "presider" over a group of Tibetan lamas. The work through Alice Bailey was presented as part of the Ageless Wisdoms and his relationship with other great Teachers was hinted upon, but no name as such was revealed.

Many of the volumes of work given by The Tibetan deal with a process known as "initiation". In the book *Initiation: Human and Solar*, the word "initiation" is explained as coming from two Latin words, in, into; and ire, to go. Therefore, it is the making of a beginning or the entrance into something. If we look at the various theories concerning the origins of the Cosmos, no matter which hypothesis may be correct, it leads one into thinking that the Creation process itself is a type of "initiation". Although on a completely universal scale, the original Big Bang explosion would have marked the entrance of the Universe into being and thus it became "initiated" into reality. It would also apply, when taken in this sense, to the creation of the Sun, Earth, and of life forms themselves. In taking this approach to seeking an understanding of existence from the initiation standpoint, we must understand the term posits, in its widest sense, and entrance into the "spiritual life", or into a fresh stage of that life. This gives the Creation a *reason* for being. Initiation is likewise a process of undergoing an expansion of consciousness, which is part of the normal procedure of evolutionary development, viewed on a large scale and not from the standpoint only of the individual. Now when applied to the Universe or the Earth, for example, the implications do become interesting indeed! It places these bodies, both collectively and individually, in the category of life forms, rather than seeming dead bodies, without consciousness or purpose of a spiritual nature. The plot thickens when we go a step further with our definition of initiation gleaned from the work of The Tibetan. Again, from the work entitled *Initiation: Human and Solar* we find these words:

"Each initiation marks the passing of the pupil in the Hall of Wisdom into a higher class, marks the clearer shining forth of the inner fire and the transition from one point of polarization to another, entails the realization of an increasing unity with all that lives and the essential oneness of the self with all selves. It results in a horizon that continually enlarges until it includes the entire sphere of creation; it is a growing capacity to see and hear on all planes. It is an increased consciousness of God's plans for the world, and an increased ability to enter into those plans and further them."

While these words are intended to apply to man, it is my opinion that they take on a whole new perspective when applied to the Universe or to a planet. In relationship to the Earth, I will now share Albion's own words that were channeled during one of the early sessions in regards to this concept.

60

"Think for a moment here concerning the Earth. Do not think of it merely as a physical sphere in the Solar System. Think of the Earth and all of the celestial bodies, both planetary and solar, galactic and universal, as personalities or egoic structure. There are many implications in this. It causes us to approach the Earth as not only having a physical vehicle but also an astral, the body of desire and emotion, as well as a mental body, which gives it the potential of having a mind of its own. It also has a Spirit. It is divine."

Albion's words continued to open up new dimensions of thought. But before going any further, perhaps we should take a closer look at the theory of the "subtle bodies" that is an important aspect of the spiritual teachings known as Theosophy, for it obviously plays a large role in Albion's teaching.

Bodies are generally thought of as the "conveyors of consciousness" from one stage to another in the process of evolutionary growth. They represent aspects of consciousness, as well as describing the nature of the service as vehicles for that consciousness. Let us take a look now at the bodies themselves as described by the general metaphysical teachings.

First of all, the physical. Bodies that reside on the physical plane are composed of purely physical matter and are useful only during the period of physical life. This vehicle is thrown off at the time of death. The gross body cannot and does not serve any other purpose. In relationship to this planet, we have already gone through a detailed description of how the Earth acquired its body including the atmosphere and radiation belts or magnetic field, which are all integral parts of its material components. When we stop to consider that the dense physical shells are composed of millions of atoms, we might also need to consider the Theosophist's view about the atom. It is seen as a living thing that is quite capable of conducting an entirely independent life. Each cell is a living thing as well as each a combination of atoms called molecules. Each atom, molecule and cell, therefore, is a combination that makes up an entire organic body, combining together to provide a vehicle for physical expression.

The second body to investigate is called the "etheric", or sometimes referred to as the "etheric double". I have found that an explanation of the etheric body as the "nutritive" body suffices quite well. It is said to surround each particle that composes the physical vehicle and appears to the clairvoyant sight as an etheric-like envelope that makes an exact "duplicate" of the denser form. It is violet-gray in color. As the dense body is refined the etheric double follows suit. The same applies to ill health or damage in the physical, that too reflects in the etheric form. The primary purpose of this "double" is to supply prana or life force, which keeps the material body functioning, thus the validity of the term "nutritive". It is a highly sensitive entity and is greatly affected by stimuli, which are transferred to the physical in the form of thoughts, mobility and feelings. When we apply this principle to the Earth, for example, we can quickly see that a vital part of the perpetuation of life on the planet and how the damages that the planet has suffered due to many types of ecological imbalances such as pollution, strip mining, and acid rain, are very good examples of what condition our planet must be in.

The next body is perhaps, other than the physical, the most familiar to the layman. It is the "astral body", the emotional body or vehicle of desire. These words tell us a great deal about the role this part of the overall constitution of a being plays. The astral body is susceptible to thoughts. It permeates the physical, extending beyond and around it in every direction. Its colors are said to vary, depending upon the condition of the nature of the being it is related to. It is the center of all passions and desires, the center of the senses. Its colors change with moods and it is affected by the purity or impurity of the physical and etheric bodies. Again, in relationship to our planet, we must first consider the implications of the astral's very existence. We are not accustomed to thinking of the Earth as a living organism, much less as a body with moods and feelings. This concept indeed challenges our previous views. Accepting for the moment that this is so, imagine the vibrant condition that this implies. Think of the Earth as having moods, perhaps reflected in its atmosphere as weather patterns or in seismic activity, which is release of pressure, and even volcanic explosions which constantly occur and alter the physical shell. Could these be evidence of the Earth's moods? Is it possible that the desires and feelings of the planet could also be demonstrated by some other unrecognized force that exists within or upon the planet that affects its life as well as our own such as memory? More about this will be taken up in a later chapter.

The mind is the next aspect up for consideration. This causes us to go even further in grasping an understanding of these subtle bodies with regard to Solar or Planetary Beings. When we think of the mind we automatically think of the intellect, the "thinking" tool within conscious entities, and this is where the Ego or "personality" comes into play. The intellect has to do with reason and logic, as opposed to aimless activity based totally on feelings. A higher still aspect of the mental body is generally called the "causal vehicle", and it constitutes the fifth aspect of consciousness. All causes come from within this body. Cause generates effect as it manifests in the lower bodies. One writing describes it as a "receptacle" or storehouse of qualities that are carried over from incarnation to incarnation. It marks growth. Consideration of this type of consciousness being true likewise of the Earth gives rise not only to adjust our thinking to include the idea of this planet, as well as all other such bodies in the Cosmos as having a higher mind of its own that responds to experience with reason, but also that it is capable of "recording" these experiences for future reference in the ongoing process of growth and development. It also stimulates thoughts of the Earth reincarnating over and over again.

63

This promotes excitement and presents us with another new approach to our views of planetary evolution.

The Buddhic or "intuitive" body adds still another dimension to our quest. Intuition is a much higher form of mental activity than reasoning or intellect. This body "connects" the consciousness of one being to another and serves as a "conductor" or pure "knowing" energy through to the lower bodies. This is a spiritual function, that again, goes far in its implications when related to a planet. If it is feasible that man and other life forms are related, it then becomes natural to assume such an at-one-ment with all bodies and life forms as well. This unites the Universe and its population completely. Everything is related to everything else. That the Earth has the potential of intuition is bound to be a new concept for many of us indeed.

A final part of consciousness is the Spirit, which is thought of as the "Divine" part of self, the Monad, that spark of purity that emits from and is the only part of any being that is immortal. All of the other bodies, even the higher ones such as the Causal and Buddhic, eventually are cast off as the consciousness continues towards perfection, and all that remains is the immortal Spirit, the original spark of Light. Is the Earth immortal? Will its Spirit survive all stages of death? The answer is yes, if it is indeed a living, evolving Being.

Albion's words add further food for thought:

"If we approach these bodies in relationship to the Earth, we find that each of these bodies is involved in its own trek of evolution. Each body is growing at its own pace. Thus, to view the Earth only in its physical sense is only to see the equivalent of a box. It would indeed seem dead or inorganic. Only when it is viewed as a vehicle that contains the various bodies can we begin to comprehend a new and broader perspective. It is a unit of Being, as well as a unit of consciousness."

The Teacher went further into this line of thought by saying,

"Consider that the body of the Earth upon which you

reside is varied in its topography. Some areas are flat and barren, while others are mountainous. There are areas filled with water and other terrains gashed with ancient canyons of great depth. It is indeed a feast for the eyes. This solid ground is very beautiful."

He continued with a note of remorse in his deep voice.

"As far as the perception of the masses goes towards viewing the Earth, they consider it little more than a solid ball of rock and for its scenery. They do not consider that it is alive, a vibrant organism."

He then began to tell us that this may not always have been the case.

"Some civilizations of the past have understood a greater sense of the Earth's presence. They knew that the planet has an astral, mental and spiritual being within itself. These civilizations, as with all civilizations, have risen and fallen and are now but a memory. The Mayans, Egyptians, Sumerians, and the Aztecs are some of these. Some have left an understanding of the Earth in writings, some of which have been discovered and some of them have not. More such writings will be found in the future."

Albion went on to mention some particular places on the planet, leaving the subject of past civilizations as if he had a special feeling about the prospect of future archeological discoveries, but said no more about it at that time. His voice picked up into a quicker tempo as he began again.

"All of the physical history of the Earth is recorded in the Grand Canyon. It is the "memory" of the beginnings of the planet."

His thoughts went to the other side of the world as he said,

"Another place that contains geological records in its topography is the Himalayan Mountain range."

Our discussion after this evening's session had centered on the Teacher's point about the Earth's being alive. Although the concept had been mentioned before, it had taken on a clearer meaning, due to his discussion on the subtle bodies and his implying that this applies to the planetary bodies as much as it does our own. I recalled the idea of planetary "Initiation" and began to formulate ideas as to where this might lead to in future sessions.

My thoughts went back to a book I had been reading, *The Little Green Book*, a guide to self-reliant living by John Labell. There was a part in it that had reminded me of Albion's words about the planet's aliveness. In December of 1968, the crew members of the Apollo 8 Moon Mission saw a sight that not only was different from what any other human being alive had seen, but must have been a humbling experience as well. The Earth from space! It surely must have given them, and eventually all of us here on the planet through their photographs, a new perspective of Home! Another famous photo taken on a later mission from the surface of the moon, Earthrise, appears on the cover of this book as a drawing. Albion specifically asked us to choose this picture so that we would be reminded of the Earth's beauty and also so that we could view it as a whole rather than just from our own space upon it. *The Little Green Book* had also called my attention, for the first time, to one of the works of Buckminster Fuller, *Operation Manual for Spaceship Earth*, which elaborates on the author's approach to "our capacity for survival on this magnificent craft, this Spaceship Earth". His blueprint for survival is sensitive and revealing reading.

Treating the planet as a living organism is imperative to our survival. So our primary concern as a people should be to care for our "Home". Ecological balance has to be maintained, for the alternatives are all fatal to man's continued participation in the Universe. Fuller's description of the Earth as a "spaceship" traveling at 60,000 miles an hour around the Sun is certainly graphic and provides us with a perspective that the astronauts I mentioned earlier must have experienced for real. I am sure many of us never stop to realize such a view of our planet or think of it as a "craft" sailing through space.

Operation Manual for Spaceship Earth brings the "spacecraft" idea even closer to our reality by likening the globe to a mechanical vehicle, such as an automobile.

"If you own an automobile, you realize that you must put oil and gas into it, and you must put water in the radiator and take care of the car as a whole. You begin to develop quite a thermo-dynamic sense. You know that you're either going to have to keep the machine in good order or it's going to be in trouble and fail to function. We have not been seeing our Spaceship Earth as an integrally designed machine which to be persistently successful must be comprehended and serviced in total."

It becomes almost laughable, if it weren't so serious, how we don't view the Earth in this perfectly logical way. We can't say that we haven't had good role models to follow. The Native Americans of North America, as an example, held the planet in such high esteem that their very religion was constructed to honor it. They believed the Earth was their Mother and they still do. They are aware of their responsibility to take care of her. They know their lives depend totally upon their ability to balance with nature and its needs.

Sun Bear, Chippewa Medicine Man, along with the majoritiy of the Indian people, believes that, "Man's responsibility to the Earth Mother has been so lacking that we have reached a dangerous point", he says. "Earth awareness is at an all-time low and that has to change". Sun Bear is one of the key people, I believe, in New Age work today. His worldwide travels have been motivated to spread word of the need to return to the "old ways" of being self-reliant and accept once again our responsibility to the planet. A vision of seeing the cities being emptied because of lack of work, pollution and wastefulness has prompted concern for our destructive and blind disregard for natural environment and resources. This, coupled with the realization of our lack of survival skills to help us get through the upcoming period of Earth changes, has caused the Medicine Man to expand the work of the Bear Tribe Medicine Society into teaching others how to live in the traditional ways. Can we really afford not to heed his pertinent advice? I got a feeling of hope when, during a conversation with Sun Bear, he said: "I am now beginning to sense a greater sense of spiritual awareness from people, in general, all over."

R. Buckminster Fuller's concept of our having had to ride on this spaceship from the very beginning without an instruction manual and how that has made it imperative for us to make the best use of our scientific experiments and make use of what they teach us, is true. But, the author also points out the equally important need for us to be able to "anticipate" the consequences of extending our survival and growth. This unites metaphysical and physical knowledge, and it shows the need for both intellect and intuition. Far too many of us give credence and allegiance to only one of these capabilities that we all have. I believe we have reached a point that this is dangerous to ourselves and to the planet. It would seem to preclude our readiness for moving out from this terrestrial sphere into other parts of the Solar System and beyond. It definitely dictates our ability to "cope with far vaster problems of Universe."

Science is coming around, or at least to the point that a new theory has been presented which is causing a bit of a controversy. That could be a good sign, for it seems as if new ideas that eventually turn out to be true, have stirred up controversy in the beginning. British scientist, James Lovelock, has proposed what is called the Gaia Hypothesis. Gaia was the goddess of the Earth in ancient Greek mythology. The theory suggests that the Earth's atmosphere and seas are maintained as "highly sophisticated buffering devices by the totality of life on the planet. The whole Earth, in other words, may function as a single self-regulating organism." Scientist Lovelock, who is laying his reputation on the line, says: "We live one life". The theory puts the Earth in the category of a living organism. It had its start from the view afforded the world of the Earth from space, which gave us all our first sight of the globe as a whole. We are all a part of Gaia. As Albion said, "We are all intertwined." It will be interesting to watch the progress of the theory, as well as its acceptance or rejection from the scientific community as a whole. If it does "catch on" and is properly explored, it could go a long way towards opening the minds of people worldwide towards viewing the planet as a living Being as opposed to a lifeless body floating in space.

Albion's teaching in our next session led to a better understanding of the concept of Initiation from the standpoint of the Earth. It also included a discussion of the Earth's astral body. The four of us settled down in my living room once again, anxious to hear what would be given. The session began with the Teacher speaking slowly and deliberately about the "bodies" of the planet in review.

"If we approach each of the bodies or dimensions within the Earth itself, we find that each unfolds one at the time and each is on its own trek of evolution. We find that each body is evolving and growing at its own pace. Thus, to view the Earth only in its physical vehicle you will see and know only 'the box', the vehicle that contains the various aspects of the total egoic structure. We must now take on a new and fuller view of the planet. It is a unit of Being, as well as a unit of consciousness."

He went on, still reminding us of information he had already covered.

"Consider that the physical body of the Earth is very different in its topography in different areas. All of the physical history of the Earth can be known by studying this topography. The Grand Canyon is an example of this for it shows you much of the historical records of the planet. The Grand Canyon is part of the 'memory'. Other parts of the 'memory' can be seen in the present placement of the continents, in the great mountain ranges, especially the Himalayas."

69

With these thoughts considered, Albion went more into the Second Initiation and its results. Keep in mind the meaning of the process of Initiation, in general.

"After the 'Fires of Creation' that brought the planets into being as offsprings of the Sun the Earth spent time adjusting to its body. The planet settled into a control of its physical body, into its orbit and formed its land masses so that all of the kingdoms of life could appear and have a place to live. This, as we have said, is the Karma of the planet. These life forms did indeed evolve, after the Earth moved closer towards being ready for its next period of major Initiation, which was to open its astral body."

I think this is a good place to stop and explain the meaning of the Second Initiation, as it is understood in the Wisdom Teachings. Once the first major initiation has passed, the second carries one into an increasing awareness which, in turn, makes one more capable of mastering his own personal situation. This period brings the Earth up to its entrance upon the spiritual Path and this opens its potential awareness of consciousness on the lower planes—physical, astral and lower mental. In the case of the Earth, and all other planets in the Universe whose duty it is to support life forms, the process of the Second Initiation activates the "fertility". This means the biosphere can come into being.

It is also important to note that the Second Initiation gives the planet its first taste of emotion, of desire. Desire, then, becomes the "motivating force" that gives the necessary impetus to gave an unceasing and ever increasing determination towards further growth and self-awareness. It is said that the time between the first and second initiatory periods with man is very difficult and dangerous, for it brings out the weaknesses that exist, if there are any. One would be very prone to "backslide" or spend many incarnations wandering about aimlessly. So it is with the Earth. This points out to us that the time that elapsed between the ejection of the planet's body particles form the Solar Nebula

70

through its hardening into a solid sphere and the development processes involved with becoming prepared to give rise to and support life forms was a delicate time indeed. Esotericism would have us believe that it was a period of the equal distribution of "prana", or life force, which would secure its existence. The Earth could have failed to become what it is anywhere along the way. Let's take a look and see what science may tell us which could be applied to this specific period of time.

The Earth was quite hot at the time of its formation. The water we see here now would have been in the atmosphere in the form of vapor, only to come down in the form of torrential rains after the planet's surface cooled down below the boiling point of water. This would have created fresh water oceans. As dry land began to appear and disappear through various periods of change, so did mountains rise and fall, erosion washed away the soil constantly changing the Earth's face. Great glaciers formed at the polar ice caps, winds blew fiercely. It is estimated that the age of the planetary body must be at least several hundred million years. The shaping and reshaping of its physical body has been going on that long.

I found it interesting that in Carl Sagan's Pulitzer Prize-winning book, *Dragons of Eden,* the author likens the cosmic history of the Universe to a one-year calendar. If we suppose that the beginning of the entire Universe was in January, it would then be that the Earth would have been born in the middle of September! Life would have begun at the end of that same month. At the earliest stage, life must surely have been in its one cellular form and have "hatched" in the primordial oceans. Dr. Robert Jastrow, another of today's leading scientists and science writers, says that the Earth is 4.6 billion years old and was formed out of atoms of gas and bits of dust. He describes it as a "sterile body of rock". Imagine the primitive oceans containing no life, land barren of life, even vegetation. Biologists have determined that life evolved from two basic kinds of molecules, amino acids and nucleotides. These were the building blocks of life --twenty different kinds of amino acids build protein and five different kinds of nucleotides, which are a complex molecular structure made up of about thirty atoms of hydrogen, nitrogen, oxygen and carbon. Life as we know it now could not have appeared until very, very late in the cosmic year. This has to do with the Earth's sexuality in the esoteric sense of the word, and is an important point to keep in mind.

This leads us to a determination that the period of difficulty the planet went through between its creation and the appearance of life, which constituted its fertility and eventually led up to its Second Initiation, was a very long time indeed!

The Second Initiation period, as with the first, also took a long time. From the appearance of one-celled micro-organisms that began in the sea through the time that the Second Degree culminated, according to Albion, with the legendary Biblical flood, when human life had evolved and become civilized on Atlantis and Lemuria, would constitute another several million years! This gives us some concept of the relationship with time that a planetary body has as opposed to the much shorter period of time with which we humans deal.

The Second Initiation not only brought the Earth to its karmic, fertile stages, but it also awakened its astral body, the body of illusion or desire. Desire is an aspect of consciousness, which brings the Earth one major step away from a mere ball of rock. This is also a process of the development of the "psychic faculties", giving the planet entrance into the astral dimension, the plane of illusion or Maya. This could not be until its physical body was stable. Now we see the astral consciousness becoming part of the planetary constitution. I believe that the astral body of the Earth can be grasped when one stops to consider the changes in the aura (atmosphere) that the appearance of biological life made. Researchers at the National Center for Atmospheric Research in Boulder, Colorado, believe that biology may be the main

72

source of the atmosphere in its present state, which could explain why other planets that have no life forms are so different. Humans and other life types are generators of atmospheric gases that affect the climate drastically, as we will see later!

The Second Degree Initiate has a firmer and more conscious grasp of his own situation, as well as being more aware of the "group", which with the Earth, would be the other planets in the Solar Family. This marks the first time the Earth is conscious of its "brothers and sisters". It "sees" them as personalities. Earth knows now that she has a place amongst them and her feelings start to be felt. They begin to work together. Also, as the First Initiation gave rise to the awakening of the anal chakra, the Kundalini, the Second Initiation gives rise to the Solar Plexus. If we take into consideration that Albion later named the Kundalini chakra as the Ring of Fire in the Pacific, we find that metaphysics places a great land mass there, which was later sunk during the Second Initiation. More about this later.

Progress becomes more rapid now. The physical body of the planet is no longer the only element that has demands and needs to be satisfied. With the appearance of life, the Earth becomes a "mother". It's general attitudes will change. Willingness to nurture, reproduce and sustain is within its consciousness and control.

Let's go back now to Albion's words about the astral body.

"The astral form pulsates within the vibration of the planet. This form is motivated and sustained from the lowest in the mineral world up to man, by determination and desire. Remember that the astral body is temporary. It incarnates only as long as the physical body exists. Its atoms contain the 'memory' and will evolve and become a star, for a star is the highest stage of celestial existence that the components of a planet can evolve to in the physical dimension."

"You may ask," Albion goes on, "What is the desire of the Earth?" Its desire is the same as that of all other

73

Earth Formation

life forms, to indulge self and to become self-aware. Its highest and still to be recognized motivation is to return to its Source, its nomadic or pure Spiritual consciousness. Perhaps this is a new concept for you and difficult for you to think of a planet as having emotions and be motivated by desire, but it is so."

Other than the atmosphere, the astral body, according to Albion, is also a part of the planet that we know as its magnetic field. This is the region of space around any magnetized body that its magnetic forces can be detected. It is created by the combination of the Earth's spinning and the iron in its core. In science this is referred to as the Van Allen Belt. This is the Earth's "vibration". This vibration extends far beyond the physical body of the planet. The same is true of your human auric field.

"As life began to appear in its various forms, from the simplest to the more complex, this was a calmer Initiation than the first. The planet was eager, too eager, to accept its responsibility of supporting life and the first life forms that were beyond one cell and more complex, were mutations. But eventually things straightened out and proceeded normally. Young life forms had a difficult time on the young planetary mother. There were times the Earth's bowels erupted, it rolled and it shook and it vibrated. But evolution continued and the life forms multiplied. The Earth became more hospitable to its young."

Albion says that the Second Initiation culminated in a great flood. It was an initiation by water.

"When the Second Initiation took place, the time of the final thrust, man was in existence all over the planet's body. This occurred some 11,000 years ago. the way you count time. The two major land masses, Atlantis and Lemuria (Antilia and Pacifica) were submerged during this time, Lemuria first."

As stated in other parts of this book, the destructive periods spanned over several thousands of years, not all at once and they caused great migrations of people to seek safety. There will be further information about these now "lost continents" in Chapter Five.

This session ended with Albion saying that once the planet stabilized, its rudimentary emotion, desire, settled it safely into a life-bearing sphere.

"Now the Earth is ready and preparing for its Third Initiation which will mark a new phase of its existence. The Earth also has a causal body, a mental capability within itself. At this time, it lies asleep within the consciousness of the Earth's being. The Second Initiation gave birth to Earth's Soul, the third will give birth to its mind. Although it now lays dormant, it is there, quietly, rhythmatically pulsating, waiting to spring into life."

The mind of the planet is to come alive!

My mind raced at the thought. Imagine the planet having an ability to calculate and understand the relationship and the interchange of the various energies within its own being! A growing, changing, evolving Being genuinely places our "Home" into being our "colleague and sister". Earth's place in my mind had evolved from merely a dead sphere into my seeing it as a "cosmic personality" indeed.

"Nature is ever at work building and tearing down, creating and destroying, keeping everything whirling and flowing, allowing no rest but in rythmical motion changing everything in endless song out of one beautiful form into another."

Muir

CHAPTER THREE

THE EMERGENCE OF PLANETARY INTELLIGENCE

"Growth is the only evidence of life."
John Henry, Cardinal Newman

The Third Initiation is an elevation in consciousness and experience. Blind devotion that handicaps the devotee from the service he must give to the higher forces, is no longer an obstacle. It equips the Soul with the ability to become aware of its True Self and open the first inklings of a mind and intellect. In short, it marks a period of Transfiguration.

There has been a vast movement, as of late, among those individuals who are interested in and involved with non-sectarian, unorthodox philosophies. It is generally referred to as the New Age. Marilyn Ferguson, author of *The Aquarian Conspiracy*, describes it as "a great shuddering, irrevocable shift" that is afoot. "It is a new mind -- a turnabout in consciousness in critical numbers of individuals, a network powerful enough to bring about radical change in our culture." Virtually every segment of society is being affected by "Holism", a total approach to living. The concept of the New Age is basically one that treats every level of body and consciousness as being interconnected and thus affecting one another. Medicine, science, politics, all are being influenced by New Age thinking. Whether the "movement" will lead to global turmoil and a dissipation of society, or whether it will bring about a real breakthrough to the next step in human evolution, is something that remains to be seen. The facts are that change is happening. Positive thinking, psychoanalysis, healing, and holistic medicine, parapsychology, meditation, yoga, astrology, and quantum physics all play a role in New Age teachings.

Ferguson does not leave the Earth out of her discussion. A view of a "whole Earth", meaning that everyone is bound together in heart and mind, living on the planet as brothers in a borderless country is presented as the desirable state of a future for mankind and the planet. This New Age movement just happens to correspond to the period that Albion has said marks the beginning of the Earth's Third Initiation. Could all of this trend towards Holism be man's response on his conscious, or even unconscious levels, to the planet's period of upcoming change?

If we turn once again to the Ancient Wisdoms, we find that the Third Initiation does indeed begin a "transfiguration". The Holt Intermediate Dictionary of American English defines the word transfiguration as: "to change the form or appearance of, to make glow or shine; illumine; make seem glorious". The esoteric explanation given in the writings of The Tibetan, through Alice Bailey, is that the Third Initiation sees the development of the causal (mental) body. The Ego is brought into touch with the Monad. As this degree is taken, the initiate can then, it is said, pass into higher levels and dimensions of awareness at will. It unites the Soul and the personality.

Now this opens a lot of possibilities and tests for the Earth. Let's consider some of these, first by sharing Albion's words about this important period.

"As you know, the Earth is already quite aware of its physical self. This awareness came as a result of its creation and subsequent processes of survival and adjustment. It is aware of its desires. It wishes to be more balanced and passive, just like you do. Now it approaches a time when, through Initiation, it will take still another step towards Self-Realization. It will begin to know its own mind. It approaches a stage of growth that will enable it to merge its Ego or personality, with its body and emotions, Mind and Soul joined together. For humans, the Third Initiation is a point when one's 'force' is recognized and brought into balance. So it will be with the Earth. It will have not only a great understanding of its own force, but also of its own faults. It develops the 'mechanism of understanding'. What are the Earth's faults? One is called the San Andreas. That is a fault and there are many, which include its storms or climatic conditions that affect the lives it must support."

When the Teacher first said this, we weren't sure if he was making a joke or if he was serious. He was serious. We were later to see more of the planet's "faults", geographically, atmospherically, and those that the life forms she supports has caused. Albion continued.

"The pressure, pressure that is rubbing upon itself, will be brought into balance during this period of preparation for initiatory change. There will be volcanic eruptions and increased seismic activity. This is not a 'doomsday' prediction. It is a natural sequence of events. This is an important thing for man to realize. You must understand that it is a glorious occasion. These physical changes that the planet must go through in order to prepare itself for its Third Initiation are necessary. The Earth will no longer be hooked to only a blind orbital path, performing its Karmic duties. No, it will awaken in its own mind and say, "I am alive. I have my own purposes to serve, too.' It will become more aware of its 'mission' and destiny. You can be sure, my friends, that when the Earth's mind awakens, it will take a look (symbolically) around and see what is alive upon itself, judge what is right and wrong with itself, just as you, in your own mind, judge what is right and wrong with yourself. Something else will change. We will pose it to you in the form of a question. 'Will all of the destruction and imbalance that has been perpetrated upon the planet and that has robbed it of its natural resources in such

79

a rapid way, continue to be tolerated?"

"Those who survive this coming period of natural and ecological changes will be the New Age Workers. Their visions will be broadened and they will have an understanding of the Earth as their Home and Mother. The New Age people are reminiscent to I, Albion, of those in civilizations past who have understood this and had it as an integral part of their lives. These civilizations, like the Hopi, knew how to live on the Earth in balance."

The Teacher paused for a bit before telling us that his next words were a very important part of understanding the Earth's evolutionary and initiatory process.

"The planet Venus is the 'sister' to the Earth. It has already undergone the five initiation cycles that a planet can go through before the Sun swells to reclaim it. Venus is a 'sacred' Planet. The Earth will have two more cycles after its third one is finished, so it is still profane. Venus has already reached and has gotten in touch with the monadic spark of Divinity within itself. Its physical body is of no use. It is a 'boiling hell'. But when one is in touch with its Spirit, its form matters not. Venus has a special esoteric relationship with your Earth. As an older sister would guide a younger sister to the 'Portal or Threshold of Initiation', so it will be with Venus guiding the Earth."

"The Third Initiation is the Time of Transfiguration. In the Biblical scriptures you find that as the disciples look on, the Christ rose out of the body of Jesus. He transfigured and became 'Pure Spirit' before their very eyes. If you consider the other planets and also the life forms that live upon the Earth as 'disciples', of sorts, they, you, will witness this event with the planet Earth. It is not to be looked upon as a time of destruction. It is not an age of cataclysmic doom. It is a time of awakening. It can be a time of 'judgement', to be sure, for those who are not in tune and those who don't know how to survive, as the mind of the Earth awakens."

"After the Initiation, the Earth will be able to hear

sounds for the first time ever. Can you imagine this? For the first time the Earth will open its eyes and ears! It will hear the universal sounds, not just be drawn to their frequency, as when its mind was dormant. It will become more cognizant of its place in the Solar System, and eventually the galaxy and the entire Universe. As the 'eyes' are opened, it will reach out and 'see' its gaseous brothers and sisters: Neptune, Uranus, Jupiter and Saturn. The Earth will learn during this period of its evolution, of its responsibility for bringing to the 'New Age' individuals who survived its change and who have the ability to live upon the planet in a peaceful manner. The Planetary Hierarchy will be watching all of these transactions very closely."

When Albion spoke of the "Planetary Hierarchy", he later designated its meaning. It is a part of the Spiritual Hierarchy, but not composed of evolved human spirits. It would, rather, be the Great Spirits of each planet in the Solar Group. This is referred to in the Wisdoms as the Planetary Logoi. Also in keeping with the subject of the Spiritual Hierarchy, there was some information that Albion gave in another session one evening, that is along these same lines. I will share that with you now before continuing about the Earth's Third Initiation.

"The Spiritual Hierarchy is composed of a large group of entities, all of which are no less than Fifth Degree Initiates. These entities have surmounted all the negativity of earthly living. They have conquered every human difficulty and have been the victors. You will know them as the White Brotherhood. These Initiates have 'personalities', egoic structures, and mental catalogues of knowledge. They 'oversee' the evolution of every single form of life that descends into matter. The members of the Brotherhood function to accomplish the unfoldment of the Divine Plan. For the most part, their presence is felt on the subjective levels of consciousness, and their work remains invisible. It is like a 'Cosmic Underground'. We also wish for you to understand that it is not unusual for members of the Hierar-

81

chy to manifest in the physical dimension. In fact, there are some who live in the flesh all the time in various parts of the world. But, for the most part, their work is on the 'Innerplanes'."

"You must not overlook that just as there are the Forces of Light, there are likewise the Forces of Darkness. The Black Brotherhood. This is polarity. The forces of good and evil are constantly at war with each other, which provides 'grist' for the mill of Evolution. Both of these Hierarchies have their place, and both are powerful."

"There was a time that the White Brotherhood was not operating in an 'invisible' manner. They were totally physical. This was during the Atlantean times. They walked and moved freely among the masses. They had great temples. They spread out and many of the ruins of these temples are still evident. They comprised a Priesthood. Their work was identical to what is now, that of directing the affairs of Evolution, constructing systems of thought and developing spiritual quality in life. This is great power and it led to trouble within the Priesthood. Material living was not compatible with their frequency. A split developed. It evolved into the White and Black Brotherhoods. Thus, the birth of opposing forces. It caused the White Brotherhood to retreat to the subjective levels of reality to do their work. You must understand that when such a split occurs, it 'trickles' down into society. You see evidence of this existing still. The split of the Brotherhood caused a division of those who use it for ill. This 'split' is recorded in your Bible as the Fallen Angels. The Black Brotherhood is willing to control the masses, the White Brothers only seek to guide. The migrations that happened at the time of the destructions of Atlantis were with individuals who listened to the message of the White Lords. Civilizations were 'seeded' in safer parts of the world to which they were guided. Within these migratory groups there were a few of the Brothers of the Light that remained incarnate among them. They were the ancient Egyptians, the Aztecs, the Mayans and the Incas and the Hopi Indians. When the White Brothers, for the most part, went into the subjective dimensions, it left man to go on what he knew was right. The Black Brothers remained to sway them from this Path."

"The so-called New Age will hopefully provide a condition of life that the Hierarchy can become externalized once again. They will once again wish to build their ashrams all over the globe, openly, in full view of an awakened society. That is the hope and the Plan. When the Hopi speak of their Great Day of Purification, they speak of a time of another 'war' between the Forces of Light and Darkness. The future beyond that will be a manifestation of the result."

"This information is to share with others to help make them aware of the Earth as a living evolving organism. It is now necessary to give information that would expand the scope of knowledge concerning the Planet. These thoughts are to take place between the years of 1982-1987. This five year cycle is a time in which the whole flow of the Scheme of Evolution will 'take a turn'. There will be great changes that will enhance and increase the input of energies into the evolutionary patterns. This will, in turn, affect the life forms on the Earth, as well as the planet itself. Within the White Brotherhood (Spiritual Hierarchy) there are changes that are taking place. They are just beginning this day (channeled on January 1, 1982) and will take seven months to complete. Let us make it clear that although these changes will affect the Earth and those that live upon it, they have nothing to do with either of these directly. They will have to do with the energies involved with the make-up or vibration of the Brotherhood itself."

"Let us explain. The collective energies that are generated by the Hierarchy serves to provide the flow of power that moves the Scheme of Evolution forward. This power determines the outcome of this Scheme. This energy, likewise, affects all of the kingdoms of life and causes them to evolve. It is the same force that sets up the Law of Cause and Effect, which yields the interactions of political, social, racial, medical and spiritual events to expand the human kingdom, as well as the perpetuation of all of the other species in existence. Each individual member of the Hierarchy has at his discretion and within his power, the decision-making that will affect all of the facets of life that exist."

"There are occasions when the members of the Brotherhood remain the same for hundreds, sometimes thousands of years of time, without change. But there are other times when there are changes in the membership that are made. Such is occurring now."

"The Hierarchy is divided into seven major groups. Each group of entities represents and contains within their jurisdiction, decisions concerning each of the seven Ray Forces that exist."

I know these from past study to be:

Ray One -- Willpower
Ray Two -- Love-Wisdom
Ray Three -- Active Intelligence
Ray Four -- Harmony through Conflict
Ray Five -- Concrete Knowledge-Science-Intellect
Ray Six -- Idealism
Ray Seven -- Ceremonial Order-Balance

Albion continued.

"The Entities that wield the force of Ray One, the Ray of Will and Power, are having to make changes within the 'inner group' in order that an increase of force might be centered in those affairs of Evolution that have to do with the force of Will and Power. This will be necessary to generate the power that is needed to bring about the physical planetary changes that are necessary for the Earth to go through in preparation for its Third Initiation. This will result in the unleashing of a tremendous amount of strong force being released upon the Earth, the three lower kingdoms and humanity. Physically, it is literally the power to move mountains and the physical manifestation of this energy will be mostly absorbed by the Earth. The life forms on her back in the two lower kingdoms, the mineral and plant, will be a part of the planet's response. But the animal and human kingdoms will each have the choice of response, based on their instinct and free will. Animals will follow their instincts to survival. In man, a negative response to this degree of potent Ray One force will result in aggression, war and violence and can manifest on all levels. On the other hand, a positive response, which is the desire of the Brotherhood, will bring about progress, growth, survival and expansion. It will carry man into the New Age."

This information requires a lot of careful thought.

Albion went on.

"The Entities involved with this, and they number twelve, will accomplish the generation and dispensing of this force by elevating to a higher frequency, releasing it telepathically all over the globe. The affects of the Force will continue to exist for 1,000 years into the future! These twelve Entities are new additions to the Ray One Force and have been selected from a group of Chohans (Six Degree Initiates) of Light. They are Planetary Spirits, concerned with human and planetary affairs. The changes that are affected will help open the mind of the Earth so that it will no longer be dependent upon humanity's collective intellect totally. The Entities have been 'waiting in the wings', so to speak and are utilized prior to major planetary initiation periods. They provide the 'thrust' for change. The specific parts of the globe that will be affected the most by this stepping-up of Force during this five year period and thus, the areas geographically, politically, religiously and socially 'charged' with the Force, will be North America, Russia, England, France, Central and South America, and Tibet. If this Force is used and absorbed for a positive end, it will do much towards that enhancement of group consciousness and brotherhood, it will be good. That will cause cooperation and collaboration between these 'energies' so that the flow of Evolution is enhanced. The dawn of the New Age will then begin. If these 'energies' are used for individual and personal power and will, it will take only one of these groups or strong people within the groups to upset the balance. This would mean that the five year cycle could bring about change that could cause stagnation and would delay the unfoldment of the Divine Plan and the ushering in of the New Age."

Albion now began to speak of still another Hierarchical change.

"There will also, during this same period of five years, be changes in the Second Ray Entities in the Brotherhood. These are those that deal with the forces of Love, Creativity and Wisdom. This group of Entities is concerned with consolidation of the world teachings and principles. They are specifically concerned with the reappearance of the Christ and have been preparing the way for this appearance for some time. They have also increased their output of energies in order to draw many 'incarnated recruits' to serve as workers for the Christ Consciousness to appear. An avatar always comes at a time of crisis and the coming Earth changes that will constitute the beginning of the Earth's Third Initiation is a crisis. Not all these necessary changes will run smoothly, there is always some degree of stagnation and difficulty. But the work of this Second Ray group of Entities is designed to minimize the negative potentials as much as possible. They will do their work. Then it will be up to each individual as to whether or not the procedures will run smooth and occur on time. These Entities do all of their work telepathically, much of it through the dream state. They pour out Love, which affects the Heart Center of the planet and of the life forms upon it."

Albion went on to explain the choices of the White Brotherhood to gain help with their work.

"Many individuals have been chosen from time to time, only to be discarded for their lack of seriousness and balance in their approach to the work. These persons are relieved of their duty with the blink of an eye due to the importance of the work yet to be done. One's motivation for the 'spiritual work' must be proper. No self-serving is needed nor tolerated. To be sure, there are times when there is no crisis or turning point with humanity, when the Hierarchy might be more considerate or tolerant towards individuals and the masses. But otherwise, in times such as this, no such consideration can be afforded. We trust you will understand these words. Think them over most carefully. This is a time of testing to see if each person can be responsible for himself."

There was further information given concerning matters within the Spiritual Hierarchy. This session was a long one.

"Although there are no specific changes that are taking place with the other major Ray Group, Ray Three, they are very busy concerning themselves with enhancement and stabilizing of communication matters of all kinds and on *all* levels, both planetary and extra-planetary. These Entities are very interested in NASA's projects of space travel, as well as the European Space Agency. They are particularly concerned with the areas to do with Radio Astronomy and space travel. They support such projects, as long as they are for good. These projects help to prepare those of you that dwell on the Earth for a future position of becoming true spatial citizens."

This last thought reminded me of a special friend of mine and my husband, Alan C. Holt, an employee of NASA at the Johnson Space Center in Houston, Texas, where he trains astronauts and flight controllers. I had met Alan in San Diego in 1979, at a UFO conference. Alan has a personal and scientific interest in that phenomenon, particularly in the possible propulsion systems involved with various sightings. However, his main work aside from his duties at NASA have to do with the concepts of an innovative spacecraft, one that could far surpass any present propulsion system. Holt

87

describes our present models as requiring enormous amounts of thrust to overcome the pull of gravity. However, Holt's proposed craft, Star Eagle I, would require no such thrust, but rather would be able to "alter local gravitational fields instead of simply out-muscling gravity". Although this feat is not possible now, it is not an impossible future accomplishment. Alan Holt believes in and is working on a breakthrough in man's current understanding of the four fundamental forces in the Universe. A thorough knowledge of these forces individually, as well as their relationship with and affect upon each other, must be developed for Holt's spacecraft to become a reality. This is similar to the belief held by the late Albert Einstein of the unity in the behavior of universal forces which he called the Unified Field Theory. Holt believes that Einstein's concepts merit further research and eventual experimentation. If a Unified Field Theory can indeed be perfected, it could possibly lead to a process of converting electro-magnetic energy to the force needed for propulsion. Such propulsion could be used to transport the space shuttles, manned planetary orbiters, satellites, and even future space colonies into space.

Another interesting aspect of Alan Holt's work includes the "dimension" he calls "hyperspace". In an article in the May, 1982 issue of Science Digest, Holt describes this topic in the following manner:

"At the time of his death in 1955, Albert Einstein was developing a unified field theory, his final attempt to describe electro-magnetic and gravitational fields in one mathematical theory. Einstein concluded that in a field theory that describes both matter and energy, mass must be dependent on moving fields, or energy currents. Since such fields or currents have not been observed, either mass may not be describable by a field theory or the required energy may flow from an unobservable, supranormal reality-hyperspace."

Holt's craft would then, instantaneously change the "polarity" of these hyperspace currents and the craft would move! Still another model would be able to generate its energy patterns that would be different from the surrounding local hyperspace current, causing the spacecraft to disappear from its location in space and time and then reappear at a more compatible energy site. This work is not only exciting but has the potential of bringing mankind into that phase of becoming the "Spatial Citizens" that Albion spoke about. In a recent visit with Alan, I asked him many questions about the coming Earth changes and man's future, in terms of new energy sources and the role that science and scientists, in general, can and will play. This interview appears in Chapter Seven of this book.

If indeed the Brotherhood is interested in NASA and other space breakthroughs, then there must be special interest in the work of Alan Holt and others like him. This is, of course, conjecture on my part. Perhaps we will soon see the day that more scientists will pour their mind-power into projects that will serve to advance mankind into a New Era and go far toward solving the current use of energy.

Albion's comments on the work of the Spiritual Hierarchy continued.

"The work of the Ray Three Entities is ongoing. They are also concerned with the education systems worldwide, particularly in North America. You can expect to see many positive changes in the educational systems in America, but the changes required will be painful to instigate. Change almost never comes easy."

The Teacher's next words were intriguing and complex in concept.

"There will be, collectively, forty-three members of the White Lodge (Brotherhood) that will incarnate, physically, during the next two years. They will incarnate in Ireland, Central America, the United States, Russia, Egypt, Iraq, Saudi Arabia, Libya, Pakistan, India and Israel. These Masters will begin to affect the policies of these countries on the international scene, particularly around the turn of the century through the middle of the next. They will help to carry these nations through many major political, social and Earth change crises to come."

The final group within the Hierarchy to be discussed was those who work with the force of Ray Seven, the ray of order and balance. Their force and work has also been greatly expanded.

"These are the White Magicians, the Manifestors. The reason for a stepping-up of the work of these Entities is primarily concerned with the 'migrations'."

Let me explain. From time to time during the sessions that were held for the book, Albion referred to "migrations" of people that would occur as this period of Earth changes began. In fact, he claimed that they have already begun! I think it best to share a compilation of his thoughts on this matter. Most of these references came during one session. First, in regards to the Seven Ray Entities that the Teacher calls the "Organizers";

"They work with survival of the Race and all life forms. Some of them are presently serving as 'Monitors' for the sixteen human channels that are being given information on Earth changes and survival, such as through our 'Instrument'."

"In order for the term 'migrations' to be clearly understood, we must explain ourselves very carefully, for an understanding of this will give a greater sense of security and direction, which is important. It will also help to understand the events that will occur in various countries all over the globe, as they unfold during this time of change."

"There have been at least three other occasions, some prior to recorded history, in which it became a necessity for migrations to occur. Migration does not merely imply the movement of people from one place to another for safety reasons, but it implies the same movement within the animal kingdom as well. You would do well to watch the migrational habits of winged and and non-winged species, to note any changes or peculiarities that occur. Watch their cycles of migrations. They will go out

90

of the normal patterns as the Earth changes become more severe. You can see how one who is not familiar with animal and bird migrations would need to know this in a general way before it could be used as a 'sign' of impending danger."

"Now let us make comment about 'human migrations'. We will consider it from three major points of view. First and foremost, migrations will occur due to climatic changes. Indeed, this has already begun. There will be areas of your country, for example, that will not be accustomed to experiencing extreme cold and/or heat, drought, flooding and the like, that will find themselves unable to cope physically, psychologically and economically, so they will migrate to other geographical locations. Climate will also have a strong affect on the etheric (health) and astral (emotional) bodies of humans. For example, people who are used to cool climates and vibrations will sometimes find themselves thrown into situations of extreme heat and drought. This will cause tempers to rise, tension to build and this can promote violence and all sorts of disharmony. The reverse will likewise be true as time goes on. Individuals who are accustomed to drier, warmer climates, or even wet, tropical, will suffer changes that will cause physical and emotional disorders. Depression, bone problems, circulatory and respiratory problems will result in migration to more agreeable areas."

"A second point that we wish to make clear concerns migrations due to seismic activity. This, of course, will become more prominent as seismically active locations become more and more unsafe. While some of this has already begun, the major portion of this remains well into the future. Such migrations will occur in North America, Iran, Italy, Egypt, South America, particularly in the area of Chile, the Hawaiian Islands, Japan and other islands in the South Pacific. Not all of these migrations will take place due to choice, but rather because of necessity. Some of these land areas will be broken apart and others will cease to exist. Although most of the migrations, both for climatic and seismic reasons, will be gradual, there will be some that will happen quickly and without the heeding of prior warnings. This can cause panic! Panic is born from emotional upheavals based on fear and also on the trauma associated with having to leave one's home and familiar surroundings. During these times, especially as the changes become intense, refugee camps will spring up all over. One of the tasks of the Seventh Ray Entities is to impress individual "New Age Workers' to care for such migrants, while others, and this is happening now, will teach survival skills before they become a total necessity. Fear is thus minimized with such skills, you see."

"Now we come to our third major point and reason for human migrations. It is economic change. Such change will be due, in part, to the climatic and seismic occurrences we have already mentioned. You can be sure that there are Intelligence Circles, worldwide, particularly in the U.S., Russia, the British Isles and the Arab countries that are keeping a watchful eye upon climatic and possible seismic conditions so that they might learn what can be expected as far in advance as possible. When there is major climatic change, food sources are threatened. Crops fail. When there are major Earth upheavals, political boundaries set by man make little difference. In order to prevent possible global pandemonium, intelligence groups are busy, you can be sure. Some of these groups are not even known to exist."

In regards to Albion's words, I ran across a book entitled *The Coming Ice Age* which is a report compiled from expert testimony, government and scientific studies, and is designed to show the truth about climatic changes and their political, social and physical implications. Some very interesting points are made in this writing, some from CIA intelligence reports, which could instigate migrations such as those which Albion had spoken about. It also confirms his use of the term "intelligence" data. Information in regards to weather forecasting was given that shows our lack of accuracy

92

and long-range predictions about the weather. At best, a one to three day forecast is about the extent of our present capabilities, and an advance forecast of thirty days is not much better than a random guess. One can quickly see how vulnerable we really are to sudden climatic conditions and how uninformed we remain as to what we may be confronted with in the future. This is a wonder to me, based on the fact that such a large portion of government funds are poured into meteorological research. It reminded me of another book that had shed some additional light on this very subject. Written by Joseph Goodavage, the book *Our Threatened Planet*, discusses, amongst other things, the sad state of affairs when it comes to weather forecasting. Goodavage points out that the American Meteorological Society and the National Weather Service know next to nothing about how the Earth's weather really operates and even less about how to predict it. In 1975, a report by then President Ford published by NASA, stated that the U.S. has made substantial advances towards achieving a better understanding of the "dynamics" of global weather. The development of satellites to gather and use this knowledge was reported to improve vastly the long range forecasts with celebrated benefits ranging from agricultural to recreational. But the author, Goodavage, feels not so elated at this prospect. The inaccuracies of weather predicting, coupled with the vast and negative implications of this problem, lead Goodavage to suggest that a long-proven method of forecasting climatic conditions be given serious consideration by the "powers that be". Astrometeorology, predicting the weather by planetary positions, Goodavage feels presents a logical arguments to such a method and proclaims evidence of its accuracy throughout the book. Concentrations of the planets, influences of the Moon and eclipses are a few examples of phenomena to be studied. Introductory instructions are given in the second part of the writing as to how the system works. The author feels that inertia, lack of interest and authoritarianism are all contributing factors to the severe and dangerous lack of knowledge and accuracy we are confronted with. He seems to feel that recognized bodies such as the American Meteorological Society are too quick to reject his recommended predicting system. I think that the results of giving such a system a decent try could prove to be very interesting, but perhaps it "smacks" too much of astrology to be taken seriously by the scientific community. But can we afford the luxury of not considering every possible avenue of improving our understanding and forecasting of long-range climatic events? I think not. Prejudices that serve to create barriers are deadly when we are talking about such pertinent issues of survival as our climate.

Other data contained in *The Weather Consiracy* that caught my eye also seemed to confirm Albion's words. He had mentioned the interest the "intelligence" community has for weather. *The Weather Conspiracy* stated: "The CIA estimates that even under the most optimistic conditions, in the years to come, there simply won't be enough food to go around." Part of this will undoubtedly be due to climate. Facts about cold weather causing us to become more dependent than we are now upon fossil fuels and foreign imports cast a dim light on our predicament.

All of this information just serves to point out to us the importance of the work of the Seventh Ray Entities. They may have to be "magicians" indeed to help us survive, considering all of the factors involved. Our cooperation is vital to their success and our survival. More data about how we can all serve as their assistants is to come in Chapter Six.

In keeping with the process of the Earth's Third Initiation, I think it best to consider some important rules that were set down by Madame Blavatsky concerning the qualifications one must meet before this Initiation can be taken. While it is true that they were written to concern human souls, perhaps it would be enlightening to apply them to a "planetary" point of view. We can see trouble immediately when we realize that the first qualification requires perfect physical health! Needless to say this is not the case of the Earth, primarily due to man's lack of concern and ecological horrors heaped upon the planet's physical body. The Earth is sore. It needs healing. But hopefully this may be on the verge of changing. As of late, along with the outcry of various environmental groups, there is a seeming revival of the Native American's view of the planet and what has been done to it. Many people are coming to the realization of just how out-of-step we are towards coexistence. Can we survive much longer? I would feel that the poor physical condition of the Earth could conceivably delay its Initiation or make its preparation period we have been discussing much more traumatic, at best.

The second rule is mental purity, with the others being unselfishness of purpose, which it seems the Earth has been; truthfulness to the Laws of Karma, also a plus; courage in emergencies, intuitional perception of its Divinity and aliveness, and appreciation of the visible and invisible worlds. Much of these rules will be met at the Third Initiation itself. But so far it seems that the Earth is doing its part, now we must do ours.

Albion describes the Earth as a "chela". This is indicative of one that has willingly offered themselves to a "Master" as a pupil so that the mysteries of Nature might be learned and thus understand its very reason for existence. It develops latent powers. If we apply this to the planet it will give the Earth the eventual ability to pass its consciousness into even high dimensions of existence at will.

With the Earth as a "chela" clearly imprinted in our thoughts, let us continue with further information Albion stated in regards to the Third Initiation that we approach. It is wise to keep in mind that his words can be redundant at times, so pardon any repetition.

This particular session was immediately following the one leading into the information on the "preparatory" period. He began with:

"The following words will bring forward the esoteric as well as the exoteric implications of the Third Initiation. Let us consider now, the number '3'. It brings an ancient symbol to our minds, that of the 'triangle' which we will call a Triad, the Trinity. Ancient tradition holds that the symbology of the '3' has always stood for 'spirituality' and spiritual growth. It likewise represents Diety in the Christian religion. Therefore, the Third Initiation becomes the first of the major initiations the planet or man goes through. Three is communication, a skill that the Earth will develop soon along with a mind of its own."

Albion, for the first time, began to speak of other celestial bodies that will play a role in the Earth's initiation aside from what has already been given regarding the planet Venus.

"The Sun, Sirius, known in the Wisdom Teachings as the Central Spiritual Sun, is the 'source' of spiritual, cosmic rays. These rays are not cosmic in the physical sense, but in the esoteric sense. Sirius will emit its consciousness to the Spleen chakra of the Earth, causing an important stimulus to occur. Although this force will be sent in a direct 'blast', it will not come in contact with its physical body for that would upset the planet's orbital path and there would be too much direct power to its life forms. Most of the energy will be captured by the Earth's aura (atmosphere), mostly by the magnetic field. This will absorb about 70% of the Sirius 'blast" which will in turn 'trickle' down to the Earth in small packets of energy, spanning a period of twenty-five years, beginning in 1990. The remaining 30% is dissipated during its journey to the Earth."

Albion's comments about Sirius prompted me to re-read some of the available material from my early years of study. Sirius, astronomically speaking, is nine light years from the Earth. It has a diameter twice that of the Sun. It is actually two stars, with the small "companion" being a white dwarf with a density 90,000 times that of the Sun. Because they are so close, they appear as one star unit to the physical eye and they reside in the constellation known as the Great Dog.

In esoteric literature, Sirius is considered a source of thought or mental force that it "sends" to this Solar System. It acts as the "transmitter" of the energies that alledgedly produce self-consciousness in man. This energy is intensified during Initiation which causes a greater understanding of Truth. It is said to affect the throat center. Now this is a most interesting point. Keep it in mind when you read about the location of the Earth's chakras in Chapter Four.

Albion continued.

"When these 'packets' of energy are released, they will be absorbed not just by the Earth, but also by the life forms in all of the kingdoms. It is dependent totally upon the free will of the life forms and their evolvement as to whether or not they can utilize it to create a rapport with the Earth. There will be programs, concepts and theories of technology that will bring man to a point of no longer being trapped on the Earth. Space travel for exploration will increase and when man leaves the planet to colonize other regions of space, the Earth will no longer have to bear the karma of being totally the support system for life forms."

The Teacher gave another session after this one that continued his thoughts on the Third Initiation.

"Before the planet goes for its full Third Degree it must be purified. This is what we have been saying that the 'Earth changes' are all about. These changes will help to break down and destroy the toxicity and putrifaction that has been created by the life forms, primarily man. It will also help to clear up the toxicity that has built up for the Earth being only a physical and astral body wandering in its orbit in space. As the energies of 'purification' are directed in a series through to the Spleen chakra, the magnetic field and the atmosphere will absorb it. Once the energy is absorbed by the Spleen, it will purify it, distill it and re-emit it back into the atmosphere. The clear energy is then drawn gradually into the Crown Center in the Gobi Desert, Shamballa. This will activate a freer and intensified flow of the Shamballa force all over the globe. It will be subtle in its nature and will take some time to manifest. But when it does, it will mark a time that there will no longer be a barrier between science and metaphysics. It will join together the forces of Truth and Logic."

"As the Third Initiation proceeds, the Earth will reveal many of its secrets. From the year 1990 through 2015 several things will be encountered. First, it will reveal its true age, for the Earth is much older than what is presently thought. It will yield many of its major archeological discoveries in Egypt and in the U.S. There will be the discovery of the tomb of Nefertiti. Records in the form of manuscripts will be found in Arizona, near the Meteor Crater, First and Second Mesas and Canyon de Chelly. There will also be discoveries in Kentucky, Nebraska, Ohio and New Mexico."

"During this period of the Third Initiation there will be more Third Degree human initiates incarnating on the planet than ever before. There are more disciples preparing now for the Third Degree than ever before and this is happening on a global scale."

"All this is taking place in other dimensions of existence and will become apparent in the physical more and more as the Earth prepares to gain an awareness of its Ego. It has the free will to do so. Will it respond negatively to its Ego as men often do? Will it be filled with pride and thus gain a sense of separateness from the life forms upon it? You had better hope not! All upon her skin will respond to the Earth's initiation's Ego. The Earth will be like a chick peeping from its shell for the first time. Will it recognize its cosmic link? Perhaps. The choice belongs to the Earth. There is no power that man can wield that will change or affect the planet's response. The Earth will decide its own destiny, in its own time and in its own space."

"When the Earth goes into its Fourth Initiation, which

98

will be many thousands of years form now, it will finally be at a point when it can pass into perfection. It can lose its physical form with no regrets. Or it can consider another alternative. It could remain 'in the body' and continue to support life, just as a Master might choose to stay in the flesh to bring disciples to the threshold of their own initiations. The Moon is the Earth's disciple. That will be the choice and choice is Divine Inheritance. The Fourth Initiation is harmony brought about by conflict. As it says in your Biblical scriptures: 'ashes to ashes, dust to dust'. Ashes are the Primeval Fire of Creation, dust the shedding of its form. When the Earth passes through its Fifth Initiation, it will be in total control of its destiny. It will be a 'sacred' planet. Once again, it will have a choice, which will be whether it will pass out of this physical plane and into another. This would make it invisible. Presently, there are suns, even whole galaxies that are invisible, but they exist. They are the highest evolved universal Beings in their life category."

His words about invisible suns and galaxies are undoubtedly a reference to such that exist in the spectrum of X-rays and ultraviolet. Discoveries of these have been made.

There was so much that Albion had to say about the Earth's gaining a "mind of its own" due to its upcoming Initiation, but only once that he told us what sort of "thinking" apparatus its mind would be. The session began with:

"Let us concern ourselves with the mental body of your sphere. When the word 'mind' is used, most people automatically think in terms of the intellect. You must discard this notion to understand the mind of the Earth. We have taken great pains to explain to you that the Earth has a physical, etheric (aura) and astral body, all gained in other Initiation periods. It is the astral body that we wish to bring to your attention now for it is this body; that gives rise to the mental body. The astral body of the Earth, as with man, resides and functions in the

99

astral plane or dimension. This plane is the plane of thought forms. The Earth is capable then of generating thought forms (astral images), but these images are not connected, the Earth does not think or feel in associated thoughts."

A.S. interrupted to ask a question. "So, in other words, those thoughts rise spontaneously?" Albion responded by saying:

"Yes, they rise spontaneously, but they are also not connected or associated such as with those based on intellect, as with man."

An example was given.

"Picture an image of an apple -- next picture a vehicle. They are not related but totally separate 'thoughts' you see. This, thus far, is the only process of thought the Earth can do. These images are important for they will give rise to an associated thought process. The thought forms of the planet have to do only with emotions, for they are astral, concerned with balance and imbalance only. That is all. For example, if there is an area that is under a great deal of seismic pressure, the Earth will create, not knowing why in the intellectual sense, an image that will show this fault line. It then knows as your body would know, that this is a symptom of weakness. Now all of these individual images have been 'collecting' for many, many years. It has formed a sort of 'collective unconsciousness', which resides in the Earth's aura. This forms a sort of unconscious memory of its past experiences and behavior, with its physical history remembered in its physical body (i.e., Grand Canyon). The astral thought patterns prepare the Earth for eventual self-conscious awareness, for they will be able to think both archetypically and associatively. Concrete thought is born."

The complexity of the material prompted A. S. to ask, "So the mental body will learn from experiences that the Earth has already had?" Albion responded;

"Yes, of course. When you are a child you learn from your experiences and they build one upon the other. So it is with the Earth, you see. As these 'chains of thought' become realized, the planet will then be able to bring mental pressure to bear upon its own physical body. As opposed to mountain chains being caused by some aimless wandering of land masses or a fault line breaking loose at random with the Earth being totally helpless, it will be able to control its own activity, as it is with yourselves. As time goes on, the mind of the Earth will grow stronger until it will be consciously aware."

We were not sure, as the session came to a close, if we understood the Teacher's words, so we discussed the depth of the material for a couple of hours trying to distinguish the differences between our own way of thinking with that of the planet. There had been some indication at the end of the session that the next phase of material would regard the Solar System. Albion wanted us to get a clear picture of not only the Earth, but our entire systemic neighborhood. We were mentally geared for that information and got together the very next evening.

I think that we all were beginning to show the mental fatigue that comes along with such intense information and we felt Albion sensed that. He spoke very slowly and carefully, making sure we understood the concepts he was presenting.

"There are millions of solar systems like yours all over the Universe. Each, along with all the bodies of matter in them, have their own individual roles to play, as well as collectively, in contributing to the evolution of the Cosmos as a whole. One must approach both the individual evolution and the evolution of these bodies as groups before a complete understanding can be gained."

"In these other solar systems there are many planets that support sentient life. Also, each planet in any given system or group contributes to the growth of their Solar Family. To better understand this, let's consider your Solar System. Imagine for a moment that all of the

101

bodies within it go together to make up 'one body' or one 'unit' of consciousness. This body would have certain energy points. These are chakras. Solar or Systemic Chakras. There are seven of these." Carefully the Teacher began to name these centers.

"First the Kundalini or Anal Chakra. This center has the capability of 'drawing' in force like a magnet. It is like the 'pulse' or 'thermometer' of the solar group. This is located in the Sun. Next, let us remind you that when any form takes in energy, it must, in turn, be distributed through the body or form in question. This is the job of the Systemic Spleen Chakra. It also serves as a filtering device to 'cleanse' the system of impurities. When the energy is taken into the spleen, it is released as cosmic rays, gamma rays, X-rays and the like. There is a special esoteric relationship between the Kundalini and Spleen Centers, as distributors of force to all other bodies in the Solar Family. This Spleen Center is also located and comprises the 'etheric' body of the Sun. Think upon this very carefully."

Before going any further Albion gave us a bit of Solar System history.

"Once, long ago, two 'cosmic wanderers' were drawn into this Solar Group by gravitational pull. One was the size of the planet Mercury, the other a bit larger. They were large pieces of debris left over from the explosion of a star in another system. These bodies collided with an infant planet, the fifth one out from the Sun. This formed what you call the asteriod belt."

He continued about the Systemic Chakras. "Now let us consider the Solar Plexus. The work of this center of force is that it retrieves and pulls negative energies from the system and transmutes it into a higher vibration. It is a higher octave of the emotional energy of the system. It is the planet Uranus. It draws and then distributes the energies to all of the satellites, such as the Moon, who then transmit them to their 'parent' planets. Planets with no moon, such as Venus, have no need for and do not attract emotional energy. There will

102

come a time that the Earth's moon will sever its relationship with the Earth and become independent unto itself."

"Now let us turn our thoughts to the Heart Systemic Chakra. This is Venus, the 'alter-ego' or sister of the Earth. Venus generates a tremendous amount of force. It pours out Love energy to all the bodies in the System."

Albion advised us to go to esoteric literature to familiarize ourselves with the particular "life forms" that reside within the vibration of Venus for it would shed further light on understanding this spiritual energy.

A quick recall of such esoteric information reminded me that Venus is not populated with physical life, but rather with etheric life forms comprised of highly evolved "Beings". They are far beyond mankind in their evolution. Sananda is said to be the Venusian Logos, who is the Spirit of that sphere.

"Now let us go to the Systemic Throat Chakra. This is the center of communication, telepathic communication. It is located within the vibrations of the planet Mercury. Mercury is so close to the Sun that it is able to absorb massive amounts of the star's energy, which it then propels to areas far beyond the Solar System. In doing so, it links the system with other parts of the galaxy. It also serves to link the planetary vibrations together, thus communication. Planets are connected together, galaxies are connected, everything is related. This is the nature of the Universe."

"Galaxies appear throughout the Cosmos in groups or clusters, not alone. The galaxies within the 'cluster' to which your own Milky Way belongs are all on the same spiritual path of galactic evolution. This is true with all clusters. Galactic consciousness is not individualistic. It is a 'group consciousness'. Remember this."

"Now let us think about the Systemic Brow Chakra and its function. This is a center that projects energy, but also the star and planetary bodies use this center to gain 'insight' in order to penetrate atomic structures and therefore gain a greater understanding of the total relationship of all matter. This particular function thus keeps a clarity and purity and does not allow just any sort of body to invade the Solar System and remain. Let us give yourselves an example. There are planets that belong here, along with the Sun. Now suppose there is a 'cosmic wanderer' such as a planetoid or a comet that does not belong here. Some of these bodies could do great harm to the vibratory frequency of the system's residents. Although all of these aliens cannot be swept away, it is not bad, for some of them are beneficial and actually 'seed' the planets with nutrients and even the 'seeds' of life forms."

This comment was reminiscent of the theory of Fred Hoyle and N. C. Wickramasinghe, authors of *Lifecloud*, which was discussed in Chapter One. Albion continued.

"So the Systemic Brow Center is like radar that filters, selects and ejects those bodies that do not belong and would be harmful in some manner. If this center goes out of balance, bodies do creep in and cause damage. This Brow Chakra is embodied in the planet Saturn."

"Finally, we must consider the Systemic Crown Center. There is not one body, in any form, that can reach the full potential of the spiritual frequency of this center. It is the planet Pluto. This is the Shamballa of the Solar Group. Its energies are still frozen in time and space, yet to be fully released. It will be millions of years, in your time, before this releasing will occur, marking a time the Solar System will have reached enlightenment. It may well not be able to happen in this Great Age. An enlightened Solar System shines far beyond the greatest of Light forces in the Universe. When such occurs, it leads eventually to the same for all systems within any galaxy. An enlightened Galaxy! This can be witnessed on the physical plane and is known as a quasar."

"What we have said here of the esoteric relationship of the planets and the evolution of systems and galaxies is very important to a greater awareness of the Earth and its own evolution."

These words had given us a lot to ponder. I, for one, felt I needed to study it and weave it into the other information we had been taught. The session ended and we broke up for the night.

The Third Initiation of the Earth was becoming more clear and more real. I was beginning to piece it all together. I was understanding that once the period of "purification" or Earth changes was completed, the planet would take its Third Degree, and that this would bring a climaxing point between the power and higher consciousness, inaugurating a new cycle of activity for the planet. It will help the Earth to become in control of its personality. It will begin to shine with a "light" of its own and eventually will evolve to the point of bathing in Pure Light. Through its "newfound" type of intelligence, the Earth will be able to begin to convey its own ideas and thoughts into ideals. It will gain reasoning ability. Its growth will become more self-controlled and more rapid. It will become aware of its creative energy and will become capable of using it to create its future. I have read that the Third Initiation, being the first major degree, causes the "neophyte" to be confronted by the Black Magicians, resulting in barriers and obstacles being thrown in its path of growth. In relationship to the Earth, I could not help but wonder if the Black Brotherhood has indeed been using mankind as the tool of such obstacles and barriers. If so, they have been successful. Perhaps Albion's words will serve to open our eyes so that man and Earth can approach this time of Initiation in harmony together.

"Teach us to know and to see all the powers of the Universe, and give to us the knowledge to understand that they are all really one Power."
                                                    Black Elk

CHAPTER FOUR

MAPPING THE EARTH

"Great things are done when man and mountain meet." **William Blake**

When the American astronauts first stepped onto a world other than our own, it marked the beginning of man's entrance into a "new age". As a technological feat, the Apollo 11 mission was applauded by the entire world, but it seemed to have an effect that was felt much deeper within man's psyche. We had left the Earth for the first time. The two men who were on the flight team stood and looked back at the "shining blue marble" suspended in space. What an overwhelming experience that must have been!

The third planet out from its parent star, the Earth is a beautiful orb. Shakespeare had called it "this pendant world". A terrestrial globe, Earth, along with the other planets of the Solar System, revolves steadily along, fulfilling her duty as a life-bearing planet. Ancient people called her their "Mother". They built temples to her glory and performed rituals to her continued fertility in their religions. The oldest of these religions known are those that are based on the worship of Nature, called Earth religions. It seems to be inherent in our own nature, as humans, to worship and offer prayers to these forces that we cannot understand. So, primitive peoples all over the world have demonstrated and recorded evidence of their respect and love for the planet.

The Earth has also done some recording of her own. Geologists are constantly discovering evidence that this home of ours has preserved records of the collossal events of her past. Such can be seen in the lofty mountain ranges, the canyon gorges, and the volcanic craters and domes that dot the entire globe.

Man and Earth go together. In the Biblical account, humans are said to have been created from the soil and to the soil our physical bodies will return. Earth has been the stage upon which the human drama of life has been played for thousands of years. The interplay between the planet and the life forms swarming on her skin has shifted back and forth with the destinies of both constantly unfolding. It seems that each has affected change within the other. Man, with his thoughts, feelings, and deeds, Earth with her cycles of growing pains and changes. They are both "keyed" into the same purpose and task: survival.

While the major kingdoms of life, the mineral, plant, animal and human, have all developed over the centuries, far beyond their "garden of Eden" existence, it is hard to determine which one of the parties involved has been more affected by the relationship of Earth and life, for each has borne a burden so that they might become "self-realized".

Perhaps the greatest tool that can be used in bringing a relationship into a state that it will be of benefit to all concerned, is that of understanding. While early, more primitive man nay have had a closer understanding and regard for the Earth with its cycles and moods, it is certain modern man has slipped into a poor grasp of the same. Our present day "space age" attitudes may be a factor that has contributed to a "slack" in our viewing the planet as our "Mother". Also, political and religious views have led both man and planet to a dangerous point. Most religions of the world, especially those in the west, have sought to lift our consciousness beyond the Earth and "earthly" things, while the time

107

spent here is not given as much emphasis. Politics has put the world into boundaries of races and nations and the protection of these is the primary aim of that part of our society. All of this has caused the relationship between man and the Earth to fall short of being really connected and has lead man into a "smug" attitude, taking for granted the ground under his feet.

I think that it was Albion's concern for this faltering relationship coupled with his feelings about our desperate need at this particular time to better understand the planet, that caused him to choose this particular sort of information for his book. Some of his first words about this show evidence of this motive. His words were,

"The 'Earth changes' have been a general theme, for some time, that has flowed throughout the New Age teachings. As we come to a point in time when these changes will be more and more apparent, for they have indeed already begun, we feel a strong need to give information that will strengthen mankind's relationship and thus his understanding of his terrestrial sphere."

These words brought our first real lessons in "Geomancy" (esoteric knowledge of the Earth for purposes of divination) into reality. What was to follow opened up a view of the Earth that none of us had ever been exposed to or thought of before. "We wish to make certain areas -- for they are power points -- of the planet known to you. We wish to call them 'vortices' " were the words that came through on a chilly night in November of 1980. "There are many places we will discuss that will be familiar and some will not, but they will all have a specific type of energy. These are not 'ordinary' spots on the globe."

His thoughts continued, with each word being formed carefully and deliberately, seeming to know our need to have the concepts he was about to speak of explained very carefully.

"Some of these vortices are positive, some are negative, some are neutral, containing no charge as such. Some are natural to the planet, while others are man-made in nature."

To say that this information peaked our interest is an understatement. My husband, Scott, and our friends A. S. and D. remembered their reaction to those words, as I listened to the tape later, in their presence.

These "vortices" continued to be his topic. "Some are natural 'creators', other are natural 'destroyers'." It was not until much later in our sessions that the choice of words in this last sentence became more clear. You too will see this as we go along, so keep them in mind. "We wish to make you aware of the specific geographical sites on which these vortices are located." The Teacher further indicated that there are other people that would be receiving, writing about and teaching this same sort of information and that surely our paths would eventually cross. This was another one of those bits of information that Albion has a way of dropping into his conversations that he rarely makes any further reference to. It is interesting how we forget such innuendos, only to have them crop up as we are transcribing a tape or remember it only when it happens as he has said that it would. I have often wondered if his "matter-of-fact" approach to these little "tid-bits" diminished their importance or if his method of delivering them to us is all that is involved. Albion does have his distinct methods of speaking and expressing himself. In any respect, such comments have served to deepen my own thoughts about this Entity that I have come to know as my "Source".

"You will go to some of these places in the future. Some of them you have already been to." Then, his next statement was another one that was not to become clear until a later meeting that Scott and I had with a Native American medicine man a year later. Sun Bear, a Chippewa, who lives in Spokane, Washington, also has an interest in educating people of all races in regards to understanding and setting up a more balanced relationship with the planet. It was he who first spoke to me about "recharging" and healing the Earth Mother. Albion continued.

"We will utilize your presence in some of these areas, through your travels, but that will not be often enough or widespread enough. This is why we choose to share our thoughts in a book, for this can help to create a 'network' of people that can help with the tasks."

"You will be told of vortices in areas worldwide. Some of these areas will be in water, some on dry land."

The Teacher's desire to bring this data together became more apparent as his words continued. "I, Albion, will explain the vibrational frequencies and the function and importance of each vortex. Hopefully, it will shed some light on our point of view of the Earth changes and of the 'karmic' conditions of the planet as well. We will speak of the most powerful vortices in the world."

This is a good place to stop and identify what the word "vortex" actually means. I don't think that I was totally sure of its meaning, or at least in the context which Albion was using it. Webster's New World Dictionary gives three definitions of the word vortex: "Whirling mass, forming a vacuum in its center into which anything caught in the motion is drawn; a whirl or powerful eddy of air, whirlwind". The third characterization seemed to fit better with the context of Albion's thoughts. It described a vortex as: "Any activity, situation or state of affairs that resembles a whirl or eddy in its rush; absorbing effect, catastrophic power, etc".

The picture our Source was painting began to become more clear and at the same time, more intriguing. "You will go to England, France and Scotland. You will also go to Hawaii." No precise indication of a specific motive was given for these trips at that time. The extent of his "planet mapping" was pointed out in the declaration that: "We want to first discuss these areas of the world that are involved with the three major 'Ray' influences." Remember, the rays are "emanations of divine force". The three major rays indicated are certain to refer to Ray One, the ray of will and power, Ray Two, the ray of love and wisdom, and Ray Three, the ray of active intelligence. All of these energies exercise a major function within consciousness, as well as activities and events in time.

"We also want to make it very clear to you that the information concerning these geographical locations and currents is really nothing new. Also, they are not 'chosen' by the Spiritual Hierarchy or any aspect of 'Divine Consciousness'. Most of them are the direct result of the beginnings of the Earth and its own evolution." This firmly established the "naturalness" of the vortices. He continued: "Some of the vortices will be in populated areas and some will not. They have to do with the Earth and the evolvement of the various life forms of which you are all an integral part. How these lives and the planet evolve in harmony is our concern."

It was becoming clearer to us now as to the characteristics the information was taking on. Albion began to quicken his pace. Every sentence seemed to no longer be composed of separate statements, but gradually began to come together.

"We wish to speak for a moment about the specific types of vortices" were the words that began to sort the information into categories. "The Earth's vortices have a relationship with all the life forms on her skin. First, let us think about the actual appearance and makeup of the vortices which could be described as 'astral' in nature." This choice of words caught my attention immediately. From years of study regarding the subtly bodies of Nature and man, I recognized astral matter and the astral dimension to be emotional in its origin and relating to feeling, as well as having a "filmy" or "misty" substance and look to it. This seemed to slant the vortices as "psychic reflections" that could only be seen with the clairvoyant sight, then they must be the result of the Earth's "emotional" body and its response to its own evolutionary experiences. These words settled strongly in my thoughts. These "whirlpools" of energy were invisible, but they were real, nonetheless. More information as to their actual appearance followed:

"If you could touch a vortex with your physical hands

it would feel slightly wet, of a watery consistency. It would seem 'thick', somewhat like a fog. It would also feel slightly sticky. It would have no actual color, but does reflect the colors of the environment, sometimes. It's essence takes on a sort of radiance.''

What turned out to be one of the most important points of the material was made next, although it was not elaborated upon at that time. Albion reminded us that the vortices are both positive and negative in their charge, plus he carried that explanation a step further by choosing words that were to become his constant terms for future identification of what charge any given vortex has. Those that are positively charged he named "electrical". The negative (negative not to mean 'bad') ones he called magnetic". There was also the term "electromagnetic", which he gave to mean an equal amount of both electricity and magnestism. Science, while it does not totally understand the nature of electromagnetism, describes it as the physics of the relationship between electricity and magnetism. Magnetism, which is produced by a current of electricity, is another bit of detail, but that is all that is currently known. Albion's use of electromagnetism in regards to the vortices seemed to be merely to point out that that type of vortex consisted of the energies of both.

Electricity and magnetism seemed to be chosen also for a more esoteric reason. Albion indicated on a number of occasions as the work proceeded that an electrical force was a male, projective frequency, while magnetism was female and receptive in nature. Electromagnetism would be of an androgenous nature. There is clarification of this as the sessions go along.

The meeting that night came to a close as the Mentor concluded:

"Electricity and magnetism are constantly reacting upon each other, with the resulting energy giving birth to evolving life. Without this interplay by these two opposing forces, there would be no life. We do not refer only to life on this planet in its various forms, but to LIFE that is the very force that gives 'Being' to matter itself."

It had been a long evening. My body was tired, for the hour was quite late, but my mind was racing! Perhaps the caffiene in the two cups of coffee that Scott and I drank didn't do much in helping us to relax either. Scott sat in his usual quiet manner and listened, while I chattered until the wee hours of the morning.

More than two weeks went by before our next session. During that two weeks, other aspects of my work began to require my attention. At the time, I was working in Los Angeles and had been since April of the preceeding year, on KMPC Radio. My choice not to live in California necessitated my traveling to and from Los Angeles every weekend. Weekends were spent doing private counselings and conducting my five hour Saturday night talk show that dealt with various subjects and guests working on the paranormal and "Holism". Thoughts of vortices danced in my head during that period and I remember feeling, on a number of occasions, an excitement about Albion's channeling a book. I was ready, for visions of expanding Albion's work excited me, but frightened me at the same time. I had not been very "verbal" about my Teacher, at least not in a public way. Maybe it was lack of confidence in myself, but certainly not in Albion or his teachings. I shuttered each time the thought of making his presence known beyond the small groups that comprised the classes that he had taught in the past, passed through my mind. I finally came to test my own confidence in myself and my own personal relationship with Albion, realizing that he would do nothing unless the time was right. If he felt that the time was right, then I would trust his judgment.

I arrived back in Sedona and quickly arranged a time for our next session. The four of us got together and chatted for a while, but we were all anxious to get started. I thought that the book would be only about vortices. I soon found that this was not to be the case.

Albion's words came out loud and strong as he began to add to the groundwork that he had laid down two

113

weeks prior.

"As we come forward here now, we wish to bring to your attention one of the most powerful and significant electrical vortices that exists in the continental United States. This eddy is an embodiment of 'Ray One' force. It is located in the primary area of Mt. Shasta, California, but extends out for just about one mile southeast."

It definitely left an impression on me as the first vortex was identified! It was a place that neither Scott nor I had ever been at the time. A quick bit of reference work & a later trip revealed that Mt. Shasta is indeed a beautiful sight! It is a volcanic mountain in the Cascade range in California and towers 14,162 feet into the skies. Albion went on."This is a 'destructive' vortex in the sense that it acts as a 'catch-all' for the negative energies for the area of California and much of the western part of the country. It draws like a magnet. It takes in negative thought-forms and energy so that they are diminished in their affect on the planet,and transmutes them into positive energies."

This was a rather different and interesting concept! The manner in which the vortex functioned was given to us next. "These negative energies are gathered by suction, creating a 'funnel-like' effect. Mt. Shasta then breaks them down and dissipates them." It was as if he was describing the mountain as a sort of astral "relief valve". He said that similar vortices existed elsewhere, although he did not name them at that time. It was later determined that all Ray One vortices serve a like purpose of either building up a power or tearing it down. Areas where there are high concentrations of negative thought forms and energies, due to population, planetary stress and various other types of conflicts, seemed to be endowed with funnels akin to the one at Mt. Shasta. He spoke of another one like Shasta that lies further to the north, approximately one and one half miles, which he labeled a sub- or mini-vortex that has the same abilities. A name was not given, which has led me to refer to both of these, since they are so close together, as the "Shasta

114

Complex". I became more interested in learning more about this great peak and the surrounding area, so I did some additional research.

Shasta is located on the northern extremity of the Sierra Nevada mountains in Siskiyou County, California. It is actually the cone of an extinct volcano that used to be much higher than it is now. The ground around it is sunken and the mountain itself has been worn away by ice. It really shouldn't be considered as an extinct volcano because it is still capable of eruption due to a sulphurous furole that lies below the extreme summit and one or two others on its northern slope. Shasta is snow-covered during most of the year.

Aside from the interesting physical data to be learned about Mt. Shasta, there is also a history of strange happenings that are associated with it. Stories are circulated about unusual looking people that emerge from the forest and hide when seen by anyone. They are most often described as tall, graceful, agile and dressed "different". Some people even describe them as wearing headdresses. They are said to have larger heads than we do, larger foreheads and they always pay for things that they buy in the local area with gold nuggets! Chants have been heard coming from the general area of the mountain and reports of "domes" that have been seen persist right up until this day. Another facet of the stories seems to suggest that there is something going on there that is a bit reminiscent of "UFO" activity. Sometimes cars are said not to function properly, as if their electrical circuits have lost their power. There have been many ufo sightings that have been reported in the area, along with "strange boat-like" objects. Some people feel that there is actually still a colony of the direct ancestors of the ancient Lemurians that live there and that they still practice their ancient rituals. A hike of the area is said to reveal the presence of carved statuary and ruined buildings. What I had learned peaked my curiosity.

"There is a second vortex that is located in Arizona. It

is located forty-five miles east of a town known as Tuba City. This is in Navajo territory,(Hopi-Navajo joint use area approximately 20 miles northeast of Oraibi) but has nothing to do with that tribe of Native Americans. It is a vortex that, unlike Mt. Shasta, is of a 'constructive' sort. It is a Ray Two vibration. It connects the energies of the planet and the life forms that are positive in their nature. This vortex appears as an astral 'cylinder' which extends down into the center of the Earth." He told us that this cylinder extends about the same distance as from the ground to the center of the Earth, out into space. This would be approximately 4,000 miles! The enormity of this power source caused us to discuss our surprise about this when the session ended. He had also added that the vortex was a "creative" force, another quality of Ray Two energies. Creativity, in man, we can all relate to, but Albion explained how the planet makes use of such energy as well. It can take all of the elements and chemicals in the soil and blend them together, making them complimentary. "This is why this Tuba City vortex is so rich in oil, natural gas, uranium and other minerals that have become valuable to mankind." He also related that this creative tide was unmatched by any other, but that there were many of its sort in the world.

A third vortex became apparent as the Teacher continued. "It is located in the area you know as the Ocala National Forrest in Florida. It vibrates to the energy of Ray Three." He seemed to relate this ray type to mind, as well as to communication. "We want to call this vortex a 'communication beacon'." He indicated that all Ray Three vortices are communication beacons. "Were you to see them with your psychic sight, they would appear as 'searchlights'. It is a lighthouse, of sorts. Communication vortices pulsate at regular intervals. The Ocala 'beacon' comes from within the ground, it is not on the surface." It is interesting to note that, according to the Teacher, beacons are one of the most common types of energy centers. Without giving specific loca-

116

tions, he said that there are many other such beacons in this country and others, just like the one near Ocala.

The session ended at this point, for the evening, but not without Albion's giving us instructions that he wanted to continue the work on as regular a basis as possible. After we were finished, we compared schedules for the near future and decided we could get together again in one week.

A week later, my living room once again became a classroom. Albion began with his usual: "As we come forward here now, we come in order to proceed with our work." His first tidbit of information was an additional comment concerning Mt. Shasta.

"In order to bring a clearer understanding of the importance of Ray One force, we might point out that through destruction, creation survives. Think about this. When the Earth was quite young it was first covered by a huge shallow sea that covered the entire sphere. As the planet evolved, it changed, causing great pressures to be built up. As these pressures were relieved, due to the heating of the core, dry land that you now call continents began to appear, built up from volcanic eruptions down under. This continued for millions of years. In the basin you now know as the Pacific Ocean, there was once a massive land mass. The whole 'lid' was blown apart, resulting in the so-called 'Ring of Fire'. This volcanic chain still exists."

He went on to say that the Ring of Fire is the single most powerful, most potentially destructive vortex on the entire planet. It is also the largest vortex of any kind and it is electrical in its nature.

After sharing these additional remarks about Shasta and the Earth's youth, he turned his attention towards still another category of vortices. Albion spoke:

"The 'Synthesizer' vortices are very important and serve some major purposes. First, they synthesize the planet into its relationship with the entire Solar Group. Without these centers of force the Earth would not be able to maintain its orbit. It would go off on its own and would not obey the law of gravity."

These words were a bit of a puzzle to me when I first listened to them on tape the next day. However, after giving them some thought, especially about the law of gravity, I thought back to a quote that I had read in one of Dion Fortune's books, *The Mystical Quaballah*, which stated that "God is pressure". These two pieces of information seemed to correlate, but I wasn't sure I understood all of the implications.

Albion's voice seemed to have a quicker and more intense pace than usual that night. The room was glowing from the embers in the fireplace, for these early winter evenings had begun to sport a noticeable chill.

"All spheres, be they suns or planets, asteroids, comets or even galaxies, have three major synthesizing vortices which serve major purposes and several minor ones. They are the North and South Poles, the opposite ends of any body. So, they are the 'polarizing' agents."

Albion continued to elaborate about the poles, saying that when the Earth was very young and was beginning to settle into its orbit, this wobbling "planet baby" had   difficulty sustaining that pattern. Four times during the first 25,000,000 years, the Earth rolled over and its poles shifted. This generated an immense amount of electrical force, coupled with magnetic force and in his words, "electromagnetic-type energy was the result." We will see in the next chapter, which concerns the Earth changes, that there are ancient legends and some scientific data that suggest a pole shift has occurred.

Albion went on to point out the other important "synthesizer". "The third one of the synthesizing vortices is the equator. Its purpose is to unite the hemispheres and keep them in balance." Keeping in mind Albion's definition of electrical and magnetic, he gave an example of his words:

"Let us consider an Earth sliced into top and bottom halves with the equator as the cutting point. In the top half, the energy is more electrical, while the energy in the bottom half is more magnetic. Throughout history, you will find that all of the northern-most civilizations, both ancient and modern, are more electrical in nature and therefore more aggressive and warlike. The cultures of the southern hemisphere are more receptive, creative and bent towards cultural matters." According to the Teacher, "such is the effect of the electrical and magnetic forces constantly at play one upon the other." He added a few more comments along this line of thought. "The 'equator synthesizer' is necessary in order to sustain the magnetic aura of the Earth itself. This field completely surrounds, but does not touch the planet. Part of this aura is what you call the atmosphere, part of the magnetic field." Also, for those who are interested in a visual, he said that the equator synthesizer appears to the psychic "sight" as a single bolt of blue lightning and completely circles the Earth. The Pole Synthesizers are likewise blue in color, except at the very center, where there is a constant flickering of red light or flame.

While it was clear that the poles and the equator were the main synthesizers, he began to share with us the location of others, the more minor ones. But first he gave further clarification of his choice and use of the word "synthesizer". "Consider the word synthesizer. You should immediately think of related terms such as balance and harmony." Upon hearing his definition I later consulted the Webster's New World Dictionary (p. 1445) to find this meaning: "the putting together of parts or elements to form a whole, in Hegelian philosophy, the unified whole, in which opposites are reconciled". These two, combined, give us a good idea of Albion's intended thought. He further stated that forces in opposition do not always create conflict, but can also create balance.

"There is another synthesizing vortex that is located in Vancouver, B.C. near the point where Canada and the U.S. join. This vortex attracts high and low pressure weather systems, especially those that are loaded with water. This energy causes currents of wind that bring these fronts over North America, that in turn, creates a large percentage of the weather patterns for the continent. This is 'synthesis'."

Another example and location of a synthesizer that the Teacher shared concerned an area of southern California known as Santa Ana.

"There is a magnificent vortex there that also picks up atmospheric conditions and spreads them towards the midwest, across the plains and on to the northeastern parts of the country. These vast and powerful winds are necessary to the survival of life upon the planet. Many wind systems are spawned by the Santa Ana vortex."

It began to come clear that these synthesizers have to do with weather patterns. He went on: "Hovering directly above Tampa, Florida, there is a most intense vortex. If it were viewed with the clairvoyant sight, it would appear as a huge tornado-like 'funnel' of pure lightning, pure electrical energy."

He described this eddy as extending 8,240 feet, which is one and three-fourths of a mile above land. This is a very important synthesizer due to its far-reaching vibrations that give it the ability to draw pure, electrical force from far out into the Atlantic and the Gulf of Mexico, as well as from land mass areas as far inland as the plains states. Another bit of conversation was added about Tampa that served to stir our curiosity. "The Tampa Vortex is second only to Mt. Everest, which is located in the single most powerful electrical center on the planet other than the Ring of Fire itself." His next words were the first indication that any of these vortices could be dangerous to physical life. "The Tampa Vortex can be a very dangerous vortex due to the lightning that it generates. Yet, without electrical energy centers, life would not, could not exist." Albion turned his thoughts to archeology by saying that: "It will be discovered that some of the earliest civilizations, even as far back as the Titans, had their existence in the area of Tampa, as well as the areas 150 miles to the north and south. Their size was due to the type of force promoted by this electrical energy in its primitive stages." A quick reference to *The Secret Doctrine*, Volume Two, will reveal information about a race of giants, Titans, that once thrived on the Earth.

"Another electrical vortex is located in the area of Chihuahua, Mexico. Still another of these 'funnels' of electricity is located on Kitt Peak in Arizona." Then, a vivid description of "synthesizers" was given. "When there is a great deal of electricity in the atmosphere, such as when the Earth passes through the tail of a comet or any type of phenomenon that causes electrical friction in the atmosphere, these vortices literally 'light' up. They also create a 'hum..mmm.mmm' that can be heard with the spiritual ears. The Tampa vortex feeds and is the source for a big percentage of the electrical energy present in the northern hemisphere. Tampa 'feeds' Kitt Peak and Chihuahua and thus sets up a triangular circuit that uses water in the Gulf of Mexico as a conductor. It goes across the Gulf as a 'zipping' sort of electrical charge."

This was the first time that Albion showed a connection of one vortex to another. We were to discover that the Earth is criss-crossed with lines of force which conduct a flow of power, like a web that creates a "network".

In later sessions there was mention of other synthesizers located in other parts of the world. One is known as the Intertropical or Equatorial Convergence Zone. This comprises a belt of converging trade winds and rising air that encircles the Earth near the Equator. The activity of the rising air produces frequent thunderstorms resulting in heavy rainfall. Oceanic regions of calm surface air, called the "doldrums", occur in this zone. This zone can and does shift seasonally with the Sun and its position varies daily. It experiences particularly large shifts over the Indian Ocean due to the Asian continent's pressure patterns.

We find that the topography of the Earth, radiation from the Sun, and the albedo of the Earth's surface all affect these vortices Albion calls synthesizers. The

Teacher said that other synthesizers are to be found around the areas of Bermuda, Cuba, off the main island of Hawaii, Iceland, Cape Cod (off the coast of New England), the Black Sea, the Sea of Galilee, the Bering Strait, plus two located on dry land in the Gobi and the Sahara Deserts.

Another weather synthesizer mentioned on this continent is the Chinook winds that originate on the east side of the Rockies. These winds are warm, dry, and catabolic and are produced by descending air currents and they blow from the west primarily in winter. Known around the world as "foehn" winds, the nickname Chinook comes from the Chinook Indians who camp near the mouth of the Colombia River. These winds really showed their force in Colorado during the winter of 1981, reaching 141 m.p.h.! This caused serious erosion to farmlands.

Although most of these synthesizers have to do with weather and electrical patterns, there is only one occasion when they are utilized for another purpose. Albion gave an example to explain the continent of Pacifica, where a vortex was located that was one hundred times more intense than the one that is now in Tampa. It was over a land mass that now barely peeps above the surface of the Pacific, Maui in Hawaii. It was this vortex that triggered the demise of that huge continent. This makes a suggestion as to what can and will be coming in the future, does it not?

I must admit that this last sentence did not thrill me a lot. I wasn't too sure where this conversation would go after this remark. Our thoughts got a bit of a breather as he went on to say that ancient people, such as the later Atlanteans and the Egyptians, knew of these synthesizers and knew how to harness energy from them. One method they used on Atlantis was to take a large quartz crystal, place it in the vortex area and it, in turn, would absorb the energies and store them like a battery. Much about this sort of practice can be read about in the Edgar Cayce material on Atlantis.

This concluded the basic information about synthesizers and ended our session for the evening. At first, we had it in our heads that the vortex information would follow some sort of a pattern. But we were soon to learn that this was not to be the case. The more than seventy-five sessions for the channeling of this material did not follow any set design or pattern, with one specific block of information following or leading to another. Although it did make the final task of organizing the material a more difficult one, an attempt has been made in this writing to present the information exactly as it came through, such as the direct use of Albion's words, but also trying to arrange it into some semblance of order.

The following two sessions were spent with the Teacher giving additional data about the location and functions of electrical vortices. Earlier mention had been made in regards to Mt. Everest and the following is a quote from Albion about this great mountain.

"In the mountain range known as the Himalayas, lies a peak that is surpassed by none other on this planet. It is Mt. Everest. This 'point of light' is the 'watchtower' with its watchful eye upon the location of two countries that contain within their national and racial consciousness, the most ancient of all religious thoughtforms of this present root race. They are India and Tibet."

Mt. Everest, known as Chomolungma to the locals, spires 29,028 feet into the sky. Chomolungma translates to mean "Goddess Mother of the Earth". It is situated on the Nepal-Tibet border. This vortex is a Ray One center and gives off a tremendous amount of sheer power! This power sustains life and spreads prana all over the globe.

Another mountain, the Teacher said, that has a special esoteric relationship with Mt. Everest, is Mt. Ararat. Our thoughts immediately go to the Bible and the deluge, remembering Ararat as the alleged landing place for Noah's ark. Visible for a hundred miles away, these two peaks stretch upward approximately 17,000 feet. It sits in eastern Turkey near the Armenian and Iranian borders.

Albion went on to another summit after identifying Ararat, his words turning our attention to Alaska.

"The peaks of Ararat, Everest, and Alaska's Mt. McKinley, are all 'electrical watchtowers' and they have their 'watchful eyes' upon the parts of the planet that are the most important to the future. There will come a time that the land of Alaska will be, not just in words only, the 'New Frontier'. These words require a lot of careful thought."

Indeed they do! They seemed to me to have an air of prophecy about them.

The Channel next suggested taking a globe and marking the three peaks of Mt. Ararat, McKinley and Everest. We should draw a line between them, being sure to pay attention to the parts of the Earth, including water, that these lines crossed. He said that these lines are the conductors for electricity from these three mountains and the areas that lie around them. These threads, like connectors, make a "humming" sound, indicative of the electrical current being transmitted through them.

More information came concerning the sounds involved. "If you were to hear Mt. Ararat, it would sound like a siren. It is a loud wail that ebbs and flows, loud to soft and back to loud again. It is a beacon . . . it is a monument to time."

"If you tune into the sound frequency of Mt. Everest, you would encounter the sound of 'high C' on the musical scale. It does not ebb and flow like Ararat, but is constantly in a spiral-like motion of sound, with the sound beginning small and getting louder and louder as time goes by. There will actually come a time that it will become physically audible!"

"Mt. McKinley generates a sound that is like the wind, a howling wind. It is an awesome power that never ceases to blow."

Distributors of life force, these three peaks resounded in our thoughts and conversation following the ses-

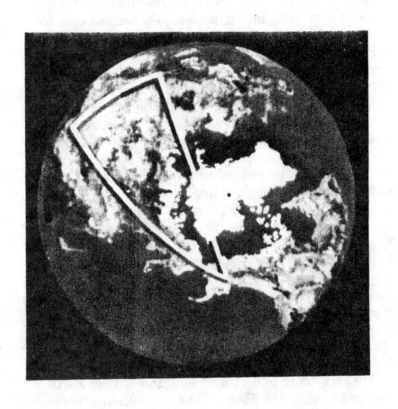

Three Peaks (Main Electrical Vortices)

sion. D. commented that he felt that he would like to go to all of these three mountain someday. His idea had already been running around in the heads of the rest of us before he spoke. We all quickly agreed to do that at sometime in the future. Knowing that there was much more to come in Albion's sessions, we decided that by the time he was finished, we could probably keep some travel agency very busy! We wouldn't worry about the small details, like money! That note of humor brought the evening to a close with all of us feeling as if we had "visions of electrical vortices" dancing in our heads.

The next session began with further data about Mt. Ararat. I have made a special point to give this information in this form, for Albion placed a special label on this summit. He related this vortex to a past period of Earth changes, the flood that is prominent in legends of civilizations world-wide. It was also the first mention of Earth changes to come, which we were to learn was to be very much a part of this work.

"Mt. Ararat is a powerful vortex that is very ancient. Your Bible speaks of a great flood that was a major catastrophic event. It was, indeed, for it marked the Earth's 'Second Initiation' in its own process of spiritual growth." These words prompted me to realize that he was going to be talking about the Earth's initiations in their entirety, which subsequently played a great role in my expanding understanding of the "living Earth" consciousness, "The flood caused many civilizations to flee and seek shelter. However, there was not much shelter to be found, and many perished. Many people believe that there was only one flood, and there was only one major one. But, what you generally refer to as 'the flood' actually occurred over a period spanning years. During that time, many floods rose and fell, culminating in 'the flood' of ancient legends. There also was not just one Noah, but many like him who were prepared for this major disaster, change period. Other 'Noahs' of previous floods that had been building up to the big one had also survived. Prophecy of these wet periods caused them to

126

be forewarned and many people were prepared. You approach such a period now of change, but not purely by flood. This vortex, Mt. Ararat, was the single unit of electrical force that coagulated at the time of the Second Initiation into a full-fledged eddy. So, we see Mt. Ararat, now, as a symbol of the Second Initiation. The 'voice of God' promised men that the Earth had passed its test and would never undergo destruction by water again." Albion went on to say: "Its astral body was born during this period. The planet opened its feelings and emotions, and it developed a memory, which can be seen physically in the records kept by Nature in the terrain. The grandest of all canyons is an example of this."

The "grandest of all canyons" is Albion's favorite way to describe the Grand Canyon located here in Arizona. He gave more about this area in later sessions. Continuing about Mt. Ararat, he said:

"This is a most powerful vortex. If you visit there (he must have read my thoughts) it is best to go in the early morning hours just at daybreak for its energy is released at that time in full force. One only has to stand there in a visual quest to understand, receive, absorb, and utilize the pure electrical force that comes from this great mountain. Standing erect, it is a reminder, a monument, that shall never again be touched by Earth changes."

This last piece of information about Earth changes and Earth's initiations were stirring all sorts of the pieces of the puzzle around in my mind. Some of them were beginning to fit together. I remembered back to the process of Initiation that I had learned about through my Theosophical studies. I was beginning to realize now that it could also be applied to a planet, so the picture was becoming more complete. Our discussion after the session that evening seemed to center around Albion's comments of our approaching such a major period of Earth changes again! His motivation for this work I was to put together into a book was clearer to me more at that mo-

127

ment than ever before.

Further data followed into the next session, which was to prove to be the rule of their content rather than the exception. He called attention to "one of the most magnificent and most important mountain regions on the continent of North America." By this time we were accustomed to having to change locations geographically, very quickly in our thoughts. "The Rockies are a highly charged electric pattern or 'grid'." Here was another new term, one that was familiar to me from other sources.

"We wish to discern the difference between a vortex and a grid. A grid is a 'pattern' of energy, whereas a vortex is a pattern of energy that has coagulated into a funnel of power. It would be correct to say that the entire Earth is an energy pattern of one form or another. Many people are aware of the grid systems. A grid indicates an area, in our use of the term, that is highly charged, but has not enough energy to actually coagulate into a vortex. As sensitive people pass through such an area, they feel its influence."

The Teacher then used a very simple analogy to relate a further understanding of a grid.

"If you imagine a weather radar screen, you would see the various weather patterns and fronts and formations, as 'blotches' of activity. Some of these patterns will be circular in motion, while others will spread out over great distances. Not all will form into actual organized systems (vortex) but will remain to be seen only as concentrated areas of weather activity (grid). Such is a grid and such is the entire Rocky Mountain range."

"There is a part of the Rockies known as the Grand Tetons. This whole spot came very close to forming itself into a full-blown vortex, but did not have enough power. In the area of these peaks is an actual electrical vortex, the only one this close to this part of the chain that is a powerful vitalizer for life forms. It too, spews out prana. All life forms can draw energy from its effects. It would be a wonderful place for a healing center, for people who are ill can be recharged there. It is a good energy for the blood circulation as are all electrical vortices. It is also wise to be cautious in electrical vortices if the blood pressure is high. You should not remain in such areas too long at a time."

Another couple of electrical vortices were mentioned in this session.

"Yellowstone Falls in Yellowstone National Park in Wyoming, has an unusual nature, as does Niagara Falls on the New York/Ontario border. Their energy is in the power of the falling of the water. Because of the amount of energy created by the downward plunge, the type of force generated is electric. But, due to the mud pools, hot springs, and the nature of the element of water itself, which is magnetic, these two forces combine and the result is that such places become electromagnetic."

Yellowstone Falls drops 308 feet in the Grand Falls area. A lot of power, indeed. After this information, A. S. interrupted to ask Albion a question. "Would this be true of any major waterfalls all over the Earth?" "Yes," Albion replied, without further comment. He added only that one cup of mud from any hot springs area would charge the physical body if it were rubbed onto the flesh.

Scott and I were preparing to leave for a lecture we were scheduled to do in Florida, so the sessions were not possible for two weeks. It was going to be wonderful to be back in the "Sunshine State" where we had lived before moving to the West. We had met in Tampa & this was the second marriage for both of us. Our desire to work together as a New Age team has been a strong point in our relationship from the very beginning. Scott's regard for Albion's teachings had drawn him into my "channeling class", and our love developed from there. We were to spend time in Tampa on this return trip, working and seeing old friends.

After a successful time in Florida, our return to Sedona was a welcome one. We always miss the red rocks when we have to be away. Our next session with Albion was set up with A. S. and D. shortly after our arrival.

The Teacher continued the work on the vortices, with his attention turning from the electrical to the magnetic ones. Before getting into new territory, however, there were a few additions to the location of electrical vortices that were made. They were Stone Mountain (Georgia), Ceasar's Head (North Carolina), and the San Francisco Peaks (Flagstaff, Arizona). All of these are in the United States for this was the place he began his discussion. You will find that as time goes on, he did make reference to more electrical energy points in other parts of the world, but they did not become evident until he began to broaden his scope beyond this country more often.

Albion began his discussion that night with a note of clarification about vortices in general.

"We have to conform to boundaries or identification by countries so the reader will be able to easily relate to the actual locations. But, we wish to make it clear that when we view the Earth, or any planetary body, we do not concern ourselves with man-made boundaries. We are only interested in the vortices themselves, no matter which boundary they lie within. The country is not what makes a vortex, but purely the energies involved. You should not consider any country or city special due to a vortex being located within it, or at fault, should the vortex be a negative one."

We later were to learn that the only real exception to this thought would be in regards to so-called "man-made" vortices, which are temporary in their nature. More about these are to come later in this work.

The groundwork for magnetic vortices began.

"The Pacific Ocean is a highly-charged electrical body of water. The Atlantic is highly magnetic. This forms a polarity. Magnetic vortices are also located in various parts of the world."

He described this type of eddy as "like a suction area, having the ability to attract energies into it. They are extremely fertile locations and promote reproduction on all levels and to all life forms. Because the magnetic vortices are feminine or receptive in nature, they also stimulate all subconscious activities, such as dreams, psychic impressions and sensitivity, creativity, and memory." Such power centers can also be very powerful, as with the electrical ones, in being conducive to intuition and spiritual growth.

The first magnetic vortex that was mentioned was a place that was very familiar.

"It is the whole country of Yucatan. It has drawn men from various parts of the world throughout previous periods of Earth changes. There are temples and other buildings in this place that were built in the distant past by 'migrants' from other civilizations. Some of these temples were used for worship, while doubling also as astronomical observatories. Some of the people that erected these structures, as is true with similar structures worldwide, were aware that their rituals and the designs of the buildings themselves, had 'drawing power'. They received energy from the solar unit (Sun), the planets, the Universe, as well as from the Spiritual Hierarchy itself."

A reference was then made relating to the beliefs of the Ancients. "The constellation of Draco was revered by the individuals in the Yucatan area in olden times, it was the serpent in the night sky." Other than my understanding of the serpent as a symbol of wisdom to many cultures, I had no further clue to the full meaning of this reference. All of us speculated after the channeling was finished that maybe he was indicating a sort of "ancient astronaut" theory, but no specific explanation was given at that time.

It is widely speculated that ancient civilizations believed that they had come from the stars. Another clue to the "Draco" comment was channeled later, so I include it here, at this point.

"There is an astral type energy that constantly bombards your planet, that had its origin in the vicinity of the Draco constellation. This energy is rather electrical in nature, filled with prana. It is received by the Yucatan vortex and is transformed into pure magnetism. This

131

makes the Yucatan a place that is quite conducive to cultural, creative and spiritual development. Art has flourished there. Telepathic ability is strong with its inhabitants of the past and the present."

His next statement gave me reason to think we might need that travel agent after all!

"There will come a time that we will instruct yourselves to make a pilgrimage to Yucatan so that you might touch into the 'vibration' of these energies. This will help you clearly to understand what a 'pure' magnetic vortex is like in terms of its frequency."

He said that there would be no other area in the world that he could discuss that would be more conducive to stimulating the flow of creative energies, sharpening telepathic abilities, as well as improving memory. With Scott being an artist, the stimulation of creative energies sounded like a grand idea. My own psychic abilities are always open for improvement, so the trip was definitely something to look forward to someday. The Teacher continued about Yucatan.

"There are temples in the form of stepped pyramids there that contain records that have long been 'lost' to man. Some of them are buried deep in the Earth." He also stated his belief that this area had once been a part of the now lost Lemuria. He elaborated.

"It was a very large continent, this Pacifica (Albion's name for Lemuria) that, up until the time of its destruction over 20,000 years ago, had supported various life forms, including man, for well over 200,000 years. These people were very primitive in comparison to the Antillians (Atlanteans), for example, who saw the advent of technology during their time. Although the Pacificans did develop technology, they did not advance it as far as the Atlanteans and others. There were power points that were scattered all over this land. Some of these, though Pacifica lay buried now beneath the sea, are still in effect to this day."

Albion's thoughts turned from the Yucatan and Lemuria.

"Since we are discussing magnetic vortices, let us turn our thoughts to an area in the Atlantic, to a group of islands known as the West Indies. There are three islands, in particular, that we wish to bring to your attention. Each of them is magnetic in nature, but only one of them has an actual vortex. The islands of Grenada and Haiti are both magnetic, which causes them to be very fertile and it also affects their cultures. The inhabitants of these islands, due to the intense magnetic energies present, have phenomenal psychic capabilities. But, the third island, Bimini, both the north and south islands, is where the magnetic vortex is, and it is so intense that it stretches for 25 miles in every direction! It is one of the oldest on Earth and is as intense as the vortex in the Yucatan."

Bimini is familiar to most of us as a result of the predictions of the prophet Edgar Cayce. It was near this island that Cayce said that land would rise in 1968 or 1969 and that that would prove that a civilization had existed in times past in this area, a civilization that Albion said was indeed Atlantis. Cayce's prophecy came true when a manmade "road" was discovered by explorer-scientist, Dr. J. Manson Valentine of Miami, along with a group of divers, in 1968. Albion's words agreed with those of Cayce when he said: "Bimini was once a part of Atlantis, a great continent."

He continued:

"Bimini was once the site of a great city, that was walled with stones and contained a Temple that was the home of an ancient mystery school. It was filled with Initiates of the highest order, known as the 'Elders'. They were wise men. The city contained observatories, which were manned by neophytes who gathered astronomical data and relayed it to the 'Elders'. They, in turn, reduced it into 'astrological' information, which they used for their knowledge of life cycles and prophecy. They lived their lives according to planetary movement and its affect on their physical lives and their psyche. From this mystery school came instructions for the masses as to when to plant and harvest, omens of weather and the like."

Again, the Teacher's words took on a prophetic note.

"In this Temple city, there was built a huge pyramid that was a place of Initiation. It was quite similar in appearance to the pyramids that still stand in Egypt. This monument still exists to this day, but is under the sea. Future expeditions will uncover its ruins and in doing so will gain many secrets of a long lost society." His next thought was an interesting one. "There are many presently incarnated individuals who will be instrumental in this discovery. Many already know that it is there for they 'remember' it from past lives.

I recalled some flap about such a discovery that had been made in the late seventies, but it had faded out of the headlines rather quickly. I also had a special interest in this prediction, for I had made a similar prophecy in an earlier book that had been written about my psychic excursions and investigations into the infamous Bermuda Triangle. A friend, internationally famous author and linguist, Charles Berlitz, is believed to know of the actual location of just such a pyramid structure near Bimini. Not having spoken with Berlitz for some time, I cannot be sure of any further expeditions in regards to locating the underwater structure.

Albion continued by saying that anyone who spends time on Bimini, especially on the North Island, would find their dream sequences and psychic thoughts going back into ancient times. There are many people who have had past lives there when it was still a part of Antillia and they are drawn there, in this life, once again, to visit and to investigate what they deeply "remember". So, it would seem that Bimini is haunted by the "ghost" of a civilization long past! Another prophetic tone was noted in his words:

"Beginning in the 1980's, there will be small land masses that will begin to be uncovered due to the coming Earth changes. Only then will there be significant inerest, once again, to instigate major excavations and research concerning Antillian existence. This will bring about the putting to rest once and for all any doubt that such a continent once existed and thrived." Albion also spoke of similar discoveries that would take place in the Pacific that would prove the existence in the dim past of Pacifica.

"Newfoundland and the Galapagos Islands are other magnetic areas that are grids, but not vortices. In these locations, many new life forms have and will continue to develop. They are 'breeding grounds'. Another such area is the Great Barrier Reef off the coast of Australia."

Although these were the only specific areas he named, he did suggest that other global areas where there are great fisheries and other types of aquatic life, would likewise be magnetic in nature, thus making for fertility, especially in water.

The next location given was the island of St. Helena, in the southern Atlantic.

"There is found a vortex that covers the land mass entirely, as well as the nearby offshore waters. It promotes receptivity and is an excellent place to meditate and listen to the inner self. Napoleon once rested here and planned his strategies."

The session was proving to be a long but interesting one. Albion proceeded, keeping his British accent at a steady pace.

"The city of Venice is a magnetic grid. This grid vibrates to Ray Two energies, the energy of Love. Venice, as are all highly magnetic areas, is conducive to sexual energy and fertility."

"Tibet is a magnetic country that forms another grid system. There is so much energy there, it will eventually coagulate into a vortex." Now this was something new. The Teacher had never before mentioned that a grid could group into a vortex. Interesting.

"When this does occur, it will be electromagnetic in its nature, due to the affect of the surrounding electrical peaks. This land is conducive to discipline and reception and is so charged, it affects the highest spiritual levels in life forms, especially man. Tibet is also a location that contains records of history that no one knows exists, save the oldest orders of the Lamas. This grid is good for psychic sensitivity, as well."

Since we were trying to get in as many sessions as we could, to make up for lost time, we planned our next talk with the Teacher for the next evening. The session began with Albion immediately directing our attention to Africa. He singled out D. and Scott, instructing them to imagine that they were floating above that continent. He said that they would remember that continent as it had looked long ago, suggesting they each may have had past lives there at some time. A comment about the continent itself preceeded his discussions of any vortices.

"Africa is a very important continent, for it has and still plays an important role in the whole scheme of things in both the physical and spiritual evolutions of mankind and of life itself. When the Earth was very young, this land mass was much larger than it is now. It went through many changes during the last major periods of cataclysmic upheaval and bore the worst brunt of these changes. In fact, there was a time many thousands of years ago, that it broke into two parts. There were a lot of volcanic eruptions, as well as much continental drifts."

I should stop here and explain that the "continental drift" that Albion mentioned no doubt refers to a well-known scientific theory by the same name. Since the fifties, there as been mounting evidence that the continents are "drifting" apart. Basically, the theory is simple to understand. There is a thin crust, consisting of the rocky surface and upper mantle that composes a layer called the lithosphere. This lithosphere is like a jig-saw puzzle, being composed of ten large plates and several smaller ones that all fit together. They float on a hot layer called the asthenosphere. The continents can drift because they are floating on a molten sea. They slam into each other, burying themselves underneath each other, causing mountains to be built. This is what

Albion says occurred to Africa during the past period of continental change. He commented on the continent's evolution, esoterically, by saying: "It has taken part of its First and Second Initiations through this process."

We were to learn that there were not many vortices on Africa's land. He said: "There are only four areas that are full natural vortices, two of which are in Egypt." First he drew our thoughts to the southern tip of the continent near Capetown. "This is a highly-charged electrical vortex, so much so that prana can be absorbed through drinking and swimming in the water of the area. The vortex there shoots up like a fountain composed of highly-charged electrical force, like sparks." Albion's knowledge of current events caught us off guard with his next words. "Do you recall, several months ago, as you count your time, that reconnaissance planes took photographs of some sort of flash that was believed to be an explosion, possibly a nuclear bomb test off the southern coast of Africa?" All affirmed that we remembered the incident, for it had made the national news. "Well, it was not an explosion at all. It was a manifestation of this vortex's force. It is rare that vortices become physically evident, but it does occur, either through sound or 'flashes' of light, with sound being the most common."

Several months after this session, Albion's reference to that flash came back to A. S.'s mind upon reading an article in the June 20, 1981 issue of Science News, a weekly publication designed to update scientific discoveries in various fields. In the category of "Earth Sciences", there was a seven paragraph write-up on "brontides", which are natural explosions and booming noises of unknown origin! They are thought to be caused by ground to air transmissions of energy. They are sometimes accompanied by a strong smell of sulphur, dry fogs, bubbling rivers and flames from the ground, but no sure cause for them has been determined. It seems that brontides are reminiscent of Albion's vortices!

He went on about the Capetown vortex.

"This power center is one that can do a great deal to re-vitalize the physical body. It is also a source of prosperity vibrations and the area is fertile in gold and minerals. This area of the world is prosperous and will be so in the future. Using this energy, which is positive, for positive results, replenishes it. Using it for negative ends depletes it. This area is excellent for the growth of crystals."

Albion's mood seemed to respond to a change in location, geographically, to one of making sure we were all attentive to this particular information about Africa, especially Egypt. Scott and I were planning a trip there in November, 1981 as artist and teacher, respectively, for a group known as Astara. A. S. was also planning a return trip to Johannesberg, South Africa at approximately the same time, to teach some self-motivation and nutrition workshops. He wanted to be sure we heard his words clearly.

"Now we go in our thoughts to Aswan, Egypt. This is a magnetic vortex. The drawing power of this center pulls from the atmosphere and from the vibration of the life forms in that area, the human life forms. It promotes a powerful degree of clairvoyant ability. There was a time that many religious organizations, called the Mystery Schools, were located there and there still remain scrolls and artifacts yet to be discovered. The land is rich in energy there. It affects some people introspectively and promotes seclusion. In Aswan, there are many ruins buried beneath the Nile."

A look at the map finds Aswan about 900 miles south of Cairo. It is the site of the famous Aswan dam, which controls the yearly flooding of the river Nile. It is also the resort area of Egypt.

Cairo was next on his list.

"This is a strong magnetic vortex. It is more intense, more powerful than the one in Aswan. It is also larger and covers more land. The ancient Egyptians knew of this vortex. They used its powerful energy to propel themselves into astral, mental, and spiritual dimensions.

138

No other culture has surpassed them in the knowledge they learned during their spiritual travels. Going there would promote the same in yourselves. It is an area that gives a greater understanding of how the subconscious works, it triggers a clearer channel, helping you to retrieve more from the 'world memory'."

The time came for the tape to be turned over. The pause must have directed the Teacher's attention to covering a different ground somewhat. He began: "There are also vortices that are encountered in water." One that was recognizable to all, especially myself, was the infamous Bermuda or Devil's Triangle. Many books and articles have been written over the years about this strange area off the southeastern coast of Florida, that alledgedly stretches down to the Windward Islands, to Bermuda and back to Florida's tip. It has been the site of many disappearances or weird accidents involving both air and sea-going craft, the most famous being the disappearance of five military planes in December of 1945. Theories ranging from UFO activity to unusual atmospheric anomalies have been proposed to explain the occurances there, but none as of yet, have been accepted as the total answer. To label that area as a vortex seemed appropriate.

"Another one is the Ring of Fire in the Pacific, and still another centered in Lake Superior in the Great Lakes region of North America." An explanation of the water eddys would seem to make them part of the general group of synthesizers described earlier, due to their interaction with the Earth's atmosphere. Albion continued, "These vortices take energy that is in the atmosphere, particularly from the ozone layer, and seek to re-balance it." The ozone layer is an important part of the Earth's aura, for it protects the planet's life from the constant bombardment of various sorts of cosmic rays that come from other bodies and sources in the solar system and beyond. This layer has been damaged by pollutants from technology and this is of major concern to scientists and environmentalists alike. "These water

139

vortices, and there are others like them all over the globe, capture the energies and pollutants that are harmful and undesirable and draw them down through their funnel and down into the depths of the undersea terrain." It would seem that these aquatic centers are magnetic in nature. "These vortices cannot 'clean' things up entirely, but they serve a major purpose in this direction."

At this point, A. S. requested permission to ask the Teacher a question. When given the go-ahead, she said: "Are these water vortices you are talking about like the Ray One kind . . . destructive for constructive reasons?"

"Yes, most definitely," was the quick reply. "Remember, we do not use the term destruction in a negative sense in these cases."

"Yes, I understand. Thank you."

Albion continued: "Were it not for these four vortices, the North American continent would be suffering from even greater damage due to the mounting negative effects of what is happening ecologically." He went on to make reference to nuclear radiation clouds that float around in the atmosphere as a result of nuclear tests being carried on in many countries around the world, including our own, and attributed at least a partial cleansing of these dangerous clouds, to the water vortices.

The session ended with a note of anticipation. Albion indicated that his next point of discussion would be in regards to the Medicine Wheels of the Native Americans. Since moving to Arizona, my husband and I had become increasingly involved with the teachings of the Indians, especially the Hopi and the Chippewa. The meeting we had had with Sun Bear, whom I mentioned earlier, had caused us to join forces with this man's energy in hopes of helping him accomplish the realization of his visions. At the age of fifteen, Sun Bear received a "vision" that was to determine his life's work. He saw a Medicine Wheel with animals of all kinds approaching it from the four cardinal directions. A closer

140

look revealed that these figures were of all colors, red, yellow, black and white. Sun Bear interpreted his vision to mean that it was time for all men to return to the traditional way of life, living and walking in balance with the Earth Mother. He also felt that it was an omen that showed that it was meant for him to teach men of all races the wisdom of the Medicine Ways. My agreement with his vision, led me to become his first apprentice to learn the "Way" and to share medicine knowledge which I am gaining with others through the vehicle of my own work. Sun Bear's application of the wisdom that came to him in his vision led him to establish the first inter-racial medicine society, which he named the Bear Tribe. Land was acquired, eventually, and the Bear Tribe is presently located on 90 acres of forest land outside of Spokane, Washington. According to Sun Bear, "Our aim is to be in harmony with ourselves, with each other, with the Earth Mother, and with the will of the Great Spirit."

The word "medicine" implies the development and use of spiritual powers. It can regard healing with herbs, chants, prayers, as well as prophecy and visions of the future. The Medicine Wheel is a stone circle. Some are built of small stones and are found from Texas to Canada on this continent. The rocks were placed on the ground in a huge "wheel" pattern, with a center hub, the other rocks coming out in spokes. It is believed that they provided a circle within which sacred rituals took place.

All this made me particularly interested in what Albion would have to say. The session began with his words taking us to the state of Wyoming. "In the foothills of north-central Wyoming, near the border of Montana, lies a vortex you know as the Big Horn Medicine Wheel." The Channel paused for a moment to insert a personal note directed at myself. "We have directed the Instrument to study the ways of the Native Americans for their knowledge of the Earth is of great value to our work." His reference to myself as "The Instrument" was his usual manner of addressing me. He continued: "Before we go into various locations, keep in mind that we will be using the Big Horn Wheel as an example of our thoughts." He also said that many of the wheels predated what we generally know as the native tribes and were built by their ancestors. He knew of their use as ritual sites, as well as their being places of astronomical observatories. However, he related what he felt was an even more important purpose, but preceeded that information with some general comments.

"Since ancient times, the circle has been used to represent eternity, the infinite and Divine Force. They knew that the Earth was circular. They knew that the Sun and stars were circular. They knew of the power points (vortices) on the Earth and considered them sacred. Upon these vortices, they built their medicine wheels. As tribes wandered, for many of them were nomadic, they would search out these vortex areas and this would often determine where they would camp. During the times of past Earth changes, many bands of people wandered or migrated for many years prior, searching out vortex areas that were safe."

Albion continued by saying that there are many Medicine Wheels here in Arizona, some of which have not been discovered yet and that there are many yet to be found in other places as well. The Medicine Wheel was a place of meditation and used mostly by the elders and medicine people of the tribe. It was the place their prophecies were received, oftentimes, a place of spiritual attunement and of celestial observation.

A quick glance at a map printed in the book *Native American Astronomy*, edited by Anthony F. Aveni, shows that there are many wheels that have been found in Alberta and Saskatchewan, Canada and also in the states of Wyoming, Montana, and Colorado in the U.S. There are also believed to be some in Arizona and other areas, but they have been lost to time or not yet identified as Medicine Wheels for certain.

Albion designated each of these Medicine Wheels as vortices. He did not wish us to think of all of them as major, except for the ones that were built on high mountains and the majority of them were not. He also designated medicine circle vortices to be electrical in their nature.

The session that night ended with Albion giving us an assignment, of sorts. Although we did not realize it at the time, his instructions were to lead to future journeys in regards to the training to be more in tune with the Earth Mother, as well as exposing us to sites easily within our geographical range, that were important "power points". The Teacher's instructions were very precise and added an air of adventure to the work. We weren't sure what to expect, but we listened very carefully.

"We wish to direct yourselves to a most important spot on the globe. You know it as the Four Corners. We wish you to leave Sedona at 7:00 a.m., on February 10, 1981. You will need to arrive in a place you can rest for the evening and adjust to the energies of the area. This is to be Kayenta. Furthermore, you should arrive at Four Corners at 7:00 a.m. the following morning. You are to fast for the entire 48 hours, returning to Sedona by 7:00 p.m. the second day. Is this clear?"

It seemed as if his intentions were to have us there so that he could channel some special information.

A. S. was the first to speak. "You want us to fast totally?"

"You may have a mild vegetable broth and a small amount of orange juice if you dilute it with some pure water."

A. S.'s studies of nutrition for the past several years came in handy at this point. Even though fasting was part of her and D.'s normal regimen from time to time, neither Scott nor I had attempted a fast, as such, certainly not for that length of time. I must admit that I was not overjoyed about this part of the trip. Having been a consultant to a medical doctor for seven years, along with national seminars given on the nutritional aspect of good health and spirituality, A. S.'s view was favorable, so fasting it was! She felt that what Albion had asked us to do was simple in its principle. Fasting would help to eliminate stress and the drainage of energy from the body that occurs as a result of the digestion process. Little digestion would be required for the vegetable broth. It would also cause any toxins in the body to surface, which would help bring about a cleansing. "Don't worry, you will survive it!" was her comment. I remained skeptical but agreed to give it a try. Scott took it in stride as all good, stable Capricorns would do!

We planned our trip. We would travel in A.S.'s truck, a Trans-Van, quite sufficient for such a journey, having plenty of room for the four of us. A sofa, table and chairs and small kitchen are part of its lay-out. I remember making a quip about not needing a kitchen, which was promptly ignored! A. S. would also make the motel reservations and the vegetable soup. Somehow her calling it "soup" instead of "broth" made it sound more hearty! Albion's choice of the number "7" was nothing new, for he had often used that time for channeling sessions, Depth Studies, or other activities based on his work. Our curiosity about why he chose Four Corners would have to wait until we arrived. We all felt there must be a good reason . . . there always was.

Our journey began with us leaving Sedona very close to the 7:00 a.m. target time. There was a chill in the air as we rode up Oak Creek Canyon towards Flagstaff. I sat and looked out the window, amazed by the beauty of this area, as I had been ever since seeing it for the first time in 1975. Oak Creek ripples through sandstone cliffs, creating a "gnomeland" effect. The drive to the first stop, Kayenta, was 175 miles away. The trip was a pleasant one. We went through portions of the Navajo Indian Reservation, including the Painted Desert. Much of the terrain takes your thoughts to what the Moonscape must be like. Miles and miles of high desert, no vegetation to speak of, except for a few places where trickles of water run, massive cliffs and jagged rock monoliths jut out of the desert floor. We listened to the tape of the last session with Albion so that we would be certain to follow his instructions to the letter.

We arrived in Kayenta at dusk and checked into our motel. We had spent some time on side trips along the way, including Meteor Crater, outside of Winslow, one of Arizona's prime attractions. I will reserve comment about that spot at this time. Albion made particular comments about the crater later in his channeling, which made us remember our visit.

We checked into our room and relaxed. Kayenta is at the entrance to Monument Valley, truly one of Nature's more spectacular sights. Composed of huge red rocks, the monoliths stand on the flat desert floor. They are all that is left of a 1,200 foot high plateau made from windblown sand dunes solidified ages ago. Navajo women can be seen herding their sheep along the way, making the ride through the monuments a memorable occasion. We decided to ride through the valley upon returning from Four Corners the next day.

Our day began early. We got up at 4:30, so we could be at our destination on time. Aside from a feeling of weakness from the fast that Scott and I had experienced, we were ready for the second lap of our adventure. A breakfast of the diluted juice tasted like bacon and eggs! A. S., Scott and I curled up on the sofa and chairs and slept the bulk of the ninety miles we had to travel, while D. drove. We were awakened by the bump of the van rolling over the stony entrance to the actual spot where the states of Arizona, New Mexico, Colorado and Utah join together in a perfect squared cross. The barren terrain was little change from what we had seen on other trips through the Navajo Reservation. It was cold and the wind was blowing strongly. The dawn was slowly lighting up the eastern sky. We parked the truck facing south, got out and walked over to the flat marker erected to the joining of the land here. The wind was so strong, we could not stay out very long. I was the first to return to the warmth of the van and the others followed

145

me shortly. Blankets were put around the windows to make it dark for the channeling and we all bundled up to keep warm. A new tape was popped into the recorder and the session, under these unusual conditions, began.

"We wish to share information at this particular spot on the Earth Mother. Be aware within yourselves that in all four directions of this place, there are great 'Thunder Beings', ancient entities created by ancient minds. They are the guardians of this sacred place and all that exists in the astral realms around it. Many come here and they see only the physical bleakness of these Four Corners. They see the Earth being stripped of its natural resources and grandeur by the mining. Only the sands of time and the sound of the wind make themselves known to most. Some people leave here thinking about the vastness, the bleakness and desolation. But, with those that can make a sensitive attunement to the areas and its vibrations have a much different reaction. Many tune into the 'astral temple' that exists deep below the surface of this sacred ground. You are aware of the fact that the inner self within the human being is that part which is spiritual in its nature. So it is with the Earth. What is within the ground is the generator of its energy, its vibrations."

"If you will peer with us towards the east, with your spiritual sight, you will 'see' the 'Thunder Being' of the East! The east is the direction of the promise and hope of the future. It is the direction of the 'Messiah' of the past and those yet to come. This Thunder Being guards the 'pink crystal chamber'. It is an astral chamber here in the Heart Chakra of the planet."

Now we knew why Albion had called this a special place. The key was in the use of the word "chakra". Most of us are familiar with the Sanskrit term for "wheels" that is used to indicate energy vortices in the human etheric body. There are seven of these centers of force and they are centers of force through which energy flows from one of the subtle bodies to another. The seven centers or chakras in the human body are located in the

146

base of the spine, commonly called the "Kundalini", the navel center, known as the solar plexus, the spleen, the heart, the throat and the brow, known as the "Third Eye", and finally, the top of the head, or the Crown chakra. Albion's words about the planet's heart chakra opened my thoughts to understand such centers exist within the Earth, as well and that Four Corners is the Heart center of the Earth.

Albion continued, his words filling the van. The wind had picked up and we could feel a slight rocking of the vehicle.

"This crystal chamber looks like stalagtites and stalagmites of pink quartz. Pink is a magnetic color, it draws the thought forms of the dreams and hopes of the future towards this sacred center."

"Now use your inner sight and direct it towards the South. The 'Thunder Being' that guards this direction dwells in a green crystal astral chamber. These green crystals contribute to and form a healing center of the planet. There is a power generated here that helps the Earth regenerate itself. Life forms also receive of this power. This healing force helps keep the planet fertile and prosperous and healthy."

"The Thunder Being in the west guards and abides in the astral chamber that contains crystals of all the colors in the rainbow. In the west, life forms, especially human, escape. They escape the over-population of the east, start 'new worlds', escape restrictions of all kinds. History will bear this true. It is most important that this area be kept intact. The Thunder Being that guards this chamber is most powerful. This western chamber has energies to keep the Earth in balance. It allows the emotions of the Earth to exist. It is like a 'relief' valve for the planet."

"Now turn to the final direction of the North, the area watched by the Pole Star. The Thunder Being that guards this golden crystal chamber, perpetuates the 'psyche' of the Earth. This is the 'Altar of the Earth'. All of the Great Beings from other celestial spheres in the Cosmos can communicate with the Earth through this direction and chamber. It is like a communication vortex and its 'eye' is always open. This center of gold is always present for spiritual travelers to reside. Your thoughts can pass through this chamber and out into space to communicate with other parts of the universal system."

"These chambers of crystals are guarded by these 'powerful Entities'. The Elders of the Navajo know of these Beings, they know that this is a sacred area."

The Teacher then instructed us to go to the spot and stand over the Heart Center of the Earth.

"Aside from the reaction to the energies that you will have, you can also make a 'love' sacrifice. Your sacrifice can become a 'sacrament' to the Earth Mother. You can give the crystals all of the thoughts, the anxieties, the fears, doubts, grief and pain that you have within you and you can experience a 'rebirth' in this release. It gives a new faith. Listen to the planet and find a new way of life and a new way of 'being'."

After the channeling, the wind had died down and it wasn't as cold as it had been when we arrived. We got out of the truck to go over to the monument. While we had been working, four carloads of Navajos had come to set up their jewelry stands. Indian jewelry is very popular with the tourists that come through the reservation. We walked from where we were parked over to one of the jewelry stands, where a middle-aged Indian woman had beautiful trinkets spread out on a table in the East. Scott and I strolled up to the table and I immediately noticed a button pinned to her dress that read "Jesus saves". I smiled and pointed it out to Scott. Albion had just described the East as the direction of the Messiahs. I couldn't help but notice the synchronicity. All four of us walked around the tables, browsing. The Navajos are friendly people and they made small talk with us at each stop we made. Just as we were about to step up onto the flat concrete monument with the emblems of the four states engraved in bronze, a pick-up truck with three Indians inside drove up on the western side. We all chuckled at seeing a cardboard rainbow swinging from the rear-view mirror! Once we were in the center of the monument, we held hands and stood together in silence, making our "sacrament" at the Heart Center of the planet. We were there only a few moments, making no attempt to draw attention to ourselves. Several of the Indians glanced at us curiously, but I noticed an older woman who watched us with a smile of "knowing" on her face. It was a wonderful experience that early morning at Four Corners, one that none of us is likely to forget.

D. went back to the van and made some hot coffee, as the three of us walked around a little longer. Off in the distance towards the state of Colorado, we could see Mesa Verde, a location of incredibly ancient pueblo ruins. The wind started to pick up again, so we returned to the van for some of that hot coffee. We sat there, sharing words about our morning, but there weren't too many words to be shared. Just the experience itself that was running through our veins was enough. We all felt good and were ready to plan the rest of the day. We would go back to Kayenta and visit Monument Valley before returning to Sedona.

As it turned out, Monument Valley was a perfect way to top off a day that had such a special beginning. Riding past the unusual rock formations was spellbinding. Arizona's wonders never seem to cease. A few days after our return home, Albion made some comments about this beautiful place.

"The area of the 'Valley of the Monuments' is not a vortex, as such, but just before you entered the area of the actual valley of monoliths, you passed a big rock that juts up from the Earth's surface. This is a 'fledgling' vortex of pure electrical force that feeds the entire area with prana."

I believe the rock mentioned must be El Capitan. A huge, jagged peak, El Capitan sits alone in the desert approaching Monument Valley. It is a beautiful and striking remnant of an extinct volcano and it can be seen for miles around.

We arrived back in Sedona, tired but satisfied with what we had learned and the experiences of the journey. We were all hoping that this "pilgrimage" would not be the last.

An entire session was to follow concerning the chakras of the Earth. My own personal reaction to the information was strong, for I had not considered the subject quite from this point of view before. Not long after the Teacher gave the locations of the planetary centers, I had the opportunity to share it in a lecture I was invited to give at the Los Angeles Medicine Wheel Gathering. This is one of the four major conferences conducted in the U.S. each year sponsored by the Bear Tribe Medicine Society founded by Sun Bear. The response I received was very positive. I have chosen this point in the writing to share this information Albion gave.

"As we have said, a 'chakra' is an ancient term used to designate an energy center in a body and there are seven such centers taught in the Wisdom Teachings. The Planetary Chakras would be, as with the human, located in the Etheric Body. We will utilize the familiar names for the Chakras of the Earth so as to not confuse anyone by coining new terms. As you know, a chakra becomes active through growth and development with man, and so it goes with the Earth. Energy builds up until the center's movement is like a whirling vortex of force. In reference to your planet, these chakras must be set above the level of 'ordinary' vortices. They are majestic swirls, indeed."

Albion settled into a verbal pace that let those listening know the information would be detailed.

"The first chakra we will consider is commonly called the 'Kundalini' or 'root' center. In a human it is located at the base of the spine and is the color of flames. It receives energy from the Spleen chakra, which we will discuss later, and is the pure electrical force that propels a body on its path of evolution. In the Earth, the

Root chakra is the area known as the 'Ring of Fire' in the Pacific Ocean."

Since it has been mentioned several times without explanation, I will stop here for a moment to explain that the "Ring of Fire" is a chain of volcanoes associated with island and mountain arcs and earthquakes around the Pacific belt. The Cascade Mountain range is a part of this ring. About two-thirds of the planet's volcanoes lie along this belt, including the South and Central American ones, the ones in the Aleutian Islands, Japan, and the Philippines.

Albion continued: This is the most powerful and largest single electrical vortex on the Earth. Through millions of years of volcanic activity, energy has been collecting. During past Earth change cycles, this area has been the triggering device that caused them to begin. It was in this ancient place that the Pacifica (Lemurian) continent met its fate. In the future, this area will set off volcanic and seismic chain reactions. It will not happen all at once, but over several hundreds of years. It has already begun."

Listening to this information later, I assumed that he must have been talking about the 1980 eruption of Mt. St. Helens in Washington state. This peak belongs to the Cascade range, which is a part of the Pacific belt and its rebirth was the first volcano to explode on the continental U.S. in many years.

Albion continued, relating the Kundalini activity in the human body to what occurs in the etheric body of the planet.

"As with a human, as the Kundalini rises up the shaft of the spine, so will this rising occur in the 'Ring of Fire', causing it to behave quite similarly. Mountains and domes are the 'spine' of the Earth. They are like the vertebrae, although not all located in one place."

This description created a picture of the electrical energy of the planet's Kundalini moving in a sort of a circle around the Pacific, creating a rise in the physical activity and subsequently the planet's consciousness. It makes good sense that the energy patterns of the Earth should be circular in motion, the globe itself is an "almost" circle and moves in its orbital path in rotation, with the orbital path in a near circle around the Sun. Knowledge leads to an awareness of this pattern and enables one to apprehend one's first glimpse into the more subtle energies of the Earth for the first time. It is also interesting to note here that the Native Americans have long been considered the "Earth" people, with all of their sacred ceremonies being a petition to the Earth Mother to provide them with their needs. To them the Earth is sacred. Their houses, tipis, hogans, and the like, their religions, stone circles, the Medicine Wheels, along with their sacred lodges, such as the Sun Dance Lodge, the kivas, the sweat lodges used for purification, were and still are, all round. This could indicate that the Indians had a knowledge of the natural energy of the 'Kundalini' Earth as being circular and this might well have been their way of keeping in tune, so to speak, with the planet.

Such thoughts made me conscious of the other ancient religions and practices that likewise are tuned into performing their ceremonies, sacraments, and rituals inside a circle, or otherwise hold the circle symbolic of some ancient, traditional truth. Stonehenge was one of the first to come to mind, followed by thoughts of ceremonial magic, Wicca, the May Pole and May Dance, and the Zodiac, itself, being but a reflection of an even greater cosmic wheel. Scientists tell us that observation data show that everything in the Universe is rotating in a circular motion or movement.

Scott lit a cigarette lighter so he could turn the tape over in the dark room. After the short pause, Albion announced that the Solar Plexus chakra was next on his agenda.

"Just as the Kundalini is purely electric, so is the Solar Plexus purely magnetic. The Atlantic Ocean's center is the Solar Plexus of the Earth. Keep in mind, the navel chakra is a receiver of energy. It absorbs vibrations, whether they are atmospheric, geological or from thoughtforms from the life forms on the planet. It was in this area that Antilia (Atlantis) met its demise. This was during the time of a 'great flood', the Second Initiation of the Earth. That period was the time of purification and awakening of the astral body into life. It marked the beginning of the planet's having desire."

"Now we come to the Spleen center. In the human etheric body, as well as the Earth's its function is to cleanse. As the Earth moves into another phase of evolution, which you call the 'Earth changes', it moves closer towards awakening its mental body, thus having a mind of its own. This is but another step towards Terra Firma becoming self-realized."

I can definitely say that the thought of the Earth becoming self-realized did give me a new perspective of the ground under my feet!

Next, Albion took us, in thought, to a portion of the world that covers a huge land mass. "It is in Alaska and it extends into some of Siberia, as well as the extreme northwestern United States and Canada." The Teacher did not elaborate any further in regards to the Spleen chakra at that time. His next words immediately proclaimed that the 'Kundalini' Heart chakra was the area known as the Four Corners. This we already knew and had experienced.

"The Throat Center of the Earth, in which the planet communicates with all the planets in the Solar System, as well as with the other bodies in the galaxy and the Universe, is located in the Puerto Rico area." Upon hearing this spot pinpointed I later remembered that in Aerocibo, Puerto Rico, there is the largest radio telescope known to man, thus far. One of the many uses being made of the giant, 1,000 foot dish that is nestled in between three mountains, is to send and hopefully, receive intelligent signals from outer space. Interesting it should have been built in this very spot! Albion must have sensed my energy levels getting low, as he hurried through the rest of the session, naming the last two of the major chakra areas.

"India and Tibet, collectively, form the Brow chakra or Third Eye of the planet, with Tibet being the most potent. The Crown chakra, on the other hand, is in the very center of the Gobi Desert."

The Teacher elaborated quite a bit about the Crown center.

"This area that you call the Gobi Desert is a most powerful and important vortex. It is the center that is the flow of Divinity; it is the opening for the Spirit of the planet to be released and linked to the creative Sun, as well as all of the vast regions of space. Each celestial sphere in its own right has these chakras and this Crown center. Like all of the Crown chakras of the celestial sphere, it is a communicating link, with the other parts of the Universe, a spiritual link. This, again, shows the at-one-ment, the brotherhood, of all of the atoms that go together in a symphony of form. In the core of the Gobi Desert, as with all centers, you can look for miles and not see many signs of a civilization, whether they be in the middle of a wasteland or on the bottom of the water. It is important that the Chakras of the Earth are kept in reserve, are kept in balance, for the energies that are present are most intense. Imagine yourselves in the Gobi and that there are thread-like spokes that are emanating—seven of them—from this Shamballa center. It might also be wise to picture that this Shamballic force does not take on the form of a spiral-like or cone shape or a whirlpool as do many of the vortices, but is like a fountain of silvery water. As these spokes are projected from this fountain of spiritual force they in turn connect and link the Crown Center with various locations all over the globe."

"In Sedona there is a vortex that is a Beacon that is the receiving point of this Shamballic force. It is Bell Rock. Bell Rock serves two purposes, as a receptacle for this Shamballic force and as a Beacon vortex. This is why there are many individuals drawn to this rock. They feel a special energy indeed. This is the energy that the

154

Native Americans in the ancient past attuned to and recognized as sacred. Secondly, there is a spoke that is projected from the Shamballic fountain to the Himilayan Mountains, and in doing so it energizes those peaks and fills the entire range with spiritual force. There are individuals that are living in the flesh, as well as some that are astrally incarnated that are living throughout the Himilayan range."

"There is a third spoke emanating from Shamballa that goes to Madras, India. This is a spoke that is most powerful, that has to do with the nurturing and flourishing of the Eastern philosophy. Fourthly, there is another spoke that is connected to Greenland, not the whole of Greenland, but a pole there to create a balance - the North Pole. There is a fifth spoke that is connected directly into the Easter Islands. It promotes spiritual growth, advancement, and even technology. The sixth spoke is connected to Japan. It has to do with spreading spiritual energy to these land masses. These places all have spiritual disciplines that are very powerful and/or serve a major purpose to the planet."

"The seventh spoke is connected to the Valley of the Kings. In this area, beneath the sands of time, there is a palace that literally has been lost. This temple, as we will call it, was at one time an astronomical observatory. The cultures, both ancient and modern, that have occupied this area have had a deep interest in the heavens. Even on Greenland there are many observatories and projects concerning the weather and various strategic exercises. These seven spots sometimes overlap each other. The Crown chakra, as well as all of the chakras, are connected, integrated and related one to the other."

A few closing remarks about there being "threads" or lines of force that connect these chakras and their energies together were coupled with the identity of the Spleen as electromagnetic, along with the Heart center. The Throat was named electrical in nature, the Brow & Solar Plexus as magnetic and the Crown, electromagnetic.

The session ended that night with all of us being tired,

so we didn't stay together to talk very long. The pace of the work had been stepped-up and I felt it was necessary to work as often as possible. We were free from travel for a while so we made plans to work again two days later.

The next session was the first time that the information didn't seem to follow the previous pattern of thought as had been the case. I was to find that fact confusing, at times, as well as it making it more difficult to organize the information into this present book form. It seemed as if enough foundation had been laid for Albion to feel he could just channel data and we would know how it all fit together. Not wishing to tackle making any suggestion as to how the information should be given and not being sure at that point if order should be the rule, I said nothing. Each session was recorded and later transcribed. This began a very long task of organizaton that has provided an ultimate test of patience.

That evening's session officially began with Albion's bringing up a term he had used only once before, that being in relation to the chakras being "connected" together. The term was "ley (pronounced lay) lines". This was a remotely familiar term to me, having read of them in one or two other books.

Many early surveyors of the various ancient megalithic sites believed they had an astronomical function, just as Albion has confirmed. Many of the alignments were known to be a few miles in length, but no one had tracked them further until 1922, when Alfred Watkins of Hereford, England, published a book entitled *Early British Trackways*. Watkins' discovery was that ancient sacred sites were arranged in straight lines that extended for several miles. He believed prehistoric people traveled from one landmark to another in straight tracks to find their way across country. The landmarks include Medicine Wheels, Neolithic stones, holy wells or trees and stone crosses. Also, ancient settlements or crossroads, chapels and hilltop beacons were included. Watkins devoted his remaining years to the accumulation of both tradition and physical evidence of "leys", as he referred to the alignments. His conclusion, published in 1952, *The Old Straight Track*, was that the patterns in British landscape like the tracks, monuments and sacred places and the lore about them, did not arise by chance. It was, in fact, a pattern laid down by Neolithic surveyors that developed over 4,000 years. He viewed the country as one vast archeological relic, a structure of lines and centers, arranged on universal principles and related to the topography and the seasonal movements of the heavens.

My growing understanding of the ley lines caused me to begin to picture the Earth as being criss-crossed with threads, along which various types of energy flows. In my mind, it gave the planet the appearance of being "wrapped" with twine. A geological ball of twine! Where each of these threads crossed each other, a powerful point of energy, a vortex, is created, of varying degrees. Some are major, some minor. Energy to feed these points come from the planet itself, along with energies that descend from space. I was beginning to get a firm grasp of what is known as the ancient science of Geomancy. This is one of the Wisdom Teachings I had not studied, but one of the best definitions that I had heard to define Geomancy is "Earth Acupuncture". Another twist to the concept of ley lines is found in British lore.

Albion added additional food for thought by saying that the web around the Earth, invisible to the physical eye, serves as a conductor of force. It stores information of the energies that flow through the ley lines and anyone who is sensitive to them, can "read" or translate the information. It is known that ancient people were aware of these lines and also the power points that I and Albion, call vortices. Sometimes they would sleep on them bypassing the conscious mind and its interferences, allowing the information to come through the dream state. Many believe this is one of the ways that prophets could make predictions about the planet and their environment, its safety and dangers. Mapping the landscape was, and still is, a part of various cultures worldwide. The Native Americans knew Geomancy quite well, though they didn't use that particular term. They knew of power spots on the Earth, but didn't call them vortices. Rather, they simply designated them as sacred.'

It is also interesting to note there are many legends that deal with "imaginary" places, although my use of the word imaginary is debateable, that man has created or been aware of. Could such places have been descriptions of vortices or power points on various parts of the globe? I am thinking of places such as the Garden of Eden, Oz, Camelot, Chardin's "noosphere", and the Seven Golden Cities of the Cibola, a legend of the Aztecs from the 1500's, and Shamballa. Shamballa, for example, generally taken to be an imaginary paradise, was indeed designated by Albion as a vortex, the Crown Chakra itself. The ancients believed Shamballa to be the center of the world and the source of all energies. I also believe that many of the locations of most powerful vortices are being used by the Spiritual Brotherhood in which to establish ashrams and other types of centers of Light. These vortices transform the electric (positive), magnetic (negative), and electromagnetic (both) energies that they generate and receive, into the energy the Earth and mankind require for their sustainance.

Albion's words about the ley lines had definitely added some fuel to my understanding of this concept. He also pointed out a major spiritual connection.

"As you know, the symbol for the White Lodge of the Spiritual Hierarchy is the five-pointed star. Look how many flags and nations use this symbol. It is also the esoteric design for the Fifth Degree of Initiation, that of Adeptship. It appears, along with rays of vitality, on the flag of your state of Arizona, as well as, of course, the flag of the United States."

"There is a configuration of energy, connected by a special group of lines of force, that involves five places on the Earth. The Hierarchy uses these unique ley lines to transmit force from one point to another, thus becoming the major 'spiritual transit system' on the planet. The lines are between Tokyo, New York, Darjeeling, London and Geneva." This confirmed my feelings of the Brotherhood using these charged areas and connections.

The next phase of the work was to prove to be of particular interest to myself, as I had long held an interest in ancient temples and their ruins. I was so excited to be able to actually visit the ones in Egypt, some of the oldest known in the world. The Temple of Isis on the Isle of Philae was my favorite. This was the subject Albion began to discuss, temple ruins from the past history of the Earth.

"Take all the major ruins, no matter what country they reside in, and connect them all together, for they are connected in reality. There are many such ruins that have totally crumbled or long been buried beneath the sands of time, but their vibrations can still be felt. Drawing lines between the ones that you are aware of, will give you a good understanding of the patterns created by such lines of force earthwide."

Research that was conducted to bring Albion's words into reality yielded many of the major temple sites in various countries. Egypt, China, England, the Yucatan and Mexico, various ruins in North America, such as cliff dwellings, Japan, ancient Greece and Rome came to my mind very quickly. I knew that there were many others and that they were virtually worldwide.

The Teacher next instructed us to pay special attention to those places that were used in a combination of worship and astronomical observations.

"These transmit a particularly powerful flow of energy from one area to another. They form an esoteric link that is unique in its effect. It is conducive to 'cosmic consciousness'. All such structures were built at vortex points, they are highly-charged and many are considered still as sacred ground."

A little more thought reminded me of some of the most notable places on the Earth. Stonehenge, long considered a site of ancient Celtic rituals, as well as an observatory. Macchu Piccu, another. Albion spoke of how the Ancients understood the heavens because of their dependence on such knowledge to plant their crops, when to hold certain sacred ceremonies for their livelihood and protection by the gods, many after whom the planets and distant stars were named, and also for their seasons and sometimes the weather. I recall an old, I believe Celtic, belief that when a halo appears around the Moon, you can count the stars inside it and that will tell you how many days it will be before it rains. I only tried it once, on a night when I counted eight visible stars. Nine days later, it did rain and I assumed I must have missed one! I haven't tried it again.

As it turns out, Stonehenge was to be mentioned several times in various contexts in the sessions held for this book. Other places used as examples, by Albion and without research, are the Medicine Wheels, most of which are located on the North American continent and in Asaka, in Japan, believed to be a temple and/or observatory. This Asaka is one of the few places believed to have used, in harmony, the data gathered by the astronomers that was, in turn, turned into interpretations of celestial activity by astrologers. They actually worked together. It would seem that modern scientists, metaphysicians, and practitioners of the Occult Wisdoms could take a lesson from the ancient Orientals.

Albion continued:

"When a person goes to one of these places, such as Macchu Piccu, and is sensitive to the information we have given, or of their natural psychic abilities, he would be able to attune, through the ley lines, to all the other places of the same power that are on the same circuit worldwide."

The next statement must be read carefully, for sometimes Albion's use of the language is not readily clear.

"All vortices are connected, in the strictest sense of the word, with all other vortices. No force operates independently of another. This is the Law of the Universe. At the same time, it should be borne in mind that some connections or power points are more powerful than another and contain different kinds of energies. This makes them appear as if they are separate. Also, energies of a like nature are connected, such as temples to temples, electrical vortices to electrical vortices and so forth, again giving the illusion of being separate. They are not truly separate, only different in their various vibrations."

The session finally ended. It had been a long one and I was tired. We sat over coffee and A. S. related to me a capsule version of what the Teacher had said. My memory was almost blank, but as she talked, the information began to sound familiar and soon my recall totally returned. It was decided that it would be a good idea to suggest that the reader might find it helpful to obtain a globe or a world map to use in conjunction with reading the book. The major vortices could be marked with different colored pens, while the chakra areas could be drawn on with magic markers. These would also work well for tracing ley lines. A visual aid can be a big help, so I decided I would do that for myself.

Before A. S. and D. left for the evening, we all speculated about a personal note that Albion had injected into the session that night. "There will be a great deal of activity in the month of March. It will seem that the four of you will be going in forty different directions to once! It will be a necessity. You must organize yourselves, for this will be a must if the work is to be projected in full force."

As it turns out, no truer words were ever spoken. March ended up being the deadline month for my writing the book. A. S. left for South Africa for three weeks, Scott and D. scheduled an art exhibit of their work in Sedona, and I had two workshops to do on Earth changes down in Phoenix. All this was coupled with arranging future travel plans in the U.S. and abroad. My private psychic readings and readings that I also do through the mail, plus the two classes that I teach were keeping me jumping. Did we remember his words when all this was going on? I must admit that I didn't. Not long afterwards, Scott and I were sitting in a motel room at the Grand Canyon Moqui Lodge where we had escaped to have a silent weekend alone to work on the book and be together, when I came across the transcript of that tape. I couldn't help but smile to myself. It brought a similar reaction from Scott. We couldn't say we hadn't been warned! It made me reflect in a quick thought of how much advice he had given me over the years that I had lost somewhere in the process of being busy with living. I felt like the horse that had been led to water but the Teacher couldn't always make me drink! But, Albion had sure tried.

We planned another session for the weekend and parted for the night. The book was beginning to develop into quite a full-fledged project, most of which was my responsibility. All the hours I could squeeze out of my schedule were spent working with Albion, either alone with Scott or with A. S. and D. The sessions became my work, classes and social get-togethers.

The next session, Albion introduced a new aspect of the vortex information. He called them "man-made" vortices and labeled them as temporary. He also categorized them, to a point.

"Vortices created by the Earth due to its process of evolution and vortices created by the activities and thoughts of man, are different. Any such powerpoints generated by man or major events are temporary and last only as long as they are fed by energy. The vortices created by the vibrations of the mineral, plant and animal kingdoms are considered as the natural force of the planet."

"Selma, Alabama and Atlanta, Georgia are good examples of man-made centers of force. Stonehenge is another one, though it is erected on a site of an Earth-made vortex, it is still made more powerful by rituals that were celebrated there. This is common with many

162

historical locations. Places of great battles are often negative energy spots or become negative or more charged due to the event that occurred there. Even memory of such events as they are re-lived in thought by man, continue to transmit energy, telepathically, to such areas, causing their energy and power to survive."

I think that a note here about the time that this session took place is required. It was during the time of the famous Atlanta child murders which reached national headlines. I also remembered my Civil War history lessons in school. I wondered if all of this contributed to his calling Atlanta by name. I also reviewed the civil rights marches in the sixties in Alabama and the violence that took place there as a result. It was not long after this session that the Selma vortex was back in the news again, with renewed marches and civil rights activities. I also remember a lesson that he had given to the regular weekly Albion class, in which he discussed the reinactment of battles worldwide and the like, and remembered how he had told us that such things could bring the vibrations of such events back to life, so to speak, and transmit them into our consciousness. I found it something worth thinking about.

He also spoke of places like the Kremlin, the White House, the Capitol building in Washington, as examples of man-made vortices, while Bethlehem, Calvary, Normandy Beach and Independence Hall were given as examples of event vortices. His next words led our thoughts to the country of England. This was when he went into detail about Stonehenge, labelling it as the major vortex in that land, although there are over nine-hundred similar stone circles sprinkled throughout England that are less powerful. He spoke of these types of vortices as being marked by great stones. My mind drifted to the huge stone monoliths on Easter Island that have long been another great source of mystery, likewise made of rocks.

"These rocks become charged with the vibrations of the area and the events that occurred around them.

163

Others are used specifically due to their natural charge, such as the pile of quarried blocks that compose the Great Pyramid of Cheops in Egypt."

He went on to point out other areas.

"Delphi in Greece is another area that is created by man's activities. Such energy can be created in any location and it can be of a positive or negative nature. Even the grave sites of pharaohs, saints and great men and women can generate a lot of power. These places are even more charged when they are created near natural vortex locations as well."

This led me to understand that most man-made power points have very little or nothing to do with the geographical location itself.

He specifically described the "Selma vortex" as a negative one, created by events and thoughts there over a period of time. Atlanta was the same type. He later included Hiroshima, location of the holocausts in Germany and Golgatha, site of the crucifixion, as other examples. The case with which a vortex of a negative nature could be created was given to us for consideration.

"We will take this room where you are seated as an example. If an event were to occur that stirred anger amongst yourselves, your feelings would set up a temporary vortex of negative energy here. If over a period of time, no energy was added to the mini-vortex, it would dissipate. However, if more negativity continued, the vortex would grow. When such eddys are created, they should always be consciously replaced with positive energy and thoughts."

A. S. interrupted to ask a question. "So, by creating a positive vortex it would essentially wipe out the negative one?"

"Exactly!" Albion's reply was loud and forceful. He also added:

"The same thing of which we are speaking about here, A. S. applies as well to geographical vortices. This is one very effective way to heal the planet. Imagine what millions of people could do to repair the Earth by healing negative vortices in geographical areas, along with dissipating man-made ones."

The Teacher also pointed out that artificial and negative vortices have risen and fallen constantly all over the Earth since man first appeared on the scene. Replacing negative energy with positive energy was not a new concept to me, but using it to heal the planet was. We were told that this could be done most effectively by going to such areas, but that it could also be achieved telepathically from a distance. There's power in numbers, so the more energy directed to a spot, the more power is transferred and the more likely the success of the mission. I had heard of groups in Phoenix that were using a similar technique to work with negative past life experiences, as well as with the planet. They called it "psycho-drama".

Albion brought the session to a close by making a more detailed evaluation of Atlanta. "You should avoid going through Atlanta right now in your travels and if you must, it would be wise to surround yourself with protection. This negative, whirling vortex is growing, being fed by the fear of people due to the rash of killings. The Spiritual Hierarchy is quite concerned with this location, as well as El Salvador, Israel and other places torn by war and strife. Vortices can build to a point that their energies spill over into the surrounding areas, whether they are positive or negative, natural or man-made. This one in Atlanta has the potential of setting off tornado-like funnels that could spread over much of the southeast, so it is imperative that there be a great deal of healing energy sent there."

It seemed as if the Teacher was satisfied that he had given enough information about negative vortices that it would be known how best to deal with them in the future, no matter where they were located. He assured us that such vortices exist worldwide and would continue to rise and fall until man's consciousness evolved into a higher plateau. Then, his thoughts turned to a completely different subject.

"When the Earth was very young, still in its prenatal and infant stages, it spun much faster than it does now. Time causes everything in the Cosmos to gradually wind down like a top. This is known as entropy. During the time when its speed was more rapid, the pressures were greater and great currents of friction were set up by this movement. This produced sound. Likewise, when the Earth began to move through its various stages of evolution, creating an atmosphere and precipitation in its primordial state, the formation of the continents and the like, this activity produced sound. Subsequent continental drift during times of upheaval, have produced sounds. Sound, in turn, produces a current or frequency that is mostly magnetic in its nature. This is due mostly to the water content and subterranean location and involvement of such chaotic activity. There are electric, magnetic and electromagnetic sound currents that exist."

"There are three areas on the Earth that sound currents, creating sound vortices, wail as they come from the bowels of the planet. These 'sound' energies are primarily produced by deep underground magma flows and the movement of the Earth itself in its orbit, and the geological history of the area. One of these is underground in the continent of Africa, in Egypt and the Great Pyramid is built over the top of it. If you were to look at this vortex with the clairvoyant sight, it would appear as two pyramids with their bases together, one below ground, one above."

"The shape forms a diamond. One part of the vortex points into the center of the Earth, while the other noses towards the heavens. At the time that the pyramid was built it was built in the center of the Earth. The ethereal subterranean pyramid is generated from a central source of subterranean energy that breaks through the crust and then spirals back into a peak out from the planet into the Solar System."

He continued. "The second sound 'well' is located just off the coast of Maui in the Hawaiian Islands. It has

166

Great Pyramid

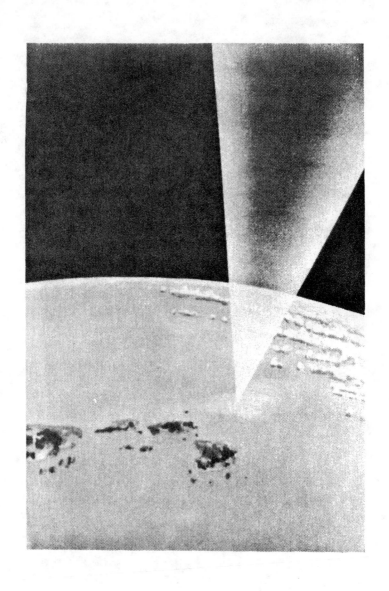

Maui

another geometrical shape, that of a cylinder. It comes from the bottom of the sea and breaks through the water surface, extending out into space for quite a way."

After this information came through, a friend of mine, Jaine Smith, visited Maui and spoke to a lady, Pali Lee, who lives there, about some of the contents of the book I was writing, including the information about Maui. She later wrote to me personally, offering some interesting lore about the area mentioned in Albion's work.

Hana is almost 25 miles east of the Haleakala Crater. Twenty two miles east of Hana are two of the deepest spots of the oceans anywhere near Hawaii. They are called "ka-maka-naho" which means the deep or hollow eyes. Knowing the history of Maui, wrote Pali, and the wars of chiefs and how everyone coveted living in or ruling that Hana area was, and still is today, protected by the kama'aina (Children of the Earth) as a sacred place and no tourist industry has been allowed to take over there. It is as it was, sleepy, calm, peaceful and quiet. "Quaint" is what most people call it. The seven sacred falls is where Kiha Wahine lived and is a beautiful spot and holy indeed. It is the "deep spots" that were of particular interest to me.

"A third sound well, the newest of the three, is in the area you now know as Florida. It is in a location that is already filled with water and when it reaches maturity, there will be no land above water around it. The energy pattern being built takes the form of two triangles, their two points together."

I felt that this must be Lake Okeechobee, which the Teacher later confirmed.

The Teacher added a bit more about Maui, describing it as electromagnetic in its nature.

"It is very alive and active. It draws its power from the 'Ring of Fire' in the Pacific. Although this vortex is dormant in its physical effect right now, its power will erupt three times by the end of this century. The electrical energy there goes and comes in terms of its fre-

169

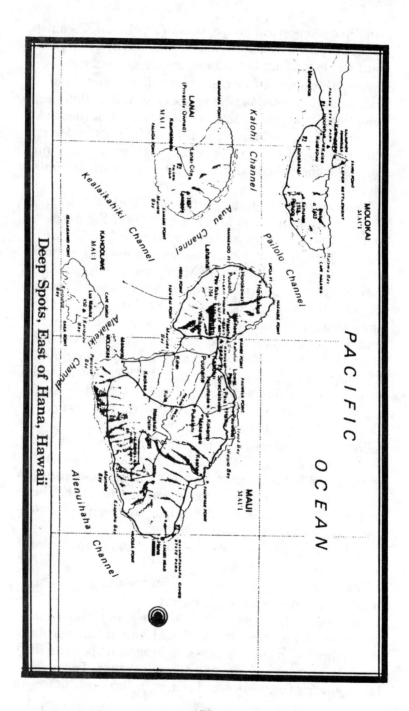

Deep Spots, East of Hana, Hawaii

170

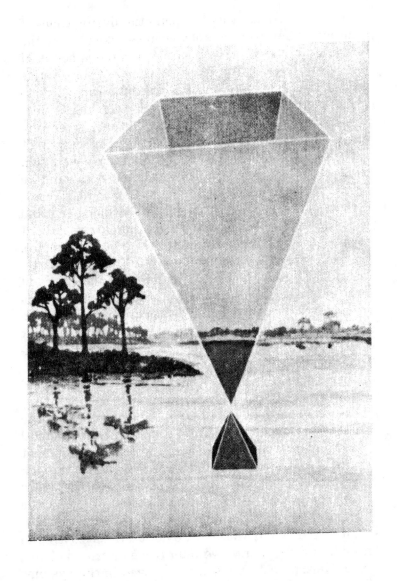

Lake Okeechobee (Beacon Vortex)

quency and is only at its full potential during times of eruption. When eruptions of volcanoes take place in the Hawaiian, Islands, they release a large amount of 'memory' stored in the Earth. Memory of the Earth's past as well as mankind's. This memory, in regards to man, is of the Third Root Race, which was the beginnings of the Lemurian civilization. This energy tends to bring out the primitive nature of those in its wake."

These words required a lot of thought. We were told that only by using our intuitive consciousness could we "hear" these sounds. He said the sounds are like records of the planet's earliest stages of development and growth. Anyone sensitive to them could arrive at a lot of past-geological information that still puzzles science. So, in essence, he was telling us how to "read" the Earth. "Such past sound records are likewise indicators of future activity, for through the past, the future is apprehended." Sounded as if he was describing a method of prophecy! I couldn't help but think of how difficult it would be to try to get some scientist to use his intuition to read the Earth's past, at least consciously. Albion must have picked up that such a thought would be forthcoming and added:

"Many geologists will do so in the future, within the next twenty years." That was an exciting thought! "There will be more sophisticated seismic equipment that will react to these sound currents that flow through the planet by ley lines. Such instruments will be useful in determining the process of the beginnings of the Earth, but also in determining its future forms, as well."

These particular words were not quite as exciting to myself and Scott until we interviewed a friend of our, Alan Holt, an astrophysicist employed in the Systems Training Department at the Johnson Space Center outside of Houston, Texas. An interview with Alan appears in a later chapter, part of which seems to relate to what Albion was saying several months before concerning the future development of seismographic equipment.

The session was proving to be another long, but intense, one. A quick pause to put in a new tape and the Teacher proceeded. "You might wonder why the sound vortices are located where I, Albion say them to be. Both the sinking of Antilia and Pacifica caused 'wounds' of sorts, to the planet. Similar 'wounds' occur during all major periods of change upon the globe, such as when great mountain ranges are formed or a big meteorite or comet hits the terrain. Earth-healing impulses are sent out to heal the wound on the Earth's body, much as the brain would do in the human form. These 'sound currents' are healing currents."

Scott mentioned later that in 1976, Albion had predicted how sound would be harnessed and used by man, both for healing and for destructive purposes. He had spoken of "sound surgery" and since that time, development and some use of such techniques is underway. Along the "destruction" line of thought, there is a lot of speculation about subterranean sound currents being generated by the Soviet Union and how they may have used this tactic to cause major earthquake activity in Iran in the early '70's, that took thousands of innocent lives!

"The Great Pyramid structure harnesses, in a sense, the major sound currents located in that area. This is part of the reason the pyramidal shape can construct or heal and preserve, in its most positive and constructive form. Sound is the oldest frequency in the Universe. It is the result of the first Manifestation of Spirit, which was 'movement'. This translates as the 'Will of God'. All life forms have some device within their physical bodies or consciousness that is sensitive to and a receptacle for sound. Sound, as a current, will be used in times to comes as the 'fuel' to carry life throughout the Universe. Sound is the current that carries the x-rays, cosmic and gamma rays, radio waves. I am speaking of a sort of 'cosmic transportation system' that uses light, sound and gravitational waves. Is this clear? There is no particle of matter, even the sub-atomic particles, that do not emanate sound. Each group of particles has its own distinct sound energy, as different from each other as the fingerprints of your own hand is to the hands of all other men. The sound is the 'signature' of the body by which it is generated. There will be police equipment developed in the next twenty years or so that will be able to identify subtle sound currents in areas that a crime has been committed. The criminal will, in turn, be captured by the duplicate sound currents he or she emits. Sound leaves an indelible print, you see, and it does not deteriorate with time."

While all this information about sound was interesting, the next phase of the session succeeded in capturing my undivided attention! "We are going to reproduce, using the vocal chords of our Instrument, the sound currents of these three areas we have mentioned." For the next several minutes, long, wailing noises came from deep within my throat. It was one of the rare occasions that I was compelled to stand up while Albion was channeling. There is really no effective way to portray the sound he made, but a musician, Ron McLain of Sedona, listened to the tape and put the sound into a recognizable form to those that can read music. They are as follows:

Sound of Maui—E flat to F—stacatto once every 1.25 seconds

Sound of Florida—A—unbroken, steady tone

Sound of Great Pyramid—B flat and C—tones alternating from low to high

"Remember, sound is the identity of matter. Not one single particle of matter in the Universe could be lost or silent, or it would strike an immediate note of discord that would resound throughout eternity. The 'Universal Mind' knows the location of every single atom in space by its sound. Electrically-charged particles have a high pitch, while magnetic atoms and particles are lower and have a stacatto rhythm. Electromagnetic particles are combinations and variations of both. Understanding the importance of sound is to understand creation."

The evening ended with that note. It was a while before any of us spoke. The information, although about sound, had a particularly silencing effect.

A. S. and D. left, taking the tape recording of the session to make a copy of their tape library. I went off to bed, telling Scott that that was definitely one tape that I wanted to hear again.

The next session brought things closer to home once again.

"Let us turn our thoughts for a moment, to the state of Arizona. We wish to bring to your attention a couple of areas of concern to the Brotherhood at this time. One is the place known as Apache Junction, close to Superstition Mountain. This is one of the most powerful spots in Arizona, but its energies have been used negatively. This vortex causes war and destruction. It spurns hatred and fear. It manifests on the physical and emotional levels of the consciousness of life forms. This area can erupt and spread an 'inky-like' astral substance all over the Phoenix valley." There was no further information about this vortex. Instead, he turned his attention to our area of Arizona, Sedona. Since my very first visit to Sedona in 1975, Albion had been telling about the "special" energy that exists in the red rocks! It was he who had instructed me to move to this location. It took nearly five years to make it, but I did.

Albion continued: "There are seven vortices in Sedona. We wish now to speak of two of them. One is quite powerful and is located at Bell Rock." Bell Rock is a beautiful bell-shaped mount, located in the area of the Verde Valley known as the Village of Oak Creek. "The other is in a place called Apache Leap." This is a cliff west of Bell Rock and it is called this name due to it being the alledged location of an event that saw a band of Indians and their horses jump off the cliff, rather than be captured by the cavalry. I have not been able to verify this legend with historical facts as of yet. Albion labeled it a negative place that compels one to death and despair. He advised against hiking in the area. He also

175

spoke of a spot that contained a "minor" negative energy pattern (not a vortex). "It is located in the middle of your town, behind a bank." The Teacher was questioned by our naming the banks in the downtown area and received confirmation when the First National Bank of Arizona was mentioned. He claimed that the energy extended west down to the Post Office. We checked the distance and it is about 1/4 of a mile. "It is one that can confuse communication." I had to listen to his words with a bit of humor. What a ridiculous place to build a post office! I wonder how different our world might be if we, as the masses, were more in tune with the planet, not just ecologically, but also with the geographical energies as well. There was a time that the Ancients had a greater balance and sense of awareness. We continue to uncover advanced knowledge certain civilizations had, some of which approach being superior to our modern technologies, pointing towards their wisdom in such matters.

The other vortices located in Sedona were identified as being on the Airport Road, Boynton Canyon, Red Rock Crossing and Indian Gardens.

Our thoughts were directed next to Flagstaff, Arizona, a town twenty-seven miles north of Sedona. His words created an image of one of my favorite sights. "The San Francisco Peaks, in Flagstaff, compose a major vortex. Their vibrations are similar to Mt. Shasta in California, being electrical in nature." We were all familiar with "the peaks", as they are called. Part of the San Francisco mountain range, the summits can be seen for almost one hundred miles away on a clear day. The highest summit is Mt. Humphries, which stretches over 12,000 feet into the blue sky. The Hopi and the Navajo have long considered the Peaks as sacred.

"Before the turn of the century, there will begin to surface some geological indications that will suggest that there is a lot of pressure building in the bowels of these peaks. There will eventually be another eruption, but not for some time. The Indians know it has occurred before and that it will occur again. The power of these mountains generates an energy so great that it can cause consciousness to heighten into God consciousness. Their internal fires are sacred."

In Jeffrey Goodman's book (American Genesis), published by Summit Books, he refers to the San Francisco Peaks. "The Hopi refer to these mountains as their traditional home. They have a number of shrines in these peaks; it is there that the Kachina people live, the spiritual beings who the Hopi say have helped them over the ages. In their ceremonies, the Hopi dress up in the costumes of the various Kachinas. Interestingly these peaks contain geologic evidence for the destruction of three previous worlds as described in myth. The destruction of the past, or third, world by water could correspond to the flooding that occurred in the San Francisco range approximately 25,000 years ago. The destruction of the second world by ice could represent the glacial activity that took place in the peaks approximately 100,000 years ago. And the destruction of the first world by fire could represent the violent volcanic activity that erupted in the mountains approximately 250,000 years ago."

This information is not only interesting and informative, but lends itself well in proving the Hopi's legends of past Earth changes discussed earlier in this book, as well as pointing out the powerful energies contributed to the Peaks by the Native people. Lawsuits have been instigated by the Navajos and the Hopi to insure the preservation of these summits. They want possession of their sacred ground. But, as of July, 1982, these lawsuits have been lost by the Indians, which has left bitter feelings that undoubtedly will simmer for some time to come. Albion said that being in the area of these lofty fortresses would provide a dose of spiritual energy and an elevation of consciousness.

We ended our session that evening by vowing to spend some time at the Peaks as soon as we could. A. S. and D. shared with us an experience they had had there earlier in the summer. They had ridden the skylift to the top and had watched a storm approaching. It had formed a sort of funnel that had made them think of Albion's description of a vortex. After our friends left, Scott expressed an interest in doing a painting of the Peaks. "Perhaps it could capture some of their power and it would be shared with those that view it." Scott said this in such a way that it seemed as if he might be able to accomplish it with any of the vortex areas. We decided we would ask Albion about this the next time we talked to him. We were tired so we went to bed, knowing that we had a busy couple of weeks ahead of us. Part of our plans included a trip to Pittsburgh for a special radio program. I have a weekly radio show there that I conduct by telephone. Now, I was going there in person to do a week-long special program and it excited me to be getting back into a radio studio. I really missed that. We were also going to do some private readings so there was lots to do to get prepared. We wanted to get one more session in before we left so we planned it for the coming Tuesday evening, three days later.

Albion opened that session by calling our attention to D. The embers in the fireplace glowed red and spread a gentle warmth through the room. His words began with the usual, "As we come forward here now, we come into this vibration in order that we might share information that we wish all of you to pay attention to, especially yourself, D." We were not to understand why he was singling out D. until the Teacher was well into his talk.

"In the ancient past, when the Hopi were still transients (we took that to mean during the time of their migrations) and had just begun to arrive at their present mesas which is their 'Promised Land', they knew the energies in this area were very potent. They constructed a great Temple which was a holy place on holy ground. It was their Sun Temple. It was a place of Initiation and the remnants of it can still be seen."

We felt that he must be referring to Mesa Verde, Col-

178

orado, a place that is known for the Sun Temple ruins. The ruins overlook a canyon and were discovered in 1915 by cowboys who were out rounding up stray cattle. It is obviously a site of ancient ceremonies. There are two kivas in the southern half of the buildings. Kivas are traditional underground rooms the Hopi prepare for the religious rites. A sun dial sits in one of the buildings. Although it is not certain, it is believed that the temple ruins are a monument to one of the almost extinct clans of the Hopi, the Bow Clan, and that the Hopi once indeed occupied Mesa Verde.

Albion's words flowed. "The energies of that sacred place, due to time and the change in the Earth's patterns, along with the movement of the Hopi people themselves, has caused its power to be 'transferred'. It is now located, mostly, hovering over the Grand Canyon. It is now an 'astral temple'. It would be most valuable for you to go to this area, the grandest of all canyons, to make an attunement to the very potent and ancient energy patterns. You are to make a 'pilgrimage'."

Aside from the information about the Hopi connection to Mesa Verde, we were also aware of their belief concerning the Grand Canyon as the site of the re-emergence from underground after a couple of the previous major Earth cycles. This spot, known as Sipapu, is believed to be at the bottom of the Canyon of the Little Colorado above its junction with the Colorado River.

Albion described our "pilgrimage" as being for the purpose of making a special attunement to the canyon itself. "You can touch into this power composed of archaic and present Hopi thoughtforms. It has an effect on the higher levels of your consciousness and it can further your becoming aware of the energies of the planet. To you, D., consider what we have said very carefully, for we wish to inform you of an entity that is present within your auric field. It is a young Hopi boy. He is simply a 'rider' within your aura and he does not influence your thinking or actions whatsoever. He is there to learn and to grow from your experience. Together, you two form a 'duality' of energy. This boy lived in another time as a Hopi in the Canyon area and you knew him in that life, for you too have lived as a Hopi in time gone by. We will call him by the name of 'Swift Creek'. We ask that when you go to the Grand Canyon that you take a pad of paper, and pencils for drawing. Go to a spot that is close to the village area, sit alone and seek to become aware of this entity's presence in your vibration. This entity will take a special form. Then allow your thoughts to manifest on paper. This will give you great assistance in getting in touch with the Native American flow of energy within yourself."

"We also wish to point out to yourself that although this young entity did not live upon the Earth for many years, in terms of how you count your time, there was a great deal of strength and wisdom within his consciousness that needs to be expressed. This can be done through yourself, D. This is not uncommon. It is accepted that spirit teachers and guides do exist. In your particular circumstance, the roles are reversed, so to speak. You are a guide to a discarnate, as opposed to a discarnate being your guide. Swift Creek's energy moves very quickly."

Albion then turned his attention away from D. and spoke to A. S.

"We wish you to also select a place of your choice. Sit for a while on a flat rock. You should also have a pencil and paper in hand, for there will be symbols that will come through to you. Don't worry yourself with any interpretations of these symbols, just channel them. The purpose is to loosen the hand and the consciousness to get them working together. This will allow, in the future, information to flow in the form of symbols so that you will be able to make an attunement to an individual. You will be able to use the symbols that you receive at the canyon as a basis of divination. When you see them with a person and have learned their meaning, you will know that concept is applicable to that person. These glyphs will be both Atlantean and Lemurian in their to go farther back into time and deeper in consciousness in your work with people."

After the Teacher seemed certain A. S. understood his suggestions, he focused his thoughts towards Scott. "We suggest that there is a need to unstop an energy 'clog' in the base of your spine. It is a 'clog' in the etheric body. There is a hollow-like cylinder that runs all the way from the base chakra to the base of the brain." This the Teacher described as being the etheric duplicate of the spinal cord. "We would like for you to also choose your own location and sit upon the Earth. Draw the energy of the planet up through this etheric column with your thoughts, for this will help to cleanse this passageway. It will bring you into a greater balance on all levels." Scott verbalized his understanding of the information Albion had given him. I was not to be left out of the journey. As is often the case, Albion told the others to pass some thoughts along to myself.

"When you visit the canyon, the Instrument will receive a bolt, a charge of energy that will serve a two-fold purpose. It will help break the congestion in the chest, intestines and bowels. It will also help to balance the chakras in the etheric body. The Instrument should sit on the ground." I gathered that I was to receive a general healing.

We were excited about the trip! We talked busily after the session to plan when we would go. We would have to squeeze it in before our travels. We finally agreed to go in two days. It seemed important to go right away, in light of the fact that part of the reason for going was for a healing to the etheric body with Scott and myself.

We arrived at the entrance to the south rim of the Grand Canyon National Park before noon. After viewing the deep purple gorges for a while, purely for the sake of their awesome beauty, we split up to find our own place of solitude. The day was sunny and the air crisp and cool. We regrouped after a couple of hours, with Scott and I being the first to wander back to the van. A. S. came back a few minutes later, eager to show us the symbols she had received. They were interesting.

While we three sat in the truck talking about the energies that we had experienced, D. appeared out of the corner of my eye. He seemed still in deep thought. I could see by the look on his face that he had had a special experience. He climbed up into the truck and sat down, heaving a sigh of satisfaction. "You guys won't believe what happened!" We were all eager to hear of his experience.

"I went climbing down into the rim of the canyon a ways, looking for the right place to sit. I spotted a small ledge and started to go to it when a saw a whole flock of ravens!" He seemed to light up as he talked. "There must have been seven or eight of them." He had tried to walk quietly and get as close to them as he could. "They heard me coming and they all flew away except for one. He stayed. He just stayed there and looked at me. He wasn't scared of me nor nothin!"

D. Related to us how he had moved within ten feet of the big bird, sat on the ledge and meditated on Swift Creek. The raven never moved. "It seemed as if I felt a sort of mental kindredship with the raven." The bird had served as a symbol of Swift Creek in D.'s mind. Since that time, many contacts and energies involved with the raven have occurred, far beyond the point of coincidence. On occasion, the raven has been portrayed through D.'s artwork. The telepathic contact that was made at the Grand Canyon that day has indeed proven to be of value.

After returning to Sedona in the late afternoon, we made plans to get together after a nap and dinner, to see if Albion would make any comments about our trip. We were tired, but we were anxious for some possible feedback.

We got our wish. As soon as we went into our session, Albion began with: "We are pleased with the results of your journey to the Grand Canyon." He made reference immediately to the symbols that A. S. had received by showing approval of her degree of receptivity, but in the same breath, pointed out to her that the third symbol at the top of the row on the right side and the third symbol on the bottom row on the left side, were a bit incomplete. He suggested that she make a re-attunement to them in order to complete and perfect them. He reaffirmed the origin of some of the glyphs as ancient and indicated that as time went by that there would continue to flow through to her concerning the symbols and how they might be utilized for spiritual growth and for sharing and identifying information concerning using them to work with others.

Then his attention turned to D. "You have learned more as to how to be in touch with objective entities from yourself." He suggested that he should draw a raven and incorporate his perception of the facial features of Swift Creek into the image.

His comments to Scott and me were brief. He said that there had been some clearing of energies in the spinal shaft with Scott and that the balancing would continue over the next several days.

Albion closed the session, sensing the experiences we had had been enough for one day. He said that he would be giving us some information in the future for the book that would deal with the continent of South America. "We are concerned with this area. Even though the physical Earth changes will begin in North America, the South American continent should be watched very closely as well."

That piqued our interest so we looked forward to the next time we would work.

The next session did get into some of the areas of our southern continental neighbor. The first vortex mentioned was described as electromagnetic. It was Angel Falls in the country of Venezuela. Discovered in 1935 on Mt. Aunyantepul in the southeastern part of that country, the magnificent falls drop 2,648 feet, making them higher than any other waterfall in the world.

"The water is very highly magnetic," Albion stated, "but the energy that is generated by the falling currents makes for a powerful electric force. Thus, this vortex is a combination of electric and magnetic energies. The constant interplay between the two creates an electromagnetic vortex that is one of the most powerful on the planet. This vortex can heal and energize the body physical."

The next place on the agenda of his thoughts was Peru. He seemed especially interested in this area and the interest could be sensed in his tone of voice. His words became slower and more precise. "This entire country is a rather extraordinary magnetic center. Let us first consider the area of Nazca." Many people involved with the "ancient astronaut" theory of how the Earth was first populated, had a special interest in this particular spot in South America. It is a place of intersecting lines that are generally accepted to be astronomical sighting lines. Seen from the air, however, they give the appearance of intersecting landing strips, leading some to speculate as to the possible extraterrestrial origin. Albion had his own version of truth about these controversial lines. He made little comment about their being of any astronomical use and nothing about extraterrestrials.

"These lines were placed to 'map' the Earth in this location. Symbols of diety were used. They also mark the spot of a re-emergence after previous Earth change periods, similar to that of the Hopi. They marked ancient underground fault lines. They likewise were places of sacred ceremonies to ward off the 'gods of the underworld' during certain times of the year. They are like the hands of a great Cosmic Clock." One can only consider this as food for additional thought concerning this enigmatic area.

In regards to South America, in general, he spoke of it as being under some negative influences, especially in the south. At the time of his channeling, the war between Britain and Argentina had not occurred, but I thought of his words after the fact. He also made remarks concerning the country of Chile and warned of seismic activity there in the near future. He also felt

184

that the negativity would spread into the central American countries and that these would be places to watch for both political and physical activity.

Next, the Teacher's words took us to the country of Japan. Several places were pointed out to us as vortex locations. "Mt. Aso is the largest active volcano crater in the world. It is called Kyushu. Such a place generates a constant flow of potent electrical energy and it can revitalize all levels of the being if you are in its physical presence."

We were also told that as with all of the vortex points, holding a rock from this area would have the same rejuvenating results, but to a lesser degree. That thought made me want to begin a rock collection for entirely a different reason than ever before. I made mental notes upon hearing the tape later, as to what rocks I already had and where they were from. I remembered my prize possessions that I had picked up at the Great Pyramid, Meteor Crater in Arizona, and some from the Grand Canyon. Oh! I would have to sort them all out and check the energy of the area that they all came from as to its type.

Albion continued about Japan. He spoke next of the highest mountain on the island, Mt. Fuji, towering 12,390 feet into the clouds and containing many sacred Shinto shrines on its slopes. "This is an electrical vortex." The same went for Mt. Misen, famous for its firewalkers and also for Mt. Koya in central Honshu. Mt. Koya is the site of a complex of temples and graves. It also houses monasteries and other schools of religious thought. "Electrical energies not only charge and revitalize, but they are 'ascending' forces and carry the consciousness into higher realms."

There were two magnetic areas mentioned, as grids or patterns of energy. Remember, these are not coagulated into vortices. They were Fukui and Tohuku. Aside from both being the sites of hot springs, Fukui also has several Zen temples built in its area. With magnetic energy being conducive to mind power for healing and introspection these temples are surely built in the right kind of spot! Albion spoke next of a place named Hokkaido on the northern island that is highly magnetic. I discovered it, through my research, to be the home of ancient shamans.

Several other countries came to the forefront as the evening progressed. Most of them were mentioned in a brief fashion. One got the impression the pace of the work had been stepped-up. At one point, the Teacher said that there was much yet to cover and that we must move over the Earth at a steady pace. He kept his word.

"In Cambodia, in the Mekong Delta, you will find a city that has long since been abandoned. It is in the jungle and is a magnetic grid location. This is one of the places whose energies need to be revitalized or they will dissipate entirely. It is like a sore on the Earth Mother. Earth needs healing here."

With this, we skipped to Korea. He spoke of Cheju Island as being electromagnetic. Research showed this located on the 7,000 foot Mt. Han Ra. "The mountain is electric, the island is magnetic." Deer Lake, a spot famous for its angelic presences was said also to be magnetic. "The water draws your consciousness into other dimensions." He also spoke of another electrical peak, Mt. So-Ark, giving us an interesting comment about a feature of this vortex. "It is surrounded by a massive magnetic grid that is made of a hundred lakes." It seemed as if a water/mountain combination was almost always turning out to be electromagnetic.

Australia was the next mental stop. Ayers Rock, located in almost the exact geographical center of that continent, is estimated to be 230 million years old. "The people who first settled in this area were some of the earliest migrants from Pacifica. One of the ceremonies that these ancient people practiced was to instill their thoughts and powers into stone or other objects to make them sacred. They believed their gods would enter into them. The rock was then worshipped as being the wisdom focus and power center for the tribe. Ayers Rock is one of these, as is Prophecy Rock of the Hopi and the monoliths on Easter Island. Each of these cultures of people had their roots in Pacifica." He also added that such a practice is the use and generation of magnetic forces.

The Teacher related that New Zealand has a powerful electrical vortex that is called the "cloud piercer", Adrangi. It soars 12,349 feet and is embraced by the Tasman Glacier. Albion pointed out that the North Island is an electromagnetic area that contains volcanic mountains that are sacred to the Maori.

By the time that the session was over we had travelled with Albion's thoughts to many parts of the world. He instructed us with the necessity of having a couple of "marathon" sessions. The world is a big sphere and there were apparently many more locations that he wished to point out. Two weeks had to pass before we could work again. We left for Pittsburgh and A. S. and D. went in other directions.

It was wonderful being in Pennsylvania and seeing old friends I had worked with in Florida. I had lined up a long list of guests for my special radio show for I had five hours for five nights to fill. The topics varied. The guests included Brad and Francie Steiger, the "New Age musicians" Golden Voyage team, Robert Bearns and Ron Dexter, along with Jeffrey Goodman. Sun Bear and Wabun were flown in from Washington to be my co-hosts. It proved to be an exciting, but tiring week and I was ready to come home by the time it was finished. The book and the information Albion was sharing had really caught my attention. I felt dedicated to the book project and I was anxious to get back to it.

Upon our return, it was almost another week before we could have another session. The Monday class was the only time we talked with the Teacher for there were many readings by mail and housework to catch up with first. I noticed that he was beginning to share some of the same information that he was giving for the book in the Monday class. He began to channel about the

Earth being a living organism, as well as an introductory bit about the vortices.

Scott and I did hold a session alone for the book, but by the time the four of us were able to get together again, we were rather surprised to hear Albion request that we take another trip. This time, we were to go to Four Corners again, the Heart chakra of the planet. "We wish for you to go to this special place within the next three days so that we might utilize that energy to channel some very important information for our book." We were not too sure why he wanted us there for a channeling session, other than what he had said about the high energy. But, I, for one, had long since stopped questioning Albion's motivations. So far, there had always been good reasons and good results! This would be our second journey to this area and we all looked forward to it. Aside from the work we would do there, it would also serve as a mini-vacation, which we all needed. We made our plans and left two days later.

We arrived in the Four Corners at dusk. There had been thunderstorms earlier in the afternoon and streaks of lightning still danced across the pink skies. We were also at the monument with the only car other than ours leaving shortly after our arrival. The Moon rose soon after our arrival and it was full. I moved to the sofa in the van because that was where I like to work. Scott sat in a chair and A. S. checked the batteries in the tape recorder. The channeling began with Albion's voice filling the air.

"We come forward into this vibration here in the 'Heart Center' of the Earth, in order that we might bring forward information that is very important to our work. We find the energies here very helpful to our task. These energies are the 'pulse of the Earth Mother', they are a 'Fountain of Love Vibrations'." His words turned to a philosophical note. "Man is a product of his thoughts, his environment, his science, and of his land. It is time for all men to come into a greater recognition of this so that they might gain a better understanding of his function and his purpose of his place in the Universe."

He went on to say that the information he was sharing would be a part of his helping others to understand and relate to the planet better. He cautioned us that it would meet with some opposition and obstacles, for there are forces on the Earth that are not interested in having such information shared. I was reminded, as he brought ego to my attention, by saying that the work must be shared with others with honesty and integrity. It did give a stronger sense of responsibility and I am sure that this was his intent.

The more the Teacher explained of the life and evolution of the globe, the more it tended to make it more "human" in my eyes.

"The Earth is affected by the thoughtforms and actions of man, as well as its relationship with the Sun and the other planets in the Solar System. It is also affected by its own 'karmic' conditions and duties. Some of this effect causes negativity in the body of the planet and three of these manifestations are part of what we wish to share with you at this time."

"These three major blemishes on the planet are places which are caused by man, primarily, but they are also natural to the Earth in some respects. No being is perfect, neither you nor the Earth Mother. There is a great deal of energy and tension that forms a funnel-like vortex over certain areas. These vibrations can cause conflict to the physical and astral bodies and they should be avoided."

"The first such area, a grid, is to be found in the country of Chile in South America. There is an area, deep within the bowels of the Earth, that rumbles with the flow of lava. There is literally a river of fire! As the Earth moves about the Sun in her irregular orbit, she moves in a manner that ebbs and flows form fast to slowing down. The slowest period of movement occurs in the winter, through the month of March. This is so every year. When the planet is moving slower, these lava flows beneath the surface have an opportunity to stagnate more than when the terrestrial orb is moving more rapidly. This causes a greater build-up of pressure. This is going on beneath Chile at this time. Not only will this cause a larger potential for seismic activity, but that 'river of fire' is esoterically connected with other such areas of its sort, such as the Pacific Ring of Fire, Mt. Vesuvius and Mt. Pele. As with humanity, one negative sort of activity will serve to 'trigger' another. Watch Chile, not only for physical catastrophes, but also for social, political and religious unrest, as well."

His next words were quite illustrative.

"Imagine a 'river of fire' in the human body! It would be like a bad case of indigestion and you would have to belch to obtain relief. When the Earth 'belches', it can wreak havoc in a given area of the planet. This land (Chile) was more flat when it was once a part of Pacifica. What is now Chile, is a more mountainous place due to past Earth change periods. It was once the site of wars and many humans have given their lives there in the past. It is a magnetic country that will become quite electric when it erupts."

The next grid Albion labelled as a "blemish" turned out to be a place that has been in the news a lot over the last several years.

"We wish to bring the Persian Gulf area to your attention. This is a full-blown vortex that is shaped like and behaves like an amoeba. It is primarily composed of an astral-like solution that pulsates and reaches out to the land masses within its grasp. It appears as black as ink. It is a magnetic vortex and it draws energy unto itself. Think carefully about this place, for it is an area that the major parts of the world think that they have to depend upon right now, due to their need for oil. Nothing could be further from the truth."

Somehow that thought was both prophetic and comforting to me.

Albion continued.

"No area could generate a greater degree of destruction to the human race than the Persian Gulf. This vortex feeds upon the thoughtforms of humanity such as greed, jealousy, fear and anger. They spread rapidly, causing the vortex to grow. There is a lot of this going on at this point in time, as you well know. You should keep a watchful eye on the Persian Gulf for it has the potential of behaving like a 'suction cup', pulling all of the energies of the world's greatest powers into its grasp. Stay away from this place."

Later discussion of this part of the information caused us to think of a mutual friend in Florida who was planning on leaving for two year's work in Saudi Arabia. Although we did not want to spread fear unnecessarily, we felt that this particular person was familiar enough with Albion's work that he would be able to take the information in the way that it would be the most valuable to him. A. S. did tell him later, and as of the time of this writing, he is still in the United States. In fact, he has recently moved to Arizona and scrapped his plans entirely. The third place the Teacher brought out was China.

"Outside of and to the south of Peking, there is an underground chamber, erected by the Chinese people of the distant past. It is currently being used by members of the Chinese government for important, secret political meetings. It is hidden from the eyes of the world. It is a magnetic vortex, because it is underground. This is a place that the future of the world depends on. The Chinese government holds the fate of mankind in the palm of its hands. We will call this energy the 'Red vortex'. It appears as an inverted funnel. All of these negative areas we have mentioned are physically connected together. They are connected by ley lines of force. If you draw lines showing them linked, you should be watchful of the land areas that these ley lines cross. These lines transmit negative energy and they create potential danger zones."

That information finished our session. We left the Four Corners and drove on to Cortez, Colorado for the night. As always, after "heavy" information, we wanted to

Red Vortex

relax, have a nice dinner and talk. The negative is as important as the positive, but it always seems to leave me with a stronger sense of responsibility. I guess I felt that now a little more than usual. I, as a psychic, had been feeling strong indications about the mideast and the conflict going on there. Albion's words had reinforced my own feelings.

The evening was rather humid and I had some difficulty falling asleep. The restlessness and the planetary "blemishes" that I thought about so much during the night faded quickly as the sunlight streamed into the open window. I woke up Scott and the others. I was ready for some breakfast.

We ate and headed back to Sedona, taking our time, driving through that part of the Navajo reservation is always a special treat. Albion's suggestion of a couple of marathon sessions was discussed as we rode through the tall pine stands just north of Flagstaff. We decided we would have another session as soon as we could, for the project had developed into a commitment and I was anxious to get it accomplished as soon as I could.

Classes and private readings took up the next couple of days. When I was able to have another session, Albion once again began to cover several parts of the Earth, naming several places, as before. The first place mentioned was Spain.

"In Spain, I don't want you to think that the entire mountain range known as the Pyrenees is electric, but some of its highest peaks are. This is also a country that contains a massive magnetic grid system. It is in the area of the Drach caves."

This was another indication of underground caves and the like, as being magnetic in nature. The Drach Caves, or Dragon Caves, in Spain are the largest in the world. The Teacher continued:

"The Canary Islands form a magnetic vortex in themselves. The ancient people of this area were extremely psychic, magnetic-type people who worshipped by seeking to connect themselves with energies in other parts of the Solar System. Magnetic people are also very telepathic. They erected many monuments to their gods of space and of Earth."

The next place on Albion's agenda was to plant a seed of thought that made similar places and events much clearer in my mind.

"There is a place in Spain that you call by the name of Guadalupe. It is a magnetic spot and was the site of the appearance of an apparition of what you know as the Virgin Mary. When an apparition occurs like this, and it matters not where, it is drawn into the physical dimension by a strong magnetic pull. It is a force, not always an entity, that is personified in the mind of the seer, the observers, for there are often more than one. The magnetic grid or vortex serves as a sort of 'receiving device'."

Upon hearing these thoughts, I thought of the beautiful church the travel group had visited in Egypt. It was in Zietoun and I had felt it to be the most "holy" place that I had ever been. It was a church in a Cairo suburb where a mirage of the Virgin Mother had appeared on the roof, with many thousands of people witnessing the event over a two week period. An artist had drawn a magnificent portrait of the apparition, based on his own experience of seeing it. This too, according to Albion's definition of Guadalupe, must be a highly magnetic place. I also thought of another such location in Portugal called Fatima. Fatima is a spot where the Virgin had manifested on several occasions to a group of children.

"Consider now the country of Italy. Mt. Vesuvius is located in this land. It is a powerful electric vortex.

This is still a living volcano and has received a lot of attention due to the prophecies of Edgar Cayce. Its possible future eruptions were somehow indicative in that prophet's mind concerning the coming period of Earth changes. Another eruption was also brought out by Albion, one of long ago.

"The ruins of Pompeii are no longer situated over a

194

full-fledged vortex, but they are the result of an electrical vortex erupting in the past. The consciousness of the people drew this destruction upon themselves due to a misuse of powers and psychic forces. This is quite similar to what happened on Pacifica and Antilia."

"Now, turn your thoughts to Rome, to the Vatican. This is a perfect example of a powerful man-made vortex. It is like a huge 'memory bank'." This statement requires careful thought. "It is like a 'subconscious' that has been created into an actual entity. It is composed of the energies of all of the followers of the Catholic religion, collectively. Between the years of 1987 and 1995, this religion will undergo many drastic changes. This 'memory' vortex will yield much of its data during that time."

I assumed that he was making reference to the huge Vatican library, which is said to contain many lost books, lost to the public, that is.

As with the information about the appearance of apparitions, the next words were very revealing to me.

"There was once a great man who lived in Italy. He was called St. Francis of Assisi. He is an example of a living person who literally created a vortex around himself, within his aura. Such a vortex is centered and grounded through the heart chakra of the individual and it is highly magnetic. Many people you would call 'saints' created such light bodies around themselves. This type of vortex is obviously man-made and is often viewed as a 'halo' with the clairvoyant sight."

This clarified many unanswered questions I had had in the past. Now I knew living people could indeed create vortices in their vibration. I couldn't help but wonder if the same would be true for evil persons, as with a saint.

There were two more countries discussed during this session before we took a break. When Albion had suggested "marathon" sessions, he had said we should work for a while and then break for a rest. This first attempt at this yielded three conversations with two short breaks in between.

France was the next stop on the evening's agenda. Four magnetic vortices were mentioned. Albion's words were strong and to the point. One almost got the distinct feeling that he was reading from a "memory file" in his own mind/consciousness. -

"There is a place in the south central part of France that is a magnetic grid. It too is like a memory pattern. It is Auvergne." I found out that Auvergne is a region of extinct volcanoes and many forests and lakes. It also sports both hot and cold mineral springs. The teacher continued.

"However, the most powerful magnetic area and it is a full vortex, is the Lourdes. This shrine has been the site of many appearances of the Virgin Mother. As with many magnetic vortices, especially those related to water, this is a place that has potent healing abilities to the physical body. It can provide 'magnetic healing' feats. Another magnetic location is St. Girons." Research show St. Girons to be the home of the Pyrennean Caves where there are many petroglyphs etched by a people in the past. Caves were the clue to the identity of the fourth magnetic area in France.

"The Dardogne Valley caves are highly magnetic in their nature too. They also contain 'memory' of times past, both of the Earth and man." These caves and caverns likewise contain old petroglyphs.

Albion continued regarding France. "An archaic site of initiations into the wisdoms is a Mt. St. Odile. This is an electrical vortex. There is another small electrical vortex that is also found at Chamonix." Chamonix is a valley located near Mt. Blanc in eastern France. "There was once an electrical vortex in Brittany, but it is no longer alive. Its energies have been dispersed. The Earth needs healing here. If given new energy, it could be drawn upon as a strong magnetic force to work with drawing down forces from other planetary bodies in the Solar System." This was not the first time Albion had mentioned healing or revitalizing certain vortices and grids on the planet.

196

In his trek around the globe, the only place that the Teacher mentioned in regards to the country of Yugoslavia was a spot known as Nin. "Nin is floored with radioactive sands. Where there is an area that is the site of a high concentration of radioactivity, this indicates a place that is extremely powerful for healing. The sands are healing to the etheric body. The soil can strengthen the virility of an electric person and can heal a magnetic person."

This was one of the first hints we had that people are also electric, magnetic, and electromagnetic, as well. During the break, I expressed a keen interest in pursuing that thought with the Channel at a later, more appropriate time. Albion's final words at the end of the first part of the session had been that we should take a sixteen minute break and then he wished to discuss the country of India.

"There is much to relate to you concerning this land and it is very important to our work that this country be more clearly understood."

Scott fired up the coffee pot. The hot liquid felt good to my throat. Albion's voice, being much lower and considerably louder than my own, left my throat a bit "scratchy" sometimes. The minutes went by quickly and it was time to begin again.

"India is a potent land mass, you can be sure. It is situated very close to the Brow Chakra of the Earth. There are many vortices, as well as grids, in this country. Let us first turn our thoughts to the Ganges River. This is a magnetic flow of water. It is very fertile with plant life and good for healing the body of man."

Next, attention turned to the majestic mountain range, the Himalayas. To mountain lovers, this range is very special. It is applauded as the most exciting and, at the same time, the most dangerous of all the mountains in the world. The Himalayas contain some of the highest peaks on the Earth, including Mt. Everest. The mountains stretch for 1,500 miles in a slight curve across the top of India and they are 100 to 150 miles in width. The eastern range is bordered by the Brahmaputra River and the western by part of the River Indus. The south finds the fertile plains of India and to the north lies the high Tibetan Plateau. The Himalayas have always been sacred to the Hindus, and the Chinese held seven of the peaks as sacred, as well.

In his dealing with the country of India, Albion pointed out several special places of interest. He seemed especially drawn in his thoughts to six temples located in southern India that hold special reverence to the Hindus of the area. It requires a pilgrimage of about two weeks to reach the area on foot. It is said that each of the Temples represents five of man's chakras, as well as being located on the site of sacred ashrams. I will list them you you here:

1. Tirupara Kunram, a location that is considered the holy mountain of the Lord. "It is an electrical vortex."

2. Trichendur, what Albion called a "magnetic" vortex of healing energies.

3. Swamimalai, also a "magnetic" vortex area. It is called "the Heart of the Universe".

4. Palani Temple, "magnetic" vortex known as a spiritual oasis.

5. Tututani, an 'electrical' vortex. This means "Lord of the Mountains". "Nowhere else on Earth provides a more powerful inspiration to do good than this temple", were Albion's comments.

6. Alakar Malai, is an "electromagnetic" vortex and represents the "Third Eye" in man.

"These six temples would make a wonderful spiritual pilgrimage, for all of the three major energies are present there; electric, magnetic and electromagnetic."

The Teacher's words carried our thoughts to several additional magnetic areas. They included Ajanta, located in the western part of India. "This is not a vortex, but a grid." My research shows Ajanta to be a place of caves containing ancient rock drawings.

The next spot, "a sacred lake called Pushkar. It is a "God-lake'. Its water is conducive to carrying one's consciousness into a very receptive state."

Almora, situated in the foothills of the Himalayas, is 7,000 feet high in some places It is the home of a well-known guru, Govinda. It is most interesting to note that above this special area, there is literally a break in the Van Allen belt. This "belt" is a doughnut-shaped region of space that contains many high-charged and rapidly moving particles, all trapped in its magnetic field. This makes this place a very "charged" location. In fact, it is said to have such a powerful energy that only individuals that are very well-balanced should venture there, for it could have a negative effect, a very destructive one, on weak and off-centered minds.

Another cave, an electromagnetic grid, is the Amaranth Cave in Kashmir. This cave is in a mountainside area, 16,000 feet high. The height and the cave being "in the earth or rock", both contributing to the makeup of its energies.

Also, several man-made vortices are to be found in India and most of them are located over grids that are primarily magnetic. They have been created by Holy Men who have chosen to live in certain places. Examples of these are: Punjab, where Ram Dass has built a healing center; Anantapur, home of Sai Baba; and Auroville, home of Aurobindo.

"Perhaps one of the most special vortices in all of India is Bodr Gaya. This is an electrical vortex of great power. It marks the spot where the Buddha attained enlightenment. Spending time here, for the 'prepared initiate', can achieve the same for yourselves." Albion also told us that a time would come when we would have an opportunity to visit this sacred place.

The next power point the Teacher mentioned was one that I wished he had also said I would visit. "A vortex that is electrical in its nature is at Darmshala. It is a place that the 'attuned' person can hear the 'music of the spheres'. It is the 'sound celestial'. It is the chosen home of one of the Holy Men of the world, the Dalai Lama. Although its energy is electrical, its power can transform such force into purely magnetic energy. It transforms 'aspiration' into receptivity! this is good for the disciple, for it is a good telepathic current so that the Dalai Lama can send his thoughts and power all over the planet."

The next area that was brought to our attention was described differently than any other, thus far. "There is an area known as Khajuro. It is the site of two temples, the Jain and the Brahmin. These spots are magnetic, highly magnetic. They are conducive to the healing and revitalization of energies of a sexual nature." Ancient teachings speak of the sexual force as the most potent of all of man's forces. We know that Tantric Yoga is based upon the total and proper use of sexual power. The Teacher also indicated that other places, particularly magnetic areas, promote sexual energy.

It seemed as if India contained more magnetic grids and vortices than any other place mentioned previously. My idea was substantiated later by his remark that ... "India contains more power points within its boundaries than any other single country in the world. Humans in the East likewise make more conscious use of these energies than do those in the West." He went on to mention a location that is quite similar to Delphi in Greece, with the exception that Delphi is a man-made vortex. It was Rishikesh, a magnetic grid that, through the constant use of its energies, has coagulated into a full-fledged vortex. Most of the inhabitants of this area are very psychic and have the gift of 'seeing' into other dimensions of time-space, as well as the future. Being there would develop anyone's psychic sensitivity and one's healing powers to a very high degree. I couldn't help but wish I could go there for a while ... a long while!

The next two places the Teacher spoke about in India were the healing springs at Razir and Kulu Valley. "Razir is a spot that is highly magnetic. It is said to have been visited by both Jesus and the Buddha. The Kulu Valley is likewise magnetic and a spot where angelic beings congregate."

This concluded the information on India. It seemed logical that the next place he took us to in thought was Tibet. Tibet truly is a place of spiritual intrigue that has long captured my imagination. The first and one of the few energy points mentioned by Albion was: "An electrical vortex called Mt. Kailas. Its energy is extremely potent and it is spirallic in its nature. it causes the consciousness to 'aspire' and 'ascend'."

My research revealed this white-domed peak is believed to be the "Heart chakra" of the Earth by the Tibetans. This, of course, does not agree with Albion's designation of the Four Corners of the North American continent as this particular sacred center, but does establish its being a special place. It is also interesting to note that on Mt. Kailas there are two lakes, one shaped like a crescent Moon, the other round like the Sun. The solar-shaped body of water has four rivers, each of which flows in four different directions. "This is a place that the Great Planetary Spirits congregate. Their power sustains the Earth. It is here their presence can be felt very strongly by the enlightened Chelas." His next words were quite revealing. "The Dark Forces have, in the recent past, concentrated their negative forces to the land of Tibet, part of the Earth's Brow Center, to disperse this 'Force of Planetary Light' of the white Brotherhood, and the force was a powerful one, indeed. One of the results was that the Dalai Lama was forced to flee to India and this kept His Holiness within the boundaries of the Brow chakra. This was to keep his finely-tuned body from being destroyed by such an input of negativity. There will be a time that, by the turn of this century, this sacred Tibetan land will not be left without a spiritual force. The 'return' of the Holy One to Tibet will herald the true beginning of the New Age! You can be sure that the Brothers of the Absent Light will try to block this return of spiritual power and this situation should be watched closely by all."

Still keeping his thoughts centered in the Himalayan region, the Teacher next spoke of Sikkim, a beautiful area that contains thick jungles, complete with orchids and exotic animal life. In Sikkim, the highest peak was described as a "powerful electrical vortex. It is an entrance-way into the 'Mind of God'." This was an interesting choice of words, to say the least. The highest summit turned out to be the 28,000 foot Mt. Kanchenjunga, which translates to mean the "Great Snow of Five Treasures". It is said to display all the brilliant colors of the rainbow.

My energy was exhausted. The session had been a long one and I was ready to quit for the evening and relax. My thoughts were full. I knew I would have to listen to the tapes to remember it all, and I was looking forward to that. The next day, Scott made a comment about the Himalayan mountains and decided to sketch out a painting. The information had inspired him. I envied his talent. If I could paint, I thought, I could paint a lifetime of work with the images Albion's channeling had always planted in my mind. My fantasies of being an artist were interrupted with A. S. and D.'s leaving. They were also tired from the session. We decided we would try to work again the next evening, but as it turned out, it was almost a week before we finally did work again. Travel plans and an overload of psychic readings came in the mail and delayed my extracurricular activities. I had begun to hope that there would come a day that the book would be my total task. But, that was not to be for a while.

When the next session came, it proved worth waiting for. At the beginning, Albion said that although he would continue with further information about vortices, he would first give some instructions for the next "pilgrimage". It was to be to the Hopi Indian Reservation. This would be our first trip there, so we listened carefully although I was not to be totally aware until hearing the tape later. After this initial trip, there was to be two other times that the Teacher sent us to this stark land of the "peaceful people". It became clear that he was "exposing" us to the vibrations of the land, as

202

well as the energy of the first Americans. I was very interested to learn some of what they knew. I also feel it was designed to lead us into a deeper understanding of the values, lifestyle and survival techniques the Hopi have from their memory of other periods of Earth changes.

Once the Hopi trip had been discussed, the Teacher turned his thoughts to the continuation of the locating of the vortices. I had previously made a list of other countries that had not been mentioned, of which A. S. informed him. He began to rely on this and it seemed to make his work a bit easier.

He mentioned again that Cambodia was in need of healing. The fact that the location was low in energy told me that a war is not healthy for any area in which it might occur. He also spoke of another magnetic spot, a grid where there is an abandoned "Temple City". It is called Angkor Wat. The one area of Light in Cambodia is composed of fifty man-made mountains, each bearing the face of the "Boddhisattva of Light". This seemed symbolic of one candle in a land of darkness, to me. "This place is electric."

Albion's pace quickened as he turned to another part of the globe. "In Arabia, there is one of the most powerful vortices in the world and it is man-made, generated from worship of Diety. It is Mecca. There, one can find the veil between the visible and invisible worlds drawn apart. Even to the unenlightened, this veil is very thin here. It is a spot that was originally chosen for its pure magnetic energies, but man's thoughts and activities there have converted it into pure electrical force."

Arabia also is the home of Mt. Arafat, which is known as the "Mountain of Knowledge". This is an electrical grid. Another magnetic vortex and very potent one, is the "Mouth of Hell", where smoke smelling of sulphur pours out of holes in the ground. "This energy is very dangerous to the emotional or astral body of man. It is of no use to the mental self, and should only be utilized by an initiate who could transform it to the higher spiritual levels. The soil is good for healing the physical for it will draw impurities, but cannot be allowed to stay on the body for but short periods of time." The Teacher later commented that this would be so for any soil or water that is high in sulphuric content.

The Middle East continued to be Albion's geographical topic. "Israel is a magnetic country, the Jews are a magnetic sort of people. They have a natural 'drawing' power, which can be used to 'draw' energies, of evil or good, to themselves. The black race is also very magnetic in this way. Mt. Sinai is a powerful electromagnetic vortex. It inspires one to receive." This we all recognize as being the mount where Moses "received" the Ten Commandments. The voice continued. "A magnetic grid can be found at the Dead Sea. Its water can be used for stiffness in the bones and muscles and being in the sea gives the physical body a good massage, of sorts." I didn't think he would go without mentioning Bethlehem and he didn't. "Bethlehem's power was created by an event, just like Lumbini in Nepal, the birthplace of Buddha."

England was next on the list. Since I had been planning to lead a tour group to both England and Scotland in the future, this information piqued my interest. His first words were of Avebury. "This is an electrical vortex with ley lines connecting it to other such places all over the Earth. It is a solar observatory that is not unique for there are many like it all over the world. Observatories of the sort were built to pay homage to the gods, as well as being a place to observe the heavenly bodies and the weather, both a part of their sacred rituals." England has long been noted for its energy and it is still a center of occult and metaphysical teachings, which is why I suspected it to be a special energy spot. I was right.

One of the most prominent of England's intriguing locations is the "mapping" of its territory by both ancient and modern Geomancers. Legends abound regarding old castles, stone circles, legendary forests and the like, and are a serious part of the country's history and charm. A psychic attunement to the landscape reveals myriads of "ley lines" that connect the power points to one another. This is, according to Albion's work, the way the etheric body of the entire planet appears. It literally is an "Earth Network". Some say that the ley lines reflect a celestial pattern. This relates the Earth to the Universe in a cosmic at-one-ment that man has constantly striven to understand. Most agree that the ancients of the earliest cultures had a greater knowledge of the planet's etheric body than we do at the present time. Part of the purpose Albion had designed this book for was to re-educate us in modern society of this archaic knowledge so as to help to prepare us for the imminent period of planetary change. Re-acquiring the ability to view the Earth through the Brow Center so that the network of global energies and power points and grids can be known is believed by Albion to give a much better chance of survival on all levels, as well as bringing the student of life to a better balance with the planet. The importance of this was becoming more and more clear as Albion's information for the book went on. It had been reinforced earlier in the year (1981) to me when I had learned of the Bear Tribe and Sun Bear. "Walk in balance on the Earth Mother", a slogan of Sun Bear's, sums up the goal of all self-reliance information.

Albion continued about Avebury. "This is an important vortex, for it is a terminal for many ley lines." Turning to a history book of England, I found that Avebury is also the site of the biggest man-made mound in the world. Some belive that it is the place of the resting place of a "spiritual" king, where he sleeps until he is needed again.

Glastonbury came out of the Teacher's next thoughts, an area that is rich in the lore of King Arthur and his knights. "This is a powerful vortex, it is man-made. It can best be described as a creation of man's thoughtforms concerning the walking of the spiritual path of life. King Arthur is believed to symbolize the New Age 'pilgrim', his grail, enlightenment."

I was to discover that a spot known as Chalice Well,

which Albion labeled as "highly magnetic and good for healing", is a grid. The entire area around Chalice Well is powerfully-charged. "Anyone living or spending large amounts of time in Glastonbury must be able to deal with the energies or they will cause negativity to those that are unbalanced, especially on the mental or emotional levels of their consciousness."

Stonehenge was next. I could feel the Teacher's vibration peaking inside my own consciousness as he began to channel this information. "This is one of the most powerful of all vortices in the world." He had talked about Stonehenge before, but never in such detail. This ancient sarsen circle is without doubt one of the most mysterious places on the face of the Earth. Why or who built this prehistoric site is a subject of long-running controversy. Most scientists will agree that it is an astronomical observatory, quite sophisticated, while most Occultists proclaim it an outdoor temple used for rituals by the Celtic Druids. A popular theory put forth by Gerald Hawkins, the author of *Stonehenge Decoded*, believes it to be representative of the Sun, that is was used to predict eclipses. Albion united two theories by describing it to be both an ancient observatory and a place of ceremony.

"It served a scientific and a spiritual purpose." He spoke of other stone circles, such as the Medicine Wheels, as having the same function and that ley lines connect them all together. "One can attune to the Universe here, for it links this planet with other parts of space and its inhabitants."

One site that is believed to be physically connected with Stonehenge is Woodhenge, located about two miles away. It is said to represent Mercury, the closest planet to the Sun. There are believed to be other circles like Woodhenge to represent other planets in the solar system in the proper pattern. England is littered with the remains of monolithic circles. Albion has said in the past that all of the inhabited areas of the Earth were once as populated by sacred circles and archaic obser-

206

vatories as plentiful as they are in England.

England's next door neighbor, Scotland, proved to be equally as powerful as any other previously mentioned except for, perhaps, India. We were not surprised to hear that Loch Ness, home of the famous monster, Nessie, is located over a magnetic grid. Findhorn, a popular "New Age farm", was said to be a natural vortex that is also magnetic in nature, which causes it to be high in its degree of fertility. "All magnetic areas are very fertile, with few exceptions. Angels, nature spirits and elementals are drawn to this type of energy. Findhorn is not really outstanding or unusual, it is just that there people have consciously recognized its energies and have worked with them in balance. Worldwide application of energies in this way could turn the entire Earth into the proverbial Garden of Eden."

A tag was placed on the Island of Iona when Albion labelled it not only magnetic, but also that it is connected to other magnetic vortices that are in water.

Other islands were brought into the Teacher's conversation as the session went on. The first mentioned was the Azores, which Albion simply described them as "mountaintops of Atlantis and that they are highly magnetic, as was that entire continent." His words again brought to my mind the legends concerning the psychic capabilities of the Atlanteans. I felt that that was partly due to their land area being of the highly magnetic nature Albion described.

The island of Costa Rica, which lies between Panama and Nicaragua, in Central America, was also described as being magnetic. The mention of Costa Rica reminded me of a delightful man Scott and I had met at the Malibu Medicine Wheel Gathering in May of 1981. His name is Rainbow Hawk and he is working in Costa Rica to build a self-reliant community similar to the Bear Tribe in Washington state. Living in a better balance and helping to heal the Earth Mother should work very well on this island. Albion added, "Cartago is another magnetic vortex in Costa Rica. Its waters can heal the physical body also."

When Hawaii was named from the list I had prepared, the information given, in addition to what I have already shared about the "sound" vortex off the coast of Maui, was very interesting. Albion considers the Hawaiian Islands the mountaintops of Lemuria. "A very powerful grid system exists on Mauna Kea, the highest peak in the Pacific. This force is conducive to aspiration, for communicating and for mental development." The island of Maui was once again brought to our attention with a remark about a dynamic electric vortex. It was Halea Kala crater.

Next, thoughts were shared about Greece. Listening to the sessions was beginning to take on the essence of taking "psychic" trips all over the world. We were beginning to gain a great familiarity with the planet and that felt good. It was clearly a part of Albion's purpose, to be sure. The information of Greece came forward with a reminder that Delphi is a man-made vortex. "It is a place that was made conducive by working with the higher forces."

In regards to the mystery schools of ancient times, Albion said that; "The Elysian Mystery Schools and all such places of Occult learning, were built over magnetic vortices that are natural to the planet or artificial vortices created by the 'magnetic' activities of the people in the area over many years of time."

Mt. Olympus, home of Zeus, is a "once very potent electrical vortex, but its force is dwindling and needs revitalization. The Earth itself is becoming weak in this area and it will be the site of some of the major seismic and tidal activity, more toward the late 1980's and all through the 1990's. Healing thoughts to this location can help to 'ease' some of this trauma."

Mt. Olympus' energy, once re-charged, is very conducive to contact with higher forces. I looked up the data on this summit and found that it is 9,793 feet high, located in the mountains of Northern Greece. Like the San Francisco Peaks in Arizona are the home of the

Kachinas, Mt. Olympus was believed by the Greeks to be the home of their gods. A pattern seemed to be evolving as the information about the famous mountains of the world continued to be brought forward. It's interesting to note how many of the peaks were held sacred to the ancient people and some modern ones, as well. This thought was reinforced time and time again during the sessions that led me to electrical energy as having the greatest potential of spirituality. Albion identified Mt. Athos as an electrical "spiral". It is curious to note that in the lore of this peak, "warlocks" were known to gather herbs form Mt. Athos for their medicine potions. This peak stands 6,670 feet into the Grecian sky and since the 10th century has been the site of major orthodox Christian contemplative centers and thirty-two monasteries.

The next location was obviously a special one to Albion. A long time before he began to channel the information for this book, he had said that in one of the two lives he had lived on the earthplane, one had been on the Isle of Crete. It seems that this land mass was once much larger than it is now, this according to Albion's own words. Located in the eastern Mediterranean, it has been the home of civilizations since before 1600 B.C. "Crete is a magnetic vortex and its energies can be best used for learning to stabilize the consciousness. I, Albion, worked to achieve this and my achievement of this ability is the reason that the work now can be done through a physical channel such as my Instrument."

Next to be mentioned was the island of Aegina, which was also said to be a magnetic grid area. The final comment made that night concerned the Parthenon. Albion described this age-old temple of the goddess Athena as a "man-made vortex, built over such a high energy spot that it burst into a bonafied funnel of energy that is electromagnetic in nature. It is conducive to learning and growth on all levels."

With these thoughts shared, the session came to a finish. The time had seemed to pass quickly and the hour was late. We sat and talked for a while, making plans for our trip to the Hopi reservation. We would have to fit it into a busy time, for Scott and I were going to have to go to California for a speaking engagement. With that in mind, we decided to go right away.

The drive to the reservation took three hours. The van rumbled along the road towards the three mesas. We had received instructions for our own personal little tasks. D. had been told to collect some rocks from which he could make "Earth change talismans". A. S., Scott and I were to be in the vibrations, apparently to the energies of the area and the people.

We arrived at Second Mesa, the location of both Old and New Oraibi. Looking around, it was hard to imagine how these people were able to grow their food on this barren and rocky ground. We investigated some of the other villages, too, going into some of the little shops, getting a first hand look at some fine overlay silver, a specialty of the Hopis, along with their coil baskets. The Hopi are fine craftsmen, taking special pride in the silver work, basketry and pottery. The day was hot and dry, like most of the days in the high desert. We left, just in time to have a beautiful turquoise and gold sunset cast shadows and hues of light over the rock monoliths that lie in the distance. Hopi and Navajoland has been blessed with plenty of space where one can really get a grasp on the vastness of the planet coming off those mesas onto the plains. It has been a pleasant day, spent basking in these ancient energies.

With Scott and I alone, a couple of later sessions were held to cover most of the remaining major areas of the world. In one, as we settled in for an evening with the Teacher, he began to pick up on the naming of countries again, naming Finland and Norway first. "These counties are extremely magnetic. You will find that there is already, and it will continue for the next ten to twenty years, an interest in extra-terrestrial life amongst the people of these lands. This is often true with people who live in countries that are highly magnetic. Such magnetic places will attract magnetic people to them. A high concentration of such people can actually 'draw down' the forces and entities from space."

"Finland and Norway are fertile, physically and esoterically, and will become more fertile as time goes on towards the New Age. These lands will attract sensitive persons." I gathered from Albion's words that a lot of so-called UFO activity occurs in potent magnetic locations, with naturally magnetic-type people. His was a curious line of thought for a serious UFO investigator to pursue, I thought. It is also interseting to note that there are over 100,000 lakes in Finland alone, and Helsinki is a city nestled among islands and peninsulas by the sea. Likewise, east of Stockholm there are literally thousands of islands. If a magnetic "indicator" is lots of water, it is no doubt why Albion designated Finland and Scotland as such, as well as other islands of the world. I gathered it would be safe for me to consider such lands as huge magnetic grids. The teacher did point out one lake in particular, in Sweden. It was Lake Malar.

"This is a powerful vortex of energy that is magnetic and is conducive to subconscious activity of all kinds."

For the first time, the USSR got into the picture. The world's deepest lake, Lake Baikal, descends 5,712 feet into the body of the Earth Mother. "This water is a highly magnetic grid and its minerals would soothe the pain and stiffness of arthritis and other stiffening problems in man's body." Of course, there is no way that this could be determined for sure without proper experimentation. I did a bet of research on Lake Baikal and found that it is located in Southern Siberia and covers approximately 12,162 square miles. A big lake. indeed!

"The Kremlin is a man-made vortex. Due to the activity that goes on there it is highly electrical in nature." I think it is important to note here that in one of the Tibetan's books, channeled by Alice Bailey, entitled *Destiny of the Nations*, there is mention of how Communism, if practiced in its purest sense, could be the highest form of government on Earth. Needless to say, there is no such "true form" being utilized today by any country, certainly not the Soviet Union. With the use of the "ascending" energies of electrical force, in a positive and balanced manner, perhaps some of the aggressiveness and potent power, alone, that is characteristic of electrical energy, would or could, make a big difference in world politics today. It disturbs me a bit that any government, in any country, is generating pure electrical force that is strong enough to coagulate into a vortex, for purposes less than spiritual! But, it has, in the past, and will continue to occur in the future.

I also remembered a reference that I had read many years prior in one of Rudolph Steiner's books that many years from now into the future, Russia will do quite a turnaround. It will become, according to Steiner, a place of spiritual enlightenment. Makes you wonder if the world will last that long with the way things are going, for Steiner said that it would take about 1,500 years. Other Russian places that Albion mentioned in passing, included the Ukraine, which he labelled as magnetic, Bukhara and Leningrad, and Zawgorsk, also magnetic, plus Moscow, which he said is electric.

The only specific place regarding the land of Iceland that the Teacher mentioned was in reference to the glaciers and the volcanoes. Iceland has more volcanoes than any place else in the world and it is also abundantly wealthy with hot springs. This entire country is a magnetic grid and the only electrical energy that is generated there is during a volcanic eruption.

I had barely had time to tune into Iceland when I was listening later to the tape, before my thoughts were diverted to Hungary. I don't recall ever having given Iceland such thought in the past, but it left me with a feeling of high energy and I had listened. I make a mental note to find out more about this land in the future, for there was something about it that intrigued me. The Teacher's words broke my line of thought. "Long before Hungary was a country as you know it, it was a place that a small number of ancient Antilian (Atlantean) migrants settled. They were the last of the survivors of the continental sinking."

Then came Ireland. "Aran Island is a magnetic grid, and you should know about a holy mountain in this land known as Croach Patrick. This is the only vortex in Ireland. Its energies ascend heavenward and it is like a giant spiral. It can enhance one's spiritual understanding and the potency of its energies can blend into the consciousness." Research revealed this mountain to be the place of forty days of fasting by St. Patrick, way back in time.

As the information continued, I couldn't help but think about how our historical prejudices get in the way as he would speak about certain countries, some of them the sites of war and strife, both past and present. It was turning into being a good lesson in learning how to look at the planet and the life forms upon it, in a neutral fashion. It felt good to me to experience this.

Next came Germany. It seemed that many of the areas in this country were magnetic. Augsburg, Baden Baden, in the Black Forest, Brennberg, Frankfurt, Gladenbach, Hamburg and Munich, all were said to be magnetic grids. The two places mentioned as the most potent in Germany overall, were the Black Forest, "a highly-charged magnetic grid, as I have said, and the Exern-stones, a site of worship dating back to the Stone Age, said to be a full-fledged, natural magnetic vortex." Albion said it was esoterically connected to Stonehenge and others of the same sort. "Ley lines run in all directions out from these stones." Additional research by the reader on this area is worthwhile, but too lengthy to mention here.

Holland was called by the Channel; "the future New Age Center of Europe," whereas Belgium was not a location of any specific vortices.

The session came to an end with Albion's urging us to work as often as possible, for there was still much to be covered yet. It didn't take much persuasion for we were as anxious as the Teacher to absorb this information. Several days passed. My class required attention. I noticed that more of the data Albion was sharing for the book continued to trickle out in the lessons he taught each week. The class of about twenty people had been studying with Albion for a little over a year at that time. I had told them about the "book sessions" and they seemed anxious to share in the information, which gave me a good idea as to how the public might also respond.

When we did work again, it had to be without A. S. and D. They were busy, and we did not wish to delay any longer than we had to. Scott and I prepared for a session together and we anticipated it to be another long one.

The familiar words; "As we come forward here now, we come into this vibration in order that we might continue our work on the vortices and grids of the Earth. We wish, first of all, to bring the country of Switzerland to your attention for the Alps are of ascending energies and they will draw the consciousness of those that are in that area from seclusion and cause it to ascend to the higher forces of the Universe. All of the Swiss Alps appear as a spiral of energy, but are electromagnetic in quality. These energies have a positive effect for healing and psychic attunement. When there is a great amount of moisture, as in these Alps, the water serves as a 'conductor' of the energies, as well as adding to the charge. This is evident in other ranges, such as in the Andes, rain forests, etc. In times past, many people who have practiced the spiritual arts and the like, have sought seclusion in these peaks."

Deleting some of the Teacher's rhetoric, suffice it to say that Denmark, like Belgium, was labelled a magnetic grid. Also, another piece to the Lemurian puzzle was added with the brief mention of some very familiar islands. "What you call the Easter Islands (which he had mentioned before) compose a gigantic and potent magnetic vortex. This land mass belongs to Pacifica." Sitting west of Chile in the South Pacific, the

214

Easter Islands, with their forty-ton lava sculptures, have long intrigued modern man. Albion contributed his theory of the statues by saying: "The Ancient inhabitants of this island were very magnetic in their nature. The sculptures are images of their gods and they were placed there as 'watchers' and as 'protectors' of future Earth Change periods. This was part of the 'Promised Land' of some of the later Pacifican migrants." It is hard to say whether Albion's theory of the great stone faces is true or whether it is but another addition to the growing list of theories that already exist. Perhaps only time will tell.

I had thought there would be more information needed to understand Latin America than given, but Albion simply stated; "The Himilayas direct their force towards the Andes. They have an 'esoteric' connection. This great range has been the home of the Mayans, Aztecs, Incans, and the Quechuas who were all very magnetic people. Much of the area of the Andes is electrical in nature, but the ancestors of these cultures came from highly magnetic lands, thus were able to adjust and deal with the electrical forces here to their advantage. This changed these people eventually, especially the Mayans, into one of the few concentrations of 'electromagnetic people' in the world at any time in history. Others, such as the ancient Egyptians, are an example of this too. These cultures are an example of how a people can create an energy that will live through the ages." I guess it doesn't take Albion a lot of words to imply a great deal!

Mexico came up next, closely akin to the previous information, being the home of the Mayans in Yucatan and Guatemala for 3,000 years! Since information about Mexico had been given earlier, he only reminded us that many of the ruins were of archaic observatories and are linked to others, such as Stonehenge by ley lines, Chichen Itza, Palenque, Uaxactún and Mayapan were likewise indicated as sites of astronomical-type ruins.

Magnetic sites were talked about, too. "Tikal is a special site of ritual. It is a magnetic vortex, and so is the Zuni Village in New Mexico. The waters there can heal the body."

The site of an ancient Aztec city was next on the list. It was Ixtapalapa. "This is a potent electrical vortex and that fact was known by the cultures of the past. This place will raise the consciousness and will arouse the Kundalini Chakra within those that are in its presence. It is a spot that can help create a balance in the consciousness." I discovered that there is a peak here called Cerro de la Estrella, which translates to mean "Star Hill". I asked Albion to comment: "This area has a double purpose, for it is also a communication vortex." That makes it a "beacon" similar to the Bell Rock one here in Sedona.

The next vortex Albion talked about was not totally unfamiliar to me, for I had read about it in my study of astronomy. In 1976, when I began my study, I had quickly developed an interest in a relatively new subject in the field known as Astro-Archaeology. I had read about ancient ruins that specialists believed were sites of probable astronomical observatories. Teotihuacan was one of those. "This is a special place, my friends, it was once a place of worship. Anyone going there can sense the relationship that the ancients had with other bodies in the Solar System. Life depended on this knowledge. The sun and moon were their sacred dieties. This location carries the consciousness into 'astral travel' through space." The temples there are the Temples of the Sun and Temple of the Moon. Albion described Teotihuacan as an electric vortex and a very potent one.

The Teacher continued. "The area you would call Uxmal, in the Yucatan, is a man-made vortex and its energy is dissipating due to its lack of replenishment. This is a spot that was once a strong electromagnetic grid. Its energies, although low, can still be felt."

The following place was likened by Albion to the Gizeh Pyramid complex in Egypt in one certain respect. He referred to Milta, the City of the Dead, as a magnetic grid.

Next, Chichen Itza was described as a "Beacon" vortex. "It projects its invisible rays that come from the center of the Earth, from the molten core." His thoughts zeroed in on a specific building there. "There once was a temple there, of which the remnants still exist, that is built directly over this magnetic Beacon vortex. It was a sacred temple but also was like what you would call an institute of 'technology'. Celestial bodies were observed and rituals built around them. It was an important vortex and still is." The Teacher went on to say that the "Elders" who manned that temple complex were extremely sensitive to the Earth and its energies, the air currents, tectonic movement and so forth. Their receptivity was enhanced due to this being a magnetic place. The Encyclopedia Britianica describes Chichen Itza as a ruined Mayan city, founded around the 6th century A.D. It is believed to be a place that was once involved with a cult known as Cenote, who engaged in human sacrifice. Chichen was invaded by foreigners, possibly the Toltecs of central Mexico and they may also have been the Itza for whom the site was named, but it is not certain. Scientists feel sure that it was primarily a sort of astronomical observatory.

The talk about Mexico was intriguing, but Albion quickly moved on to other thoughts of other places. An old city in Honduras, known as Copan, is "a place that drew people to it due to its potent energies. Copan was erected over a region where there is a major ley line 'terminal'. Stonehenge and the Externstones are also connected to Copan. The effect the other bodies in the Solar System has upon the Earth and its life forms (Astrology), as well as the movement of the heavenly bodies (Astronomy) became the primary function of the Priesthoods that once thrived there. This is one of the birthplaces of technology and it is a powerful electromagnetic vortex. Both energies are prevalent and can be used to activate the human chakras, especially the Brow and the Crown centers."

I have deleted much of the commentary Albion made

as he moved through the geographical areas of Latin America and Mexico, leaving only the most pertinent information for purposes of time in this writing. His pace was steady, his voice moving at a confident clip. "In the country of Nicaragua, there are intense areas that are highly magnetic. A lot of it is centered under the city of Managua, which is a very unstable location. Unsettled or negative thoughtforms building up in this region can cause the Earth underneath to break loose. Like California, this is not a safe place to live." After Albion's comments, I expected the recent conflict in Nicaragua could trigger seismic activity in the not too distant future.

The session came to a close with Albion stating that this would cover, for the most part, the major energy vortices of the world.

I suppose I, for one, had never realized the vastness of the Earth before now. So many hours had been spent pinpointing the vortex locations. Some had been apparent, some had been new to me altogether. The Earth, in its five billion years of life, indeed represents far more than a sphere of rock floating around the Sun. Albion's words had given it not only life, but a distinct personality, as well. It was easy to see how the activity of the planet's evolutionary changes, along with the positive and negative activity of the myriads of life forms that live here, have all contributed to its geological and esoteric bodies.

Time goes on. As many more millions of years pass by, the personality and body physical will continue to change. Old mountains will be washed away and new ones will rise. Man will find new places to create his vortices. He will continue to "search out" the natural spots. He will still follow the ley lines as threads of navigation of the vast terrain.

What happens on the Earth will continue to be determined by the Sun. The distant future of the Earth will culminate as the Sun dies, exhausted of its central fires. But until then, the Earth will no doubt, continue to provide man and all the other kingdoms with a home. Trying to understand the world upon which we live has been a challenge since the dawn of prehistory. Perhaps we move closer, once again, to a time that the knowledge of the Ancients is very important to modern man. Albion's "Spiritual Geography" is presented as a way to seek to "walk the Earth Mother in a greater sense of at-one-ment and balance".

LIST OF ADDITIONAL VORTICES
OR GRIDS

MT. KENYA—grid (electric) Africa
MT. KILAMANJARO—grid (electric) Africa
EINSIEDELN—electrical vortex, Switzerland
VAL COMONICA—magnetic grid, Switzerland
WILD VALLEY—magnetic grid, Switzerland
TAOS, NEW MEXICO—electric grid
DEVIL'S TOWER, WYOMING—Beacon vortex
MATTERHORN—sound vortex, Switzerland
KENNYBUNKPORT, MAINE—synthesizer
PIKE'S PEAK—electrical vortex
LAKE TITICACA—electromagnetic vortex
MT. WHITNEY, CALIFORNIA—electrical vortex
MT. BLANC, WESTERN EUROPE—electrical vortex
SIDI BON SAID, NORTH AFRICA—electrical grid

SWITZERLAND

The Alp area is mountainous and therefore an area of ascension. It will draw those for seclusion in order to ascend to the higher elements of consciousness. The energy of the entire range is spirilic in nature. The magnetic quality, due to the significant amount of

219

moisture there, has a significant effect in healing and psychic attunement. It is electromagnetic. This means that when there is a mountainous region with a significant amount of moisture, the energies are charged further and use the water as a conductor. Other examples are the Andes, Yosemite Falls, and rain forests.

CHAPTER FIVE

EARTH CHANGES: PAST AND FUTURE

"Earth changes, but Thy soul and God stand sure."
Browning

"The Earth is now passing my window. It's about as big as the end of my thumb."
Astronaut in Apollo 8

It's easy to fall into a false sense of security during our lives upon the Earth. Although we are constantly exposed to the plight of the victims of various natural and man-made disasters, we tend to remain trapped in the "it only happens to someone else" syndrome. Our attitude about the planet is one of taking it for granted. It's always been here and it always will be! Or, will it?

Nowadays, this complacency may be changing. We are experiencing a wave of interest in prophecies, both ancient and modern, that predict a coming period of Earth upheavals and change. There is more concern about the destruction we have heaped upon the planet and its ecosystem. Perhaps some "mechanism" within man's psyche has triggered an "instinctual" warning of some kind. Books and articles about the Earth's past periods of cataclysms have definitely gained a wider audience. Legends of the lost continents of Lemuria and Atlantis are subjects of intrigue, while phenomena such as earthquakes, tidal waves, and the changing weather patterns, are becoming more and more of interest to the average man.

The Earth may not be as stable as we once thought. Geological evidence shows that "terra firma" has undergone major changes in the past and speculation has it that this can and probably will, occur again. When? No one knows. We have the geologists and the prophets to rely on, a strange marriage of scientific and non-scientific advocates, each with his own ideas about what kinds of changes we might expect. A quick glance at both of these disciplines leads to the unsettling discovery that they are pretty much in agreement. The methods by which the geologist arrives at his conclusions are by far different from that of the prophet, but the results seem to be the same!

Although we generally think of "Earth changes" as a natural process, part of the "chance" we have to take to live on this planet, we are becoming increasingly aware that man himself may play a more contributive role in the fate of the planet than we had ever realized before. Tampering with environmental conditions like the weather, along with the plundering of natural resources, is a source of mounting concern. The question is: How will all of this affect the future of Mother Earth? This question is one that requires searching out an answer. If the prophecies are indeed indicative of what's to come in the future, then we may need to know the answer to this question much sooner than we expect.

In order to gain a clearer picture of what both the scientific and the non-scientific predictions are really saying, we need to explore both sides. An examination of intuitive responses to the planet comes to us from almost all cultures from the ancient past right up to modern times. Perhaps one of the most well-known and accepted of those sources would be the Bible.

"Immediately after the sufferings of those days the sun will be darkened and moon will not give her light and the stars will be moved out of place, and the power of the

heavens will be shaken."

Matthew   24:29

"...and there will be signs in the sun the moon and the stars, and on the earth distress of the nations and confusion because of the displacement of the sea."

Luke   21:25

"...the earth is utterly broken down, the earth is utterly moved, the earth is staggering exceedingly. The earth shall reel to and fro like a drunkard and shall be shaken like a hut and its transgressions shall fall and not rise again."

Isaiah   24:19   and   20

The Bible is a book the Christians all over the globe respect as a "rule" to live by. Critics will say that it is a marvelous history book, but nothing more. Others take a totally fundamental approach to it and consider its source to be God and its prophecies as inevitable. Whichever is true lies within the mind and choice of the individual, but there is no mistaking that the Bible warns man of a time, perhaps due more to evil deeds and thoughts than natural planetary cycles, that the Earth will pass into another period of great change, to be followed by a time of peace; a New Age. This New Age is common amongst various sources of prophecy, as we will see.

Another prophet, Nostradamus has also been getting a lot of attention as of late. Many books have been written that have sought to interpret the famous "quatrains" of that sixteenth century seer.

Before dying in 1566 Nostradamus predicted that his grave would be opened and the one responsible would die. In May, 1791, his grave was dug up, coffin opened, and Nostradamus' skeleton bore a plaque around its neck reading, "May, 1791". A stray bullet from a peasant farmer's rifle struck and killed the man responsible for opening the grave, true to the seer's words. Of Nostradamus' predictions, over half have come true. Some say he predicted the rise and fall of Hitler, the Second World War, the assassination of John Kennedy and

Robert Kennedy, as well as other major historical events. Following are selected future predictions.

July, 1999—World War III—Missle attack on New York City. "Inhuman and cruel heart, blood will pour, mercy to none."

1986—Great world-wide drought and famine. "...Man shall become a man-eater."

May, 1988—a great earthquake will occur (New York) after a series of volcanic explosions in the American Northwest." "...a fire from the center of the earth shall make an earthquake in the New City."

A deluge of floods shall precede a great war. "...No spot on earth for a firm foothold."

In regards to a great war, some scholars of Nostradamus' predictions have interpreted the quatrains to say that in July, 1999, World War III will begin. They believe there is reason to believe that the seer "saw" nuclear attack on the U.S., namely New York City. Likewise, an Arabic master of Islamic Law attired in a blue turban will wage war across the west. It is said that this leader will invade all of Europe and bring the world face to face with annihilation. Soviet nuclear power coupled with Islamic manpower will occur and the war will last for twenty-seven years. But it seems that they go further to interpret that the barbarian will be driven back but not before the world is undone and desolate. They say the U.S. and the Soviets will become friends. Peace will be achieved! This Golden Age is predicted to last for a thousand years.

It is important to remember that Nostradamus, like other prophets, believed that the future can be changed. He wrote that the tragedies he saw could be averted allowing man, if he chooses to, to be the master of his fate. More about Nostradamus later.

No discussion about coming Earth changes would be complete without recognition of a famous modern prognosticator, Edgar Cayce. Cayce's "readings" for thousands of clients in the early part of this century, were sprinkled with glimpses into the planet's past and its future. The Cayce prophecies speak of events that he said would begin to occur as early as 1936 and continue through the turn of the century. Some of the predictions speak of catastrophes, but not all of them. There was also the prediction of the appearance of new land in both the Atlantic and Pacific Oceans.

However, the most familiar and quoted of Mr. Cayce's views of the future include:

The sinking of Japan into the sea.

The transformation of northern Europe "in the twinkling of an eye". The land sinking, the oceans rolling in.

Los Angeles and San Francisco will be destroyed before New York City.

The North Atlantic coast of the U.S. will undergo many physical changes. New York City, the Connecticut coastline will go under the sea.

The southern Atlantic coast, Georgia, South Carolina and possibly North Carolina, will disappear beneath the ocean.

The Great Lakes will empty into the Gulf of Mexico.

The western coast of North America will be inundated for several hundred miles inland.

Similar cataclysms will occur around the globe -- in the Arctic, Antarctic, and the South Pacific, for example.

These excerpts from the "readings" of Edgar Cayce have been studied carefully by a great number of people, laymen and scientists alike. Although obviously none of the above predictions has occurred as of yet, many feel that they are probable and in the not-too-distant future.

A recent book released by the A. R. E. Press and authored by Edgar Cayce's eldest son, the late Hugh Lynn Cayce, entitled, *Earth Changes Update*, takes another look at the prophecies and the probability of their occurrence. Headlines that quote accounts of seismic activity and volcanic eruptions seem to verify some of the events predicted and show that patterns of change predicted in the 1930's are coming to pass. This substantiates the forecasts of the next twenty years or so, as highly likely. The thing that I feel is of particular importance with the "update" book is the section that deals with the positive steps that are necessary for preparing for the coming changes. "The need for centered individuals seeking guidance through prayer and meditation is emphasized." Hugh Lynn's book also reminds us that the predicted upheavals are only a prelude to a New Age of spiritual awareness. In this we see but another indication of the "cleansing" period bringing the world to the threshold of balance. That promise makes survival all the more important. In light of this, Chapters Six and Seven of this book deal with the matter of survival on all levels of being, from the physical to the spiritual.

Seeing the Earth changes as a cleansing, led me into thoughts of what the Hopi Indians of Arizona refer to as the "Great Day of Purification". You will recall the account of the "Four Worlds" in the First Chapter, which described the change periods that have occurred in he past. Could that also serve as an indication of what could happen again if certain rules of living are not followed, namely living in the traditional ways, as laid down by the Great Spirit? Let's take a look. The prophecies tell of their land, which is essentially comprised of three large mesas, being the "center" from which all the Indian people will be reawakened. They also believe their land to be a "safe" place to be when this age of reawakening begins. A "true White Brother", white taken to mean pure, will come in the form of a "Light from the East". The Brother would be clothed in a red cloak or red hat and he would have the corner piece of the sacred stone tablets that is now missing. The tablets

Hopi Tablets

referred to are said to be real and contain the etchings in stone of how they should make their migrations to this land, how they were to know the place they should settle and the way they were to live when they go there. Alledgedly, there are four of these tablets, one with a corner broken off. This is the corner the True White Brother would have. It is believed that the Hopi still, to this day, hold these tablets in their possession. It is said that only the True White Brother will be able to read the ancient stone plates. He will come with two helpers. One will bear two important symbols and wear an odd-shaped hat. The other will bear the sign of the Sun.

Their appearance is supposed to herald the Great Day of Purification which, if it happens, will affect the entire world. They speak of the Earth shaking three times for short periods, in advance of the trio's appearance. Some believe the "helpers" to represent groups of people rather than actually being only two individuals. The task of the three will be to petition the world to return to the traditional ways of living. Should they fail, it will spell death to many numbers of humans. The Hopi believe that if enough of their people remain true to the ancient ways, that the True White Brother will not fail and global disaster will then be avoided. The Hopi believe the time of the True White Brother's return is near.

Recently, an article appeared in the newspaper of the Hopi Tribe, the Qua'toqto. It concerns a meeting held at Grandfather David Monongye's home in Hotevilla, where Hopi spokesman, Thomas Banyacya, recounted a recent trip (early June, 1982) that he and Monongye and Dan Evehema took to New York City to be a part of the demonstrations against the threat of nuclear arms buildups and to try to deliver a message at the United Nations' General Assembly devoted to disarmament. There were about ten people present at the meeting, where Banyacya recalled his own involvement with "the Hereditary 'kikmongwis' (village chiefs)" and the high religious leaders of the Hopi.

In New York at the U.N., Banyacya's group tried to appear before the General Assembly agenda. They were offered, however, five minutes by David Brower of Friends of the Earth organization's presentation time. But, this was cancelled because it did not meet with the approval of the U.N.'s established procedure.

The Hopi Message for the Second Session on disarmament at the United Nations, June 24, 1982, is as follows:

TO THE MEMBERS OF UNITED NATIONS SPECIAL SESSION ON DISARMAMENT

My name is Evehema. I am one of the religious leaders from Hotevilla in Hopiland. As a member of the Greasewood Clan, I have a special duty as the town crier for the high religious leaders and Kikmongwis. I have been instructed by my leaders to present this message to the House of Mica. We are amazed to see the world leaders now gathered, just as our ancient prophecy foretold. Since we only have a small amount of time, I will have our official interpreter deliver the message from the Hopi at this time.

THE HOPI MESSAGE FOR THE SECOND SESSION ON DISARMAMENT AT THE UNITED NATIONS, 24 JUNE 1982

My Hopi name is Banyacya of the wolf, fox and coyote clan, and I am a member of the Hopi Independent Nation. Since 1948 I have been an interpreter for the hereditary Kikmongwis and the high religious leaders of the Hopi. Our presence here today, to deliver this important message to the United Nations and the people of the world, is a fulfillment of one of our ancient prophecies. When faced with many unresolved problems, we first were instructed to go to a White House, which our elders say should represent purity and justice. If turned away, then we were instructed to go the House of Mica that would be standing on the eastern part of our homeland, where world leaders of all nations would be gathered.

229

The Hopi have made three attempts to address the House of Mica, but the doors were not open to us, nor to the original native people of this land. We questioned why the doors of the United Nations have not been opened to the native people, since the United Nations stands upon our land?

The oldest continuously occupied villages on this continent are in Hopiland, and we are the descendants of the ancient survivors of the last destruction of the world by a great flood. Our purpose is to share the knowledge of survival in hopes of preventing another global catastrophe by the invention of a gourd full of ashes, the atomic bomb.

We wondered who would help us in our fourth and final attempt to open the doors of the United Nations. Since Hopi means the People of Peace and we are all children of the Earth Mother, it seems appropriate that the doors were opened by a group called the Friends of the Earth. We would like to extend our warm appreciation to their president, David Brower.

The traditional Hopi follows the spiritual path that was given to us by Massau'u, the Great Spirit. We made a sacred covenant to follow His life plan at all times, which includes the responsibility of taking care of this land and life for His divine purpose. We have never made any other treaties with any foreign nation including the United States, but for many centuries, we have honored this sacred agreement. Our goals are not to gain political control, monetary wealth, nor military power, put rather we continue to pray and to promote the welfare of all living things. Our goal is to preserve the world in a natural way. Now is the time when the Sun enters his summer home, when our Kachinas are performing ceremonies to bring gentle rains for the plants, animals, birds and all forms of life. In contrast, we heard the United States, the Soviet Union and other nuclear powers are performing an evil ritual which threatens to bring down a rain of fire that would destroy all forms of life.

It was said by Massau'u that if and when a gourd of ashes is dropped upon the earth, many would die and the end of the materialistic way of life would be near at hand. We interpret this as the dropping of atomic bombs on Hiroshima and Nagasaki. If this happens again with the present powerful weapons, this world may come to an end. For this reason, the Hopi wish to remind the people of the world that their land is a sacred trust, that it was designated by the Creator as a refuge for all living beings. Therefore, any and all desecration of this land must cease.

According to ancient traditions, the previous world was destroyed when men became greedy, corrupt and lost the spiritual path. Upon emergence into this world, the Great Spirit gave us a life plan, the secrets to survival. Our White Brother was directed to go eastward, and he was given a special mission to go to another land where remarkable inventions would be developed. We knew our White Brother would one day return, and he was to use inventions to help his young brother in preserving the beauty and balance of this land. But, since the White people have returned, many have been blinded by the lust for wealth and power, and once again have lost the spiritual path. As we stand before you today, we are still looking for our true White Brother. Where is this true and honest person?

We, the Hopi People, have watched man destroy the earth, the air and the water in the name of progress. Uranium for nuclear bombs now is being mined on our Hopiland area without our consent, nor approval of the traditional Hopi leaders. Hopiland is recognized as the spiritual center of the continent. The exploitation of our land is not only a violation to the Treaty of Guadalupe Hidalgo, it is a sacrilege which will not go unpunished.

The Hopi have a realistic plan for world peace, but it is too complex to explain in 5 minutes. We ask for at least three or four representatives to come to Hopiland. We also invite world spiritual leaders to come with them as soon as possible. Our wise elders are waiting patiently for you in their sacred Kivas to reveal the ancient secrets of survival. There should be three or four nations who are willing to accept our offer. We do not want the world to be destroyed in a nuclear holocaust.

The Hopi are doing all they can to warn the people of the world to take positive action, so as to avert nuclear or natural disaster. If this positive action is not made by the nations of the world, the Hopis will direct their prayers for help to a spiritual power which will come from the Western direction. We are entering a critical period in the existence of mankind.

We await your response.
Thomas Banyacya Interpreter/Oraibi

David Monongye
Kursgova
Evehema
Howesa
Will K. Mase

TO THE MEMBERS OF UNITED NATIONS SPECIAL SESSION ON DISARMAMENT:

We the undersigned Hopi innitiated leaders and members of the Hopi Sovereign Nation, on behalf of our highest hereditary kikmongwis and all traditional Hopi people, hereby present to you our most urgent petition calling upon all of you to immediately put aside all forms of instruments of warfares including the development of nuclear energy for destructive purposes.

As spiritual leaders knowing our ancient Hopi prophecies, warnings and religious instruction all of which were given us the original native people in this western hemisphere we strongly believe that the time has come for us to remind all of you that only by humbleness, kindness, and true love for all living things on this mother earth can we solve world problems. Great Spirit Massau'u has warned us not to develop any "gourd full of ashes," atom bombs or nuclear powered missiles and drop them upon our Mother Earth. Whoever does that will surely have to face eventual punishment which will be great.

We have many ancient prophecies, religious instructions and warnings which we wish to share with all our white brothers and sisters but only by words of mouth in our pueblos and by our spiritual kikmongwis. Therefore we sincerely call upon all of you to do away with further development of these deadly instruments of warfare and come and meet with our highest Hopi spiritual leaders as soon as possible.

> Earl Pela
> Sidney Sekakuku
> Wayne Susunkewa
> Byron Tyma
> Augustine Mowa
> Amos Howesa
> Paul Sewemaenewa
> David Monongye

It is also interesting to note that right now, the "politics" on the Hopi reservation involve a split between the Traditionalists (whom Monongye and Banyacya belong to) and the non-Traditionalists. The Traditionalists wish to remain true to the rites and beliefs set down in the past and they do not wish for the onslaught of the white man's world to destroy their way of life. The preceeding speech shows that they are sure they know what will happen if this occurs! Others seem more prone to the "modernization" of the people and the reaping of the monetary rewards to be gained by stripping the land of its valuable natural resources. To do so is a federal issue, involving the Bureau of Land Management. So the battle quietly rages, out of sight to the masses of the world. The Traditional people are struggling to remain "true" to the spiritual laws, while the forces of progress push on. It is barely imaginable that these precious few could make the difference in the fate to befall us all, but they believe they can if we will but listen.

During one of the sessions held for this book, Albion instructed me to obtain an interview with a Hopi Elder. Fortunately, on a trip to the reservation with a friend from Sedona, Randy Richmond, Scott and I discovered that he was acquainted with the well-known Hopi Elder, David Monongye, mentioned in the group attending the U.N. Generally called "Grandfather David", David is a resident of Hotevilla on Third Mesa. He is said to be well past one hundred years of age and is very concerned for the fate of the Earth and mankind.

As we entered into the small, spotlessly clean home of the Hopi Elder, I could not take my eyes off him. His advanced years did not show on his face, but his words reflected the wisdom of a time I could only read about. I told him I was in the process of writing a book and the general theme that I was following. I don't think he was as impressed with that as he was in telling us about himself and his travels. We learned about his trip to Sweden, Germany, and to the United Nations in New York. His words reminded me of the Hopi who went to speak to the United Nations once before, which in and of itself was a fulfillment of part of their prophecies. Their prophecies had told them of a "House of Mica" that would be on the eastern shores of this land and that it would house the nations of the world. When the Hopi realized the plight of the world back in the 40's and the condition it was in, they realized that their prophecies were coming to pass. So they sent a delegate to the United Nations to let the world know of their beliefs. They wanted the people to change their destructive ways way back then. I think that it's safe to say that very few, if any, listened to them or took the Indians seriously. Grandfather David had been one of these who had spoken.

One got the feeling he had told many others who had come to him of his experiences and we were getting the full course. As he talked, I glanced across the room at my fourteen year old daughter, Mary, who was hanging on every word. Mary had become quite interested in the Native American path. She had been given the name of Bright Bird by Sun Bear and she had recently begun to study the ways of the Pipe. She seemed to sense that she was privileged to be in the Elder's presence. I couldn't help but think about the nearly ninety years difference in their ages. They knew and lived in two completely different worlds. But, here she was, totally intrigued by his world that she could only imagine. I saw that as a sign of the children of the present drawing upon the experiences of the "Keepers of the Past".

Grandfather David made comment, speaking in quite clear English, about how people come to his home all the time and ask of the prophecies and the great periods of change about which they speak. He reminded us that the Hopi Mesas are safe. He strongly stressed the need for people to return to the " old ways". As he talked, the modern world with all its diversities and strife seemed so far removed from this peaceful setting. But yet, that was only an illusion, for the global state of affairs was obviously weighing very heavy on the old man's heart.

The Hopi prophecies indicate another world war that will be started by those people who first received the "light". Many believe this to be the people of India, Egypt, China, Palestine, and/or the Africans. Current conflicts in these countries, especially in the Middle East, would seem to make the prophecy imminent. I get the feeling that people all over the globe are frightened by the prospects of war in this part of the world because it fits so many of the various predictions, including the Bible. In fact, there has been a rash of books written by several different Christian theologians that have been popping up over the last decade, all centered on Biblical references to a period of strife and global change. The constant drama of the Forces of Light and Darkness is replayed in every one of them. One of the most popular of these is a series of books by author Hal Lindsay, which began with the title *The Late Great Planet Earth*.

The Hopi, the "Peaceful People", feel that there will

come a time that things will get so bad in our country that people will flee to their mesas for refuge. I know that this is already beginning to happen, at least in a small way. Grandfather David had indicated how people were coming to the mesas seeking his information. This can be witnessed most any time you visit the reservation, for there will be many non-Indian people browsing in the various villages. I doubt that all of them are merely curious tourists!

One of the most intriguing of all the Hopi prophecies that I have heard concerns an end to their ceremonialism. It is to begin with a Kachina, the Blue Star Kachina, unmasking himself in front of uninitiated children. The Blue Star Kachina represents a Blue Star that is far away, so invisible. The Kachina will unmask in the Wuwuchim Ceremony, which is held in the month of November every year. This will end the ceremonies for a while, and the sacred dances will not begin again until the beginning of a "new cycle". Old Oraibi, the longest continually inhabited settlement in North America, over 4,000 years, will be the site of the renewal. No specific date is given, nor is the length of time that the ceremonies will be discontinued.

The remainder of the prophecies comment more on signs of the changing times, that mostly have to do with the advances of technology and the attitudes of people, in general. They tell of the Eagle landing on the Moon and we all know this has happened. The Apollo II lunar module was named "the Eagle". They also speak of a "house in the sky" that is to be one of the last inventions allowed mankind. Some believe that to have been Skylab, while others feel it may yet be a "space colony", which would certainly give us more time before the final days on the Hopi time scale. They speak of strange starlike "things" that will come to the Earth. Speculation has it that this could imply the worldwide UFO sightings that have been on the increase since the 1940's. It could also be the satellites that drift in space, some of which have fallen to the Earth. They tell of a time that two brothers will build a "ladder to the Moon". Could this be the "space race" that took place between the United States and Russia? It seems so. They knew of the coming of the white man. They knew of the contraptions he would drive, boxes moving without animals pulling them. They knew of the ribbons he would build to stretch across their lands and if you stand on the mesas, the highways do indeed look like ribbons. The prophecies spoke of a "gourd of ashes" that, if dropped on the Earth, would kill many people. I believe the explanation of the "gourd of ashes" as the bomb that was dropped on Hiroshima and Nagasaki to be correct.

It's hard to say, but if the future prognostications the Hopi share with us prove to be as accurate as the ones just mentioned, we may indeed be in for a lot of trouble.

Many of the other North American Indian tribes have their own "prophetic" glimpses into the future of man and the planet, one of the most prominent ones being the Iroquois Tribe. It was given by a prophet named Deganawida long ago and is generally known as the "Red and White Serpent Prophecy". It, like many of the Hopi prophecies, deals more with changes that will be brought about by the actions of man rather than natural phenomena. This serves to further substantiate the belief that man has much to do with the so-called "Earth changes" as will the natural growth processes of the planet.

The Iroquois prophecy, also common to the Seneca people, tells of a White Serpent that will come to live in the land with the Indians. These people would attempt to destroy the red man and things would be very bad. This situation would draw a Red Serpent who would come from the North, that would, in turn, terrify the White Serpent. He would release the Indian people who would be like "helpless children". For a short while, the White Serpent and the Red Serpent would get along, but then they would begin to argue and fight. The Indians would regroup and renew their faith and live by their old principles. This is another indication of how the

Native Americans believe their way of life is pertinent to surival and being in balance with the Earth. The prophecy states that the Indians will remain neutral in the fight.

During the battle, the Native people would receive a message. It would come to them through a young Indian male who would have great powers. He would be heard by thousands. I understand the prophecy to say that at about this time, a Black Serpent would come from the sea, dripping with salt water. He would look to the North and see the fighting going on between the Red and White Serpents. The battle, which had begun very slowly, would increase and become more violent. The violence would become so intense, it would cause the mountains to split and the rivers to boil, causing the fish to turn up on their bellies. There would be no leaves left on the trees. There would be no grass.

The next part of the prophecy is very interesting. It tells of "strange bugs and beetles" that would come from under the ground and attack the battling serpents. A great heat would cause the smell of death to permeate the air and sicken both serpents. Commentators have expressed belief that the description in the vision is indicative of the affects of nuclear war, yet nuclear weapons were not in existence at the time this prophecy was made! Many other Indian predictions speak of "blinding lights", again, seeming to point to the widespread use of nuclear weapons.

After the war of the Serpents had raged for a while, it is said that the Red Serpent would reach around the back of the White one and pull out a hair. Then the hair will be caught up by the wind and carried to the South into the hands of the Black Serpent. He studies the hair and suddenly it changes into a white woman. She begins to tell him things that the prophet says he already knows, but upon hearing them again, the dark serpent is angered! He heads towards the North and becomes involved with the violent battle, defeating the Red and White Serpents who have become weary in their fight.

When the war stops, the Red Serpent will stand on the chest of the White one as if he is the conqueror, looking around for another enemy to attack. He looks to the hilly country and sees the Indians, but knows they are not the ones he should fight.

It is then said that the Red Serpent will face the east and see a "blinding light" that will seem many times brighter than the Sun. He will be terrified and flee back into the sea, never to be seen again by the Indians. The White Serpent, divided in half by the battle, will revive and he, too, will see the bright light. A portion of the White Snake will make its way towards the hilly country, where he will join with the Indians in love. It will be like a reunion with a lost brother. The rest of the White Serpent will go into the ocean and be lost for a spell, then he will reappear on the surface of the water and swim towards the light, never again being a source of trouble for the Native Americans.

The Red Snake will also revive and shiver with fear upon seeing the light. He will crawl towards it, leaving a bloody trail in his wake. The Red Serpent will never again be seen by the Indians.

As you can see, this prophecy is quite detailed and involved. I have spoken with some who feel that the Red Serpent could represent the Chinese and the White could be "Americans". Could the Black Serpent be indicative of the Arabs? Some feel it could represent oil, which is the reason for so much conflict. Could the Black Serpent represent OPEC? Who is the white woman? Is the "light" nuclear war?

It's interesting to note that the Hopi prophecies also speak of "a race of people that will cover this country in one day". Could this also mean the Chinese? Deganawida said he would be the light, likening himself to a Messiah. Is the prophecy but a figment of the imagination of a self-styled prophet? Only time will tell.

The Native American prophecies seem to all have the same general theme. The Blackfeet have a "Sun Dance Prophecy" that is a forebode of the Sun being overshadowed by turbulent black clouds that will transform into a bright light before finally becoming like a human figure. They believe it to be a "messenger" or a "savior" of the Indian people. He will let them know it is time to return to the old ways. Sound familiar?

Black Elk, respected Holy Man of the Oglala Sioux, left the heritage of his vision to posterity. At the age of nine, he had seen the races of the world uniting in living the traditional Indian ways.

Perhaps it can all be summed up, insofar as the prophecies of the American Indians are concerned, by once again considering the haunting words of the Hopi. They believe that man is "tampering" with the Moon and the stars, and they see this as wrong. They say that it will create earthquakes, hail storms, floods, dramatic seasonal changes and famine. It's hard for us not to consider this statement as mere superstition, but can we so easily dismiss the comments of a people who had knowledge of the arrival of the white man into their society and the changes that his presence would make?

It is easy to see that an investigation of prophecy concerning the future of the planet will give us varied scenarios as to the manner in which the period of changes will be triggered. I think that it makes more sense to reason that the different scenarios may all play a role, each in their own time, rather than to see them as all incorrect simply because they differ.

Making the transition from the psychic perspective of future reality into the more "scientific", will lead us into just as many problems as well as theories as to how these problems might manifest.

I have observed during the time I have spent listening to Sun Bear and other Native Americans lecture, that one of their major concerns, based not only on their prophecies, but also on their urgent desire to have all mankind return to a more balanced lifestyle, is the sensitivity they have to climate. The Indians depended totally on their understanding and relationship with the Earth for their survival and they are familiar with the adverse affects bad or drastic climatic changes can have. Albion has referred to the "aura" of the planet as the atmosphere and, of course, the atmosphere is the origin and source of global climatic conditions. The Indians believe the climate is changing. They see it as apart of the approach to the next major phase of change. They believe their sacred ceremonies, such as the rain dances, will keep them in the "good graces" of the planet, perhaps lessening the severity they will experience.

The scientific community is certainly in agreement with the notion that the climate is indeed changing. In 1976, a report released by the Central Intelligence Agency, indicated that the Earth is entering into a "mini" Ice Age! The evidence, based on research done at the University of Wisconsin, reveals that the agency's interest is very political. Average temperatures in the Northern Hemisphere, where most international power struggles take place, are expected to drop by one degree centigrade and the intelligence community feels that this could lead to global upheavals. The function of the CIA in regards to climatic conditions is how they could affect intelligence problems. Aside from accurate weather predictions giving us a military edge, they seem to feel that weather will have a definite affect upon economic and political collapse, which would be caused by a worldwide failure in crop production, resulting in famine. Also, there is concern that good weather conditions over the last fifty years has lulled us into a false sense of security. How does one begin to initiate a change of thinking on a global scale? What can be done to make us stop taking the stable weather for granted? If changing weather patterns are not to have a totally devastating effect, then how we think and act must change immediately.

This weather predicting matter is very serious. The budget of the National Meteorological Service is tremendous! And still the predictions are just a little progressed from educated guesses! A massive computer known as CRAY-I, located at the National Center for At-

241

mospheric Research (NCAR) in Boulder, Colorado, is currently the terminal that seventy-five U.S. and Canadian universities and research institutions are hooked into.

Weather is an illusive subject and scientists are often puzzled and surprised by their inability to predict it, especially over long-range periods of time. They watch carefully, not leaving any stone unturned, so to speak, looking for clues that will make the art more accurate. There are questions such as, how do solar eruptions effect the Earth? They have learned, for example, that such eruptions intensify the flow of particles that can dramatically shift the Earth's high-altitude winds. Wind speeds of 450 m.p.h. have shot up to 1,433 m.p.h. very quickly! The flocking habits of birds, even the moving of the ants transporting their eggs to higher ground are being studied as clues of an impending weather disaster.

The single most major factor that is involved with a cooling of the Earth is the Sun. The Sun is considered to be a rather ordinary star, one of two hundred billion in the galaxy. It is estimated to be 4.6 billion years old, just about middle-aged. Most astronomy texts will tell you that it won't change its properties appreciably for another five or six billion years or so. But is this truly the case? Maybe not. New research shows that the Sun is getting cooler. It is already 1/10th of one degree colder than it was twenty years ago. But, that will reverse itself for the Sun warms up and cools off in seventy-six year cycles. It shrinks and expands in similar cycles. Thus, a cooling trend on the Earth is due to the same on the Sun. This could help to counteract the warming trend due to the carbon dioxide buildup.

There have been some theories recently that point to a possible "change" in the behavioral patterns of our star. Scientists at the Center for Planetary Studies at Lowell Observatory in Flagstaff, Arizona, believe they have detected a slight variance in the amount of energy the Sun is putting out. This could be a temporary phenomenon or it could lead into our having to redefine the type of star that the Sun actually is. It certainly would be premature for us to react like "Chicken Little". But, it would be just as unwise not to be aware of the activity of our source of life. The research goes on.

There are three other factors that have to do with a cooling of the Earth, each affecting our planet's activities and well-being. Volcanic dust that is thrown into the atmosphere during times of eruption is one, plus man-made dust in the form of pollution and carbon dioxide two others, all of which are contributors to determining exactly how much sunlight reaches the Earth and how much is reflected back into space, thus causing temperatures to drop. Volcanic eruptions we cannot control. But, the pollution factors are almost purely man-made. Even though the natural levels of carbon dioxide can be increased a lot, it is fast approaching the danger levels due to so many automobiles and other polluting vehicles. In his book *Man and His Whole Earth*, Gary Null says that every year there are sixty-five million tons of exhaust fumes coughed into America's air. That book was released in 1977, so it could conceivably be more by now. Environmental groups have sprung up, especially in the United States, and some of them have become major political factions to be dealt with. But still, the pollution continues. Public outcry towards the increasing damage being done by man's lust for money and progress is growing in potency and that's something to be happy about. But we still have a very long way to go. Tips will be given later in this book as to how each of us as individuals as well as groups, might do our part in helping to counteract the damage being done.

Regardless of the cause, the change of climate is now a critical factor in our survival as a species. With climate directly affecting our ability to farm the land successfully, the "politics" of food is predicted to become the central issue of every world government.

As previously stated, volcanic eruptions are not within our control. It is interesting to note however, there has been a steady increase in the amount of volcanic dust in the atmosphere since the mid-1950's. All of these major "shields" combine to affect the temperature of the Earth in a drastic manner. If the cooling trend continues, we could indeed be faced with another ice age.

History tells us that the first Ice Age occurred about 400,000 years ago, during the time of Peking Man, with another one 200,000 years ago which would be about the time of Neanderthal Man. It is believed that the last such freeze was approximately 100,000 years ago.

There is another side of the coin, however, and it concerns a natural rule in science known as the Second Law of Thermodynamics. This law states, for one thing, that the Earth should be warming! One of the reasons for this is due to the energy that humans use eventually being degraded to heat. This amount of energy consumption is forever growing, which can have a dramatic effect on the Earth's climate. Many experts in the field share the belief of a warming trend and they attribute their opinion to the city's additions to global heat, "heat pollution" caused by burning of fossil fuels, coal and gas. All this has some experts worried about the long-range and not so long-range results. A major concern is for damage being done to the ozone layer of the atmosphere because of the use of fluorocarbons. We all remember the scare generated by the widespread use of spray cans in the early '70's. This also contributes to the warming trend. Eventually, all of these things could lead to the melting of the polar ice caps that would cause flooding in major populated areas.

Scientists at Columbia University reported that the Antarctic ice pack during the summer has decreased by one million square miles from 1973 to 1980. The melting is being blamed on the greenhouse effect, again, being created by the burning of coal, oil and fossil fuels.

Additional information on the warming was given in an article that appeared in *Science News* in the November 8, 1981 issue. The evidence given is unsettling to say the least. "Polar ice caps, known to be efficient indicators of climatic change, may be showing the first signs of response to global warming caused by the buildup of carbon dioxide in the atmosphere." This data was reported to have been worded very cautiously. It was presented by researchers George Kukla and Joyce Gavin of Columbia University's Lamont-Doherty Geological Observatory at Palisades, New York. Satellite photos show that between 1973 and 1980, the Antarctic ice pack decreased in the summer by 2.5 million square kilometers. This translates to about 35% of its average area. Scientists are not absoutely sure how much of the change in the amount of snow and ice is due to natural climate variations or to other conditions that are not related to carbon dioxide. They say it is too soon to tell. The report is very important because it does follow the pattern expected because of increased levels of carbon dioxide, the result of industry waste and auto exhaust pollution. It is also just as important to note that findings at Princeton indicate the opposite is true. Warming is greater over the Arctic Ocean in the summer than in winter. So, it's too early to draw conclusions. A longer data base has to be established, models have to be more carefully observed and compared. We have to wait until the true nature of seasonal variability is better understood.

A strange twist in the warming trend came to light due to research being done on climate, including excess amounts of carbon monoxide in the atmosphere, at the National Center for Atmospheric Research in Colorado. Scientists there who have been described by Smithsoian magazine as "scientific druids in their space-age megaliths", suspected that the sudden and abundant buildup of carbon monoxide gas over the Amazon jungles, which was as great as that over some city suburbs, could be due to the cutting and burning of the rain forests to make way for farms and roads. The fires were intense and the burning vegetation was felt to be the culprit. But, the scientists were in for a shocking surprise! Termites, who occupy two-thirds of the dry land on the planet, were flourishing on the cut-up vegetation.

It was found that tiny micro-organisms in the termite's system which break down the wood, caused the insects to emit carbon monoxide and methane gas! Who would have ever guessed such a thing! We cannot upset the natural balance of the Earth without causing potential disaster. We must learn this. We have to.

There is a lot of evidence that the warming trend is indeed going on. Over the past forty years, an estimated 10,000 cubic miles of polar ice has been discharged into the oceans, raising sea levels by five inches. This slows the rotation of the Earth! This is due to the transfer of the huge amounts of ice into a thin layer of water spreading over the oceans, just like an ice skater extending his arms reduces the speed of his spin. The result, since 1940, has been a lengthening of the Earth's day by 0.00075ths of a second. This is according to a report by two scientists from the National Oceanic and Atmospheric Administration. The melting is believed to be caused by a global warming trend from 1890 to 1940. However, since 1940, the mass of discharged ice has counteracted this greenhouse effect.

Heating or cooling? The question remains as yet unanswered. But one thing is for certain. Changes in termperature affect circulation of weather patterns and this leaves us with no doubt that something is going on. The weather is changing. We see evidence of it worldwide. In October of 1981, in India, heavy rains caused major flooding. The same occurred in China with more widespread loss of life and devastation. Here in the State of Arizona there have been periods of severe flooding that are supposed to occur only once every 200 years, but have occurred three times in the last three years. While some areas have been saturated with unusual downpours, others have been beseiged by drought. Concern is mounting in regards to water supply for crops and human consumption. Water is a valuable commodity in more ways than one. In some places it is being transported from one area to another in order to help less abundant regions. That in itself has been creating even more potentially destructive problems with the natural ecological balance. If these trends continue, one expert at the University of Wisconsin expects the following to be the result:

- More rain in the northern half of the U.S. and drier in the central Gulf states.
- The winter wheat areas and rangelands of the high plains will be much wetter. These changes should not affect this country's food production very much.
- More drought in India.
- Shorter growing seasons in Canada, the northern areas of Europe, Russia and China, resulting in reduction of grain output.
- More frequent monsoon failures in the Philippines and southeast Asia.

Most scientists studying the problem agree that it is reasonable to assume a continuation of the cooling trend will result in changing weather patterns. After the severest winter since records have been kept having just ended in the Midwestern and Eastern parts of the United States it would not be hard to find plenty of people who might be frustrated enough to agree with the Hopis. Tampering with the Moon and stars? Could this be the problem? That we don't know. But, we do know for certain that man's actions are playing a major role in affecting the weather drama.

In further regards to climate, we are aware of the predicted changes and are also aware of some of the natural and unnatural means by which this could occur. Science is constantly learning new information about the Earth's atmosphere that convinces them even more as to how very fragile the situation really is. Facts that seem to prove the at-one-ment of all things can be grasped when data determines that insects can affect the atmosphere because it is so sensitive.

Albion has made some comments and predictions about the climate and how that might condition our lives in various ways. The predictions first. They were given in December, 1981.

"All over the continent of North America in the last several weeks, there have been weather systems that have caused a great deal of distress and damage to property and human life and consciousness. We wish to comment about these weather systems, for there will be many more. They will continue into the month of April, 1982. (It did.) What would appear to be destructive as well as distressful on an emotional and physical plane is not all to think about when one considers the effects these systems have and will continue to have on the country as a whole. It is rather interesting from our point of view how prophecy and futuristic comments can be given over and over again about the so-called Earth changes, and still humanity will tend to view those changes as some event or trend that would occur in the future, but not now. It is always the future or so it would seem. This is not so, only a popular misconception."

"Don't think that bad weather is always something negative. The areas of California and the Pacific Northwest are areas that have needed cleansing and thus the need for additional moisture. You will see a great deal of wetness. There will be supplies of water as well as cleansing in these areas. Revitalizing the soil is of importance and could not be more timely in terms of what is necessary. What could be more devastating than to approach a period of major seismic activity and not have the soil vital and properly attuned. So what appears as disaster, is not. We would also suggest that there is an increase in seismic activity that is global in proportions."

Another thing that he brought to our attention had to do with another aspect of man's "tampering", this time directly with the weather.

"This time you are presently living in is very critical. The Earth is ill. There is a great sense of disease that rumbles within her aura and her bowels. You have been made aware of it through the media, through written

248

words, the spoken word, and through prophecy. But, for the most part, it seems to be 'floating above' your heads rather than being absorbed into the Being. Man has reached a point that he sees himself as objective from the Earth. He takes the planet for granted. Most men behave as if the Earth is subservient to his human will! This attitude is as dangerous as taking your automobile and driving it at high speed into a brick wall."

"Let us consider the weather. The Earth moves about the Sun in a rather unstable orbit." (This is surely referring to the Earth's "wobble", known as precession. It makes the planet spin in a "wobbling" motion, like a top.) "Due to the short span of man's life, plus his lack of true understanding of the true concept of time, he tends to regard the planet, the weather, and so forth, as unchangeable. Nothing could be farther from the truth."

The Teacher went on to say that the Earth's orbital path had been upset in the past, more than once. He likewise pointed out that there have been drastic changes in the weather in the past and that there would be again. He stressed a need to look at climate from an esoteric point of view as well as a scientific one in order to gain a more intimate understanding of these patterns.

"Let us consider the weather in terms of the four elements; earth, air, fire and water. Water, of course, manifests as rain, sleet, snow and the like. If we relate water to the symbols in the Wisdom Teachings we would know the water constitutes change, fluidic motion. It brings growth and cleansing. Fire comes forward as lightning, volcanic eruptions and heat. Air forms the Earth's aura, while earth is the body of the planet itself. Through the law of cycles, life is constantly being created and destroyed in the activities of the elements. You are aware that there was a time when all of the present land masses were joined together. Interaction of the elements caused them to separate into continents."

Albion's next comments about the weather took an unexpected turn. "The natural periods of change the

Earth must go through in order to evolve is a spiritual matter. This includes climatic, seismic and all other geophysical changes. But, there is a matter that is rapidly becoming of concern to the Spiritual Hierarchy. It has to do with man's taking weather patterns into his own hands, seeking to manipulate them to his own liking. This is 'planetary black magic' and it must cease or man will complicate the Initiation the Earth is about to go through. It will confuse the planet and will instigate 'artifical' or false responses from the planet. Think of the weather as the moods of the Earth's personality. Anyone who imposes upon that personality will create premature change as well as upsetting the natural balance. The planet has a right to be left to her own devices for living and functioning as an evolving Being."

There is no doubt that he was making reference to man's tampering with the weather. I had not been exposed to much real information about this until reading the excellent book I mentioned earlier by Joseph Goodavage entitled *Our Threatened Planet*. The author makes comment on various bits of evidence that exist that point to what Albion considers "sinister" sets of circumstances. The government of the United States is becoming increasingly more concerned with the fact that the Soviet Union's weather modification program far exceeds that of any other country, even its own! By 1959 there is reported to have already been 36 official weather modification projects in the U.S. This seems much like the pot calling the kettle black! It is a matter of fact that the U.S. government used "weather warfare" during the Viet Nam war. There are also stories that say that hurricanes have been created and aimed at other countries. Special interest groups, including an assembly made up of thirteen senators have tried to get this stopped, so far, to no avail.

Goodavage quotes a weather official as commenting upon a "freak" rash of tornadoes that occurred in the short period of 18 hours, killing 315 in thirteen states and doing a half-billion dollars in property damage.

"Nature simply doesn't behave that way normally, the twisters were freakish . . . almost as if they were artificially generated." Huge storms appear in certain parts of the Earth that are absolutely colossal and no one really knows how they are formed. They do know that conditions don't naturally exist to form them. I remembered getting a strange "psychic" impression about the rainstorms that hit southern California in February of 1979. It poured for days, causing mudslides to devastate many residential areas. Weather radar screens on television showed the storms literally lined up in a row off the coast, coming inland one at a time. It didn't seen or feel natural to me, they seemed planned. I thought that my thoughts were too far-fetched to mention, but now I wonder!

Repeated warnings have been given to the Senate Foreign Relations and other committees by Dr. Gordon J. MacDonald of Darmouth College regarding his opinion that global weather warfare could be waged against a country without its awareness. Weather is automatically taken to be a natural phenomena by the general masses, so it would be easy to pull something like that off without raising suspicion.

Another area of a possible "triggering" mechanism to Earth changes is the planet being struck by another celestial object. Comets, asteroids, meteors or other spatial debris or bodies are all candidates for such a collision. You will recall a quatrain of Nostradamus that reads:

> "A great spherical mountain of seven stades
> At a time when peace will give way to war, famine and flooding
> It will roll end over end, sinking great nations, Many of ancient origin, of great age."

This would certainly seem to indicate that "a great spherical mountain" could be referring to some sort of extraterrestrial object that will bombard the Earth. I would think that this could be a comet, meteor or asteroid body. We know that this has happened before and it is only a matter of time before it will occur again. Other, more contemporary psychics have also predicted this, including myself. My feelings were more prone to believe that it would be a piece of a cometary body. There was also some information about this given by Albion.

"The Earth will be struck again. It will occur in or around the year of 2010. Remember this. Any such event can be changed by a change in consciousness or eased somewhat. It is most important that the consciousness and life that exists upon the Earth be as cooperative with the Earth in her orbital patterns and changes as possible. You can be cooperative by not taking and robbing her of resources. Yes, a whole environmental plan should be implemented, or otherwise the changes will be very difficult and could be disastrous."

These prophecies don't seem so far-out when we learn there has recently been a division set up within NASA that is designed to "watch" for asteroids or other bodies that could be on a collision course with the Earth. Various suggestions have been made as to how such a clash might be avoided, including the possible use of nuclear weapons to steer the object off it course.

In the search of prophecies to determine what lies ahead, one of the most devastating omens we may have to contend with is the phenomena known as a poleshift. John White, internationally recognized author and lecturer, is quite the expert on this subject. White's monumental work, *Poleshift,* (published by Doubleday in New York), contains a remarkable collection of poleshift data from both prophetic and scientific sources.

No one is absolutely sure that is has occurred before, much less whether or not it will occur in the future. The physical concept that is involved here is twofold. A "flipping" of the Earth's axis could occur, causing a radical displacement of the globe's axis of rotation. This could be brought about by a collision, such as that we have just been discussing, or some other "interference" with the planet's normal orbital pattern. A second theory has to do with a "slippage" of the planet's solid crust that lies over a molten interior sea of lava. This also could cause the polar locations to change.

It's difficult to imagine the Earth rolling over, end over end, in space! However, with the acceptance of the theory commonly known as continental drift, the possibility of such an event seems more plausible, simply because we know that land masses have moved before. Whether or not it ever caused a poleshift still remains unproven. In any case, proponents of the poleshift theory feel that such a colossal phenomena, if it were to occur, could take anywhere from a few days to as little as a few hours. For what it may be worth, the prophet of Virginia Beach, Edgar Cayce, did predict a poleshift would occur again.

Reference to the tectonic plates reminded me of an article in "Geo" magazine (April 1982) in which a theory of how these plates were formed received its first bit of physical evidence. The discovery of a huge sub-surface crater under North America suggests that the crater may have been formed due to the bombardment of a giant meteorite. The crater measures 1,700 miles in diameter, stretching form the Hudson Bay to the Great Lakes. It is believed that the meteorite would have fallen about four billion years ago and would have been about the size of the state of Delaware! It would have triggered millions of years of volcanic activity which would have discarded the granite shield of the continent and covered up the crater. The discovery is of real importance and is consistent with what is known about the plates and continental drift. It explains how granite continents were formed.

The only way science can determine whether or not a changing of the pole positions has happened in the past is to investigate, geologically. As Albion has said, "the Earth does indeed have a memory and it can be seen in the strata of rocks that compose its body." He always says that the Grand Canyon is the most complete example of this. It is also possible to carefully study the fossil records, which are also a part of the Earth's terrain. For example, paleontologists know that at one time giant mammals that once roamed the Earth, were decimated rather suddenly. The dinosaurs' lives that were snuffed out covered over three-fifths of the Earth's surface and it is generally believed that some sort of "sudden" event must have happened. It would have to have effected a major part of the entire planet, not just one isolated area. It is estimated that some forty million animals lost their lives as a result of some unknown cataclysm.

Two recent newspaper reports highlight the situation. A 1978 United Press International article headlines "Alaska was Tropical, Expert Says", states that tropical rain forests bordered the Gulf of Alaska 45 million years ago. The expert quoted is Jack Wolfe, a paleobotanist with the U.S. Geological Survey in Menlo Park, California. If his findings are supported by further studies, Wolfe told U.P.I., "it would mean the Earth's axis of rotation was once less inclined toward the Sun. This could help explain major changes in climate."

The second article that appeared in the New Haven Register (March 5, 1978) reported the discovery of fossil amphibians and reptiles as big as deer in a mountainous region of Antarctica. The animals lived during the Triassic Period, about 200 million years ago. Today the largest land animal in Antarctica is an insect (penguins and whales being sea creatures). The research team making the discovery was headed by a biologist, John W. Cosgriff, Jr., who noted that many of the species found there were also found in rock deposits of the same age in Africa, India and Australia. This supports the theory that all present land masses were originally joined into one supercontinent that broke apart, he said. He also noted that Antarctica's climate apparently was temperate to sub-tropical when the fossil animals were alive, adding, "Clearly, the south pole was elsewhere than on the Antarctic continent."

Because nearly all of the northern Hemisphere was encompassed by the event, it is feasible how it could have been caused by the Earth being struck by another object.

Although science is still hesitant to commit itself to endorsing the poleshift phenomenon, some of the Wisdom Teachings speak of it openly, as a matter of historical fact. One example of this can be found in the second volume of the *Secret Doctrine* by H. P. Blavatsky. Blavatsky states emphatically that the Ancients knew well, perhaps even better than do the modern scientists, the general behavior of the heavens and the Earth. They knew that the behavior of the globe has changed more than once since the primitive state of things.

The *Secret Doctrine* (Vol. II, Stanza II) tells of a time, in the youthful stages of the Earth's life, when it first began to support life, of a period of change.

"The Wheel (planet) whirled for thirty crores more. It constructed rupas (forms): soft stones that hardened; hard plants that softened. Visible from invisible, insects and small lives. She shook them off her back whenever they overran the Mother (Earth)."

"After thirty crores she turned round. She (Earth) lay on her back; on her side . . . She would call no Sons of Heaven, she would ask no Sons of Wisdom. She created from her own bosom. She evolved water men, terrible and bad."

Comments like "turning round", "laying on her back, on her side", certainly seem to imply an early poleshift did occur. The *Secret Doctrine* implies other such occasions that it happened, as well.

If we are to consider the Earth change prophecies, we cannot overlook Blavatsky in this department either. A woman who was very "in tune" and educated in regards to cosmic cycles, H. P. Blavatsky has left us with a legacy of "calculations" about the future of the planet. She presents a lot of data, based on her acquaintance with astronomy and mathematics, that state that the next shifting of the poles will come in16,000years. Not anything pressing for us to worry about! But, we also have to consider her warnings that the "ultimate disaster" will be preceded by many smaller submersions and destructions, brought about by tidal waves and volcanic fires. It would be anybody's guess as to when these "preceding" events might begin.

Another very prominent advocate of cataclysms that have rocked the Earth in the past is a Russian-born physician, Immanuel Velikovsky. His book, *Worlds in Collision*, released in 1950 under fire of controversy, literally created a convulsion within the scientific community. Keep in mind that at the time of its appearance, it was generally assumed that all of the fundamentals of science were known and there was only room for details and decimals. No one was ready for a man who was not even a cosmologist, but a medical doctor, to come along and present new data, much less a scenario that would turn the accepted version of the solar system's history around. *Worlds in Collision* describes a primeval chaos, when it rained fire from above, when continents buckled and broke apart, and when most of life, including mankind, was destroyed. Velikovsky's popularity plummeted with the scientists even more when he described Venus as having once been a comet that charged into our solar system, upsetting the orbit of Mars, bringing them both close to the Earth, resulting in major catastrophic events! Poleshift, fragmentation of the land masses, a discovery of a giant submarine canyon that runs twice around the globe, as well as phenomena involving other bodies in our solar group, were all claimed by Velikovsky to be the result of the cataclysmic theory he proposed. What is interesting to note is that much of the evidence presented in his book was not known to be true at the time it was published, but since then, space exploration and travel have helped to substantiate some of his theories.

One example concerns the planet Venus itself. As I have said, Velikovsky believed that orb to be a "newcomer" to the planetary family. It had, as a com-et, had a stormy and short history and if so, it must then, be still giving off heat and still be very hot. He also described it as having a gaseous envelope of hydrocarbon gases and dust. All this went totally against what was known in that decade.

Modern space missions to Venus have caused great surprise! The ground temperature was found to be 600 degrees Farenheit! It was expected to be just a little more than that of the Earth. The gaseous envelope was vindicated when NASA announced that Venus is enshrouded with an envelope of hydrocarbon gas and dust, fifteen miles thick, forty-five miles above the ground of the planet! It is also an interesting point that Venus is rotating in a retrograde motion to all of the other planets in the solar system known about to date.

Even though Velikovsky has died in the last couple of years, the controversy did not die with him. There are those in his "camp" that will proclaim his vindication from the terrible onslaught imposed upon him and his theories while others, still look upon *Worlds in Collision* as blasphemy!

"Interestingly, the most recent date for the mammoth's death, 690 B.C., is the time that the foremost poleshift theorist (Immanuel Velikovsky) offers as the occasion of a poleshift." (John White, *Poleshift*, page 22)

While it may be yet unproven as to whether or not the poles have changed places, there is another sort of polar shift activity that is receiving a lot of attention. It has to do with the Earth's magnetic field. We can think of the Earth as being a huge magnet, due to its nickel-iron core. In John White's *Poleshift*, he describes the core as acting like a "dynamo due to convection currents in the mantle." It fluctuates in strange ways. The magnetic "poles" should not be confused with the geographical North and South Poles. These magnetic poles vary in strength, sometimes dropping to zero. They've also wandered as much as 80% over the past millions of years. At the present time, the magnetic north pole is in northern Canada about 11 degrees away from the true North Pole. But the magnetic pole has another quality, that being to reverse polarity. White reports that more than 170 changes of polarity have happened in the past 80 million years. It is also known that the strength of the Earth's magnetic field is weakening steadily right now and that it has been doing so for the last 2,500 years. So far, it has decreased by 50%. If this continues, it will decrease until it disappears altogether, presumably to reappear with reversed polarity. It is not known exactly how long the reversal takes, but speculation has it that it is instantaneous, though it could take several thousand years to reverse and build up to another level of high-level intensity. What does it do? The following indications from John White explains.

- Magnetic compasses would not work.
- No magnetic field to shield the Earth from cosmic and solar radiation. Skin cancers, sunburn and yet unsuspected results.
- Entire species in the past have become extinct in correlation with magnetic field reversals.
- A drop in the magnetic field strength to zero could disrupt the weather because it influences upper atmospheric pressures.
- Average pressure system seems to drift westward with the magnetic drift."

A poleshift may be a triggering device for a future period of Earth changes, if indeed it is 16,000 years into the future. If not, and the phenomenon is a valid occurrence, then let's hope that the preceeding period of unrest is not scheduled by the Cosmic Clock to begin anytime soon! Even if we get a reprieve of time, which is not likely, or if Blavatsky's time table is wrong, there are many other prophets and prophecies that believe we don't have that much time.

One of the most common events that plays a primary role in most people's minds about the concepts and predictions we call Earth changes, is the earthquake. It has become almost a standard comment that accompanies the very mention of California. Perhaps this is one of the negatives that comes along with prophecy for predictions about "California falling off into the ocean" have reached epidemic proportions. I find that this is mostly the result of prophecies, usually those of Edgar Cayce, being misquoted or misunderstood entirely. At the same time, it is a matter of the prophecies being added to by more contemporary psychics and by the addition of the strictly scientific prognostications that have been coming out in the last several years. We cannot afford to be sensationalists in our approach to the Earth changes. We have to be careful in our study of both the prophetic data and the scientific data. I think we should look at both, as we are doing together in this work, so that we are better equipped to not only get a clearer understanding and therefore a sensible picture from both sides, but also so that we can stand a better chance for survival, on all levels.

Since the Cayce prophecies are perhaps the most well-known and certainly the most quoted, let's take another look at the specifics of the seer's words in regards to future earthquake activity. Cayce felt that the poleshift would be heralded by several decades of severe seismic activity worldwide. Earthquakes then, were the cause of the major predictions he made. He portrayed the quakes to be of such magnitude and so frequent that they would literally change the topography of the entire planet.

Most of Japan will go into the sea are familiar Cayce words. This part of the world seems to suffer drastic change. Japan is certainly known to have a major amount of earthquake activity. When Cayce made reference to Northern Europe being transformed "in the twinkling of an eye", with land submerging and the sea rolling in, it would seem to indicate sudden chaos, caused by seismic activity accompanied by extreme tidal surges. Most of the time, we have to keep in mind that the topographical changes given in most of the prophecies would more than likely take place over a long period of time. There is no time factor mentioned about Japan, but the phrase "in the twinkling of an eye" definitely gives the impression that the "transformation of Northern Europe" would be all at once! That covers a big land mass but there is a lot of water that could be involved with seismic or tidal events. The Atlantic, the Baltic, the Mediterranean, Black, Adriatic, Caspian and North Seas are all located in that general area.

I think that it is safe to assume that the predicted destruction of Los Angeles, San Francisco, New York, the Connecticut coastline, the Southern Atlantic coast; the inundation of the western coast of North America for several hundred miles, the Great Lakes emptying into the Gulf of Mexico, along with similar cataclysmic disturbances around the world, will be triggered by earthquakes. Whether or not the majority of this activity will happen all at once or in a short period of time is hard to say. No "time" description was given by the "Sleeping Prophet".

Many articles and books have been written about earthquakes that have been predicted. Many of them have either been written by psychics or about their feelings and additional prophecies. A large percentage of them have tried to pinpoint the dates for major earthquakes, especially the "super quake" that both psychics and scientists alike are saying will occur in California, particularly for Los Angeles, at some point in time. One such book, *California Superquake 1975-1977?*, written by Paul James, former engineering designer, technical writer and editor in the aerospace industry and champion of the Cayce prophecies. James presents a good overview of the probability of an earthquake over 10 in magnitude on the Richter scale, though a large part of the book is a survey of the Cayce predictions. The author also gives the feelings of other prophets, as well as the opinions of the scientific community. But, like many others, his timetable was obviously wrong.

One of the most interesting prophecies that is given in the James book is by neither psychic nor scientist.

In fact, not by a human being at all, but by a computer! In 1963, the IBM 7090 computer at UCLA, was fed data from seismographs and other instruments by a group of earth scientists. The data contained readings on the Baldwin Hills dam in Los Angeles and on the San Andreas Fault. The results obtained through computer processing and translation from math into words, was astounding.

"California will soon experience the greatest earthquake of it's history because of the breaking of the San Andreas Fault. Southern California can go into the sea."*

I think that once the information sinks in, that the first thing that should be noted is that this data was given in 1963! Nineteen years have passed. In light of the rendering of the word "soon" in the prediction, it does make one feel even more alarmed. It would seem to indicate that the "super quake" is long overdue! Some feel that the longer the quake is in coming, the more devastating it could be. James states that "this startling seismologist-computer consensus was immediately hushed up by someone in authority who decided such realism was not good for Californians". Rumors flew that two seismologists refused jobs in Los Angeles due to their knowledge of the San Andreas Fault line. We all know people who would not live in California because of the predictions, but we have all probably known those who remain there no matter what, so it would seem.

Los Angeles is not the only part of California that is believed to be in grave danger. San Francisco is also a concern. Since 1967, experts have felt the vulnerability of the Bay Area. Concern for the famous bridges, the Golden Gate and the Bay, is coupled with opinions of the loss of skyscrapers, highways, and water and sewage lines. Superquakes in Northern or Southern California would be disastrous to the entire country, perhaps the greatest in world history.

*California Superquake 1975-1977? James, Paul. Second edition. Exposition Press, Hicksville, New York: 1974-75. Pg. 23

My thoughts go back once again to the warnings of the Hopi people. Their predictions include famine. What has famine to do with earthquakes? The famed San Joachin Valley in the southern part of the state is called "the salad bowl" of the country. Any earthquake of a fairly strong magnitude could interrupt produce and fruit supplies leaving California to other parts of the country and within five days the U.S. would be in sad supply of these foodstuffs.

Most experts agree that the expected quake will be much bigger than the one that hit San Francisco in 1906. Reports from various sources, including one from the United Nations, state that the first "one-million victim" quake could happen before the end of this century!

The evidence is pouring in. HughLynn Cayce's update of the increase in seismic activity, such as predicted by his father, is impressive. Recently, Time-Life Books sent out a package offering "disaster" books for sale, designed to make the public more aware of the same. The advertisement states that we should also be aware of other areas of the world that are earthquake-prone. Charleston, South Carolina, Cairo, Illinois and Washington, D.C. are all mentioned as vulnerable locations. Using the U.S. Geological Survey as their source, the coastal areas of California, a major half of western Nevada, parts of Utah, Idaho and southern Montana, the western coast of Washington state, Hawaii, southern Alaska, northwestern New York State, western Tennessee, southern Illinois, and the northeastern tip of Arkansas, are all listed as areas that are likewise prone to suffer major damage due to earthquakes.

An article in "Science News" in 1981 shows that twice as many significant quakes rocked this country in the year of 1980, "in keeping with a worldwide trend in increased tremblors". In order to qualify as "significant", a quake must register at least 6.5 on the Richter scale, cause casualties or considerable property damage. In 1980, the strongest quake occurred off the coast of Northern California. It injured five people. Quakes are also beginning to shake the U.S. in areas that are not usually associated with seismic activity. Long Island, Connecticut, New York State and Kentucky are all examples. From "Science News", October 10, 1981, Volume 120, #15:

"In less than two months during the winter of 1811-1812, three quakes shook New Madred, Missouri -- 8.6, 8.4, and 8.7 in magnitude. They expect it again."

Seismologists, those who enforce the building engineers, met in Knoxville to report new data in the developing field of seismology east of the Rockies.

But they can't tell exactly all risks from lack of instrumental data on severe eastern quakes. Earthquakes in the east are different from those in the west. Most in the east occur on ancient fault systems that formed as early as Precambrian times and are reactivated by the spread of the Atlantic seaboard. They occur five times less frequently than those in the west. This makes people feel there is no hazard. Eastern quakes don't break the ground like those in the west. Faults in the west can be easily identified. In the east, energy travels for hundreds of miles and still damages buildings. It would certainly seem that Cayce and others have been accurate in the areas that they have specified in their predictions.

The San Andreas is probably the most infamous fault line in the world, but there is another one that we don't hear as much about. It's the Wasatch Fault in Utah, which is very active and very dangerous. Salt Lake City sits right on top of it. There is one school of thought that the United States will someday be split into two major halves. This theory would seem to be supported by Edgar Cayce's prophecy of the Great Lakes emptying into the Gulf of Mexico. This fault line could prove to be of major significance in the upcoming change period.

Earthquakes, though in our thoughts so much because of the current surge of interest in the earth change prophecies, are not necessarily really understood by the average layman. Evidence of that is seen all over the Los Angeles Basin, where houses have been built, on stilts, no less, and on the sides of the cliffs. It would seem to me that a lack of knowledge or caring is the only answer to such poor judgement. In light of this, perhaps one of the most important things that we can do is to educate ourselves about the natural phenomena that are part of the Earth change prophecies. Any part of the world that we might live in is vulnerable to one or more of these aspects of nature. Knowledge helps us to be more aware and thus better prepared in the event that we are in a position to have to experience one of these dramas of Nature. Surely a more educated public is a safer public. Knowledge can serve to bring us into a more mature relationship with Nature and the planet, whereas fear of these phenomena surely serves only to rob us to our peace of mind. Fear is emotional and thus a "magnetic" energy. It can, at its most negative, tend to "draw" that which we fear to us!

Geologists know that the Earth has elastic waves that propagate through its body, the source of which is various deformations in its crust. This crust builds up a lot of pressure in different places due to its inability to withstand the tension. This causes the crust mantle to crack. These "cracks" are the fault lines. They cause underground catastrophes in the general neighborhood. Seismologists learn about the interior of the planet and how the seismic waves are increasing and what new "cracks" are being formed as a result. Earthquakes occur most frequently where two continental plates meet or where a continental plate and an oceanic plate meet. Some fault lines move vertically and other horizontally.

There is a lot of general knowledge about the so-called "super quakes", but there is another form of quake that is much smaller in proportion from the super quake called "microquakes" or "creeps". They occur all along fault lines all the time. They too, have been on the increase along the San Andreas. Scientists are not in total agreement as to whether the creeps are of benefit to the planet by releasing tension that builds up on the major dangerous faults or whether they indeed contribute to the tension and therefore make things worse. The true answer to this question is very important for it could help in giving scientists a better timetable to work with in regards to quake predictions. If the "creepers" build up pressure to a greater degree, then the California super quake could be more imminent. If the opposite is true, then this could be why the more severe quake has been longer in coming. This would make the micro-quakes like safety valves. The final theory about "creeps" is that they have absolutely no affect at all. At this time, no one knows which theory is true, but the last one mentioned is the least to be considered true of them all.

Another book that takes a perusal of the psychic-type predictions and compares them to the scientific ones is the popular *We Are the Earthquake Generation* by Dr. Jeffrey Goodman. This material also finds the psychics and scientists in remarkable agreement. The thing that I feel was most valuable in this writing is that Good-man compiles a good time frame reference for the predicted seismic happenings. He reports the psychics as believing the large-scale quakes will be between 1980 and 1985. We will have some time for this to pass. From 1985 through 1990, Goodman's "seers" felt the land shifting and coastal changes in California to Alaska. It is the year 2000 A.D. that the psychics mentioned felt that the poles would switch.

It is a good idea to give some thought to what has already taken place on the Earth for this may also give us a better idea as to what may occur in the future. I once heard it said that only through the known can the unknown be apprehended. The past is a future indicator. In the May 2, 1981 issue of the weekly "Science News", an article written by Susan West, tells of how the Earth's tectonic plates and volcanic "hot spots" were mapped by Paul D. Lowman, Jr. It was accomplished by photographs taken from space. The space photos were described by Lowman as a big help because of the sharpness of their physiology. They showed him whether areas whose activity was not as known about had been active in the last million years or not. Thousands of pictures were viewed. Other than getting an excellent map, Lowman also learned some obscure things that were never before included, such as being able to definitely determine whether a particular fault line moves vertically or horizontally. Lowman was even able to map blocks of rocks that have fallen in between faults. The results have also added to the existing knowledge of the tectonic plates. They are found to be not always as rigid as once thought, which makes the boundaries between the plates not as distinct. It was also learned that almost everywhere two continental plates meet, as in the Himalayas, volcanoes exist. It is hoped that the map will raise and answer all kinds of questions about the Earth's interior activity.

Another subject of the past that may play an important role in the future Earth changes and that may play an even greater role in how we respond to the predictions is the legends of lost continents. Though tangible proof of the existence of these two continents has not been able to win the open approval of science, belief in the two has continued to be widespread for centuries. Repeated references are to be found in almost all occult and metaphysical literature.

One expert on the subject of Atlantis, educator, lecturer and author, Dr. Maxine Asher of California, expressed her frustration when she appeared as a guest on my radio talk show in Los Angeles. "How much proof does one need?" Dr. Asher has led several controversial expeditions in search of remnants of the lost civilization that allegedly sunk into the sea during the last major period of Earth changes. She has managed to recover artifacts off the coasts of Spain and Ireland. The ones found on the Atlantic floor off the Spanish coast near Cadiz, Asher believes to show the existence of an Atlantis or of Lemuria, said to have been in the Pacific, does a lot to determine the believeability of it happening again. We tend to become smug and cannot imagine our entire continent sinking into the sea. But, if it happened once, maybe twice before, it could very well happen again.

Maybe it doesn't really matter so much whether science accepts the fabled Atlantis or Lemurian stories or not, for it seems that science has a "lost continent" of its own! It is called Pangea. Based on the theory of plate tectonics and continental drift, the "super continent" would have been made up of one large land mass that is now separated into pieces. Researchers say that about 150 million years ago Pangea began to break up and the present-day continents are the result. But they don't know how long the continent existed before it began to break apart. That question is particularly important because its answer will have critical implications as to what the driving force might be that caused a land mass to break up to begin with. It is also thought that Pangea may have changed form more than once. The research goes on. If Pangea did exist, then something broke it into pieces, upon one of which we presently live. Whatever the "something" is, could it be triggered again?

You will notice in many of the prophecies that some of them, from various sources, speak of planetary positions and alignments as playing an important role in what occurs on the Earth. Not all of these mentioned suggest influences like those proposed by the science of astrology. Rather, some tell of the Moon and Sun having unusual color or being in different places in the heavens entirely.

Nostradamus' quatrains are an example of the inclusion of heavenly bodies as "signs" of periods of major change.

Mars, Mercury and silver joined together.
In Southern lands extreme drought,
Beneath Asia the world will tremble,
Affecting Corinth and Eugheus, in perplexity. (III,3)

267

J. R. Jochmans, author of *Rolling Thunder: The Coming Earth Changes*, is a scholar of Nostradamus, along with other prophets. He offers some help in translation of the French seer's prognostications. Jochmans says the "silver" is the Moon. He reports that the next time such a configuration will occur is in April—May of 1983 and again in June of 1985. He also takes the "Southern lands" to be Africa and southern Asia. Corinth is Greece and Eupheus is Turkey. There are other places in his work that Nostradamus talks of the planets, very similar to that just described, one of which says an eclipse of the Sun will bring more darkness than ever before.

The Bible provides us with another example. In the book of Revelations, Chapter Six, the writer relates that the Earth changes will be accompanied by strange events in the heavens. It seems to point to a shift of the Earth's axis. An earthquake of great proportions precedes the Sun's becoming black and the Moon turning red, and the stars falling to the Earth, are all part of the scenario of the "dreamer" who authored Revelations. There are likewise other similar references contained in other parts of the Scriptures that suggest catastrophes that will affect the visual appearance of the heavenly bodies. A poleshift would cause the Sun and Moon to be in new positions in the sky. This is believed to occur in the year 2000 A.D. and a poleshift is specifically stated by the Frenchman, Nostradamus, to happen.

Another matter that has gained a lot of attention as of late is that of planetary alignment. Triggered by a book released in 1971 entitled *The Jupiter Effect* (Vintage Press, 1974). Its two authors, John Gribbin and Stephen Plageman, are both respected scientists. The entire world was put "on alert" for major seimic activity in the year, 1982. The writers were most specific in their opinion that the most probable area to be affected would be the San Andreas fault in California. The trigger for this action they believed to be the planetary alignment. Not since Velikovsky has the scientific community been in such an uproar over the "far out" opinions of other colleagues. Believers of the book, which was surely greater because the authors were scientists, were braced on March 10th, the day of the alignment, but nothing happened. What is not generally known is that one of the book's writers, John Gribbin, in an article in a 1980 "Omni" magazine, had retracted his predictions by saying that his mathematical calculations were wrong.

I think that Gribbin's retraction may have been "throwing the baby out with the bath water". Although their dubbing the position of the planets in 1982 is not an actual "grand alignment", I feel that the vast majority of the information contained in *The Jupiter Effect* is worth consideration. Gribbin and Plageman proposed the theory that there is a definite relationship between earthquake and climate and believe both are influenced by sun spots. Sun spots are regions of strong magnetism on the Sun. Scientists have been studying them for the last 350 years, trying to determine more about them and their strange behavior. They have learned that they don't last very long, only a few hours. But there are conflicting reports about this, with some reports saying that they can last for up to a year. Only the biggest ones may last for a complete revolution of our local star. The blemishes seem to appear every eleven years or so, but this has varied in the past, which makes the puzzle of the sun spots even more difficult to figure out. Most of the spots are relatively small, but there are occasions that they stretch for thousands of miles across the Sun's surface. They are also usually accompanied by solar flares, which are like storms or eruptions on the Sun's surface. It's interesting to note that sun spots contain gases that are about 3,000 degrees cooler than the other gases that compose the Sun's body. Solar flares are just the opposite, containing gases that are much hotter than the other. Well, 1993 is a "peak" sun spot year, as is 2002 and 2014, so some of these dates do seem to correspond with some of the various phenomena associated with Earth changes!

269

The curious thing about the so-called "planetary alignment" of '82 that was touted by the authors of *The Jupiter Effect* as the possible "triggering" mechanism of major earthquake activity, is that it is not really a true alignment at all. Generally, an alignment of the planets is signified by every planet being in conjunction with every other planet, causing the planets all to be positioned on one side of the Sun. This is only supposed to occur about once every 179 years. Even though 1982 does not see all the planets in conjunction, we do find them on one side of the Sun. This will continue through 1984. The actual planets aligned are Jupiter, Mars and Saturn.

Close, but not close enough. The argument presented in *The Jupiter Effect* was primarily based upon the gravitational pull that all the planets would have on the Sun, along with other factors, such as sun spots. Since it was not a Grand Alignment of conjunction such as the writers indicated, we may have been spared major seismic disturbance. In reading back through the book by Plagemann and Gribbin, I couldn't help but take special note of one particular sentence. "The Age of Aquarius will be, we are told, a time of peace and love. But will it be ushered in by a major slip of the San Andreas Fault and a wave of earthquake activity around the globe, unprecedented since seismology became a true science?" *

It's amazing that just exactly that is what most of the various Earth change prophecies indicate!

The Jupiter Effect by J. Gribbin and S. Plagemann. Vintage Books, A Division of Random House, New York. Copyright 1974, page 128.

Gribbin and Plagemann were not as interested in the effect the gravitational pull the planets would have on the Earth as they were in how it would affect the seismic activity and climate. I don't see how there could be any question about the dramatic climatic conditions of the winter in 1981-82! Also, remember that the authors say the possible effect will continue through 1984.

Newspaper clippings collected in regards to the winter of 1981 are startling! A Republic Wire Services report printed in the Arizona Republic on January 23, 1982, stated that 75% of North America was covered with snow during the week before. Comment by the National Oceanic and Atmospheric Administration claimed that this was very unusual for this time of year. The area covered was 7.5 million square miles!

Another newspaper article proclaimed in January as well that arctic weather had killed at least thirty-nine people in fifteen states, had moved to the South, sending record lows across Dixie. Subsequent freezes took a devastating bite out of Florida fruit and vegetable crops. Snow plows broke down from trying to move the heavy snow in Chicago.

A curious note that appeared in January's 1982 Arizona Republic tells of an Alaskan glacier that would be dumping millions of tons of ice in the paths of ships that summer. The curious thing is that scientists say the glacier is "out of step with geological time"! Apparently its rate of melting is quite rapid and therefore, unusual.

The list goes on and on, with newspaper and other media reports giving data of hard freezes, loss of property, crops, and human life. The great amount of volcanic ash and dust thrown into the atmosphere, particularly due to the eurption of El Chichon in Mexico, brought an early and even more severe winter in 1982-1983.

As to whether or not sun spots can trigger climate changes or earthquakes, it is clear that the evidence is not totally in. Even though the scientific community, at large, is still labeling the findings of *The Jupiter Effect* as "hogwash", it may not be wise to toally disregard the information and predictions of this book. Earthquake predicting is still an infant technology and much more bizarre methods are being tested to determine their accuracy in such matters. Animal behavior, even cockroaches, are being observed on a regular basis to check for altered behavioral patterns before seismic activity occurs.

Since the retraction of the calculations in their book by John Gribbin, it was hard to carry the matter any further. However, just recently, a new book was released by the two scientists entitled *The Jupiter Effect: A New Look*. In this work the scientists Plageman and Gribbin defend the sun spot theory, while realizing their timetable was wrong on the California quake. One important thing that cannot be overlooked, I think, is that there is a real need to discard our sensational approach to the planetary alignments or any other prophecy, no matter what its source. If *The Jupiter Effect* had not smacked so much of astrology, perhaps it would not have aroused the attention of the authors' scientific colleagues. It's a fact that new theories have a rough go of it and the theorists are often labelled as "kooks".

Before we leave the subject of earthquakes, it is important to realize that California is not the only place that is threatened by major seismic danger. China is another one. Actually, there are two primary belts of quake activity on the globe. One is the "Ring of Fire", extending around the Pacific from Chile, including the west coasts of North and South America, the Aleutian Islands, the Philippines and Japan, Indonesia and New Zealand to New Guinea. The other is called the Alpine belt of Asia and Europe that extends from the Azores through the Mediterranean Sea, the Middle East, the Himalayas, through Asia to Indonesia and New Guinea. The Ring of Fire has a much larger percentage of the quake activity. Although quakes do occur in other areas, they remain in these designated areas for the most part.

A large part of Earth is vulnerable. The scientific and the psychic predictions do specify many of these vulnerable areas.

Albion has pointed out areas that he felt were in potential danger from seismic activity in the next twenty-five years. His exact words were: "In terms of land breaking apart, the areas of the most concern are the coastlines from the middle of the state of Washington all the way down to forty miles south of Baja, the link connecting Central and South America, Chile, Japan, the Philippines, the Mediterranean (both undersea and land activity primarily from volcanic eruptions), Nova Scotia, off the coast of West Africa, Iran, Pakistan, China, Nepal and Turkey."

It is true. Earthquake activity is on the increase! Twice as many significant quakes rocked the U.S. alone in 1980 and 1979. One positive note that concerns the U.S. is that no one has died in a quake-related death since 1975, although there has been a sharp rise in such deaths internationally.

Edgar Cayce also made reference in his prediction about the eruption of volcanoes playing a role in the Earth's future. Not until the eruption of Mt. St. Helens in Washington in 1980, was this phenomenon brought so close to home to those of us living on the North American continent. Eruptions of Mt. Etna, Mt. Vesuvius and sometimes Mt. Pele were given as "signs" of the beginning of global disaster. While the others have gone off since Cayce's words made history, Mt. Pele has not erupted since 1903. Within three months of Mt. Vesuvius in Italy or Mt. Pele in the Caribbean, the southern coast of California and the areas between Salt Lake City and southern Nevada are supposed to be "inundated" by earthquakes.

Volcanoes, often the triggering device for earthquakes, are one of the most ominous forces of Nature. Their power led the Ancients to believe there was a "hell" underneath their feet, awaiting "sinners" after death, while others believed the craters led to the center of the

Earth. Clouds of black smoke, red-hot lava oozing down the slopes of the gaping hole in the Earth's crust, along with hot springs and spouting geysers are all a part of this powerful phenomenon.

Even though the Earth's surface averages 68 degrees F, the deeper one goes into the ground, the more the temperature rises. Approximately thirty miles below the surface, rocks are molten and reach temperatures of 2,200 Degrees F to 3,300 degrees F. Heat builds pressure that seeks to escape, weak spots in the Earth's crust give way, and a volcano is formed. This is the way the land masses were formed. The Earth along with the recent discovery of activity on one of the nine moons of Jupiter called Io, are the only volcanically active bodies in our solar system that we know of. Any planetary body that has an actively erupting volcano has water and warmth and these are two very important ingredients of life which leads us to think that volcanoes and life are definitely linked. Interestingly, our own Moon is believed to have had active volcanoes at one point in its history. That could mean that it once had water, for volcanoes are also suspected of being the source of most of the water on our planet. Mars is also thought to have once been volcanically active since the discovery of about twelve volcanic mountains on the Martian surface. It too would have been wetter and warmer in the past, as would the Moon. Perhaps there will come a time that the Earth's volcanoes will cease to be alive, but for now, that is not the case.

An ongoing research project designed to help scientists become even more acquainted with the Earth is being carried on by the Hawaii Institute of Geophysics. Barbara H. Keating, assistant professor of Marine Geology and Paleomagnetics at the institute, explained to "Science News" that: "a hot spot is a source of hot rock that may come from the mantle". The hot rock melts through the oceanic crust and forms a chain of undersea volcanoes and volcanic islands. Seismic activity and other pertinent data gives a clue as to the location of

274

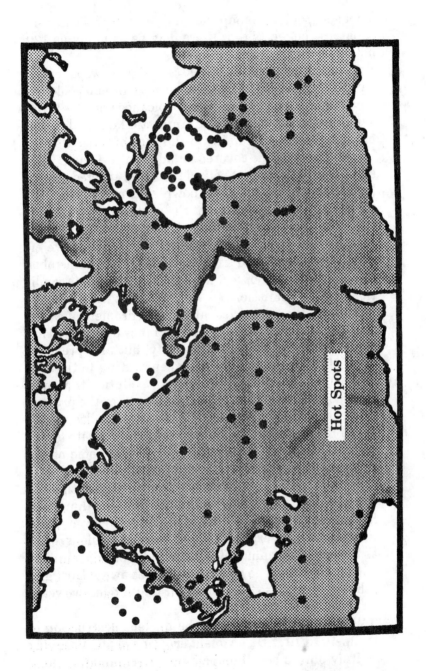

Hot Spots

a hot spot region. A map showing possible "volcanic incubators" suggests that there may be as many as 120 hot spots worldwide.

A U.P.I. article appeared in the newspaper in early 1982 concerning the efforts of a Chilean geologist who has discovered two active volcanoes on the little-explored eastern side of the Antarctic Peninsula. One of them was still steaming at the time of the discovery and volcanic debris covered an adjacent ice shelf. This seemed to indicate that both of them had erupted recently. This brings to five the known volcanoes in the Antarctica. They also represent the southernmost section of the Ring of Fire rimming the Pacific.

Volcanoes, other than with their eruptions, have effects on the Earth and its life forms. You will remember that one of the major factors that affects climatic conditions is the emission of volcanic dust into the atmosphere. Dust particles, along with droplets of water and ice crystals, affect the transparency of the air. This serves to not only reduce visibility, but also prevents some of the Sun's energy from penetrating to the surface of the planet. Even with the air pollution that man is responsible for, it is only a small part, at the present time, compared to the natural dust from volcanoes.

The Earth change prophecies seem to indicate an increase in volcanic activity. It is true that some of the major volcanoes have been beginning since 1955 to show signs of eruption and there is no question that there is a connection between volcanoes and earthquakes. Seismic activity is both the herald of an eruption, and the result of the eruption itself. Some explosions, such as the one of the famed Krakatoa in Indonesia, emitted a noise that could be heard 3,000 miles away! Dust and ash were thrown so far into the air that it took two years for it to settle onto the Earth.

We are all familiar with the ancient destruction of Pompeii. In 79 A.D., a violent eruption of Mt. Vesuvius in Italy buried both Pompeii and Herculaneum, along with a neighboring city, Stabiae, beneath a massive flow

276

of hot lava and muck. The cities had first been damaged by a major earthquake in 62 A.D. which the locals were still digging out of when the eruption occurred.

Mt. Vesuvius has also earned quite a long and infamous reputation for eruption. Its last activity was in 1944, which makes one feel as if the "giant" may not be sleeping much longer!

The other volcano mentioned in predictions as an "omen" of global Earth changes is Mt. Etna. Etna, stretching 10,902 feet into the sky, has had several recent eruptions, including three times during the 1970's, the last one being in 1975. We should not underestimate the power of Etna. Its eruptions in the year 1669 killed over 20,000 people! Vesuvius, Etna and another one on Stromball Island, all rest on the same fault system in the Mediterranean.

Mt. Pelee is another star in the drama of the volcanoes and the affect they have on the future of man and his planet. Located on the Isle of Martinique, there seems to be some correlation between the eruptions of Mt. Vesuvius and Pelee. Pelee's last eruption in 1902 took a heavy toll on human life, killing over forty thousand people. Lava flows, shock waves and earthquakes are not the only villans of a volcano, but the poisonous sulfurous gases can choke the life out of any life forms around. As we have said, many of the predictions single out these specific furnaces, along with others and the data is beginning to show that the trend is indeed developing. Albion feels that Mauna Loa on Hawaii is the one to watch, for it will be a "truly major eruption, the likes of which the Earth has not seen since the passing last hundred years".

Maui, the "Valley Isle", is the fastest growing island of the 50th state of the U.S. 70,000 people live on its 729 square miles. Maui's "soul", Haleakala Crater, could hold Manhattan Island. Its name means "House of the Sun" in Hawaiian. This volcano is 10,023 feet high and last erupted in 1750. It could, however, be active.

Albion had also made comment about some places that

we may look to for future volcanic activity. They included one off the coast of Hawaii that I just mentioned, to occur in about eight to nine years, along with an eruption in Alaska, Mt. Hood, one in Chile, two in the Mediterranean, Japan and the Philippines, and off the coast of Iceland plus South America's west coast. It's interesting to note how similar the list is to the areas that he felt would be affected also by seismic disturbances. There is another mention further along in this chapter that adds a few more places to this list, but I won't take them out of his context.

Volcanoes are also responsible for the appearance of new land. In both the major oceans, the Atlantic and the Pacific, cracks opens, allowing hot magma to flow upward from the Earth's interior. Increased volcanic activity could indeed cause Cayce's prophecy to come true about the appearance of new land. In fact, it already has. In 1963, a new island appeared off the coast of Iceland. It was named Surtsey.

It's no wonder that any psychic or lecturer who gives information about the possible future of cataclysmic change has to contend with being called a "doomsdayer". Earthquakes, volcanoes, poleshifts, ice ages and a "Great Day of Purification", don't go down well with a luncheon or, God forbid, on an empty stomach! But, we can't just dismiss the past or run away from the future. Time stops for no one.

The following material is direct from Albion and it gives his views and comments on the future of the Earth and the lives that call it home. Some of his information is identical or similar with prophecies already discussed, while others are completely different. These words are not given to substantiate any other source of prophecy nor to contradict it, but rather to show things as they are from this Teacher's perspective and how they may affect our future.

This session on prophecy was held in our home as usual, with A. S., D., and Scott present. The Teacher began, assuming our familiarity with what was to be his subject.

"Let us concern ourselves now with the future of the planet. We wish to recognize that all of the activities, which you call 'disasters', are a natural part of the factors involved with the Initiation of the planet. As the Earth approaches the Third Initiation, tidal, gravitational and seismic activities will all contribute to the 'tests' and 'lessons' the Earth must learn and experience in order to come closer to becoming "Self-Realized". Don't forget that the atmosphere, the aura of the planet, will also be involved, affecting climatic conditions and climatic change. If you were to view the Earth from our perspective, it would appear as a sphere, surrounded by an aura of blue light. The activity of the Earth's aura is one of the most dominant factors in determining the quality of life that you may enjoy. The aura itself is an essential characteristic of the planet's activities."

"Keep in your thoughts that growth, on all levels of consciousness, is the result of change. Nature's task is to transform existing forms into new ones, better ones. Its concern is the planet. The life forms that live upon her skin are linked spiritually with the Earth and therefore grow as a result of the many diverse influences that bombard it from outer space, as well as those that emanate from the lives that inhabit it. It selects, changes, rejects these forces in progressive ways, showing evidence of its own free will. Just as a human soul's evolution is determined by how one responds to the objective and subjective forces, so it is with the Earth."

"Many of you question what is the future toward which you and the Earth are traveling? All of the devices of present technology, coupled with the prophetic minds of men, cannot reveal any scenario of the future that is totally accurate, for neither is aware enough of the Earth as a 'living organism' so as to be totally sensitive to how it will respond to each of its Initiations. This has not always been so and there will come a time that it will be that way again in the future. Each civilization of man has risen and fallen during past Earth changes,

279

man learning from his mistakes and lack of sensitivity. Man has always been, now more than ever, one of the most important factors in what course the changes will take. Man has reached a point that he can make the Earth tremble due to his building of great dams and the testing of his sophisticated weapons. He can make rain and change the path of great storms. He risks melting the polar ice caps with the debris of his industries. His cities make hail fall to the ground, while his pollutants block out the light of the Father Sun. So, it is not hard to see how the health of the planet is linked with the actions of man. The destinies of both are tied together in a tie of cosmic proportions."

"The period of Initiation which is described by the prophecies has already begun. It started in 1976. All of the natural phenomena that have occurred since are a part of the beginnings of the great period of change. While quakes, storms and volcanic eruptions are constantly occurring, the drastic increase and major rearranging of the 'face' of the planet by such, are indicative of the Initiation periods. This is the sort of cycle that has begun and it will take well into the year 3000 A.D. to complete, with the most intense activity being between the years of 1986 through 2050."

"While it is certain that seismic and volcanic occurrences will play an important role in the Third Initiation, climate will be the most effective condition of all. There will come a time that your science of meteorology, as it presently exists, will not be an accurate method for understanding or predicting the weather. New methods will have to be found. There is already a great deal of concern about this. Millions of dollars are presently being spent by various governments in the world to determine what the weather and planetary changes will be in the future. Your own government, Russia, France and China are some of these. Weather conspiracies have been concocted and experimented with and this is as detrimental to the natural evolution of the Earth as your neutron bomb."

The seriousness of the Teacher's words were evident in his voice. He spoke in a tone that suggested concern, but truth. He continued, naming lands that would be affected in the future.

"The country of India will go through an increasing population problem during this present decade (1980's) and the next (1990's). Food, due to great droughts, due to fluctuation of the monsoons, will be scarce. Appeals will be sent out to all corners of the world to send water to this part of the globe. Water to fertilize the pitiful crops."

Almost a full year after Albion made this prophecy concerning India, an article appeared in the newspaper written by United Press International. It was datelined New Delhi, India and it stated that famine triggered by a five year drought in the desert of Thar is threatening more than twenty million people with starvation. The drought has dried up wells in one-thousand villages, located mostly in remote areas along the Pakistan borders. People must walk several miles to fetch water that could not be brought in by trucks due to the fact that there are few paved roads across the sand. It is also estimated that there are over 700,000 heads of emaciated cattle that nomads have had to drive into greener pastures in other states. No relief is expected through the summer of 1982.

The Teacher continued:

"Perhaps one of the hardest hit of all countries, as far as food is concerned, will be Russia. It will become almost totally benign in its ability to produce food on its own. There are already underground silos and storage bins that have been built to store grain secretly, but that's not enough. Russia will make many attempts to befriend nations that have long been its enemies so that it might obtain foodstuffs in the future. This is the true underlying motive of all international Soviet politics. It will seek to overrun countries and steal their food and control their fertile soil."

Albion's thoughts turned next to Japan.

"In Japan there will be undersea and underground volcanic and seismic activity. Three of the four large islands and all of the smaller ones will be affected. Most of this will occur just off the eastern and western coastlines. Japan is one of the areas that will be affected catastrophically, not gradually. Most of its land mass will not last past the year 2025 A.D."

"The island you call Samoa will be almost toally devastated by tidal activity. It will sink beneath the sea."

A glance at the world map shows Samoa is actually a group of islands located in the southwestern Pacific.

"You can look for this towards the turn of this century."

"It is not necessary to single out North America alone. There will be such activity in Italy, Iran, Egypt, South America, and specifically Chile. There will be activity in Siberia, Alaska, the area of the Hawaiian Islands and other islands of the South Pacific and in Japan."

The next prophecies draw our thoughts much closer to home.

"The grain belts of Nebraska, Kansas and other prairie lands of the U.S. will be hit by great droughts. They will flourish only for short periods during the early 1980's and 1990's. But that will not be sufficient to ward off food shortages and difficult economic problems for farmers. There will be water shortages in some areas of southern Canada and in the northern Andes mountain range, while there will be others parts of the world that will suffer from massive floods. China will be one of these, as will the state of Florida, the Mississippi Delta, some areas of the Himalayas and the northeast states in your country. Too much water will be just as devastating as too little. There will be panic among the peoples of the world, especially the uninformed. Knowledge promotes survival. This is the main purpose of our work."

It was not at all unusual for Albion to remind us of his intent. He seemed eager to make sure that his words did not frighten or attract only curious listeners. He wants us to use the information to become better acquainted with the planet and her period of change, as well as to help ourselves to adjust to it.

His predictions continued:

"Greenland will go through a period of warming and there will be huge melts between now and the year 3000. By that time, that land will begin to support forms of sub-tropical life. This will mark the end the the Third Initiation the Earth is going through. It will be preceeded slightly by a shifting of the poles."

If you will recall, this is a much sooner time thant the 16,000 years into the future prophesied by Blavatsky in The Secret Doctrine.

I can only speculate as to the exact meaning of the Teacher's next words. They seem to indicate a sort of "esoteric energy" as opposed to a physical one.

"There are great magnetic build-ups within the atmosphere. As the weather patterns carry these magnetic particles across the face of the Earth, they will be conducive upon the consciousness of man to turn within himself and to rely on his instinctual, thus his animal responses. This will cause fear. The electrical charges in the Earth's aura will also increase. These charges will cause all electrical vortex and grid areas to be bombarded by lightning storms. This lightning will be purple, green and gold in color. It will be highly dangerous. This will promote violence in these areas."

It would be wise to stop here and suggest that the reader go back and re-read the parts of Chapter Four that locate the electric vortices and grids. This will give some idea as to where the violence can be expected.

Albion continued.

"Closer towards the year 2000, it will become less desirable to live in the cities. More people will become a part of groups that are like communes. Steps can be taken on all levels to promote and understanding of survival in these times."

Many tips were given regarding just this. All of this

information is contained in Chapter Six and Seven of this work.

During the time that I spent listening to Albion's predictions about the changes that would occur to the face of the planet, it reminded me of a session Scott and I had had with the Teacher back in the Fall of 1977. It had been a session in which he had given us instructions to study astronomy. The reason he had given us of learning about the planets, the solar system and the universe from a scientific point of view was to gain a greater perspective about the various constellations. We should pay particular attention to the one called Cygnus. No particular reason was immediately given, which made his words even more curious. I guess it's like anything else, once a person mentions a name or object to you, it seems to start turning up everywhere. In a relatively short time, Cygnus was the area of the sky in which astronomers believe they have discovered the first black hole caused by a star collapsing on its own weight into infinity. It is known as Cygnus X-1, a source of intense x-ray activity. It was also the location of the largest object ever found in the Universe, a giant gas bubble that is eighteen light years across! Much later in time, Albion did have quite a bit to say about the reality of extraterrestrial life. It was then that I understood his directing us to be familiar with this constellation, for he identified it as an area of the Universe where an inhabitable planet exists. I won't pursue this any further in this writing, but it is an interesting thought to tuck away into the back of our minds.

Albion feels that due to the expanding into space that man is experiencing now and will continue to experience in the future, that basic astronomy should be known by all. A few years later during a conversation I shared with A.S. about Cygnus, we were viewing some astronomical slides of nebulas and galaxies. Nebulae are clouds of interstellar gas and dust. The different types of gases cause them to glow in various colors, making them splendid celestial sights to behold. The slide showing a time-released photograph of the North America Nebula, located in the constellation of Cygnus, popped onto the screen. A. S. zeroed in on the photo and became very excited. "You know something? I've seen this picture many times before, but I've never noticed this!" She got up and pointed to parts of the nebula, outlining its basic shape with her finger. "If all of the Cayce prophecies were to come true, the topography of North America would become almost identical with the shape of this nebula!" She was right! We decided that it was just a coincidence, but it sure did excite us for a moment.

Whether the Earth changes are a reality or the prophecies of earthquake and volcanic disasters ever occur, only time will tell. It seems hardly coincidental that so many seers from the past ages up to the present would tell almost the same tale. The evidence is mounting regarding the "tell-tale" signs of the coming chaos. The span of man's life in each incarnation is so short, it is difficult to imagine our planet undergoing such drastic change. But, scientific and non-scientific, geological and historical records of both planet and man tell us that this has happened before and chances are it will happen again. Perhaps, as Albion has suggested, a fuller knowledge of the earth and its physical and spiritual behavior will help us to not only survive, but to cultivate a much needed and better relationship with our planetary home.

But, a knowledge of the Earth is not the total answer. Man himself is perhaps the biggest disaster of all that we have to fear. We have to struggle to survive from our own willful destruction and disregard heaped upon the terrestrial sphere. Technology must be used more wisely in the future or there will be no need to worry about any sort of natural phenomena. Used wisely, our devices can heal the sick, provide even better and cleaner means of transportation, explore new, spatial worlds, and even someday provide us with extra-planetary homes. Used unwisely or out of fear, it could lead us all into unspeakable horror and probable annihilation. An

North American Nebula

example of this can be seen in an article written by Richard Saltus of the Heart News Service where he talks about where the current arms race could lead.

"A technologically thrilling but fruitless chess match in space, played out with missle-destroying lasers, killer satellites and orbiting booby traps, is likely unless the two superpowers move to ban such weapons."

A warning is given that scientists believe and warn that such an arms race in space could result in a nuclear war between the U.S. and the Soviet Union. It is a fact that both countries are working to develop such weapons.

Sound like science fiction? It isn't. Weapons are currently being developed that could be used against satellites orbiting the Earth or to destroy missiles soon after their launch. Lasers, atom smashers, killer satellites, are all proposed for development and future use. All of this makes it imperative to reach agreements between nations to limit such weapons.

A more reasonable approach to the dumping of nuclear and other toxic wastes must be reached and soon. Pollution from autos and industry has to be diminished from its present levels. Water in our lakes and streams has to be given a chance to recover from our wastes and the haphazard care we have given them. It is a fact that one to three species of plants and animals are made extinct every day according to the President's Council on Environmental Quality's Annual Report. At least 150 mammals and birds have disappeared since 1600. All of this is due to pollution, tropical de-forestation and desertification, which could eliminate 15-20% of all species of plants and animals in the next twenty years.

No doubt, useful things will continue to be invented. But the use we make of them will have to be more sensible in the future. Existence goes on in cycles, always new and changing, renewing itself and moving forward toward higher and higher goals.

How we treat our world will not go unnoticed. Men of tomorrow will record the past just as we consider the ancients and the cavemen today. Let's hope that we will not appear to a future society as men who had as the only objectives of our lives money, possessions, power, pleasure and the suppression of those whom we feel are obstacles to a more balanced relationship with the planet Earth.

The question of man's future, as well as the future of the Earth is perhaps more important now than ever before, due to the fast pace we move as a result of technological advances. It would seem that any of the ancient methods of determining the future or that have been valuable methods of sustaining life on the planet are slowly being discarded. Yet science with all its technological wisdom is still just as baffled as ever concerning the apprehension of planetary disaster.

"We must obey the Law of Change. It is the most powerful law of Nature."
                        Edmund Burke

CHAPTER SIX
THE ANT AND
THE GRASSHOPPER
(BEING PREPARED)

"These are times that try men's souls."
— Thomas Paine

It becomes apparent that the period of Earth changes
has purpose and that purpose overall is spiritual in its
nature. It is foolish for us who are alive during this important time to be afraid for that only wastes valuable
time and energy. It is also foolish to be apathetic. We
must learn to live with and love our Earth Mother and
the other beings who live upon her. That's how we can
use our emotional force we spend so unwisely on not caring and fear to a positive and constructive end. In the
words of Wabun, one of Sun Bear's Medicine helpers,
"When you learn to do this you will transform yourself
and help the transformation of the Earth. Some people
are able, naturally, to love the Earth in this manner.
Others have to learn how to give themselves the space
to do it. It is helpful to find an area that feels real good
to you one in which you feel safe, protected and loved."*
   A friend once made the comment that if one-third of
the Earth change prophecies came to pass, we have problems. If one-half are fulfilled, we must know how to
survive and be physically and emotional sound. If all
of them become reality, then the road ahead will be fit

*The Bear Tribe's Self-Reliance Book, by Sun Bear,
Wabun, Nimimosha and the Bear Tribe. Bear Tribe
Publishing Company, Spokane, WA. 1980.)

289

only for those that have a balanced and harmonious relationship with Nature and her Earth child.

The real question is: What do we have to lose? For many years now we have been faced with huge problems, most of them of our own making. Energy shortages, pollution of air and water, decaying cities, economic deficits, all play a role in the state of human and planetary affairs. Technology, while it has brought us many benefits, has reached a point of "diminishing returns". How much of it is really providing us with a truly better life? It is the contention of many sources today that we must develop more self-reliant alternatives. Living the good life must become a reality again. Can we continue to allow the Industrial Civilization to rob us of the responsibility we have to ourselves and the Earth? The time has come to begin a return to what the Native Americans call "the old ways". We *can* develop a lifestyle that is in keeping with producing and sustaining our needs. we *can* move from a point of being so totally dependent on government and society into a life that is independent and in that, we can seek a new sense of freedom and security. We *can* respond to the problems of our environment and our lives in a positive manner. If we must indeed face a period of major planetary change, we *can* be prepared. We *can* survive. On the other hand, if the prophecies are wrong, what have we lost?

The information in this chapter has been gathered from many sources including Albion. His instructions as to what should be included have been followed here, all designed to help us become more self-reliant, not just physically, but on all levels of our being. The choice is ours to make. I think we have the personal responsibility to be aware of what is going on around us. What can we do as individuals? What can we do as a society? We have looked at some of the signs. Are there others? Perhaps these can be the guide that will carry us safely through this period.

On a recent trip to the Hopi reservation, D. was told

by one of his Indian friends who lives on Walpi on First Mesa, that the Hopis are preparing to store 25% of their corn crop this year (1982). It is to be a "community" project. *That is a sign.* There are Medicine people from various tribes that are trying to bring Indian and non-Indian alike into a renewed respect for the Earth. Many of them, namely Sun Bear, Harley Swiftdeer, Hyemeyohsts Storm, Wallace Black Elk, to name a few, are motivated by their "visions" of what the future will bring. *This is a sign.* The Worldwatch Institute contends in a recently released study that "the world is engaging in 'biological deficit financing', bringing it to the edge of an environmental crisis that is undermining the global economy". "Biological deficit financing" is explained as the consumption of the productive resource base. We are fulfilling our current needs with resources at the expense of future generations and we have to change our policies. *This is a sign.* One-fifth of the world's cropland is approaching non-productivity. Soil conservation is a must! *This too, another sign.* The signs are all around us. We need but look. The signs and instructions given in this chapter are not designed to cause fear or panic, but rather to inform and educate. This must be kept in mind in order to insure full benefit from the information. This chapter is designed to investigate survival on a physical level so that should we have to go through earth, economical or any other form of drastic change, we will be as secure as humanly possible. It is also designed to show how becoming safe and self-reliant can bring us into a greater balance with the Earth Mother.

Albion began his discussions about surviving the periods of Earth changes by telling us the state of mind we must have, as well as where the "safe" places will be as time goes on.

"You must pay a great deal of attention to those things that have to do with the health of the Soul. When fear is rampant, man's soul is rampant. There is no better method to calm the soul of a 'wanderer' than to keep in its proper and natural perspective and in balance with the planet upon which he lives."

"This period of Earth changes will be a gradual one. As they develop, taking various forms, there will be many places that will be safe. Some of these places will be 'way stations', places where many self-reliant people will have been previously led to so that they can help with the masses as they migrate to safety. This has already begun on a small scale and it will become more apparent as time goes one. Sedona is a 'way station', as is the area around Asheville, North Carolina, the Hopi and Navajo lands, Spokane, Washington and the area of Oklahoma, Colorado Springs, and an area around southern Saskatchewan, and Santa Fe, New Mexico, on this continent. In other parts of the world, Moscow, South Africa, Madras, the whole of Holland and Costa Rica."

After this particular information had been shared, I began to notice how many times I have run into people who speak of having been told by some "source" or have been inwardly led to come to Sedona and/or to move to Asheville, North Carolina! Coincidence? I think not. Albion continued.

"Places that are also safe are New Brunswick and most of the land that is in the Atlantic time zone. Many will be drawn to upper New York and lower Massachusetts and the Western shores of Michigan. Some will know why and others will not. Through to the turn of the century, the states of Kentucky, Virginia, West Virginia, Tennessee, the Carolinas, and Georgia will be safe. It will likewise be secure, geographically, in the countries of Egypt, Bolivia, Sudan, and Ethiopia. It would have been safe in Uganda, but in the recent past, the negative thought forms created there have destroyed that capability. It will not be safe in Italy, Iran or China. These are places of imminent increases in seismic activity and flooding. It will be safe in some parts of Turkey and all of Mongolia. It will not be safe in central and western Siberia. It will be safe in the Antarctica until the year 3000, also in Greenland. There will be tidal activity in New Zealand. Close to the year 3000 A.D. the continent of Australia will break up into three or four parts. By that time, South America will be only about one-half its present size. Man cannot change what the Earth must endure. But, he can understand and be aware of it and survive it. Only the greedy and the skeptical will regret their ignorance."

"What we have said would appear to make this period seem negative, like punishment. It would seem to degrade man from his position of 'the darling of the gods'. Those who look upon this period as a time only of grief and destruction are those who would try to see the brilliance of a sunset with their eyes closed! It is truly a time of renewal and survival, a time of replenishment and release of negative pressure. It will bring a New Age when man will live together as brother and sister. People will be drawn together."

In keeping with the information Albion had given us about the "safe" places, I would like also to share part of an earlier session he gave on what he called "Light Centers" in this country.

"Picture in your minds an aerial view of America. In the area that covers the western area of the country, covering Arizona and the Four Corners and part of New Mexico that includes Santa Fe; and in the Midwest, in the area of western Michigan, the whole of Arizona, Washington State and Colorado. These three areas are major 'Centers of Light' for your country. Each of these are suitable places to establish study and healing centers or groups".

"During the period from the mid 1950's through the 1970's, the area of Florida was most active. It drew a tremendous number of individuals into a state of self-consciousness and promoted a state of spiritual growth. Now that energy has greatly subsided. The center of force in the Arizona and New Mexico area has been gaining in strength since 1975 and will continue through the turn of the century. The Michigan 'center' will come to its full potiental after the Earth changes."

This information will become more valuable, perhaps, as time goes on. In line with the Teacher revealing to us his feeling about the "safe" places to live, he continued on to more details about his reasons.

"The closer we move towards the year 2000, it will become less desirable to live in the cities. Rural areas will be in great demand. Individuals who seek to buy land should do so now. The wise person will buy land that can be farmed. Fertile ground will be scarce and very expensive in the next ten years. It would be foolish to purchase land in or near a city. Many will tend to wait until such land is scarce and the prices prohibitive. Finding proper and good acreage is our primary concern."

Before the session was completed, Albion suggested we learn about land and its proper uses. Homesteading. Since we were ready to get some land, this information couldn't have been more timely.

These words led me to begin to think not only about obtaining some land to settle down on, but more importantly how to care for and sustain its productivity. As per Albion's instructions, a research project began that took several months. Needless to say, Scott and I are interested in searching out property in areas Albion had designated as safe. Also the choice should be a farmable one, sufficient to provide basic needs. Consideration of needs with land led to the following list.

1. Land that is fertile.

2. Good water supply.

3. Space for animals.

4. Access.

5. Building codes.

6. Utility availability.

7. Waste disposal.

8. Fair price.

All of these points are extremely important and cannot be overlooked. You must also be realistic in your search. Often city dwellers dream of a "little country farm house with a white picket fence", only to end up with land that is poor quality. People tend to buy for the "view", which is equally unwise. Just remember your initial attitude and motive can spell the success or failure of your mission.

You must also decide what you can handle financially. There are many ways to get land, ranging from cash to time payments. A "down to earth" approach to this aspect of homesteading is an obvious necessity. Some pertinent points along this line are found in the *Bear Tribe's Self-Reliance Book*. "If you have the money, there are lots of cash deals available through private parties." Be sure to check such property out carefully to be sure that it is not being sold due to some undesirable reasons. "The Bureau of Land Management puts land up for sale. These are cash deals, but reasonable. Contact the office for the area in which you are interested."

One source that can be quite helpful in learning what land is available is the United Farm Agency, Inc. Founded in 1925 for the sole purpose of selling country real estate, it is presently a network of over 600 offices. Four seasonal catalogs, covering three regional areas; Eastern, Central and Western parts of the United States, are published every year. There is also a national edition that combines all three regional editions. The Agency likewise provides counseling on the various forms of financing and any other factors involving the buyer's specific needs. One particularly attractive feature of the services offered by the United Farm Agency is their outlets for lower interest rate financing. A free catalog with regional or national real estate listings may be obtained by writing:

United Farm Agency, Inc.
National Headquarters
612 West 47th
Kansas City, MO 64112

If you would prefer to read about how to purchase property first, the following books are recommended:

Finding and Buying Your Place in the Country
Leo Scher. Macmillan Books.

Buying Country Property
Herbert R. Moral. Garden Way Publishers, Co. VT.

Each of these is an excellent "way shower" in equipping you with pertinent information on rural land buying. For those of you who may already have property, but wish to sell and relocate, the United Farm Agency also provides "selling" services. If you choose to retain and put to the highest and best use the property you already own, the following books are recommended:

Country Women Jeanne Tetrault and Sherry Thomas
Anchor Books, Doubleday

Living the Good Life Scott and Helen Nearing
Schocker Books, New York

Building for Self-Sufficiency Robin Clark
Universe Books, New York.

Country Comforts Christian Bruyere and Robert Inwood
Sterling Publishing Company, New York

The Owner Built Homestead Ken Kern
Charles Scribner's Sons, New Jersey

Shelter II ed. Lloyd Kahn
Home Book Service, California

As Albion has said, many people have already migrated or are contemplating doing so. Finding the right place for yourself can go a long way towards "riding out" this period of change with much more comfort and safety than many will have.

In looking at land, you must remember that the water supply is very important. This will be especially true in arid areas. Drinking water will not be your total consideration. You must also have water for irrigation and animals. Putting in a well can prove to be very expensive and in severe cases, quite futile.

An ideal site for settling would be spring or stream fed property. Having such on your land is ideal, but not totally necessary. Be sure to check on water and mineral rights on your chosen site, for this can be a source of legal difficulties. Abstract companies are available, for a fee, to check out clear land titles, water and mineral rights, as well as future development plans that have to do with building and highways. This is for your protection. Fees are usually based on a percentage of the total price of the land involved.

In regards to water, you will want to make sure the property is high enough up the flow of the river, stream, or spring, so as not to have pollution above you presently or in the future. Any industrial development nearby would obviously eliminate that choice of sites. Pay attention to ground water, the run-off from rain, snow melts, or permanent marsh and/or springs. Generally, the more surface water, the more trouble. It will necessitate high basements, special septic systems and possible mosquito problems.

Another major concern with water is conservation. If we consider the amount of water that is polluted and the amount wasted, we are up against some strong odds! Learning to use a minimum amount of water is just good sense. Habits such as letting the kitchen sink water run while doing dishes or cleaning veggies can be broken. For example, when washing vegetables, you can fill the sink with a few inches of water and wash them all in that. The bathroom is another place we can conserve. Flushing only solids is one way, but you might also want to consider putting a large plastic jug into the water tank on the toilet that will fit, making sure you clear the flushing mechanism. This will reduce the water used in each flush. These tips can be used by anyone, no matter where you live, and at any time. The minimal average water use per person per day in the U.S. is staggering!

> Flushing—11 gallons
> Personal washing—11 gallons
> Laundry—3 gallons
> Dishwashing (hand)—3 gallons
> Garden—1½ gallons
> Drinking and Cooking—1 gallon
> Car Washing—1/2 gallon

That is 31 gallons a day! If you have an automatic dishwasher or swimming pool, these figures would rise drastically. Where will such huge amounts come from in a survival or drought situation? Also, changes in weather and season can affect the amount and the quality of your water.

There are many other alternatives to excess water use. Gardens can be irrigated with the run-off of other projects as long as it doesn't contain soap or other contaminants. Showers use less than tub baths. When doing laundry, wash as many articles of clothing as you can. Automatic washers are wasteful. In short, try to recycle water as often as you can.

Next, let's consider water storage, for drinking and cooking, as well as for washing, animals and the like. First of all, choose appropriate containers. The FDA approved polyethylene type are best. Don't use glass or plastic milk containers. Glass breaks too easily and the metal caps often will rust. Plastic milk jugs are not designed for long-term storage and can adversly flavor the water inside. You will need at least½ gallon per person per day just for drinking and cooking. Three to ten gallons per person per day would be needed if all other uses are considered. This would be especially needed should you find yourself in an emergency situation due to Earth changes or weather predicaments. City water supplies are likely to be the first that would be disrupted or contaminated. With storage, a one-month's supply should be the minimum to have on hand. (Two people X ½ gallon X 30 days equals 30 gallons minimum). Keep in mind, a 55 gallon drum of water weights 400 pounds, so consider carefully before putting a drum in a closet and filling it up! In a real emergency, water beds whose contents have been treated with the standard algacide are an excellent source for cleaning and bathing purposes. Don't drink it or water gardens or plants.

Water is the life blood of the Earth Mother. Keeping it pure and sparkling is up to us. We must respect it and care for it because the alternatives are fatal.

Albion designated his next point of concern.

"The storing of foods, in particular those that will last the longest is our second most major concern. Do not store food just for yourself, for there will be others who will need to be fed but did not have the foresight to store it on their own. You may be called upon to feed your brothers and sisters when the severe changes begin. It would be wise to have a root cellar. It would be wise for you to store meat, but be selective in your choice. Don't store red meat, for it contains the vibrations of fear and panic and this is not good, particularly during times of the great changes." Albion's words were designed to make us aware of the need for having food on hand during Earth changes, but it is good advice for any sort of situation.

The following research on this subject includes information that will see you through any major survival situation and several different ones are covered. The four main "survival" foods are wheat, legumes or powdered milk, salt and honey. These will keep indefinitely when stored properly. The enemies of any food in storage are moisture, light and heat. In planning the amount to store, you must consider the needs of infants and small children, pets, and those members of your family that are on special diets.

During times of a major emergency, such as an earthquake, use the food that is in your freezer first. This is due to the possibility of power failures. When opening cans, don't throw away the water that they are packed in. It could be a source of water if there is a severe shortage. If you suspect any liquid for any reason for drinking or cooking, strain it first through a clean handkerchief.

For long-term food storage, the following list will serve as a good guideline. You can increase the amounts as to the amount of time you wish to store for accordingly.

One Month Supply for One Adult
27 lbs. wheat
5 lbs. skim milk (dry)
4 lbs. legumes
3 lbs. honey
1 lb. salt

The following is a suggestion for food storage purely for short-term emergencies. It is for a family of four for four days.

MILK: Powdered non-fat dry, 2 packs and 4 cans (14 oz.) evaporated milk.

JUICES: 6 cans (14 oz.) tomato, orange or grapefruit. (Larger cans will lose their vitamins if left open)

FRUITS: 4 cans (14 oz.) of variety of fruits, and 2 lbs. dried fruits.

VEGTABLES: 12 cans (16 oz.) of variety of vegetables.

SOUPS: 8 cans (10½ oz.) of variety of soups, and 4 packs dry soup mix.

MEATS AND MEAT SUBSTITUTES: 2 jars peanut butter, 2 jars cheese, 12 cans miscellaneous (hash, stew, tuna, etc.)

CEREAL, CRACKERS AND COOKIES: 3 boxes each.

BEVERAGES: 4 oz. instant coffee or tea (or bouillon), 2 packs instant cocoa mix, 24 bottles soft drinks.

Because Albion mentioned a root cellar, research was done on this subject. Basically, a cellar, closet, pit or basement will serve the purpose quite well. An area 6' x 8' will store food for four people. In making your choice of root cellar locations, the north or cold side of the house, away from any fireplace or furnace is best. If the location chosen is an actual cellar in your home, cover the concrete floor with a layer of earth. You will need two thermometers, one at the ceiling and one for the floor. Green vegetables should be kept near the floor in moist bags, with the temperature at 40 degrees. Foods such as squash, pumpkin or sweet potatoes can be stored in the upper racks at 35-65 degrees. Should you choose an outdoor pit for your cellar, a ditch 12" deep and 3' wide is plenty big enough. Insulation can be achieved with a lining of straw. A screen over the ventilation openings will keep out unwanted pests. Seal your cellar after the air temperature reaches 33°F.

Whether you are storing actual food or the seeds for sprouts and future crops, some basic skills are necessary. Dry ice will keep out mold, preserve the seeds and kill larvae that might invade them. A suggestion would be to clean a one-gallon jar, being sure to varnish the metal lid to prevent rust. You may also use five-gallon paint cans or PVP plastic containers. Cover an "ice cube size" hunk of dry ice with a piece of cotton cloth to prevent freezing seeds. Place the ice in the bottom of your container and fill it with the desired seeds. Next, lay the lid on top, don't screw it down. When the ice melts, you may then seal and store at 45-50°F.

Another manner of seed storage is the "dehydration method". For this, you can buy permarex trash cans or just ones with a tight lid. These can be purchased from

Sears. You will also need to choose heavy plastic bags and calcium chloride from an industrial supplier. The cost would be approximately $7.50 per 100 pounds. On a dry day, put your seeds in heavy bags and close loosely. Then put them inside the cans. In a shallow round pan, such as an aluminum pie tin or plant saucer, put 1/4" calcium chloride and place on top of the bag. Seal the lid and keep in a cold place. When the calcium chloride becomes liquid, which should be between one and six months, replace it as needed.

Earth changes or even temporary weather conditions are not the only reasons that food storage makes good sense. Government reports as of late seem to point to food shortages that may not be too far into the future. In the book *Weather Conspiracy: The Coming Ice Age*, several reports are given, some of them gained through intelligence sources. "The CIA estimates that even under the most optimistic conditions in the years to come there simply won't be enough food to go around. The situation is not new. It has long existed." Population increases are another source of concern. It is estimated that by 1985, the world's population will be up to 5 billion!

So, it seems that no matter from which angle one looks at the potential causes of food shortages, there is room for concern. Rain forests are being hacked down at an alarming rate. The estimate in 1977 was 14 acres every minute! It must be even greater by now. Farmable land is fast diminishing. Deserts presently cover about 57 million square miles of the planet. That's 40% of all land! And they are growing. It is estimated that in the last fifty years, deserts have increased by 3.5 million square miles. That is equal to the size of Europe! the Sahara alone has grown by 400,000 square miles, with its southern border increased by 60 square miles in less than 20 years!

This all adds up to trouble for future generations. How far into the future remains an unanswered question. Climate is another major factor in food availability, as we have seen. You will recall that cold weather, for example, increases our need for fossil fuels and foreign imports. Drought cuts sharply into growing power, as does flooding. Psychics and scientists alike are predicting climatic changes that will be unprecedented, as I have pointed out. These predictions are coming to pass. All over, people are talking about how the weather isn't "normal". It is even conceivable that the weapon of the future could become food! We have to realize that food storage is, then, bordering on being a necessity.

A bit more food storage information will help even further towards preventing problems in an emergency or for posterity. You will recall that Albion has recommended that meat, such as jerky or smoked meat, not be stored, as red meat causes "humans to become more animal-like, thus fear and panic". This is for consideration during severe Earth changes, but not necessarily during times of more temporary crises. Wild game is generally nutritionally superior to confined, food-raised animals. This is due to the animal's instinctual control over diet as opposed to feed-lot nutrition. Likewise, an additional few points to bear in mind are that all parts of a sacrificed animal should be used. Hides make good clothing or bedding. Animals should be at peace when killed if at all possible. Chicken, turkey, duck and venison have the best ration of protein to fat. Also, remember that if the animal's origin has been contaminated, don't eat the liver. If you would rather eat fish, fish as well as meat can be smoked. Small fish fillets can be salted well and hung to dry. Storage of dried foods is important, but most important, the first step is making sure that the food involved is completely dry. You may want to package it in small plastic baggies, sealed tightly with twister seals. The drier it is, the longer it will keep.

Now let's think about fruits and vegetables. It is advisable that fruits, for example, should only be eaten in season and within 500 miles or less of there they are grown. Fruits are cleansing foods, whereas vegetables

303

build up the body. All fruits and vegetables, including homegrown, must be soaked in one tablespoon of clorox or chlorine mix (sea water) in a sink or tub for ten minutes. This removes residual pesticides, such as arsenic, that have been sprayed on soft foods and non-soluble coatings that have been sprayed on for preservation. It will also remove any larvae. Keep in mind that most fruits and vegetables are 75-95% water, so if your diet is high in fresh fruits and vegetables, little additional water is needed. Also, most fruits and veggies can be dried in the sun. Slice them thin and spread out so that no two pieces touch. You can choose flat pans or cardboard. Cover with cheesecloth so as to protect them from bugs and birds while drying. Be prepared to rescue the food should rain or storms threaten. Then, store the food in ziplock bags and place in five-gallon cans, sealed in dry ice. With dried grains and beans, mark quart jars with purchase dates of the dried foods. This is in order to establish use rate. How many pounds of any given food stuff used in one month, times twelve, will equal a full year's supply.

The following is a list that has been compiled as a guideline for foods that will lend themselves well to storage for short or long periods.

    DRIED
        Eggs and Milk
        Protein powder made from egg or milk
        (not soy primarily)

    GRAINS
        Brown rice, long and short grain
        Wheat (hard)
        Rye
        Millet
        Corn
        Barley
        Oats

BEANS
- Split peas
- Limas
- Chickpeas (garbanzos)
- Aduki
- Pinto
- Black Beans
- Soy beans
- Lentils
- Navy beans

FRUIT
- Raisins
- Dates
- Prunes
- Apples
- Peaches
- Pears
- Cherries

CONDIMENTS
- Salt
- Kelp
- Pepper
- Sugar
- Honey
- Agar-agar or gelatin
- Tea
- Coffee
- Molasses
- Maple Syrup
- Rice syrup
- Vinegar
- Oil
- Baking soda
- Baking powder
- Vanilla
- Tamari
- Sesame salt

Rock salt
Soy sauce
Mustard
Spices and herbs

SEEDS AND NUTS
Alfalfa
Mung
Radish
Sprout seeds
Sesame
Poppy

PET FOODS

HOUSEHOLD SUPPLIES
(Biodegradeable only)
Laundry soap
Dish soap
Hand soap
Toilet paper
Steel wool
Heavy duty cleanser
Linseed oil
Alcohol
Paste wax
Boot polish
Saddle soap
Turpentine

For more information about food storage, the following is a list of books for recommended reading:

SURVIVAL FOOD CATALOGUES

Alia, Inc.
Box 8411
Asheville, NC 28804 Catalogue price: $3.00

Sam Andy
525 South Rancho
Colton, California 92324

Perma-Pak
3999 South Main Street
Salt Lake City, Utah 84115

Simpler Life
Arrowhead Mills
Box 671
Hereford, Texas 79045

Reliance
1990 North California Boulevard
Walnut Creek, California 94596

Albion's feelings about the value of securing land that was suitable for farming made us all more aware of the growing need to learn to grow our own food. Scott and I had had our first try at gardening in the Spring of '81, but others we know have been at it a while longer, with better results, I might add. Inflation alone is motivation enough to grow as much food as possible, but the prospect of the Earth changes ahead drove the point home even more decidedly. You will recall Albion's rather gloomy predictions about the scarcity of farmable land in the future, not to mention the escalating prices. Many of you may already know how to plan and care for a garden, but for those of you who do not, here are a few helpful hints.

Perhaps the first important point that should be made has to do with attitude. When you garden, you are not only motivated to grow food or other members of the plant kingdom, but you are also cultivating a relationship with the Earth Mother. I have learned from Sun Bear and Wabun that it is a relationship that should be respected, for the plants and the soil will work hard to produce a crop for you. It is a good idea that as you begin to turn over the ground and develop your garden to explain to the spirits of the area why you are breaking the Earth. This creates an understanding between you and the "energies". You must approach your task in a positive manner and have respect for yourself as a gardener as well. Without this self-respect, you will do poor work and are apt to harvest a poor crop.

Choosing a good spot for your garden is also very important. The condition of the earth, the amount of sunlight and water available are points to look for before you begin. You should decide what you will plant which will determine the space needed. A family of four can grow most vegetables on a plot 30' x 90', 1/16 of an acre. Soil will vary in different geographical areas so you may need to fertilize it with organic compost to insure good growth. It is a good idea to keep a compost heap nearby. This will also save you a lot of time and labor of hauling it from a distance. The Bear Tribe, who grow a large percentage of their food, suggest that an "ideal spot would be a gentle south slope (sun and drainage) just below a water source, with loamy soil, not shaded by trees." Be sure to remove any rocks, the type of watering system you will use will depend upon what is available and the type of climate you live in.

If you are going to grow wheat, a plot 60' x 90' will supply one person with enough grain for one year. It will take approximately ½ acre for four people. Self-sufficiency with food is possible if you have 1-7 acres, taking soil and variety of plants into consideration. If you have acres of land, the ideal way to divide its use would be to leave 2 acres wooded, 1 acre for an orchard, 2 acres for livestock (will keep a cow, 2 goats and 2 sheep), 1 acres for a house and garden, and one acre for wilderness.

Provided you are settled fairly permanently, the following diagram shows a three-year rotation plan for crops. This rotation allows the soil to regain balance as different crops require different combinations of nutrients from the soil. It will also reduce pests.

YEAR	1	2	3
	B	A	C
	C	B	A
	A	C	B

CROP ROTATION—3 YEAR PLAN

A - parsnips, carrots, early potatoes (followed by turnips), potatoes, and beets.

B - cabbage, brussel sprouts, broccoli, kale, globe beets and early dwarf peas.

C - dwarf peas (intercrop with spinach and lettuce), onions, (follow with spring cabbage), shallots (follow with winter lettuce), broad beans (intercrop with summer lettuce), and runner beans.

A greenhouse or a hole with glass over it is a good idea, for it extends the growing season at least one or two months. Don't forget to compost your garden again after your final harvest. Mulching the soil, ideally with a layer of straw or dead leaves (any organic matter) will serve as a good maintenance program and should be done throughout the growing season. This will help to retard weed growth, retain moisture and keep the soil from hardening and eroding. It's a good idea to keep a "garden diary" to record the types of seeds planted and where, dates planted and so forth. I put various gardening hints and reminders in mine, along with various Native American "sayings" and poems about the Earth and growing. This helped to improve my attitude about myself and the garden.

Scott and I were planting in a very rocky soil that had never been used for a garden. Our plants came up but gave a poor yield. Soil has to be proper for a garden and we had the opportunity to learn this. Thank God we were just renting the property!

309

Everything you should know about planting, soil cultivation, seasonal planting, and tips about the growing of various types of crops, can be gained by reading *The Bear Tribe's Self-Reliance Book*. It is published by the Bear Tribe and can be ordered through them.

The Bear Tribe Publishing Company
P.O. Box 9167
Spokane, Washington 99209

The book is a "gem" of self-reliance information and practical skills, as well as being filled with Indian legends and prophecies, a guide to community living, poetry and prayers to assist you in developing a better relationship with the Earth.

Along the lines of growing and eating foods, sprouts are the fastest, easiest way to obtain living food. In a homestead situation, they provide an excellent source of fresh, green food during winter, as well as a source of "live" food all year long. Albion has expressed many times the need to eat "live" food as much as possible. Sprouts contain high concentrations of prana (life force) due to the fact that the seed's dynamics are released in the first 72 hours of growth. After 72 hours, the sprout becomes a vegetable. It is still an excellent source of nutrition, but the "aliveness" factor diminishes just as stored food diminishes in nutritive value. Any seed, grain or bean can be sprouted. All sprouts contain complete protein, vitamin C, trace minerals and as many as nineteen different enzymes.

During any crisis situation that forbids planting as a source of green vegetables or when the Earth is sore and weakened so that the removal of wild food would further damage an already fragile eco-system, sprouts can be the major source of fresh, living food. Sprouts can even be grown while you are migrating or traveling, as well as in a survival situation, as long as water is available.

Seeds that can be sprouted are: alfalfa, cabbage,

radish, sunflower, mung, lentil, garbanzo, wheat, and rye. For sprouting, special screen caps are available at most health shops. They will fit wide-mouth jars so that the sprouts can be rinsed. You can also use cheesecloth or a nylon stocking for the same purpose.

To sprout all small seeds (alfalfa, cabbage and radish), soak them for four hours in 1" of water in a wide-mouth jar. After the soaking, drain off the water, Remember, this water is quite vitamin-enriched so don't throw it out. You can drink it, use it as a soap base or to water your pets or house plants. Rinse the seeds with cool water and pour out again. This will dampen your seeds and reduce the germinating temperature. Repeat this prodedure three times a day. Be sure to shake the seeds around in the jar and leave it tipped to allow the water to drain. The sprouts will be ready to eat in 72 hours. The sprouts can be refrigerated in a closed jar or plastic sack. All larger seeds will need to be soaked for at least 12 hours.

The following is a list of where you can obtain organically-grown seeds and herbs.

SEEDS
Abundant Life Seed Foundation
Box 772
Port Townsend, Washington 98368
Catalog: $2.00

Self-Reliance Seeds
Box 335
Hudson, New York 12534
Catalog: $2.00

Johnny's Selected Seeds
Albion, Maine
Catalog: Free

**Vita Green Farms and Taylor's Herb
Gardens**
Box 878
Vista, California 92083
Catalog & listings: Free

Graham Center Seed Directory
Route 3, Box 95
Wadesboro, North Carolina 28170
Directory: $1.00

HERBS

Otto Richer and Sons, Ltd.
Goodwood, Ontario
LOC 1AO, Canada
Catalog: $1.00

Greene Herb Gardens
Greene, Rhode Island 02827
Catalog: Free

Meadowbrook Herb Garden
Whispering Pines Road
Wyoming, Rhode Island 02898
Catalog: $.50

To further assist you in your efforts, you may wish to
consider the following lists:

FOOD SKILLS

Putting Food By, Ruth Hertzberg,
Beatrice
Vaughn and Janet Greene
Bantam Books, IL

Fat Years, Lean Years, Ann Elliot, et al
(a food storage compendium)
Creative Living Center, CA

Passport to Survival, Esther Dickey
Bookcraft Publishers, UT

How to Prepare Common Wild Foods, Darcy Williamson
Darcy Williamson, Pub. Box 1032, McCall, Idaho 83638

Laurel's Kitchen, Laurel Robertson, et al
Nilgiri Press, CA

Unmentionable Cuisine, Calvin Schwave
University Press of Virginia, VA

Getting the Most from Your Game and Fish, Robert Candy
Garden Way Publishing, VT

Survival Scrapbook –2, Food, Stephen Szczelkun
Schocken Books

GARDENING

Encyclopedia of Organic Gardening, Staff of Organic Gardening Magazine
Rodale Books, PA

Grow It!, Richard Langer
Avon Books, NY

Easy Gardening with Drought Resistant Plants,
Arno & Irene Nehrling
Dover Books, NY

Good Food Naturally, John Harrison
Keats Publishing, CT

Intensive Gardening Round the Year,
Paul
Doscher, Timothy Fisher and Kathleen
Kolb
Stephen Greene Press, UT

Successful Cold Climate Gardening,
Lewis Hill
Stephen Greene Press, UT

Small Scale Grain Raising, Gene
Logsdon
Rodale Books, PA

Organic Gardening Under Glass,
George and Katy Abraham
Rodale Books, PA

There was reference made earlier to having animals on your property. Remember that all animals are time-consuming and slave you to their needs. You must provide their food and remove the manure, as well as providing any medical or housing needs they may have. In a migration situation, this would obviously not be possible or practical. But, again, during settled conditions, should you choose to have them, here are some helpful hints.

With poultry, you will need fresh straw each week for the nests and the poultry house will require a whitewashing two to three times a year. Most fowl will eat table scraps and/or a handful of grain. It would be best to buy your chicks when they are 3-6 months old, to avoid rearing. You will need one rooster to twelve hens. The Bantam breeds are best, such as Sebright or Leghorns.

If you wish to have rabbits, they breed quickly and are easy to keep, require a small amount of space. They are a good meat stock and fur source. Rabbits can live mostly on garden wastes or wild green food. Their manure is good for the soil. Should you be living primarily on a diet that is high in cereals, rabbit meat provides lysine, an amino acid that is low in cereals.

Goats do need attention, but they, like rabbits, require little space. You will need an 8-foot square shed to house two goats. Each female goat will yield about 200 gallons of milk each year. Your goats will need daily milking.

Cows are good animals to have around. Some breeds, particularly the Channel Island type, are docile and require only a small plot of ground to live. Cow grazing is good for the soil, too. You will need a shed that is at least 10' x 20', along with additional food storage bins and a concrete floor in the dairy room. Two cows will need 2-3 acres to graze. Those two cows will give from between 1200-1600 gallons of milk each year. Two cows will also insure your having milk year round. Four hundred and sixty gallons of milk will yield 200 pounds of butter and 200 gallons of skim milk. The same amount will also give 200 pounds of cheese.

Ducks, who begin laying at five months of age, lay one more season than hens. Adults will need to be fed once a day, 8-12 months out of the year, with you providing supplemental foraging during the winter months. Ducks need dry bedding. Geese are even more self-sufficient.

Bees are a good idea, not only for honey, but to provide fertilization for crops. A five-pound swarm is good to start with. If you buy them in May, the honey harvest will be ready in July.

Finally, fish farming is a possibility, but does require some basic knowledge. If you are going to farm, use a pond, not a muddy or stagnant pool. The pond must be kept clean of falling leaves and other debris. The best fish are mirror carp, trench, jack and bream. Even a½ acre homestead can support a pond. It's a good idea to plant food-rich cattails around the pond itself. Good fish foods to use are cholerella algae and yeast.

When feasible, having animals is not only a good source of food stuffs, but it also helps to build the eco-system around your homestead and gives you an opportunity to build a good relationship with yet another kingdom of life.

Albion made suggestions that also had to do with articles that would be desirable to have during severe Earth change periods.

"We would suggest that it would be necessary to collect books that are of an encyclopedia type. This is so that they might be used to teach the young and for posterity, so that the events and history of the past will not be lost. The Ancients stored their manuscripts, both historical and spiritual, some of which are still yet to be found." I assume a Bible, the Gita or other chosen spiritual literature would also be a good idea.

The Teacher took a more practical approach to storage by mentioning things such as: "matches, which should be placed in a moisture-proof container to prevent spoilage and ignition". The following is a list of supplies necessary for major or minor emergencies. These articles are also good to have on hand whether any sort of emergency situation arises or not.

TOOLS
Ax
Flashlight, bulbs and batteries
Files, broad and 3-cornered
Fishing kit
Butcher and skinning knives
Gun oil, rod, etc.
Nail assortment

Kerosene lantern and camp stove
5 gallon gas cans
Canvas tarp
Hammer
2 screw drivers, screws
Water pails
Fire grill
Wash tub
Canteen
Washboard
Slingshots
Saw
Hacksaw
Hoe
Spade
Traps
Mesh wire
Rat traps
Pliers
Pitchfork
Trowel
Water hose
String
Duct tape
Nylon rope
Rubber cement
Rubber patches

KITCHEN TOOLS
Hand mill for grinding grains
Distiller
Stainless steel or enamel pots (no aluminum)
Steamer insert
Bake and bread pans
Pie pans, cookie sheets, casserole
Stainless, enamel or cast iron kettles and skillets
Big fork, spoon, ladle, kitchen utensils, can opener, etc.
Storage and serving bowls with lids

Unbreakable tablewear, plates, cups and glasses
(wooden bowls work well for anything)
Canning jars, bands and lids (extra lids)
Cheesecloth
Air and waterproof containers

SUPPLIES
Don't forget extra car parts . . .
Batteries
Tires
Fan belts
Oil
Gaskets
Sealer
Major parts, brakes, clutch, muffler, etc.
As well as replacement parts for generators, pumps,
etc.

The Teacher had also suggested various medical supplies "It will be important to store medical goods, a first-aid kit, bandages, etc. Compile a list of non-perishable first-aid supplies that can be stored in air-tight containers." Again, the following list of medical supplies along with recommended reading on this and related subjects.

MEDICAL SUPPLIES
The most common injuries are cuts, sprains, bruises and fractures on hands, fingers, feet and toes.

First aid book
Bandaids
Butterfly bandages (3 sizes)
Bandages
Telfa gauze pads, 2" and 4"
Baking soda
Cotton slings
Tape, l" and 2"

Ace bandages, 2" and 4"
Safety pins
Snake bite kit
Sutures, 3-0 and 5-0
Scissors for bandages
Manicure scissors
Flashlight
Needles
Hemostat, mosquito size
Tongue depressors
Tweezers
Rubber gloves
Q-tips (cotton swabs)
Eye cup
Eye pads
Syringe
Catgut, 3-0
Oil of cloves
Tooth repair kit
Douche/enema bag
Nail brush
Muslin
Thermometer
Mirror
Hot water bottle
Medicine dropper
Ice pack
Magnifying glass
Moist towelettes
Cotton balls
Candle
Alcohol
Finger splints
Instant ice packs
Aloe
Charcoal tablets
Aspirin
Inhaler and guide
12 tissue salts

Castor oil
Iodine
Slippery elm lozenges
Linament
Lip balm
Ammonia wash
Massage oil
Eye drops
Insect repellent
Vaseline
Purified clay
Antiseptic soap
Epsom salts
Antibiotic ointments
Salt tablets
Zinc chloride
Halazone tabs
Ipecac
Iodine purification tabs
Sweet oil
Cider vinegar
Calamine lotion
Rock Rose
Scalpel blades (ll bard-parker and curved blade)
Antifungal, Desenex or Sopronol
Razor blade to shave hair

MEDICAL KITS

DENTAL EMERGENCY KIT
Dental aid Products
Box 1164
Rahway, New Jersey 07065
$19.95

FAMILY BLACK BAG
Health Activation Network
Box 923
Vienna, Virginia 22180
$91.59 pre-paid

TIMBERFALLERS FIRST AID KWIK KIT
Bailey's
Box 550
Laytonville, California 95454
Regular, $42.00 pre-paid
Mini, $28.00 pre-paid

Here is an additional list of books that will provide
sound medical practices and advice you can do on your
own. It includes information on children and childbirth.

How to Be Your Own Doctor, Sometimes, Keith
Sehnert, M.D.
Grosset & Dunlap, New York

Medical Self Care, ed. Tom Ferguson
Medical Self Care, California

Just in Case, John Moir
Chronicle Books, California

When There is No Doctor, David Werner
Hesperian Foundation, California

Medicines from the Earth, ed. William Thomson
McGraw-Hill Books, New York

How to Get Well, Paavo Sirola, N.D.

The Way of Herbs, Michael Tierra, C.A., N.D.
Unity Press

Care of the Dying, Richard Lamerton
Penguin Books, New Jersey

A Manual of Death Education and Simple Burial,
Ernest Moroon
Celo Press

A Cooperative Method of Natural Birth Control,
Margaret Nofziger
The Book Publishing Company, Tennessee

Emergency Childbirth, Gregory White, M.D.
Police Training Foundation, Franklin Park, Illinois

Childbirth Without Violence, Frederic LeBoyer

Spiritual Midwifery, Ina May Gaskin
The Book Publishing Company, Tennessee

Babysense, Frances Wells Burck
Simon & Schuster, New York

Well Baby Book, Mike Samuels, M.D.
Simon & Schuster, New York

Just to make sure you are ready for any emergency, the following "readiness" checklist might come in handy.

..-READINESS CHECKLIST..

DO YOU HAVE:

--- A first aid kit, and extra medication for family member who takes specific medication regularly?

--- A fire extinguisher?

--- A transistor radio and extra batteries? Do you know the emergency broadcast dial setting?

--- A flashlight and pair of shoes by each bed?

--- At least four gallons of water for each member

of the family?

--- Enough food stored for at least four days?

--- A charcoal grill and a bag of charcoal? (For outdoor use only.)

--- A supply of hygiene necessities?

--- An assortment of "paper supplies"? Water for washing may not be available.

--- Tools and useful items available? (Shovel, crowbar, axe, rope, wire, wire cutters, pails, tarps, can opener, etc.)

--- An extra pair of prescription glasses?

--- Sleeping bags or extra blankets?

--- Leashes and pet foods available for your pets?

--- A minimum supply of needs in the trunk of your car, plus a good book and games for the children, in case an earthquake or other blockage stalls you on the highway for several hours?

HAVE YOU DONE THE FOLLOWING:

--- Held an earthquake drill?

--- Read the Earthquake Safety Hotline packet completely?

--- Eliminated as many earthquake hazards as possible?

--- Made arrangements for a neighbor to care for

your children and/or pets in your absence?

--- Decided on three places family members can. meet if separated by an earthquake and unable to return home?

--- Taken a Red Cross First Aid Course and CPR Training?

--- Taught family members the location of main electric, water, and gas shut off valves, when to turn them off, and tools available?

--- Made an inventory of your possessions, including pictures for insurance purposes?

--- Put all valuable papers in a metal box?

--- Written telephone numbers of local police, fire, and ambulance services near the phone?

--- Made a list of key addresses and phone numbers for each member of the family?

--- Discussed what to take should you have to evacuate your home?

--- Selected an out of town relative or friend as your "family contact center"? Is that person's address and phone number known to all family members?

--- Discussed earthquake preparedness with a neighbor and developed a support plan with them?

--- Made your will? It could happen, but you will lessen the chances as you check off the above items.

In becoming more self-reliant, all areas need to be covered. Money is a part of that. If you are genuinely concerned about times of severe Earth changes or of an economical failure, you may choose to keep your money in Canadian banks, which will fail after the banks in the U.S. You could also convert your funds to junk silver that you can store, Keep in mind, however, that such attitudes, reinforced by action, can tend to create a sense of fear. Fear, in turn, can give you a distorted perception of your feelings of need and security financially. Being self-secure and prepared is quite different from being so out of fear which causes you to take unnecessary measures.

One important matter that concerns money and is applicable during safe and non-safe times, is bartering. More and more people are becoming involved with creating and participating in this form of providing goods and services that you cannot provide for yourself. It has worked in the past and it still does. You can make it work for you and it is also an excellent way to relieve your total dependence upon money.

There are several bartering companies in some cities but you can establish such a realtionship with your own circle of friends and acquaintences fairly easily. It is important to note that there are certain tax advantages to trading and good records should be kept for the IRS does consider your trading activities as income. Your personal behavior in this matter is yours to decide. Nonetheless, it is a true alternative to the system that presently exists. There are many "survivalists" who take a rather strong approach to their belief that the longevity of the present system is definitely questionable. Whether they are right or not, trading, whenever possible, makes both good economical and social sense. You will find in *The Bear Tribe's Self-Reliance Book* a "code of ethics" to follow when bartering, very much to your advantage to read and understand.

The prophecies of Albion and other seers discussed in

Chapter Five point to seismic activity as being one of the major phenomena to be expected. Many of you live in "earthquake country". It is a fact, as we have learned, that earthquake activity is on the increase, occurring in some areas of this country whose residents are all but totally uneducated to the event itself or how to deal with survival procedures should one occur. If you live in such an area, it is a good idea to familiarize yourself and those that live with you with these procedures.

Many cities and towns use an "attention or alert signal" on outdoor systems when threatened or impending natural emergencies happen. Learn your local warning signals. A 3-5 minute steady blast on sirens, horns or whistles is the most common. It is an indication that you should turn to the local radio (hopefully you have one that is battery operated) for further instructions. Use the telephone (when possible) only to report damage from fire, flash floods or tornadoes. Keep the phone lines clear. Learn how to disconnect your water, electric and gas supplies. Since one of the most common results of an earthquake is fire, it is wise to keep basic firefighting equipment, such as an extinguisher. You can inquire at your local fire station as to how to handle preliminary fire control from both wood and chemical fires. Don't forget that well-stocked first aid kit, it could really come in handy.

A free pamphlet on the hazards of earthquakes and how to prepare for them, along with what to do during and after the quake, may be obtained by sending a self-addressed stamped envelope to:

The John A. Blume Earthquake Engineering Center
Department of Civil Engineering
Stanford University
Stanford, California 94305

If you wish to spend the necessary $4.50, you may call

(415) 858-0323, a 24-hour earthquake hotline, and order a "basic earthquake preparedness packet". It includes a booklet on protecting life and property from quake damage, along with advice to parents and preparedness games for children. It also includes Red Cross information on first aid, material on water storage and how to form a neighborhood cooperative for safety. Staffers are also willing to research your individual questions on earthquake readiness. Long distance inquiries can be addressed to:

EARTHQUAKE INFORMATION
P.O. Box 5847
Stanford, California 94305

In light of Albion's words about the "migrations", I feel it wise to help you to prepare for such an event. It is also information that you can pass along to others, especially young people, for Albion did feel the massive migrations would occur quite a few years yet into the future. This information is not only for "just in case" reasons, but it is also information that is just plain good to know. All of it can be used for hiking, wilderness camping, and other situations in which you must live off the land.

To begin with, food is not the ultimate priority in a survival situation. Water is. You can exist a month or longer without food but only a few days without water, Anything that walks, crawls, swims or flies can be eaten. This includes snakes, worms, ants, lizards, crickets, grasshoppers, frogs (no toads), termites, rodents, and birds. Life forms that have been killed on the road and are still warm and have liquid blood, can be a good source of fresh meat, fur and feathers. Also, surface fish in open water are good, especially white fish with fins and scales. Shellfish like crabs, clams, lobsters and mussels, and bottom fish like flounder and catfish are scavengers, so toxins will concentrate in their flesh at 100 times the concentration in the surrounding waters.

Remember the rule, if you wouldn't drink the water, don't eat the fish from that water.

Always take drinking water from a high point in the river's flow, but only after checking at least one-quarter of a mile upstream for latrines, pollution dumps, cattle lots or dead animals. Use caution to smell and taste the water before using it. If you are in doubt, boil the water for at least five minutes, then shake it back and forth between two containers so as to re-oxygenate it and so it won't taste flat. Chlorines, iodines or halazone tablets will also purify a questionable water source. With halazone, use one tablet to one pint of water and wait thirty minutes before drinking it. With chlorine, prepare one rounded teaspoon of chloride of lime to 8 quarts of water. Use this solution with one to one-hundred parts water, about a shot glass full to a gallon. Wait thirty minutes before using. Iodine tincture is used six drops to a quart of clear water and wait thirty minutes. Iodine purification tablets are also available. You can purchase purifiers and they are available from pocket to home size. Most of them depend on a replaceable carbon cartridge.

Springs are preferred when there are flash floods or runoffs for less pollution is likely. However, don't trust the water just because it is clear. It's best and safest to purify it. Even a small dribble of a springs can provide upwards of 500 gallons of water a day when sent through a 1/2" pipe down a 100' grade of one foot. Never drink from a watering place or where no green plants are thriving.

To catch the dew as a water source, put a cloth, such as a blanket, out away from plants at night. In the morning, wring it out into a container. Small cloths may be raked through dewey grass and leaves until soaked.

Rain can also be collected on roof tops by gutters and barrels. A plastic tarp can be laid inside a shallowly dug indentation in the soil to pool water. One inch of rain over a ten square foot tarp will collect fifty gallons.

The next lists, one of survival clothing, the other of

things to put in a survival pack, are very important.

SURVIVAL CLOTHING

Hiking, work or leather topped rubber boots.
 Optional: high topped sneakers or snow boots.
Boot wax.
Two to three pairs of loose wool socks.
Open net underwear (for insulation).
 Windbreaker
 Plastic/nylon poncho
 Lightweight wool pants and shirts (cotton in
 tropics only)
 Light down or thinsulate jacket
 Gloves and mitts
 Hat
 Scarf/handkerchief
 Underwear

SURVIVAL PACK LIST
(Pack should not weigh over 35 pounds)
Candles
Canteen
Zip-lock bags
Magnifying lens
1' Square foam pad, 1/4" thick
Metal match
2 compasses (pin one to clothing)
Paper and pen
Watch
Binoculars
Glasses or contact lenses
Duct tape
Bandages
Non-stick gauze pads
Sewing kit with darning tool
Square rubber and rubber cement
Plastic tape

File
Map of area
Mirror
Sleeping bag
Ensolite pad
Cocoon tent
Hudson Bay ax
Can opener
Insect repellent
Snake bite kit
Whistle
2 screwdrivers
Walle-Hanke tool
Kleenex
Scissors
Coil of light wire
Rawhide lacing
Tweezers
All-purpose adhesive
First aid kit
Pliers
Soap
2 Metal (waterproof and unbreakable) containers of matches (pin one inside clothes)
12" sheathed knife with carborundum stone
2 sheets plastic, 6' and 10' square
Halazone tablets or iodine for tropical areas
Swede lightweight saw blade (ribbon thin steel) with tube steel handle
Fishing outfit (6 hooks, sinker, few yards tough line, float)
Length of rope, 3/8" manila, or few yards of nylon cord
Cook pot and deepside fry pan with lid or nested set of pans
Toilet kit (toothbrush, dentifrice, comb, razor, dental floss)

First aid kit (no liquids)

       Lomotil, 2½ mg tablets for diarrhea
       Sulfasuxidine, to sterilize intestinal bacteria
       Pyrrdum, urinary anethesia
       Empirin
       Compazine, vomiting, cramps
       Penicillin, for infection
       Butyn Opthaline Ointment, eye anesthetic
       Neosporin Opthaline, prevent eye infection
       Sutures, four 3-0, two 5-0
       Hemostat
       Tweezers
       Butterfly Bandaids
       Bandaids
       Soap
       Non-stick gauze
       Tape
       Zinc oxide
       Salt

30 ounces Pilot bread
16 ounces butter
14½ ounces strawberry jam
12 ounces Klik food
14 ounces condensed milk
10½ ounces chocolate bars
28 tea bags
50 vitamin/mineral tablets

Survival cards, composed of info-packed lists on shelter, water, orienting, plants, first aid and the like, may be obtained for $3.00 from:

Survival cards
Box 1805
Bloomington, IN 47401

The following is a list of recommended reading. Each book has been selected because of the excellent treatment of the subject matter involved.

Survival with Style,
Bradford Angler
Vintage Books, (Div. of Random House), New York

Outdoor Survival Skills,
Larry Dean Olsen
Pocket Books, New York

Basic Orienteering,
Michael Riley and Robert Cremet
Contemporary Books, Inc., IL

A Field Guide to Atmosphere,
Vincent Schaefer and John Day
Houghton Mifflin Co., MA

Survival Scrapbook –2, Food,
Stephen Szczelkun
Schocken Books

Wilderness Doctor,
E. Russell Kodet, M.D. and Bradford Angler
Stackpole Books

Advanced First-Aid for All Outdoors,
Peter Eastman,M.D.
Conell Maritime Press, MD

Wild Plants in the City (NE U.S.A.),
Nancy Page and Richard Weaver, M.D.
New York Times Books, NY

Survival Guns,
Mel Tappan
Janus Press, OR

Starvation is not an easy death nor a necessary one. We must be willing to give up our ethnic, regional and emotional food prejudices in survival situations. Albion has spoken of the unwillingness to change and how destructive it can be. Don't look at any food as "beneath" your social station. The possum, squirrel and wild meat diets may be considered as undesirable main courses right now, but may well be a banquet in survival conditions. Also, we must not be fastidious. Our finicky eating habits are repelled by the Polynesians' eating of raw fish, yet we eat raw oysters! Aged fish is considered a delicacy by the Eskimos.

It is also very wise to know what species of plants in the wild are edible and which are not. I'm not including any identification of wild plants, as the wide distribution of this book could not cover all the bio-regions needed to make such a list comprehensive. Many good books are available for this purpose. Here are a few:

Edible and Poisonous Plants of the Eastern U.S.
Edible and Poisonous Plants of the Western U.S.

52 cards (each identifies a plant)
$5.95 postpaid from:

> **Plant Deck**
> 2134 SW Wembley Park Roak
> Lake Oswego, OR 97034

A Field Guide to Edible Wild Plants of East and Central North America
Lee Peterson

Western Edible Plants,
H. D. Harington
University of New Mexico Press

The following is a test for plant edibility:

TEST FOR PLANT EDIBILITY

1. Avoid unknown plants that are brightly colored.

2. Many, but not all, poisonous plants have milky sap.

3. Eat no fungus, mushrooms, toadstools, PERIOD.

4. Put small test piece inside lower lip for 5 minutes.

5. If there is no burning, bitterness, soapy taste after 5 minutes, swallow.

6. Wait at least 2 hours, best to wait 10 hours.

7. Increase amount gradually for 24 hours.

8. If no bad effects after one day, plant is safe.

Wild plants rarely cause fatal poisoning.

Grass, ferns, inner tree bark, algae, seaweeds can all be eaten.

Next is a brief description on building different types of shelters. Each is designed to serve a specific purpose, under various circumstances. First, the bough bed. This is designed, of course, for good weather. A bed of young, thickly needled stand of spruce, fir or pine can be made with bare hands, although a knife or ax will speed the

334

job. Overlap layers of branches and needles toward the bottom of the bed. Continue overlapping until the bed is 1" thick. This type of bed is good for a few nights before it needs replenishing.

A shelter that you can live in a lot longer than the bough bed is the "lean-to". It should be a bit longer than your body and tall enough so you can sit up at its open side. It can also be tall enough to stand in if you plan to use it more than a few nights. If you slant the roof at 45 degrees, it is a good compromise between water protection from weather and space available inside. The open side should be away from the prevailing winds. This also offers good protection in canyons and other areas where the air currents change from day to night. Prevailing wind can be determined by observing fallen dead trees and by the slant of the live ones.

The lean-to can be erected using the plastic tarp in your kit or by using natural materials. Cut a thin sapling about 8' to 9' long so that they can be suspended between trees or mounted on y-shaped logs four feet above the ground. Slant the trimmed saplings at a 45 degree angle onto the ridgepole. Cross the angled poles. This forms your frame.

Next, cover the frame with thickly-placed needle boughs, hooking them onto the frame, beginning at the bottom support. Shingle the layers at least 6 to 10" thick. Build your bough bed inside. You can build your campfire the length of the opening and lay your firewood at one end of the lean-to for easy refueling during the night.

In bad weather conditions, use your plastic top over the boughs. Then, add a few more boughs over the plastic. This will protect against wind-driven rain or melting snow. Remember, moss, bark, grass and the like can also be used a insulation and protection. You will be wise to look for safe, over-hanging ledges or rocks created during high water at the bends of rivers and streams. Caves should also be checked carefully for animals by throwing rocks into them and then backing off so any animals that may be inside can get away.

Then there is the "cocoon" tent, which is available in most pre-packed survival kits. It is just a tube of plastic to protect you in inclement weather. This, along with a 4' x 8' sheet of plastic will provide all the protection you need in most circumstances.

Finally, a shelter can be built by burrowing into deep, firm snow at a cross angle to the wind to prevent drifts from covering your opening. Even a trench dug into snow will block some chilling wind. Never sleep or sit directly on snow. The melting will wet your clothing, a big danger in freezing weather. Use bark or sit on a bough bed to separate you and the snow. If you are in an extremely hot and arid zone, a trench dug in the desert will keep you cool. It will reduce temperatures as much as 50 degrees.

When you are out in the wild, telling time and finding direction is an important and life-saving skill. We all exist, man and animal alike, on a clock, a clock that pulses to the beat of the various kingdoms. Ignorance of these natural rythms is dangerous for it causes a misalignment, thus less of an opportunity for survival and adjustment. Direction finding is equally important.

If you don't already have a compass, here are some tips on buying one. It is a good idea to get one that has illuminated dial and needle. A magnetized needle in metal housing won't do. Consideration for waterproofing and other damage is important. The most practical ones seem to be the Silva-type or Orienteering, made by Silva and Suunto. Remember, the longer the needle, the greater the accuracy. A damped (liquid filled) compass is best for being hand held. Also, again, with the needle, the best are mounted in a synthetic sapphire or ruby to reduce friction. While out, keep one pinned to your clothes and the other in your survival pack.

There are some rules you should follow in regards to your compass.

1.   Keep compass away from iron and steel objects.

2. Never use a flashlight close to the compass.
3. Don't store near a power source or another compass.
4. Don't buy a compass from a stack of them. They may never have reversed polarity.
5. Don't store in glove box of the car. It will be affected by the electronic ignition.

The compass circle is divided into 360°. It is numbered clockwise, beginning with 0° North. A quarter of the way around at 90° is East. Each cardinal point (N, E, S, W) is 90° apart. South, then, is 180°, West is 270°. Halfway between cardinal points, 0° North and 90° East is 45° northeast. So, 135° is southeast, 225° is southwest, and 315° is northwest.

There is true north and "magnetic" north. The magnetic north pole is 1400 miles from the geologic north pole in the Northern Passage above the Hudson Bay. We must make correction between the two norths, as we want true North. The compass needle points to magnetic north "drifts". The allowance between true and magnetic north is generally marked on local maps. You can find the local difference by marking on the ground true north at night, as found by Polaris, the North Star. In the morning, compare true north with your compass north. The number of degrees difference indicates the local magnetic variation. So, the compass may show north as 10° east of the line marked on the ground. Then, true north is not where the needle indicates, but 10° to the right of the needle. An error of 1° equals 92 feet for each mile travelled.

The North Star, Polaris, is in the constellation called the Little Dipper, Polaris is actually 1° from the celestial North Pole. This is the major direction finder. First, find the Big Dipper. It is quite obvious in the Northern sky, except in the summer, when it is low on the horizon. The two stars on the outer bowl of the "dipper" point to the Pole Star. A line between the two stars on the side of

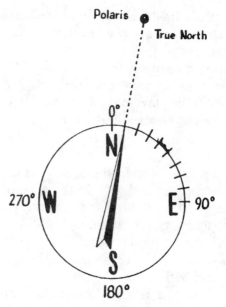

True North Vs. Magnetic North

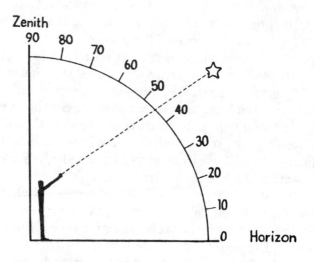

Measuring Degrees of Asimuth

338

the bowl farthest from the handle, extended five times the distance between the two stars, ends at the North Star. There are no bright stars in between. The pointers are 5° apart, about half the width of your fist held at arm's length. If it is summer, when the Dipper is not easily seen, especially when there are northern mountains, you will need to find the Casseopia constellation. It is equidistant from Polaris on the opposite side and appears as a poorly formed "M" or "W". Also, Polaris will appear at the height in the sky that is within one degree of latitude. In other words, if the star Polaris appears at 45°, or halfway up the sky between the horizon and your zenith (straight overhead), then you are at 45° latitude.

To measure degrees of azimuth, or height, hold your fist out at arm's length, with the base of the fist on the horizon. Each fist-width is equal to 10° of arc in the sky. So, if Polaris is 4 1/2 fists up in the sky, it is at 45°.

To use the Sun to find direction is also a very important skill. The Sun rises exactly due East and sets exactly due West only two days a year. They are the first day of Spring, March 21st, and the first day of Fall, September 23rd. These are the only days when both day and night are twelve hours long. Between March 21st and June 21st, the Summer Solstice, the nights are shorter. June 21st, the first of summer, the longest day of the year, is fifteen hours, the night nine hours. The Sun then, is 23 1/2° North of East and appears to move back South as the days shorten back to twelve hours on the Autumnal Equinox on September 23rd. Then, the Sun appears to move South coming to 23 1/2° South of East on December 21st, the Winter Solstice, shortest day of the year. The day is nine hours, the night is fifteen.

At dawn, North is to the left of the rising Sun. At sunset, North is to the right of the setting sun. Your latitude determines whether the Sun is North or South of your midday. If you are North of 23.4°, the Sun will be South at noon local time. It will be north at midday if you are South of 23.4° latitude. Learn your latitude.

You can do so by calling your local airport or Chamber of Commerce.

You can also find your direction by shadows. Any sun or moonlight that is strong enough to cast a shadow will, with the aid of a pole or stick, point the way for you. Push a short stick into the ground. Check its vertical accuracy by holding a weighted string plumb. Loop a string or vine around the stick's base. Mark the current shadow at the tip. With taut line, circumscribe a circle the diameter of the shadow. The shadow will shorten as noon approaches. As the shadow lengthens in the afternoon, mark when the shadow crosses the circle again. A line halfway between the two shadow marks and the pole will run North.

Finding Your Directions by Using Shadows

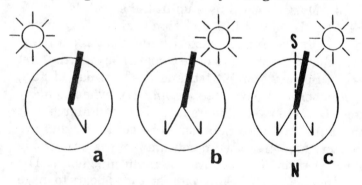

a *Push a stick vertically into the ground. Loop string or wire around stick's base. Mark current shadow at tip. With taut line, draw a circle, the diameter, that of the shadow.*

b *The shadow will shorten as noon approaches. As the shadow lengthens in the afternoon, mark when the shadow crosses the circle again.*

c *A line half way between the two shadow marks and the pole will run north.*

Now, let's consider star navigation. Used by sailors on the high seas, this is good information to know. Stars move East to West, like the Sun and Moon. You can sight them over two different length sticks plumbed straight into the ground.

Star Navigation

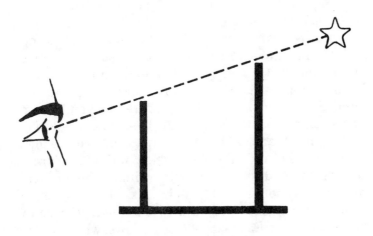

Line up a star with two stick tops. Within a few minutes, you will see the star drift off the line of sight. If the star is falling, it is west of you. If it is looping flatly to your right, you are facing south. If the star is rising, you are headed east and, finally, if the star is flat to your left, your are facing north.

Line up a star with the two stick tops. Within a few minutes, you will see the star drift off the line of sight. If the star is falling, it is West of you. If it is looping flatly to your right, you are facing south. If the star is rising, you are headed East and, finally, if the star is flat to your left, you are facing North. You might want to mark your North direction to use when morning comes.

Nature is also a helpful "way shower". The following signs can be of great advantage to you.For example, moss does grow thickest on the North side of a tree, if it is in the open sun. But, remember, other lichens and moss-like growths can grow on the sunniest side. Next, cut tree stumps have wider rings on the sunny or, most often, the South side. Using trees again, pines and hemlock tops point East unless there is a prevailing wind. Softwoods such as pines, spruce and hemlock are fullest on the South side. Poplar tree bark is white on the South side and dark on the North side. A couple more hints are that ant hills are on the South side of trees, while goldenrods point to North. Animals and birds can also be of help in pathfinding skills. A pileated woodpecker digs on the East side of a tree. Flying squirrels nest on the East side of tree hollows, while spiders erect their webs on the South side in the Sun. Water birds such as ducks, geese and so forth, prefer the West side of a lake for breeding, as do frogs and fish.

A helpful gadget you may wish to purchase is a planisphere. It shows the directions and the stars in this hemisphere. They, as a rule, are less than $5.00 in cost and may be purchased mail order, from the Astromedia Corporation, Order Department, Box 92788, Milwaukee, Wisconsin, 15320. Navigational Maps are another inexpensive aid. The following is a list of places you can obtain such maps.

Sectional Maps—Superintendent of Documents
U.S. Government Printing Office
Washington, D. C. 20402

U. S. Geological Survey (East of Mississippi)
Map Information Office
Washington, D. C. 20242
(best are contour maps, also topographic maps
and aerial photos)

U. S. Geological Survey (West of Mississippi, including
Minnesota and Louisiana)
Federal Building
Denver, Colorado 80225

U. S. Geological Survey (Alaska)
310 First Avenue
Fairbanks, Alaska 99701

Library of Congress Publications in Print—free,
available from:

Secretary of the Library
Library of Congress
First Street and Independence Avenue SE
Washington, D. C. 20540
Catalog, priced and free maps

When out in the wild, you will undoubtedly be using
fire. Proper use is a must! You must respect its
capabilities and its negative qualities. It is the biggest
destroyer of animal and plant life. Here are some important safety rules to follow. It is best to use established pits when they are available. Don't scar the Earth
Mother any further when it can be avoided. When you
must, scrape the top soil away to replace later or build
your fire on top of a large rock. Clear away all nearby
debris. Fire can burn underground in the rich humus,
so putting out a fire sufficiently is much more important than starting it. Carry kindling with you when hiking. Even a few dry sticks can be a blessing in wet areas.
Keep several stashes of safety matches in metal containers in your jacket or clothing or car. Be sure they

are protected from moisture. Ring your fire with rocks or between large logs for safety. Trench fires can be made in a long hole, lined with stones. This is a good way to support pots or other utensils.

Sleeping fires should be as long as your body. Put a log behind you to reflect the heat back to you. Don't build large bonfires, except for rescue purposes. They are dangerous and waste our tree "brothers". Also, never leave a fire unattended.

Fires can be started in many ways. Matches, a piece of glass such as a binocular lens, flint or steel, a couple of iron pyrite rocks (fool's gold), a magnifier, or the bow and drill technique which can be found in all survival books. Remember, don't ring your fire with stones from a stream bed. Water trapped in the stones can cause them to explode.

You can be a survivalist. Unfortunately, there are many groups around that call themselves "survivalists" that feel that guns and violence are the best insurance one can have. Such attitudes have their pro's and con's, but they need to be considered carefully. It is a common misconception that gun-carrying crowds will descend on those who have stored food. First of all, hungry people are lethargic. A hungry person or crowd will not walk for miles and miles to search out remotely located homesteads. There is more concern in the cities, where food will run out in a few days. Secondly, during World War II, many Mormons, especially in the south of France, had food stores. They were not raided. Protecting your stash is not among your greatest concerns, so handguns are useless as survival weapons. They are not worth their weight and bulk if there is any choice. If you must have a gun, a rifle is superior to a shotgun. Shotguns require bulky ammunition and are good only for small prey. A flat, rugged, repeating shooter for big game is best, such as a rifle with a small telescopic sight. A .22 is good for an area where there is only small game. Why not just avoid guns and carry a big sling. David didn't do too bad with it!

The following list has been selected to provide you with places you can order or purchase good survival equipment.

EQUIPMENT

The Next Whole Earth Catalog, ed. Stephen Brand
Point, California

Gear

Stephenson Warmlite
RFD 4, Box 145
Gilford, New Hampshire 03246
Catalog: $3.00

Eastern Mountain Sports
Vose Farm Road
Petersborough, New Hampshire 03458
Free catalog

Early Winters
110 Prefontaine Place South
Seattle, Washington 98104

Clothing
L. L. Bean
Freeport, ME 04032
Free catalog

C. C. Filson Company
205 Maritime Building
Seattle, Washington 98104

Fishing and Hunting

Orvis Company
Manchester, Vermont
Free catalog

Edmund Scientific Catalog
101-E Gloucester Pike
Barrington, New Jersey 08007
Catalog: $1.00

This next list is a collection of New Age magazines and periodicals, each containing articles and helpful hints on survival in these times of change.

MAGAZINES AND PERIODICALS

CoEvolution Quarterly,
Point
Box 428
Sausalito, California 94966
$14.00 per year

Science News,
Science Service, Inc. (subscriptions)
321 West Center Street
Marion, Ohio 43302
$19.50 per year

Organic Gardening,
Rodale Press
33 East Minor Street
Emmaus, Pennsylvania 18049
$10.00 per year

Small Farmers Journal
Box 197
Junction City, Oregon 97448
$12.50 per year (4 issues)

NewShelter,
Rodale Press
33 East Minor Street
Emmaus, Pennsylvania 18049
$10.00 per year (9 issues)

Medical Self-Care
Box 717
Inverness, California 94937
$15.00 per year (4 issues)

Prevention,
Rodale Press
33 East Minor Street
Emmaus, Pennsylvania 18049
$10.00 per year (12 issues)

In conclusion, times are changing. These survival techniques and suggestions are purely for the purpose of giving you the information necessary to carry you through safely should the changes become severe in your lifetime. That is all. It is not my purpose nor intention to frighten you or stir up controversy as being a "doomsdayer". There is a definite pattern of things to come, as foretold in the prophecies, and we can see evidence of the same all around us. I think that it is important to keep in mind that prophecy is to instruct and to warn. Entering into the New Age will eventually be recognized. We all look forward to a time of peace and brotherhood. But, if the Earth must go through a "cleansing" period before becoming a Third Degree Initiate, so be it. We can survive the Transition. We can learn from it. It can serve to make us a better and stronger people.

We can also realize that many of the prophecies are a result of mankind's misuse of the land and technology. We can begin to do our part. We can care for and cultivate the soil. We can save precious water. We can take positive action to grow into a higher consciousness. We can use our technologies more intelligently. The technological treasures we have and will have in the future, can be put to positive use. We can come into harmony with the Earth Mother. We can transform ourselves and help to transform the planet. We can survive.

"Walk in Balance on the Earth Mother."

Sun Bear

Chapter Seven

WALKING IN BALANCE

"We, the religious leaders and rightful spokesmen for the Hopi Independent Nation, have been instructed by the Great Spirit to express the invitation to the President of the United States and all spiritual leaders everywhere to meet with us and discuss the welfare of mankind so that Peace, Unity, and Brotherhood will become part of men everywhere."

Thomas Banyacya
Mrs. Mina Lansa
Claude Kayangyakkewa
Dan Katchongua

So far, this book has been devoted to "change". The moment of creation starts the "change syndrome" and time perpetuates it. The issue now is to decide how we can best flow with time and changes that it brings. Whether those changes are major or minor in their affect, we need to learn to deal with them in a more intelligent manner. Survival is not just a matter of physical concern. It is, an emotional and mental and spiritual one, as well. Albion has stressed this over and over again. The following is an example of his words: "We find that man's emotions tend to propel him, in terms of his relationship to time, into a positive direction . . . . one of progress and growth and balance, as well as one that is free from fear. Time, in its negative connotations, creates fear, as well as depression, anxiety, worry, and grief. That's right. All of these negative emotions are the result of a poor understanding and relationship with Time."

We can learn a lot about Time from the Hopi, for they have a different perspective from ourselves. Their view is truly a psychological one. They do not see time as a motion, such as in past, present and future. It is duration. Madame Blavatsky, in her writings, also refers to Time in this manner, saying that the only true definition of Time is duration. We don't always see it that way. Physically, Time is a process of living. It becomes a "method" of or a "Vehicle" within which we exist. Emotionally, we find that it becomes a matter of *how* we relate to Time as to how it affects us individually. Mentally, Time has not so much of an effect, but rather is viewed purely as the "space" in which we might accomplish, learn, and thus grow. It is also taken for granted in many ways. Spiritually, Time as an "entity" ceases to be. It becomes a nebulous concept that is a part of the reality of dimension and Being. Time begins and ends on this level.

So, you see, Time is an "entity" unto itself. It is a force that manifests itself throughout the objective universe. it is also an energy, for it comes from and is built into each cell that comprises form. No matter what kingdom, it encompasses movement and cycles of motion.

Albion continued: "Security. What does this word really represent to you? This is a very important question and your approach to it is more important now than ever before in your life span. Is security purely a material matter? Is it emotional balance? Security is peace of mind, some might say. I, Albion, suggest that true security only comes with a clear understanding of your place and role in the universe. To achieve such a level of security is a life-long — on going process. To be aware of this as the task is half the battle, so to speak."

"As the earth changes begin, there are certain reactions, based upon what we have just explained, that will make security even more important and realistic. The ultimate resource for solving the crisis of the future is yourself. Survival depends on you! Never before has your relationship with the planet and all the other kingdoms of life, been so intricately involved, which will determine the survival of both. A balance between man, life forms and the planet...this is the key. In balance, they will all survive and grow into Light. Remember, everything in the Cosmos moves to a rhythm and that rhythm has to be maintained. But, it cannot be so unless it is truly understood. Understanding is the responsibility of each one of us. Every type of conflict that exists is the result of the lack of accepting this responsibility on some level of Being. Think about this very carefully."

"Now it is the Earth that is about to go through major changes. It is the responsibility of all life forms to be aware of these changes as they unfold. When this is so, your degree of perception will expand and grow. This is a major step towards true security."

Physical survival has already been considered and dealt with in depth. This final chapter is designed to give you, the reader, a better understanding of emotional, mental and spiritual survival. These are the more subtle levels of our consciousness, but just as important. They must work together with the physical body for us to remain whole. Survival of the body is not very appealing if we stop to consider that it would only be an "empty shell" if our emotions, mind, and Spirit were not nourished as well.

Perhaps we can gain a better perspective of the different levels within ourselves if we consider a guideline that Albion has given. You will recall the three major types of energies that the vortices manifest themselves; the electric, electro-magnetic and magnetic. All through this writing we have been relating what we normally think of as "human" energies, chakras, and so forth, to the Earth. Now, we will once again, relate these energies back to a human. Let's turn once again to Albion's words.

"As we have said in the past that as these Earth changes evolve, different people will have different responses. There are two major factors that will play a role in determining that response. One is the geographical location in which one lives. The other is the type of "energy" the person is composed of in terms of their natural "Soul" frequency. We will explain. Some people are electrical in their nature. There are more with this frequency on the North American continent than anywhere else in the world, at this time, but they are found everywhere on the globe. Such individuals are capable of, by nature, transmitting a lot of electrical power, the power of will, progress, and movement (evolution). Electrical people will go into this period of change with just this sort of energy and impetus within their consciousness. They are the ones who will tend to take matters into their own hands. They are the pioneers of every Age. They will tend to organize groups and communities for survival."

"On the other hand, individuals who are magnetic in their nature, will approach and go through the earth change period by seeking to 'draw' energy unto themselves and to further 'ground' theirs and others' vibrations into a greater sense of balance. They are also found worldwide. Such people are in a closer attunement with the planet and can, therefore, be more aware of the planet's condition at various times. The one you call Sun Bear is one of these. They are also able to heal and balance the planet and their fellow human beings. They will be better "Planetary Caretakers" and they total the greatest in number."

"Finally, let us consider that there are those individuals who are electromagnetic in their nature. They comprise the smallest number of people on the planet, but they are very valuable to the Hierarchy, due to their greater degree of perspective in terms of the energies that exist and the interplay between those energies at

352

work. They help to provide a balance and they are composed of both electric and magnetic energies. When in balance with these forces, they display the best qualities of each. When out of balance, they will usually display one or the other qualities more prominently."

This was not the first time that the Teacher had made reference to these three categories in relationship to humans. In order to gain a better understanding of the three types, I have compiled a list of the various qualities of each from different sessions. Albion feels these energies determine not only our emotional behaviour to a large degree, but also the health of the body, as well as our egoic likes and dislikes. These "people types" also correspond with geographical areas and vibrations. The following is a general list of qualities:

ELECTRIC
Male (positive) energy
Fair or ruddy-like complexion
Freckled or body blotches likely
Extroverted
Self-expressive
Talkative
Pioneering Spirit
A generator of force (emitters)
Needs red meat or red food in the diet
Those who will bring in the New Age
Lives in "tomorrow"
Likes bright, strong colors
Strong constitution

Electric—too much (negative)
Aggressive
Manipulative
Hyperactive—speedy
High strung, nervous, edgy
Unsettled
Burns out easily
Hypertension prone

Electric health patterns
Hypertension
Heart palpitations
Elevated body temp
Prone to heat stroke
Strokes
Rashes
Complexion problems
Exhaustion of all types

MAGNETIC
Best as vegetarians
Dark hair and eyes
Olive or dark skin tones
Close to the Earth
Creative
Introverted
Receptive
Feminine qualities more prominent
Passive
Lives in "yesterday"
Often in jobs or hobbies to do with agriculture,
    real estate or receptive positions.
Supportive to others as a "Wayshower"
Dependent

Magnetic—too much (negative)
Lazy
Sleepy
Unresponsive
Apathetic
Laid back
Will stagnate

Magnetic health patterns
Inclined to put on weight
Digestive problems
Sluggishness
Poor circulation

Low blood
Arthritic conditions

ELECTROMAGNETIC
Smallest numbers on the planet
A stable blend of energies
Mixture of physical and emotional qualities
Creative manifestors
Pillars of strength
Androgenous
Diplomatic

Electromagnetic—too much (negative)
Tends to respond totally to one of the energy qualities
Frustration
Nervous tension
Lack of expression
Gentleness that masks a masculine strength
Ambitious and also dependent at the same time
Peace at any price

Electromagnetic health patterns
Prone to both mentioned with electric and
magnetic people

Based on Albion's categorizing humans into these three types, it makes me wonder how we may be affecting the planet due to the energy we emit. Relying once again on the wisdom of Madame Blavatsky, I recall a comment that she made concerning how magnetic currents develop themselves into electricity upon their exit from our bodies. Subsequently, this interplay of forces will show how unbalanced each of our human emanations could or probably does reach a point of tension that causes a violent reaction upon the Earth itself. Blavatsky felt that the "exploding" point would coincide with the changing of a Great Age or Cycle (marked by earth change period?) and would produce convulsions in the form of earthquakes, floods, fire and ice! Man's vibrations coupled with the gases and solids of the earth is an interesting perspective, indeed! We, as man, are definitely like dynamos of energy, making, storing, projecting, and attracting all the while. Could it be that there is such a resulting affect on the earth that could be so cataclysmic? It is a valuable thought. A lot of people believe that our vibrations, made up of our deeds and thoughts, can bring events to us according to our nature. In any respect, man is, so it would appear, a child of cyclic destiny and none of us can escape our mission of learning to cooperate with natural law.

Another important tool for living "in tune" with the Earth's natural cycles, was given by the Teacher. This information was channeled in the month of September of 1981 and concerns alignment of the various bodies of man with the seasons.

"We go now into the cycle of Autumn, the 'harvest.' It is a time when the seeds of activity that have been sown give their yield. You all sow seeds. They are in the form of new ideas, new relationships, new directions in life. Such seeds, if sown and cultivated properly, will now come to fruition. As you go into the winter, you will need to 'hibernate' in order to consider new projects and make plans for the future. It is a time of rest and withdrawal, a time to 'regroup' your energies. Watch carefully the opportunities that open up to you. You must use this time to re-evaluate your errors in judgment, your successes, your unfulfilled missions and the like. It is a time for planning life's strategies for the coming new cycle."

"Then will come Spring. The planet and all it's forms of life are renewed. It is the time for planting new seeds of thought and activity. New prana (life force) is abundant. It motivates and stimulates. It creates the 'fuel' for new growth, new strength. The Summer is a time for cultivation and caring for the new 'life seeds'. Don't begin new projects at this time, but perpetuate those you have already begun."

"Since 1975, there has been a steady stream of pure

Cosmic force released onto the planet and all of its life forms, by the Spiritual Hierarchy. It is designed to elevate the consciousness of both. It will help the Earth to get safely through its period of change and Initiation. It will enhance the evolution of consciousness. You will encounter more and more people in all areas of the world who are thirsting to discover and fulfill their missions in life. Many of them will find that that purpose is indeed tied into a role they must play in this period of Earth changes. Many of them have incarnated specifically to go through this period and some of them have gone through such periods in the ancient past and have come to guide others through this time, those who have never lived during such a period. Others have gone through periods of upheaval before and have not survived and thus have a 'karma' with the planet. Such souls have incarnated solely to go through it again, to survive and thus free themselves from bondage to the Earth. Remember, karma does not only affect and exist between humans, but a soul can also have karma with other kingdoms, as well as the planet itself. This is why it is so important to realize the importance, spiritually, of this period of time."

When we turn our thoughts towards accepting the validity of Albion's words, we each find ourselves more or less prepared to go through this time, than others. Albion says: "You are each on a different rung of the evolutionary ladder. You each have your own measure of knowledge and understanding of yourselves. Some of you may even have the advantage of 'remembering' lives in other times of earth upheaval. To some of you, such recall may equip you to survive this new change period, while it may cause others of you to be afraid. No matter where you are in evolution, you are all human, living in a fragile balance between life and death. You are all subject to the 'will to live'. You all have an astral body or emotional body and are full of feelings that you must learn to deal with successfully in order to grow. It is, perhaps, more difficult to some than others. It is certain that you are all endowed with the 'will to live'. All life forms will fight to survive, you can be sure. You all encounter life-threatening circumstances as you exist on the Earth. You all see evidence of the fight for survival amongst the other kingdoms. Doctors and nurses are full of stories of their withnessing patients that survive trauma and disease in the physical body, due to the sheer force of will. Such will must be a cooperative effort of all of the dimensions of your Being, working together for one goal...to live! I dare say that when the Earth changes, and all that accompanies that period begins, and becomes apparent enough, no teacher or informer would have too much trouble getting most people to comply with the physical survival techniques. Even those who may have scoffed at those of you who have seen the need to prepare ahead of time for this period, and have considered you as 'doomsdayers'. Perhaps the majority of these people will be able to survive physically, but will they have their other bodies as prepared and in balance? This is an important question, to be sure."

I think that in order to prepare ourselves, whether it be for this period of earth changes, or just for living a better life, we have to come into a greater understanding of our emotional bodies. We are tormented by them, and elated and made "whole" by them.

Our feelings change from moment to moment, constituting the fervor of life within us.

I am reminded of the words of well-known psychiatrist, Gerald Jampolsky, in his book *Love is Letting Go of Fear*. "There are better ways to get through life than to be drug through kicking and screaming!" I think that this presents to us a rather graphic picture of the way most of us seem to live our lives. We don't really seem to gain a true sense of balance with our emotions, especially those of a negative nature. I think we could all tend to handle joy and love much easier than we could pain and fear. We want things to go right for us, but we seem to not be willing enough, most of the time, to put in the needed effort it takes to truly understand our negative feelings, so we continue to be victims of our own lack of self-knowledge and understanding. This must change and the need for this change now, I believe, is greater than ever before.

While emotions are common to us all, perhaps the most common of all of the negative feelings we experience is fear. Fears come in all shapes and sizes, from many origins and causes. Although most of us tend to consider fear a totally negative response to some condition or circumstance, this is not completely true. Fears can be both constructive and destructive in their nature. Let's consider both of its aspects.

In his book, *Faces of Fear*, the late Hugh Lynn Cayce, famed author and lecturer, points out that fear of a constructive nature is quite valid and can indeed save our lives. As I read both the Edgar Cayce material and the literature available on fear, I very soon recognized that there were many usable, helpful fears. Some of them had preserved people throughout history. Cayce states that it had been important to learn to respect prowling tigers and other wild animals, as well as modern, speeding autos. Also, sometimes people are constrained from stealing and killing by fear of punishment. Certainly the fear of "what people will say" helps us discipline many of our crude, primitive tendencies. Cayce's thoughts do a quick and to the point job of showing us fear's positive qualities. We can readily expand upon his thoughts and think of other examples of constructive fears. But it is the common debilitating fears that cause us real harm. It is this type of fear we cannot afford, for it causes pain, stagnation and even death.

I think we would be hard pressed to come up with one fear that is the greatest and worst of them all. Some might say the fear of death, while others might say the fear of life! We have all met people who seem to be afraid of their own shadows. We are most familiar with fears that deal with loneliness, inadequacy, diseases, the dark, getting lost, and so forth. Some fears, such as those just mentioned are quite ominous, while others, such as that of public speaking, the opposite sex, flying, and the like, are more individualistic and not as common to such great numbers of people.

While the knowledge that fear is a deterrent from a meaningful and happy life, dealing with it can be a very different and difficult matter. It seems to rob us of our will power to deal successfully with that which we fear and this creates a "trap" that eventually leads us into a state of fearing the fear itself! Fear, thus, becomes an "entity". I think that the phenomenal insight of Edgar Cayce says it all: "Fear is the greatest drawback in the proper development of any well-balanced, normal individual." This gets right to the soul of the matter. Also, a very important thing to keep in mind, is that fear takes a lot of valuable energy. It wastes energy and drains us of strength that could be put to much more constructive uses.

While we can and should examine our individual fears and try to seek a proper course of action to dispel them, it is important to recognize that this may be more critical a task now than before, due to the upcoming economic, religious, political, and planetary changes that we face. It has been said that to be more aware of the future, being able to read the "signs", leads us into a greater understanding of Nature. Understanding definitely dispels fear. I have found that some people are against the knowledge of earth changes. They don't want to hear it! Some even ridicule the prophecies and I think that much of this is due to fear. So, how to deal with fear in regards to the cycle of change we approach is a most important question. How can we get the emotions and the body working together?

First of all, I think we have to be informed. We can all read the prophecies and thereby glean from them the warnings of future upheaval. We can judge for ourselves, through the vehicle of our intuition, those that seem to apply to our present times and our own individual circumstances the most. "Feel" the prophecy.

360

Not all prophets and their predictions are accurate. Check the number of sources, the repetition involved. I think that a true future event will be revealed through many "sources". How long a time has the prophecy been around? Does it conform to all the laws of physical science? Remember, natural phenomena must obey natural laws. While many prophecies such as those in the Bible and those of Nostradamus are relayed in symbolic language, the symbols can usually be easily related to the corresponding physical phenomena. "The Moon turning to blood", as stated in the Book of Relevation in the Bible could refer to the coloration caused by accumulated volcanic dust in the atmosphere. A "mountain" tumbling end over end in the sky, plumetting to the earth,stated by Nostradamus, could refer to a large meteorite or even a small to medium-sized comet or asteroid. We don't have to be afraid to reason out the predictions and try to determine their probability. In fact, it's just good common sense to do so.

It's also wise to weigh the prophecy, whenever possible, against the present and available scientific data and research. Though most people who believe in the validity of prophecy and those that are members of or in the same space as the scientific community are different, the two can work together. I have shown in this book how much scientific data exists so far that does seem to support, surely without intention, many of the earth change predictions. Aside from gaining supportive or non-supportive information concerning the prophecies, much valuable information can be gained from such research that is of benefit to you in many other ways and areas of your life. Knowledge of climate, seismic activity and the like, educates us to our own advantage. There are excellent periodicals and magazines that provide good sources of information on a broad variety of scientific subjects and are written in laymen's language. I would particularly recommend the following: *Science News* and *Science Digest*. Each of these give up-to-date news and articles on various subjects and some even deal indirectly with the prophecies, especially in *Science Digest*. Pay close attention to new data on the earth sciences, climate, erosion, and technology. Ecology is also of special interest, in regards to the fact that many of the predictions, such as those of the Hopi, suggest that the planetary changes will be brought on, or at least affected by man's own activities and his lack of care of the Earth.

There are also organizations, some of them worldwide, that have the ecology of the planet as their main focus. Perhaps some of you will be so moved as to wish to join or look further into the premises of these types of organizations and committees. Some of them have taken on special interest projects which they feel endanger the Earth's balance and threaten its and our future survival. Some of these groups are very politically oriented, while others are not. It does seem, however, that the one thing that they all have in common is the preservation and concern of the Earth and its natural resources. I have compiled a list of some groups for your information, should you care to pursue this matter further, for purposes of information and possible involvement.

Friends of the Earth
124 Spear Street
San Francisco, California 94105

Greenpeace USA
240 Ft. Mason Bldg. E
San Francisco, California 94123

The Cousteau Society
Box 2002 Grand Central Station
New York, New York 10017

Sierra Club
530 Bush Street
San Francisco, California 94108

This list is by no means complete but it is a start. Some of these groups put out newsletters but they do require a subscription. So, check for free information first.

Next there is the matter of where you live. Do you live in an area that is high in unemployment and apt to be one that will suffer especially badly during a time of economic change and difficulty? Can you grow your own food? How much storage space do you have? How obligated are you to be where you are? Do you live where you do because you have to or because you want to? How free are you to move? Is your area earthquake prone? Is it in a severe or rapidly changing climate belt? Is it flood or drought prone? I think that all of these are valid questions. Should you determine the same is true, it may be a good idea to change or consider changing your residence to a more safe and/or desirable place. Never make a panic move! Never make a move based totally on the advice of someone else. This is a decision that only you should make, and only then after careful thought and planning. Panic moving is like panic buying. It is based on fear, as a rule, and could cause some geographical areas to become over populated and thus dangerous. Keep in mind that the Earth is big! There are more safe places than unsafe places to live. Also, becoming more self-reliant from the economical system cannot hurt anything. These are already hard times for many of us financially and being more self-sufficient can help us save money.

Since many of the prophecies have to do with problems in the cities, it will be to your advantage, should you care to leave a city, but don't yet have land to settle on, to be aware of the established communities, many of which are teaching how to live in a more self-reliant way and in a greater balance with the planet. You don't have to become a permanent resident of such communities or tribes, but they do provide an alternative life style. The following is one such community that you may wish to check into for further information and guidance:

363

The Bear Tribe Medicine Society
P.O. Box 9167
Spokane, Washington 99209

For those that feel a move is out of the question for whatever the reason, I recommend your learning all you can about a more self-sufficient lifestyle and how it can be applied to city living or in other special circumstances that might apply to you. Such information can best be obtained from the kind of material that I have listed below. You may know of others.

All of these suggestions are designed not only to inform you about a more safe and balanced way of living, but also to make you realize that knowledge produces understanding and understanding reduces our fear. Fearing anything is said to attract it to us, whatever "it" may be. If this is so, we have an even better reason for wanting to face this difficult period in a realistic way.

Another point, albeit a simple but helpful one, that can keep us informed of what is taking place around us, is to keep up with the news. I find that reading newspapers and tabloids is very beneficial for my purposes, as they do contain a broader range of geological, ecological and economical finepoints. A disaster has to have already occurred, or certainly be highly likely, before it will be discussed or broadcast on radio or television news. A daily newspaper is a good source for additional information, and so are some of the national tabloids. Although most of the tabloid publications deal with celebrity gossip and stories of human misery, there is quite a bit of information and news given in them concerning predictions of both a psychic and scientific nature, especially if the latter is sensational enough. As an example, I found some rather interesting data in the *National Star* early in 1982. The headlines spoke of a "giant comet" that is hurtling towards our planet. The object in question is known as the Swift-Tuttle comet, and it is said to be passing "uncomfortably" close to the Earth, sometime soon.

Astronomer John Bortle, a comet specialist, who has his own observatory in Stormville, New York, while not well known as a public figure, has won a NASA medal for his work, along with having his research papers published in scientific journals. He also authors a regular column for *Sky and Telescope*, a magazine, which makes his opinion valuable to a lot of qualified people. If such a comet as the Swift-Tuttle did hit the earth, it would cause major damage to the tune of 100 of the most powerful atomic bombs exploding! The article also indicated that, and rightfully so, all the experts do not agree with Bortle's theory that the earth is in any real danger. I found this information valuable to know, in light of many of the prophecies, including one of Albion's that indicates that such an event will occur. If nothing else, it gives evidence from the scientific community that such an event is possible, if not probable. Another short blurb in a science magazine is the source of my knowing that NASA has formed a committee to watch the skies and calculations for such events in the future that would endanger the earth and its populace from being struck by other celestial visitors. It is worth the few minutes each day that it takes to be well informed, as an informed person is apt to, while respecting the dangers, not fall into the unrealistic world of fear fantasy!

It is hoped that as we learn to deal with any fear of earth changes and their possible consequences that we may have to encounter, it can prompt the discipline that is necessary to successfully deal with other fears that may plague us. The result can be a fear-free life and that is the goal of us all.

Violence is another strong emotion that has to be reckoned with. Perhaps born out of the fears we have, we definitely live in a world in which violence is more common and less controllable than I can ever remember in my lifetime. The news is full of horror stories every day, which is why a lot of us have shied away from being "informed". The worse the economy gets, the more violence. Studies have revealed the role that climate plays in human behavior and with the severe winters and summer heat waves of the past few years, violence and the fear of violence grows. In regards to general and society-type earth changes, there are many "survival" groups that have sprung up all over this country. I am not aware if such groups exist in other lands. Some of them are being led and taught by ex-military personnel. They promote the use of firearms and war-like maneuvers in order to protect your land and possessions from intruders and poachers. This is not exactly my idea of approaching this difficult period without promoting fear. If anything, it would seem to encourage violence and separateness at a time when both should be set aside. I am sure that not all groups who teach the use of firearms are being led by dangerous people and warmongers. But it would behoove the searcher to check the motives of this type of group and their practices out very carefully before you get involved. Know exactly what you may be getting into.

Some of the various earth change prophecies seem to indicate a type of disaster that is very prominently on our minds today. As I have said, the Hopi predictions of the events leading up to the Great Day of Purification, some of the predictions of Nostradamus, the Bible and other, more modern prophets and seers, seem to suggest a sort of cataclysm that is man-made, rather than due to any natural causes. Of course, I speak of a nuclear holocaust! I think that most of us tend to not think about the "unthinkable". But, the state of international political affairs have rung a bell of alarm in many people worldwide. We have watched a previously slow moving, barely audible group of protestors, mushroom into groups of world citizens outraged about the ultimate disaster that we have no control over at all. We can make a difference in whether such a thing befalls the earth and mankind or not. Pleas for disarmament are rising from religious and special interest groups, as well as whole countries and governments. We have seen people in Europe protesting the use of their countries as storehouses for nuclear weapons. One organization in the United States that is composed primarily of medical men and women, is combatting the future manufacture of nuclear arms and the continued possession of those already in the hands of the U.S. and Russia. People from all over the world and all walks of life are concerned about the propaganda that is circulating about the good chance we have, as a country, of surviving and rebuilding from a nuclear attack! An emergence of many Native American groups has occurred, some of which have appeared before political forums to try to steer man away from his destructiveness to himself and to the planet. There is a surge of individuals and groups who are against the use of anything nuclear for any purpose, including nuclear power plants as a source of energy. One tends to get the feeling that nuclear attack is more of a probability than a possibility as before. More and more nations, some of them not known for their good judgment, have or are capable of manufacturing nuclear weapons and bombs. Is it realistic to say that this manufacturing is only for protective purposes? I think not. We seem to find a need or maybe, unconsciously create a need, to use such weapons. It has already happened with the atomic bomb and many believe it will happen again with a nuclear bomb. Attack without warning is unspeakable. But, even if we were to know in advance of an imminent attack, we would have about fifteen minutes notice! That could turn into fifteen minutes of hell and the results would be untold damage to life and the earth.

I remind you of the Hopi and the Iroquois prophecies

of Deganawida. Phrases such as "blinding light", the "mountains will crack", and the "rivers will boil", and "the fish will turn up on their bellies", "no leaves will grow on the trees", "no grass", "strange bugs and beetles will come up out of the ground", and finally, reference to a "great heat that would cause the stench of death to sicken both serpents." Many experts on these Native American predictions believe that they speak of nuclear war. The symptoms fit. Some of the quatrains of Nostradamus seem to suggest the same type of event.

If these prophecies do indeed indicate such a terrible disaster could happen before we wake up to the damage that could occur with such an event, then is it not just good common sense to not allow these predictions to become self-fulfilling? It is well to keep in mind that almost all of these prophecies I have mentioned were made long before nuclear weapons and their affect on human life and property were in existence. Who could have guessed such ominous disaster would or could ever be, much less having it be made of man's own mind and hands!

Albion has had quite a bit to say concerning the perils of nuclear war. I have chosen a part of a class session that made a particular impression upon those who heard it to share with you here. I think that is serves the purpose of sharing the Teacher's views about nuclear war, but also to give his ideas and predictions about the position we find ourselves in and how we might deal with this threat to our survival.

"If we were to choose a tool that is affective on all levels, even the spiritual, that is employed by the Brothers of the Absent Light (Black Brotherhood) to wield control over the consciousness collectively of mankind, it would be fear. The 'seeds' of fear are the fastest growing seeds, taking but an instant to germinate in the consciousness. This instant germination releases a photon of light energy then returns into the fabric of the memory. It becomes difficult, at best, for some, and impossible for others, to shake this fear that

368

is growing inside their Being. Fear has a way of not reflecting reality, it is true darkness. They (the Black Brotherhood) do not deal with reality. They do not need reality, for the fear itself is quite enough to confuse you as to what is real and what is not."

"All of the recent (1981 and 1982) conversation about the possibility of nuclear attack, although based enough on truth to generate real concern, is being planted in the subconscious of people all over the world. Such a tactic is designed to drain the resistance towards, and appreciation and desire of, a world free of destructive weapons. These fear seeds promote a fear of nuclear war and annihilation as well as the fear of not having such weapons for protection. Is this not confusion? The media, government officials, warmongers, and the like, are all used as tools for spreading this confusion worldwide. It promotes all of the negative emotions that make a man vulnerable to his own self destruction. Draining your resistance to such cataclysmic potentials is indeed dangerous and allows mankind to be controlled by the 'Forces of Darkness'. Fear cannot live in Light."

"On the contrary, when the White Brotherhood has a task to be performed that is in keeping with the proper unfoldment of the Divine Plan it cannot and does not use tools of such illusion. They must perform the task in the open light of reality. But the Black Lodge continues to spin the web of illusion and this is a problem."

His thoughts clearly established, Albion went into some thoughts concerning future dealings we might expect. "In terms of who has the most nuclear weapons, the Soviets are far ahead. (This statement was proven to be true a couple of months after it was made by President Reagan in early 1982 while he was speaking on the subject of national security, which was his reason for not favoring (as of this writing) nuclear disarmament.) Albion continued. "In terms of a summit between the major powers of the world, there can be no appeal from any country or groups of countries, such as the

369

United Nations, that will bring the Soviets to the true and honest bargaining table with the United States, until such a time that your Soviet brothers and sisters are literally on the verge of panic due to major food shortages and subsequent threat of massive starvation. The only country that could possibly bring about such a meeting before that would be China, but we have no reason to believe that such will be the case. But, there is reason for us to say that the Chinese will make it known of their various bargaining powers, time and time again, to various countries."

The Teacher never made it exactly clear on what he meant by the term "bargaining powers". He did refer to the U.S., Russia, and China as the three Superpowers.

"There is not any real danger of an all out nuclear attack or use of nuclear weaponry until 1986. But between now and then there will be at least three occasions when, through tests and accidents, that the release of nuclear radiation will happen. This will cause an increase of fear. If large scale nuclear war erupts, it will be between 1986-1993. The Hierarchy has no greater and more important task than to do all it can to prevent nuclear war and to restore the planet to its rightful status as a healthy organism. The earth has work to do and experiences towards its Initiation to accomplish, just like yourselves. Its inner light cannot be blocked so that its aura might be strengthened and its life forms may continue to evolve, thus fulfilling its karmic responsibilities. The Hierarchy knows that once the Earth's task of supporting life has been fulfilled, man will have by then reached a point where he will have created, through the proper use of technology, a spinning house in space for himself."

I assume Albion's last words to refer to space colonization which is in the minds and future of scientists, even today.

If it is some sort of nuclear holocaust that looms in the prophecies then don't we have the responsibility of using the prophecies as indicator of turmoil and destruction to be avoided? I am reminded once again of the advice given by J. R. Jochmans in his book entitled *Rolling Thunder: The Coming Earth Changes*, that the only successful prophecy is one that fails to come true! This is a very important point. What good is the gift of foretelling the future if we cannot take the warnings given and change our course of direction? Not doing so would seem to smack of the vulnerability to some sort of pre-destination. I don't think that most of us really believe that we don't have any say in what the future will be. Perhaps it is time for our voices to be heard to protest nuclear weapons and call for future disarmament. We can each make a contribution to this in whatever manner we see fit. But can we really afford to remain silent and unconcerned or merely puppets of our own fears? I think not, but the choice is up to each of us as individuals. I suggest that the first step, as with all global problems, is to be informed. We should know the dangers of living with the presence of nuclear arms and we should also know the dangers of not having them. An intelligent protest is one that is more likely to count.

We have learned that dispelling fear is one way to insure emotional survival, so now let's turn our attention towards the thoughts and ideas of mental survival. I propose that being of a sound mind, both intellectually and intuitively, is very important. The inability to think can cripple us and certainly cause us much damage and danger. Again I turn to the words of the late Hugh Lynn Cayce. "Constructive attitudes are built of thoughts that are reactions to events in which you have been involved or to what you have heard, seen or read about a particular condition, person, situation, or group. We all constantly add to or modify our attitudes. Every time we think, speak, or act while holding a particular attitude, we strengthen or change it slightly." I think that these words clearly show the need to think and to think properly. The mind can help us deal with the body and the emotions. It can help protect and heal both. The mind can help us to distinguish between the real and the imaginary and help us reason out a course of action, well thought out, and to our advantage. It can cause us to be prepared during this period of changes, based on logic and reality. Not "using our heads" leaves the door of fear wide open! Being informed helps feed the intellect, but there is another part of the mind that must also be nourished. The intuition.

In many of the writings that we consider a part of the general category of the "Wisdoms", there is much reference given to a need for an understanding of the Divine Plan. My thoughts are particularly drawn to the works of the Tibetan, channeled through Alice Bailey, earlier in this century. So much of the information and instruction given in these vast works point to a need and capability of "intuiting" the Divine Plan and our role within it. It helps to dispel fear if we, for example, are able to see that this period of earth changes, as well as such times in the past, have a definite purpose in the whole scheme of things. I think that it is important to realize that everything in the Cosmos is evolving and must go through various experiences in order to do so. This includes the Earth. Being able to be sensitive to the planet and to the other life forms upon it would seem to allow us to live life with greater meaning as well as understanding. Developing our psychic and intuitive abilities is, therefore, a matter of necessity and primary concern.

During the time that Albion was giving us the information on the vortices and ley lines, he stressed on several occasions the manner by which we could increase our own degree of sensitivity to the planet and thereby learn where such places exist. Although his teachings covered the location of most of the major power centers and their connecting lines, no writing could cover them all. Thus the need for our own sensitivity to the planet and a contribution from another level of our consciousness to insure survival. We need to be able to sense the safest places. We need to be able to discern the type of energy that is present in any given location. We need to be able to feel and determine the pulse of society and the dangers that we must avoid or help to change. The following is some instruction-type information Albion gave for us to use to help us to become more in tune with these concerns and to stimulate our abilities in this area.

The Teacher began by saying that we tend to be sensitive to an area of the earth that we already know is sacred ground or a power point, the very knowledge itself helping to open the door of our perception. "But," he continued; "when you are left to your own devices to discern this information, there can be difficulties, as all of you are not at the same point in your degree of perceptive qualities and capabilities. Knowing how to 'map' the planet, which was common as a practice amongst the Ancients, has been lost. This is primarily due to the loss of the great libraries at Alexandria. In that action many records were lost. I wish to also mention that prior to the burnings at Alexandria, there were some Priests and Elders that foresaw that such an event could occur and made valuable copies of some records and manuscripts which are now buried in various parts of Egypt. Similar manuscripts have been preserved in other global locations such as the Himalayas, Tibet and the Yucatan, to name a few. So, all is not truly lost and will someday be discovered or revealed."

"Globe mapping, which we prefer to call Earth Acupuncture or Geomancy, is inherent in most cultures that have sprung from ancient origins, like the Hopi Indians, the Mayans, Egyptians and Aztecs. The procedure becomes easy when we visualize the globe from out in space and picture the vortices like little whirlwinds, each connected together by what we have called the 'ley' lines, carrying energy from one power point to another. It might be a good idea for you (the reader) to construct a world map so that you might mark the vortices that we have already discussed, plus the ones that you will undoubtedly become aware of on your own."

This was the second time that this suggestion of working with a map had been made. I might inject here that a flat world map will serve your purposes very well. There are multi-colored stick pins that can be obtained for use of type-casting the different varieties of vortices. A fine point magic marker type pen will work well at drawing the ley line connectors from vortex to vortex. I have used the color red for electric vortices, blue for magnetic ones and yellow for the electromagnetic ones. You can choose another color for the grid systems, the man-made ones and the historical ones, if you like. This project becomes quite helpful towards giving you a tool to view the Earth's "nervous system". Remember, the ley lines serve two very significant purposes. One, they act as conductors of force, and two, as recipients of energy. This is a good point in the work to share some information that was given by Albion in an In-Depth Study for a student a few years ago concerning his notion of the distinct difference between a "force" and "energy".

"Force and energy are two distinct manifestations. I wish you to think of a force as external to yourself, in the objective universe. Its primary function is to generate motion and to link the forms of matter in the Universe together. It is creativity. Energy, on the other hand, is generated from within yourself or any given life form and is caused by and perpetuated by consciousness. There can be a synthesis between forces and energies. Forces are attracted to your energies and this, again, applies to all life forms. Beingness is the constant interplay between these two vibrations or 'frequencies'."

As you begin to take on the task of becoming more "Earth conscious", it will be an important step in renewing your balance and your attunement to the planet. Albion has said that much of our abilities of this nature was lost during the Piscean Age. He feels that the Aquarian Age is conducive to developing and expanding upon such abilities again.

To be able to detect the location of a power point on

the Earth, you must first realize that the use of the "astral" vision is necessary. You have all been in locations that you felt a simple positive or negative response to, primarily through the emotional or astral body and the solar plexus. Just allowing this simple, basic response to send signals to your consciousness as you are present in various geographical locations is a sufficient beginning. Feeling positive or negative about a place can give you initial indications as to the vibrations present. Let's for clarification purposes, consider a positive response as a likely indication of an electrical area and a negative one as magnetic. This will serve to give your subconscious a category to fit "feelings" into. Don't fall into the habit of interpreting positive and negative as good or bad, but as electric and magnetic. This will serve to give an already "natural" ability a new use. If you feel a combination, clearly, of both frequencies in a given location, you may label it electromagnetic. Some areas will be easy to diagnose, due to the terrain, history, or presence or absence of water. You might want to go back and re-read the information given in Chapter 5 about the nature of the different types of vortices. Also, keep in mind that some areas will have more energy present than others; while some may have none at all. If the frequency seems coagulated in the one primary spot, it may very well indicate a full-fledged vortex.

However, if it seems to be more scattered it may indicate a grid. There is no need for the use of "psychic" tools such as dowsing rods and the like. It is better to learn to rely on your body and consciousness for the information.

A helpful hint concerning the ley lines that I would like to share is that when I see them clairvoyantly, streaming out from the vortices in different directions, they appear as "silver threads". The color is bright and they seem to have a "quivering" or "shimmering" quality about them. Albion has indicated to me that when the silver color is dull or seems to be a bit slack, it shows a lesser amount of energy and also that it needs revitalization because it has been drained or its energy is being used up very rapidly. You will find this often in areas where natural resources have been or are being robbed from the Earth Mother. This gives you an opportunity to heal and recharge these threads and the entire area. Albion says that there are many places worldwide that are badly in need of new energy. This is what he calls healing the planet. Being able to sense the power points and especially those that need recharging, is a useful task to perform, both for your benefit and that of the planet. It also helps you to develop your sensitivity to the Earth better if you practice by going to areas that are already well known for their energies. Battlegrounds, sacred mountains, certain lakes, and so forth, are good choices. Sacred shrines are also a consideration. When going there, choose a place that you can be alone, if possible, and deliberately sense the energies...tune into the spot. Sit on the ground. Talk to the earth. Some cultures in the past have had as a part of their religious ceremonies the act of sleeping in high energy areas so that the subconscious can be totally in operation and open to the vibrations. This was particularly desirable on the sacred mountains and in spots that were called "terminals", where the ley lines crossed each other. Once you are correctly able to identify one of each of the different types of energies, you will only need to remember the feelings you received from each one and when you feel it again in another area, you will recognize it. With the information given previously that helps you determine what type of energy you are as a individual, electric, magnetic or electromagnetic, you will usually find that you will more quickly and naturally respond to that same frequency geographically. As with all things, the more you work at your earth attunement, the better at it you will become.

The following is a final piece of information that Albion gave that may also be helpful to your development.

"Some people are able to work with mountainous areas and force better than any other type, they are able to follow the ley lines of force better, are able to deal with and transcend time better, are able to work better with ascending energies that are generated by the earth and extend out into the universe. They are good "telepathic senders" of thought and establishing energies. On the other hand, those that are more drawn to fertile, wet areas, magnetic areas, as well as land that is more flat, are more receptive people who can draw energies from the Cosmos down and into themselves and the earth. They are the 'seeders' of new energies and the healers. There are some who can do both quite well and they are the ones who, as a rule, work well with the electromagnetic frequencies."

As I have said, being intellectually informed and developing the intuition keeps the mind alert and useful. An alert mind is ready to deal with whatever comes along much more so than one that is lazy and in the "rut" of the routine of daily living that we so often convince ourselves is secure and will never change.

Now, what about spiritual survival? Certainly it is desirable to be aware and solid in our personal belief system and how that functions in our everyday lives. For some this is provided primarily by some type of religion, while for others, Nature and all its wonders is their religion. Perhaps the surest way to remain or become solid spiritually is to know the purpose of life, understand the unfoldment of the Divine Plan, and be comfortable in our relationship with the Great Spirit. From time to time, Albion has made suggestions as to how we might gain not only a closer relationship with the spiritual forces around us, but more of an at-one-ment of all kingdoms of life as a whole. The following is one of his suggestions and it concerns the making of an altar.

"In the ancient past, when the Mystery Schools were prominent, each contained a 'center' or focal point; an altar. Whether it is in a temple or in your home, an altar can purify physical, emotional, mental, and spiritual energies that are placed upon it...usually in the form of objects. An altar creates a vortex within itself. It is charged by your thoughts, your motives, your desires, your failures, your wisdom, all of these things. It becomes a personification of your power. While we have been teaching about vortices, dare we pass up an opportunity to teach you how to consciously create your own?"

"You should choose a suitable place for your altar...indoors or out. There should be a portion of the earth, some soil, on this altar. There should be fire, perhaps you may wish to use candles. There should be a small amount of purified water. (You may purify it with a few drops of olive oil) You should also choose a fragrant herb or incense to represent the air. You can use this altar for charging objects of power (talismans) for healing, for sending and receiving telepathic thoughts, or for whatever purpose you consider a part of your personal spiritual work. Once you have constructed it, use it, keep it active. Don't let it lay dormant."

Albion's opinion of the absolute importance of our being aware of the Divine Plan and our purpose within it during each lifetime, leads me to share with you a bit more information on this subject. I think a primary example that has that came through during a weekly class session serves to point out the knowledge and gratification that comes with an awareness of the Divine Scheme of Things. You will readily see that the subject deals with the death of Egyptian President, Anwar Sadat. Pay close attention to the energies involved and the forces unleashed by that action and how the purpose of it all can be a little better understood. Seeing things from this sort of perspective is being aware of the order of the universe. This information was channeled on the evening after Sadat's death.

"There is a period of crisis that has been brought about by the untimely death of Anwar Sadat. Many incarnated souls are sensing a tremendous loss of his energy, particularly in Egypt and North America. The reason for

378

this sense of loss is that there are so many souls that have a 'psychic' link with the esoteric (spiritual) work of Sadat...work that goes far beyond what the physical eyes can see. Also, many such souls remember Egypt as their 'homeland' due to having lived lives there before. Sadat's death is indirectly the result of the so-called 'mideastern' conflict. There has long been a karmic condition with the Jewish people, one that has affected them and many others of different nationalities. It is a 'group karma', similar to a racial karma. This condition has been active for almost three thousand years. For many years now, a special facet of the Hierarchy has been sending light forces to try and bring balance to this karmic condition and the resulting wars it has caused and perpetuated. We will call this group of Brothers the Blue Lodge. They work through incarnated individuals for peace and balance. The members of the Lodge are fully aware that this part of the world could be the true incubator for forces and energies that could trigger a global war. Such an 'incubator' is very highly magnetic and is drawing other countries into it. Many of these countries have nuclear capabilities within their grasp."

"Often times the Blue Lodge will pick a person who has all of the necessary qualities of a peacemaker, such as Sadat. Sadat qualified well. He was a third degree Initiate (he completed his fourth at the time of his death) He was also chosen for his willingness and capabilities of entering into the 'battlefields' on the astral plane, rather than the physical and work on this level to bring about peace. His strength was drained by the high emotional (astral) conflict. His 'helpers' were not strong enough, long enough. The emotional energy against him caused an unleashing of the 'dark forces' out of the astral and onto the physical. On this day, after his death, he has become prepared for Adeptship. This untimely event has given control to those individuals and forces that do not stand to gain from peace in the mideast. They are the enemies of balance, they are the 'blockers' of progress on the planet."

"Sadat's death has caused the Blue Lodge to increase the Light Forces to this area. Many Light Workers are directing their energies towards Egypt and the mideast. A Network of Light is being created. Sadat's death symbolizes the death of love, of individuality, of compassion, and hatred is rampant on the planet. Such acts push the planet into its own period of change much faster and can do much to cause that change period to be more difficult. The more difficult it is for the earth, the more difficult it will be for the life forms that live upon it. Such acts stunt evolution and the unfoldment of the Divine Plan. The Forces of light and darkness, of good and evil, are constant. Such is the fuel of evolution, as long as they are in balance. But, when negativity reigns, growth is stunted. Think carefully about this. Only when there is a balance of the two can they cooperate and insure the unfoldment of Divine Order."

This gave us some insight and enabled us to gain that quality of perspective on other facets of world affairs. Many things and conditions and people take on new, more expanded meaning as a result. There are many people who have such a degree of perspective and are busy about putting that perspective to work. These types add to the development and progress of various areas of thought and activity, many making a major contribution that can eventually benefit the whole of mankind.

One such person is a scientist I mentioned earlier, Alan C. Holt. Aside from his official duties at NASA and his interest in developing more advanced propulsion systems designed to give us more freedom for future space travel, Alan takes his technological perspective and knowledge and applies it to the future society. During an interview with Holt in Houston, Texas, in March of 1982, I asked him about his views concerning technological breakthroughs that were likely to occur, including some new sources of energy, that he felt might greatly and positively affect man.

Giving his words careful forethought, he replied;

"Solar energy will play a greater and greater role. What we have in the way of solar cells are being improved constantly. They are being made thinner and lighter and at a much cheaper cost. Various people are trying different techniques in this area. they will be workable for housing in the future."

I asked: "What about the proposed solar satellites?" My question concerned a proposal of solar energy collecting that would beam same back to the earth from space.

"Definitely. A primary advocate of that project is the Johnson Space Center. It does have possibilities but I am not personally enthusiastic about that specific approach or that it would work." Alan continued on into another subject.

"The area that I feel the government is working the hardest on is fusion. You see, theoretically, fusion action would not result in radioactive fuel." I thought back to Albion's comments on the dangers involved with nuclear war and remembered that the severe problem of disposal of nuclear waste only adds to the dangers of using nuclear power for energy. Alan continued, showing his enthusiasm. "Trying fusion experiments, we are already discovering anomalies which may help achieve a breakthrough in physics. This may help us convert one type of fundamental force into another. Gravitational forces into electromagnetic forces or nuclear forces into gravitational ones. And, if you develop this 'grand unified theory' and find techniques for interchanging, then you have energy sources that are almost unlimited because you could tap the gravitational field of the earth. I think that by the year 2000, nuclear fusion would be a reality."

I asked if there were other, less known, sources of energy that might be developed.

"There are geo-thermal energy sources that can be tapped coming up from the center of the earth. This is volcanic-type heating. Volcanic heating can be more possible if the earth becomes more geologically active.

We should be able to tap energy from these eruptions."
I couldn't help but think quickly back over some of the prophecies that would definitely indicate that the earth will become more geologically active, but I decided that I would pass making any comment to Alan Holt about the earth changes at this point.

I asked instead; "What about any supplement to fossil fuels?"

"If you develop good battery sources you could go to electrical vehicles. This is closely tied to further development of solar energy."

As it turned out, I didn't have to mention earth changes or catastrophes. Alan did. "There are economical drivers in the energy systems that would tend to stay with that which we already know, what we already have. But, in case of a catastrophic war or major geological change that would cause us to no longer have what we are used to or little of it, then I think that you will find that alternative energy sources are waiting in the wings, so to speak. Such pressure would cause them to be developed. The need will be the determining factor."

I thought that so typical of mankind...wait until we have to!

Holt's next statement excited me and my husband very much. We listened intently as the scientist continued. "Eventually we will find ways of working with crystals, on a fairly small scale, maybe by subjecting them to different types of electromagnetic fields and we will find ways of coming up with energy sources by certain configurations of crystals and lasers."

I asked him to elaborate. "In my approach," he replied, "crystals have a very regular atomic structure. There is nothing more precise than a pure crystal. The key to the approach I am taking is the coherence of energy patterns that they create, the electromagnetic energy patterns. It is not the amount of energy as much as the precision or coherence. Also involved in that is the pulsation of those patterns."

382

I could see a bit of hesitance. "I am reluctant to say too much about this as it affects all of mankind. There is first an important need to continue step by step so that it will be available when it is needed." I began to sense strongly this man's possible role in the continued unfoldment of the Plan. He did, much to our delight, say a bit more about crystals.

"The crystal energy could be used for motive power (transportation), maybe a generator." He clarified his position carefully as he went on. "When you mention crystals, some people tend to think of the metaphysical uses for them. In actuality, it will be as common as plugging into a socket. Not to say you could go out and pick up a rock and use it. They will be grown and used for their specific cohesion. Skylab (Alan was a part of the Skylab project at NASA) teams have grown crystals in space because of the lack of gravitational pull we have here on earth. Just about everything uses a crystalline structure. In fact, crystals are just about at the heart of all of our new technology. It could be very economical for NASA to do such things as growing crystals."

"Where will it all lead?" was my question. Alan replied: "You could get closer to what Nikolas Tesla was trying to do...generate certain electromagnetic patterns and, in a way, generate a resonance effect...pick up energy." He explained. "Say you had a closed area and you were generating certain patterns of electromagnetic fields and you achieve a resonance effect in the magnitude of the magnetic field. You could tap off the magnetic field. You could tap off that energy. It's like tapping into a 'hyperspace' energy field."

I stopped the conversation for a moment and asked Alan to explain for myself and the readers exactly what hyperspace means and implies.

"Hyperspace can be thought of as having additional dimensions. We have the four dimensions of space, three energies of space and time. Hyperspace would have other dimensions, other ways of describing energy patterns. And, he added thoughtfully, "who knows how many

383

other dimensions we might find?" There could be many kinds of hyperspace. If someone were to ask me right now if hyperspace is real, I would have to say that I don't know. Time will tell. Hyperspace would allow you to travel from one place to another without your having to travel through space and time."

Needless to say, the thoughts being shared with us by this remarkable man were most exciting! Having known Alan for some time as a friend, I was aware of his purely personal interest in the UFO phenomena. I feel that his main reason of interest in the phenomena is due to his interest in the possible propulsion systems that some such craft have reportedly demonstrated by eyewitness accounts. He brought the subject up sort of an after thought in regards to his theories on hyperspace. "Some UFO's seem to exhibit teleportation characteristics. It is also the only way that I can see that we could possibly be being visited by other civilizations. If we were limited to the speed of light, the time factor would be too great. Even for an alien living 100,000 years in one lifespan, it wouldn't make sense to come visit this planet as much as they appear to be visiting us."

I pursued the UFO question a bit further. "Could some of the sightings be 'holographic'?

"Yes, some of them could be." He didn't continue that line of thought, so I asked; "Where does the ingredient of mind come into all of this?"

Alan repeated my question aloud, seeming to search his thoughts carefully. "It goes back to the energy patterns, the type of energy pattern, its precision. We are all aware of what we call space and time. Our physical awareness detects these things. For example, if we could detect magnetic fields and gravitational fields, we would have a completely different type of awareness. We could have a very large space station by the year 2000 if we could afford it. It's a matter of cost. If we got a breakthrough in propulsion, this could be rapidly accelerated. You see, the reason for this, if you had a way of negating the earth's gravitational field, then all you

384

would need would be a few thrusters and the thing would go right up in orbit."

Now I understood.

"But, it will require a greater understanding of what the gravitational field is and how we can interact with it to alter it. Colonization of space is dependent on the development of our advanced propulsion system. We can do it with the space shuttle. It's beginning."

The final topic of discussion that evening came as a result of my mentioning, specifically, the coming earth changes. "Are you aware of all the prophecies and the general pulse of the masses concerning an apprehension of the period that we are moving into?" Alan nodded that he was. "Are there any technological developments that you feel can help us through should this time come?"

"Yes, I think that in the not-too-distant-future we will be able to be aware of energy blockages on the surface of the earth, or in its interior, and be able to develop technologies to allow the energy to flow around these blockages and relieve them to some degree. And, lessening the violent change that would otherwise have to occur, this could prevent catastrophic changes that would make the earth a place that mankind could no longer evolve, unless a different kind of physical man would take his place. Man should, I think, try and lessen the severity of the changes. I would like to pull together open-minded scientists who are willing to respond to and use whatever is available to get back the technology that was lost when whatever catastrophies have occurred in the past, or, at least, rebuild it for man's survival."

These thoughts ended our session for that evening. I definitely gathered that Alan did believe, at least to a degree, that the earth is changing and that we must do our part, in our way and with our expertise, to help those changes to be less severe. There are not too many scientists with the broad degree of foresight as Alan Holt, but I do believe the number of them is growing. These "New Age" scientists, in all fields, are making and will continue to make their minds work towards the benefit of all humanity. Such individuals will undoubtedly play a major role to help insure our survival on all levels.

Survival is definitely the goal. It involved, as we have seen, every area of our lives, environment and society. An article in the October, 1981 issue of *Science News* speaks loudly about the need and our ability to stave off a future of doom and gloom. The article points out that the present picture of the future is not a very "pretty" one. The growing world population is a major concern, along with the activities surrounding and the policies surrounding the earth's natural resources. I was particularly impressed with this article because it went beyond simply stating the obvious problems to offer some solutions.

One of the principals in the writing, author Lester Brown, in his book *Building A Sustainable Society*, pleads for governmental and systematic backed global conservation of national resources, simply using less and recycling more. This helps to insure such resources for future generations as well as ourselves presently. Brown "sees" that we don't have a lot of time to dream up solutions for such problems as food shortages, good agricultural land and mineral resources, and over-population that is already using up the biological systems upon which we rely. Unlike some of his critics, Brown simply does not think we have a long-term future. The only solution, he feels, is to stop the population growth, by a reasonable, regular timetable. For those of us that are here now, we must create a more resource conserving lifestyle. There is still time now for such action, but, Brown and many like him, from all walks of life, firmly believe that time is running out.

Brown's thoughts, along with others, have not fallen totally on deaf ears. Over the past several years, medically supervised clinics have sprung up in the country to help women and their spouses create the family desired. With statistics showing that by the end of 1982 the world population is estimated to exceed five billion, such organizations as Planned Parenthood seek to provide a practical voice. Free information concerning population control and family planning can be obtained by writing:

Planned Parenthood
Education Department
380 Second Avenue
New York, New York 10010

Making sure that all levels of our consciousness receive the proper attention and care, the following is a portion from one of our personal sessions with Albion. I think it will go another step in helping us maintain clarity of thinking and feeling. I will pick up the session at the point that it serves our purposes here.

"First of all, we wish to speak concerning the benefit of being near a body of water. Water generates an energy, whether it be but a small stream or pond or an entire ocean. It is a magnetic energy, primarily, and can do much to affect a balance of the auric field. You don't have to be submersed in it, but as near to it as possible. It soothes and relaxes the emotional vibrations and helps to regenerate the astral body. For example, if due to some upset or conditions, you happen to have an excess of red in your auric field, the water will help calm this down and dissipate it. It won't do it totally, but it will help. Water can cleanse mind and body."

"Oftentimes the reverse will be true. The aura will need some charging or input of energy. Such input can serve to counteract imbalances and negativity. Choosing more arid and especially mountainous areas for this purpose is good. You could also choose, for those who do not live in such places, to be outside just after an electrical storm or otherwise seek out a location that seems to be high in electrical power."

Another facet of the survival techniques that cannot be overlooked has to do with the perpetuation of the

387

planet itself. While most of us may not be directly involved with companies or actual jobs that require us to be a part of the injustices that are being heaped upon the earth, in terms of overuse, misuse and destruction of the natural resources, we still don't necessarily make enough of a purely personal contribution towards those activities being brought under control. There are several ways we can approach this matter, as individual voices.

First, we can take a political approach and write our congressmen to voice our opinions. We can contact the Department of the Interior, which handles these complaints and makes the decisions about the land. On an even more individualistic basis, we can lend our own energies towards healing and recharging some of the areas of the world that are so depleted of their own natural energies, often due to the upset in balance brought on by some sort of technology or construction of highways and other types of facilities. One matter that comes foremost in my mind has to do specifically with the sacred mountains of the world.

In our discussion of the vortices, worldwide, you will recall that many of these power points take form within and from the vibrations of mountains. Nearly every culture one can recall, whose terrain included mountains, considered selected peaks to be sacred, "homes of the gods", so to speak. I remind you of the frequency of such practices among the American Indians, especially those of the West. The Navajo, as an example, have five peaks that are held sacred in their legends, one of which is the San Frnacisco peaks in Flagstaff, Arizona. The Hopi, Sioux, and others follow similar patterns of belief. At the same time, we are familiar with Mt. Olympus, famed summit of Greek mythology, and Mt. Fuji in Japan and Mt. Croach-Patrick in Ireland. In many of these countries, yearly pilgrimages are still being made, for the faithful to partake of the psychic forces of these great mountains and to perform various rituals. Is this unlike worshipping in a great cathedral? The sacred mountains are Nature's cathedrals. It has been so within some cultures for thousands of years. We might be appalled, if we took the time to know, if we were to take a look at the treatment of these peaks. I will narrow my observations down just to this country alone.

In his magnificent work, *Mountain Dialogues*, Frank Waters speaks frankly about the wasteful destruction that is being imposed upon some of the country's sacred peaks. Waters makes special mention of the uranium mining being done on Mt. Taylor, one the holy summits of the Navajo people. He also brings sorrowful information about Pike's Peak, the San Francisco peaks and others. But, I think his most valuable point is that we have both a psychic and physical part to our nature and that both are essential to living and surviving. He believes, and I agree with him, that the sacred mountains of the world are repositories of the much-needed psychic energy that we sorely need and that they are being destroyed or, at best, mistreated!

It seems to me that the sacred mountains of the earth would be connected by ley lines of force too, for so many of them are vortices. Waters states that the holy peaks are "located on a global grid of lines of forces." He also believes that they are focal points of energy and are also "distribution" centers located worldwide.

We can speak out about this destruction. Whether we choose to do so politically or just by not being guilty of this type of destruction and work to send our healing thoughts towards these peaks, then so be it. I think Frank Waters said it all and said it well when he wrote of the need that we have for maintaining these sacred spots.

To be sure, the mountains are not the only locations that are suffering due to our environmental madness. Lakes and streams, farmable land, rain forests and our air itself, is being polluted and destroyed to "make way for progress." While we don't have to be against progress, does it have to be, as it seems to be, at any cost?

It may be of interest to note that, in this country, certainly one of our most prized heritages is the Grand Canyon in Arizona. Through this awesome landscape flows the Colorado River, that, along with time and past earth changes, has been carving the rocks for 10 million years. During all this time, life there was virtually free and undisturbed in its evolution. Now that has changed and the change began about fifteen years ago. The Grand Canyon is experiencing an ecological crisis. The cause is due to the construction of the Glen Canyon Dam which is located at the eastern gateway to the Grand Canyon. Spring and summer periods have been depleted drastically and the river no longer carries the tremendous and necessary amounts of sediment to rebuild the shoreline. As a result, the beaches inside the chasm are slowly washing away! The temperature of the river used to be between 30 degrees in winter and 80 degrees in summer, but now it is a constant 45 to 50 degrees. You can imagine the implications this had had on the aquatic life of the area. Many species have simply disappeared. In short, the consequences of building the Glen Canyon Dam to supply demands for electrical energy were not looked at closely enough and the Grand Canyon is paying the price.

You don't find much political muscle on the San Francisco peaks or at the bottom of the Grand Canyon. In passing the 1964 Wilderness Act, congress recognized that this country needed land that would be permanently free of commercial and industrial exploitation. But, this is simply not enough. Respect and care for the planet has to be widely reinstated and this has to be done now. One voice may not be loud enough, but it helps.

Perhaps the most important thing to remember and the thing that will make the biggest contribution towards survival is that the Earth is alive! If we treat it as such, our lives and our relationship with it could be more rewarding and more safe. Let us imagine ourselves into Reality! Approach every rock and tree, every life form as a brother or sister. Think of the wind as the voice of the Great Spirit and let it speak to you.

Know the atmosphere as the planetary aura and the rain as her tears.

I leave you with a scenario given by Albion several months prior to the book being finished. I leave it up to you to decide if the Teacher was speaking literally or symbolically.

"In the beginning, when the Earth first began to support life, she realized that this was a tremendous responsibility. She knew, however, that it was her Karma in this her planetary lifetime, and so She accepted the task of providing a home for millions of species of life."

"It is not understood in this day that the Earth is trying desperately to fulfill her spiritual task. This lack of understanding or caring, particularly on the part of humans who are her pride and joy, has saddened the Earth Mother and She is beginning, once again, like any frustrated mother, to reconsider whether She should continue on or not. (Don't we all reach that point spiritually?) The decision must be made. The Earth must make it. As the life forms have evolved through the ages, a point has been reached that is causing the Earth Mother to seek counsel in regards to her dilemma with her wayward children, Humanity."

"So, Earth Mother has begun to question some of the most ancient of her children, those that carry civilizations and times past in their memories. In the Water Kingdom, She has asked for advice of the most self-realized and most evolved, the great whales. The whales have replied in fear of their own survival... 'we have been overcome by man and many of us destroyed. We have not been allowed, as of late, to pursue our natural way of life. Members of our domain are being slaughtered. Only a few of the humans care.' "

"Then the Earth Mother turned to the various members of the Plant Kingdom. The pines and the oaks replied: 'We are not protected. Many of our tribes, the great forests, are being taken.'

"Many of the Animal Kingdom cried similar tales of woe. 'Many of us are extinct and there is little land upon which we can live. The fumes of pollution hurt our lungs and kill our young.'

"The Earth is calling out for change through the use of her volcanoes, her winds and the energy of her chakras and vortices. She asks: 'Where stands the evolution of mankind?' Where is the flow of civilization leading? She has listened to a few of the 'men children' who see the misbehavior and know of the Mother's dispair. She has heard the cries of the Hopi who have been crying out to the Earth Mother to take action against the raping and plundering of the land. She hears even the insects petitioning to her to help them pursue their lives in freedom and safety. All the kingdoms, except for a very few of the humans, are aware of their endangerment and that of their Mother. They want to live!"

"The Earth Mother has decided to give us a short time to mend our ways and stop threatening the lives in other kingdoms as well as Herself. She will spend that time observing mankind. What will you do to save other lives from extinction? Will the plants who give their bodies and lives for your food rot in the silos or feed the hungry of the world? Will you once again allow the mineral kingdom to rebuild and restore itself?"

"If these changes are not made, will the Earth Mother give up? Will the change period that is upon you now cause the planet to unleash her full force? Will you do your part?

The Earth is a "Pilgrim of Evolution." You are a "pilgrim" of the same. It is indeed a wonderful and thought-provoking matter to think that we are making our journey through the Cosmos in such good company, for each star and planet alike is the body of some indwelling celestial Being! The universe is a scheme of things that is so vast, so natural, that just to be a part of it is mind-boggling in itself. And remember, the destinies of both are intricately entwined.

"Give us the strength to encounter that which is to come that we may be brave in peril, constant in tribulation, temperate in wrath, and in all changes of fortune, and down to the gates of death, loyal and loving to one another."

—Robert L. Stevenson

EPILOG

THIS TIME OF CHANGE

This is a time of rapid change upon the Earth Mother -- a time when the earth is cleansing herself of the poisons that have been put into her soil, her waters, and her air. During this time it is important for all of us humans to recognize the truth about the earth, and all of our relations upon her.

We live now in a society that tends to see the earth as a mere stage set for the affairs of humankind. This society has forgotten that the earth is alive, that she lives and breathes and evolves just as we do. We have forgotten that there is a sacred web of life, a sacred circle that joins us to all the rest of the beings who live on the earth with us. Not remembering this web, we have misused and abused our brothers and sisters in the mineral, the plant, and the animal kingdoms. We have dumped our wastes into the soil, the water, and the air, with no thought of the generations to follow.

How different our life is from that of our ancestors, the Native peoples of the earth who knew how to live in harmony with all of the rest of creation. The Native peoples all over the world, at one time, had a great love and respect for the earth and for all of the lives upon her. They recognized that they were a part of the sacred circle of life, not setting themselves apart from this circle, as we do.

394

They knew that we humans, the fourth kingdom upon the earth, were dependent upon the other three kingdoms for our lives to continue. They knew the first kingdom, that of the elementals, was the most independent form of life on the earth. The earth herself, the fire, the air, and the water are the cornerstones of creation. They can exist alone, without aid from any of the other kingdoms. The second kingdom, that of the plant people, is more dependent because it cannot exist without the help of the elements. The third kingdom, that of the animals, is even more dependent because it cannot exist without the help of both the elements and the plants. We of the fourth kingdom, the humans, are the most dependent of all because our lives cannot continue without the help of the other three. While, through our ability to dream and have visions and bring our visions into reality, we are most like the Creator, we are still dependent upon all of our relations on the earth for our lives to continue.

Knowing this, our Native ancestors loved and respected all the rest of the Earth Mother's children with an active love. They knew they had to give back to the other kingdoms something for all of the goodness they received. So, they would pray to the elements, the plants, and the animals knowing their prayers were a way of giving energy that would help these other kingdoms to continue to have good and healthy lives. They would sing and dance and hold ceremonies in honor of all of their relations. All of these activities were done with the knowledge that the gift we had to give back was the special energy of our own closeness to the Creator.

The Earth and all the things upon her are the result of the Great Spirit, the Creator bringing his vision of life into reality. We humans have been given the gift of vision, and the ability to turn our visions into realities also. This gift is not something that should make us arrogant, as it often has in this society. It is a thing that should make us feel humble in our connection with the sacred circle, the sacred medicine wheel of life.

During this time of rapid change we must begin to remember some of the things that we have forgotten. We must learn again how to honor and respect all life upon this planet. We must watch the trees and the animals, and learn the dances that need to be danced. We must learn to walk upon the earth as our ancestors did, with a prayer of thanksgiving always in our hearts. In these ways we begin to give back to the earth and our relations some of the energy that will allow them to become healthy and whole.

Ceremonies held a very special place in the lives of Native people. They were ways of giving large amounts of energy back into the earth, and into the other kingdoms. We must once again learn about such ceremonies. The earth is very sick at this time because of our ignorance. In order for her life and evolution to continue, she needs the energy of all persons who can learn to become sensitive to her.

In some prophecies of the Native American people, it is said if we humans do not remember our original instructions, we will go the way of the dinosaur — we will not survive this cleansing of the Earth Mother. That thought saddens me. As a race of beings we have made some colossal mistakes, but we have also made some good steps forward. It is so easy for us to remember how we should live, if we will only open ourselves to the earth. The earth is a very patient teacher. She is very joyful when another one of her children awakens and remembers the sacred circle.

I have worked for the past ten years with Sun Bear, the medicine chief of the Bear Tribe. When I came to him I was a city woman, a former New York free-lance writer. I, too, thought of the earth as a stage set. The narrow viewpoint I had been taught often left me feeling lonely, afraid, and half-alive.

Over these years I have learned I *was* only half-alive, because I was cutting myself off from so much of the world. The first summer I spent out West I learned about gardening, about hunting, and about collecting wild plants. I learned to pray as I did all of these things. I came alive as I remembered my connection to the sacred circle.

Since that summer I have worked with the Bear Tribe Medicine Society, the organization that Sun Bear founded according to a vision that he had. In his vision he saw people of all races coming together to be a medicine society of teachers who would share with others the ways they had found to bring themselves into harmony with the earth, and with all of the beings upon her.

The Bear Tribe has a center near Spokane, Washington, out on the land. Here we have built most of our own buildings, grown much of our own food, and shared with other people the skills we have learned. Several hundred people come to our center each year to learn self-reliance, earth awareness, and to go out on vision quests to learn the purpose of their own lives.

Part of our medicine is communications, and we reach out to people in may ways. We publish *MANY SMOKES,* a Native/Metis Earth Awareness magazine now in its twentieth year of publication. We publish books: Sun Bear: *THE PATH OF POWER;* The Bear tribe's *SELF RELIANCE BOOKS;* Sun Bear's *BUFFALO HEARTS;* and Grandmother Evelyn Eaton's *SNOWY EARTH COMES GLIDING.* We travel throughout the world telling people about this time on the earth and how they can prepare themselves to help the earth during her cleansing.

We sponsor Medicine Wheel Gatherings, large ceremonies that are attended by 600 to 1000 or more people. During these Gatherings many teachers share with participants their knowledge of the earth, and other wisdom that life has given to them. Participants all join in the building of a medicine wheel, and in other ceremonies that honor the earth, and all of the beings upon her. In this way, we begin to learn again about ceremonies, and how they can help the earth.

Native people all over the world, for many thousands of years looked upon life as a sacred circle -- a medicine

397

wheel. In this circle, there was a place for human beings, but there were also places for all of our other relations upon the earth -- the elements, the plants, the animals, the winds, the sky, the sun, the moon, and the earth herself. All were considered to be equal co-creators of this life that we experience.

Slowly at first, but then with increasing speed, this viewpoint was lost as mankind maneuvered to manifest his destiny -- a destiny that set him apart from all of the other beings inhabiting the earth with him.

By setting ourselves apart from the sacred circle of life we have placed ourselves in a very lonely and precarious position. We no longer see that our actions, here and now, effect much more than the here and now we experience. We no longer judge our actions as our ancestors did, not only by how they effect us, but by how they will affect all future generations upon the earth.

Native people speak of the earth as the Earth Mother, and they really feel that the earth acts as a good mother would. She nourishes and sustains our lives. As we have grown apart from the concept of the earth as mother, we have also grown away from a love and respect for our own mothering energy. In order to help with the cleansing happening now, we must also remember what female energy really is. We must go within and find the healthy female aspects within ourselves and help them to grow. By doing so, we can come into a much larger and clearer understanding of this time in which we have chosen to live. By seeing the earth as a living being, by finding the reflections of the earth that lie within each one of us, we do help the earth, ourselves, our children, and our children's children for generations yet unborn to live.

May we all learn to walk with a good balance upon our common, and always beautiful Earth Mother.

—Wabun of the Bear Tribe

BIBLIOGRAPHY

A

Abell, George. *"Drama Of The Universe."* Holt,
Rinehart and Winston, N.Y., N.Y.; 1978

Aveni, Anthony F. *"Native American Astronomy".*
University of Texas Press. Austin and London:
1977

B

Bailey, Alice. *"Destiny Of The Nations"* Lucis Trust.
New York, New York: 1949

Bailey, Alice. *"Initiation: Human and Solar".*
New York, New York: 1951

Bentov, Itzhak. *"Stalking The Wild Pendulum."*
Bantam Books, 666 Fifth Avenue, N.Y., N.Y.;
1979

Besant, Annie. *"Man And His Bodies"* Theosophical
Publishing House, Adyar, India; 1971. Madras 20

Blavatsky, Helena Petrovna. *"Secret Doctrine".* Vols.
I & II. Theosophical University Press. Pasadena,
California; 1974

C

Capra, Fritjof. *"The Tao Of Physics."* Bantam
Books, 666 5th Ave. New York, New York; 1977

Cayce, Hugh Lynn. *"Earth Changes Update."* A.R.E. Press, Virginia Beach, VA; 1980

Cayce, Hugh Lynn. *"Faces Of Fear": Overcoming Life's Anxieties.* Harper and Row. San Francisco, California: 1980

Cerve, Wishar S. *"Lemuria: The Lost Continent Of The Pacific."* Supreme Grand Lodge of AMORC. San Jose, California; 1931 (Sept.)

D

Don, Frank. *"Earth Changes Ahead": The Coming Great Catastrophies.* Warner-Destiny book: 1981

E

Encyclopedia Brittanica. William Benton, Publisher; 1943-1973. Vol. II B-C page 827. Chichen-Itza.

F

Ferguson, Marilyn. *"The Aquarian Conspiracy"; Personal And Social Transformation In The 1980's.* J. P Tarcher, Inc. Los Angeles, Ca. 1980.

Ferris, Timothy. *"The Red Limit."* Bantam Books, 666 Fifth Avenue, New York, New York; July 1979

Fuller, Buckminster R. *"Operating Manual For Spaceship Earth".* A Dutton paperback. E.P. Dutton, New York, New York. 1978.

G

Gamow, George. *"A Planet Called Earth".* Bantam Books, 666 Fifth Ave., N.Y., N.Y.; 1965 (Pathfinder Edition)

Goodavage, Joseph. *"Our Threatened Planet".* Simon and Schuster; 1978

Goodavage, Joseph. *"Storm On The Sun."* Signet New American Library; 1979. 1301 Ave. of the Americas, New York, New York.

Goodman, Jeffery Ph.D. *"American Genesis."* Summit Books, N.Y., N.Y.; 1981.

Goodman, Jeffery Ph.D. *"We Are The Earthquake Generation."* Seaview Books. New York; 1978

Gribbin, John. *"White Holes".* A Delta book. Dell Publishing Company, Inc.; 1977

Gribbin, John and Plagemann, Steven. *"The Jupiter Effect."* Vintage Books, a Division of Random House. New York, N.Y.' May 1975

H

Hoyle, Fred Sir and Wickramsinghe. *"Lifecloud: The Origin Of Life In The Universe."* Harper and Row, Publishers, New York, N.Y.; 1978

I

Impact Team, The. *"Weather Conspiracy: The Coming Of The New Ice Age."* Ballantine Books, N.Y., N.Y.; 1977

J

James, Paul. *"California Superquake 1975-77?"* Second Edition, revised and enlarged. Exposition Press, Hicksville, New York. 1974 and 1975

Jampolsky, Gerald. *"Love Is Letting Go Of Fear."* Celestial Arts, Millbrae, California; 1979.

James, Paul. *"California Superquake 1975-77?"* Second Edition, revised and enlarged. Exposition Press, Hicksville, New York. 1974 and 1975

Jampolsky, Gerald. *"Love Is Letting Go Of Fear."* Celestial Arts, Millbrae, California; 1979.

401

Jastrow, Robert Dr. *"Red Giants and White Dwarfs"*
W.W. Norton & Co., Inc. New York, New York.
1979

Jochmans, J.R. *"Rolling Thunder: The Coming
Earth Changes."* Sun Publishing Co. Albuquerque
New Mexico; 1981

L
LaBell, John. *"The Little Green Book: A Guide To
Self-Reliant Living In The 1980's."* Shamballa
Publications. Boulder, Colorado; 1981

Leadbeater, C.W. *"Chakras."* Theosophical
Publishing House, Wheaton, Illinois; 1927

M
Many Smokes: Metis Earth Awareness Magazine.
Vol. 15 No. 1. Spring 1981. *"Earth Chakras."*
Page Bryant.

Miller, Albert. *Meteorology."* Bell and Howell
Company. Charles E. Merrill Publishing Company;
1976.

*Mitchell, John. "Secrets Of The Stones: The Story Of
Astro-archaeology."* Penguin Books, 625 Madison
Avenue, N.Y., N.Y.; 1977.

Munitz, Milton K. *"Theories Of The Universe: From
Babylonian Myth To Modern Science."* Free Press
Paperback. MacMillan Publishing Company, Inc.

N
Null, Gary. *"Man And His Whole Earth."* Pyramid
Books, New York, New York; 1977.

P
Playfair, G.L. and Hill, Scott. *"The Cycles Of
Heaven."* Avon; Hearst Corp.
N.Y., N.Y.; 1979 (Aug.)

Ponte, Lowell. *"The Cooling."* Prentice-Hall, Inc. Englewood, New Jersey, 1976

R

Ross, Lydia M.D. *"Cycles: The Universe and Man."* Point Loma Publications, Inc. San Diego, California; 1975

S

Sagan, Carl Dr. *"Dragons Of Eden."* Ballantine Books, New York, 1977

Science News. June 6, 1981. Volume 119 No. 23 page 356. *"Spotting A Hot Spot."*

Science News: June 20, 1981 Page 392. Earth Sciences Volume 119, No. 25

Science News. October 10, 1981. Volume 120 No. 15 *"Quakes In The East."* Cheryl Simon.

Science News. November 8, 1981. Volume 120 No. 20 page 311. *"CO2 Warming: Proof May Be In The Ice Caps.*

Sun Bear, Niminosha, The Bear Tribe, and Wabun. *"The Bear Tribe's Self-Reliance Book."* Bear Tribe Publishing Company, Spokane, Washington; 1977

W

Waters, Frank. *"The Book Of The Hopi."* Ballantine Books, N.Y., N.Y.; 1963

Waters, Frank. *"Mountain Dialogues."* Sage Books, Swallow Press. Athens, Ohio, N.Y., N.Y.; 1981

Webster's New World Dictionary Of The American Language. Second College Edition. David B. Quralnik, Editor In Chief. William Collins Publishing, Inc.; 1979 page 1445

White, John. *"Poleshift."* Doubleday & Co., Inc. Garden City, N.Y.; 1980

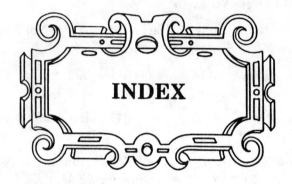

INDEX

acupuncture
earth 157

Adept (see guru)
Adeptship 158, 379

Aeagina 209

Africa 136-38, 166, 219, 254, 268
Capetown 137
Ethiopia 292
Libya 89
Johannesburg 138
North Africa 219
South Africa 161, 292,
Sudan 292
West Africa 273

Age(of)
Aquarius 270, 374
Piscean 374
Pre-Cambrian 263
Neolithic 157
Stone 213
Triassic Period 254

Alabama
Selma 162-4

Alaska 124, 153, 254, 262, 265,
271, 278, 282, 343

Albion 43-52, 54, 57, 60-1, 65-6,
69, 72-3, 75-6, 78-81, 84-6, 89,
92, 94, 96, 99-103, 105, 108-9,
111-13, 116-18, 123-4, 126, 129,
132-3, 135-7, 139-40, 143-45,
150-53, 156-65, 169, 173-75,
177-83, 186-88, 190, 193-99,
201-09, 211-13, 215-18, 234, 241,
247, 249, 253, 273, 277-78,
281-85, 290-91, 293-94, 297, 299,
301, 303, 307, 316, 325, 327,
349-50, 352-53, 355, 357, 365,
368-70, 373-76, 381, 387, 391
Accent 135
Concepts 55
Instructions 117
Mood 138
Vortex-connection 121

algae 316

Almora 199

Alpha
Alpha-Omega Theory 22

Alps (see mountains 214, 219

altar 377-78
of earth 147

Amazon (see river)
jungle 245

America - Americans 203, 239
Northwest 224

Ames Research Center 38

Angkor - Wat 203

Anatapur 199

Ancients (see man)

Andes (see mountains) 214-15,
220

angels 186, 200, 207
fallen 82

animal (kingdom) 40, 85, 294,
343, 359, 391, 394
dead 328
hides 303
livestock 308
medicine 140
pets 300, 311, 324

Antarctica (arctic) 225, 244-45,
254-55, 292,
Peninsula 274

Ant people 32

Apollo (missions)
Eight 221
Eleven 236

Arab 239
Master 224
countries 92

Arabia 45, 89, 203

Arafat (see mountain) 203

Archeology 120
artifacts 138
astro-archeology 216

Arctic (see oceans) 225

405

Argentina 184

Aries 55

Aristotle 19, 21

Arizona 98, 115, 127, 140, 145,
149, 158, 175, 208, 226, 246,
388,
   Apache Junction 175
   Bell Rock 154
   Boynton Canyon 176
   Flagstaff 130, 176, 193, 242,
388
   Four Corners 143-46, 149, 153,
188, 201, 293
   Grand Canyon 32, 65, 69, 100,
127, 179-82, 390
   Kayenta 143-45, 149
   Kitt Peak 121
   Medicine Wheels 142
   Monument Valley 145, 149
   Oak Creek Canyon 144
   Oraibi 116
   Painted Desert 144
   Phoenix 161, 165, 167, 175
   Sedona 113, 115, 143-44,
149-50, 154, 161, 174-76, 182,
193, 216, 234, 292
   Verde Valley 175
   Village of Oak Creek 175
   Winslow 145

Arizona Republic 271

Arkansas 262

Armenia 124

Aerocibo, Puerto Rico 153

Art 132, 180
   artists 194, 202
   spiritual 214

A.S. (Albion's student) 43-4, 46-7,
100, 109, 129, 137-8, 140, 143-45,
161-2, 164, 175, 177-8, 180-2,
187-8, 202-3, 210, 214, 278, 285

Asher, Maxine Dr. 266

Ashram 158, 198

Asia 121, 247, 267, 272
   Alpine 272

Astara 138

asteroid(s) 118, 251-2, 361
   belt 102

asthenosphere 136

astral 91, 99-100, 138, 153, 189
   body, 62, 70, 73, 75, 97, 127,
203, 375, 387
   conflict 379
   dimension 111
   green chamber 147
   images 100
   plane 100
   realms 146
   solution 190
   substance 175
   temple 146, 179
   travel 216
   vision 375

Astro-archeology (see archeology)

Astrology 78, 133, 217, 267
   astrologers 160

Astro-Media (Corp.) 342

astronaut(s) 106, 221 (see Apollo)
   ancient 184

Astronomy 56, 184, 216-17, 242,
255, 284, 365
   Native American 142
   observatories 131, 155, 204,
206, 217
   radio 20, 87
   ruins 215

Athena 209

Athos, Mt. (see mountain) 209

Atlantic (see oceans) 120, 130,
132, 135, 152

Atlantis (Antilia) 36, 72, 75, 82,
122, 132-3, 135, 153, 173, 180,
195, 207, 221, 266-7,
   times 82
   migrants 213

atmosphere 97, 119, 153, 244-5,
247, 276, 279, 283, 391
   anomalies 139
   electric 121
   ozone 139

407

411

412

hydrocarbon(s) 257

hydrogen 22

hyperspace 383-4

Ice 245, 276, 356
  crystals 276
  dry 301
  polar 246, 280,
  Age 244, 246, 278, 280, 302
    mini 241

Iceland 122, 212
  Surtsey 278

Idaho 262

Illinois 262
  Chicago 271

Incans 83, 215
  (see Indians)

Independence Hall 163

India 89, 123, 154, 197-9, 201,
207, 235, 246-7, 254, 281
  Ajanta 198
  Bodr Gaya 199
  Brahmin 200
  Darjeeling 159
  Ganges 197
  Jain 200
  Khajuro 200
  Kulu Valley 200
  Madras 155, 292
  New Delhi 181
  Razir 200

Indian(s) 28-9, 41, 67, 94, 116,
140-1, 149, 152, 155, 158, 180,
226, 235, 238-9, 241, 291, 309-10,
367-8, 388, 394
  Aztecs 65, 83, 158, 215, 373
  Blackfeet 239
  Chinook 122
  Chippewa 140
  Elders 142, 217
  Eskimos 333
  Hopi 140, 176-8, 184, 202-3,
210, 376, 388
    (also see Hopi)
  Incans 83, 215
  Iroquois 237, 367
  Mayans 83, 215, 373
  Navajo 148, 176, 177, 210,

388-9
  elders 148
  women 145
  Nomadic 142
  Oglala Sioux 240, 290
  Quechuas 215
  Seneca 237
  Sioux 388
  Sun Bear (see Sun Bear)

Indonesia 272
  Krakatoa 276

Initiate(s) 203
  elders 133
  Fifth Degree 81
  Sadat, Anwar 379

Initiation 53, 60, 70, 78, 94, 99,
105, 250, 357, 370
  Earth 80, 127
  fifth 99, 158
  fire 55
  first 73, 137
  fourth 98
  place of 134
  planetary 52, 66, 279-80
  second 70-3, 76, 126-7, 137
  second earth 153
  third earth 76-9, 95-8, 105,
279, 283, 347
  threshold 80
  Tibetan 59

Inner Light 53

Inner Planes 43, 82

insect(s)
  (see bugs)

Instrument 48, 141, 181, 207
  Channel
  (see Page Bryant)
  class 129
  deadly 233

Iran 45, 91, 124, 173, 273, 282,
292

Ireland 89, 213, 266, 388

IRS - Internal Revenue Service 325

Islamic (Law) 224

419

421

423

424

425

evolution 54
formation 33
gaseous 81
Heart center 149
heavenly body 204
infant 102
sacred 80
wounds 173

plate(s) 264
continental 264
tectonic 265, 267

Plato 19

planetary 205, 290
Caretakers 352
chakra 150

Planned Parenthood 387

plant(s) 197, 228, 307, 311, 343, 392
edible 333-4
poisonous 333-4

Pluto 34, 104

Polaris 88
(see poles)

polarity 258

pole(s)
icecaps 244
North 155, 257-8
North/South 31
polar 253
South 254, 257
Pole Star 337

poleshift 252-3, 255-7, 268, 278, 283

politics 108, 212, 230, 233, 243, 360
collapse 241

pollutant(s) 139-40, 243
air 276, 287, 328, 392
auto 245
heat 244

Pompeii 194, 276

population 387

Portugal 194

pottery 210

poultry
(see food)

power
failure 300

Pralaya 27

Prana 71, 149, 356

predestination 371

Priesthood 217

Princeton 245

Progenitor 41

Promised Land 178, 215

prophecy 126, 133-4, 141, 221, 223, 225-6, 229, 234-37, 239-40, 247-48, 252, 259-60, 262-63, 265, 272, 276-77, 279-80, 283-85, 289-90, 307, 310, 325, 347, 360-65, 367, 370-71
Black Serpent 238
Hopi 33
Red and White Serpent 237, 239
Rock 187
Serpent 368
Sundance 239

Prophet 157, 222

propulsion
advanced 380, 384-5

psyche 133, 221
man 106

psychic 193, 200, 207, 224, 240, 252, 260, 265, 278, 303, 372, 379
attunement 204, 214, 220
clairvoyant 138, 166, 195
faculties 72, 160
forces 388
impressions 131, 251
powers 195
psycho-drama 165
readings 161, 172, 193, 202, 225 (also see Depth Study)

427

true 77
self-reliance 296, 325

serpent 131
(also see prophecy)

Sewemaenewa, Paul 233

seven (7) 144
(also see rays)
Centers of Force 146
Golden Cities of Cibola 158

Shakespeare, William 106

shaman
ancient 186

Shamballa 98, 104, 154-5, 158
White Island 54

shellfish 327, 333
(see food)

shelter 336
how to build 334
lean to 335

shrine(s) 177
Lourdes 196
Shinto 185

Shustah 42

Siberia
(see USSR)

Sidi Bon Said 219

Sierra Club 362

sign(s) 291

signal(s)
alert 326

Sikkim 201-2

silver 210, 267, 375
threads 375-6

Sipapu 179

Sirius 96-7

Skylab 236
(see NASA)

Sky and Telescope 365

Smith, Jaine 169

Smithsonian (magazine) 245

snake
(see serpent)
dance 30
Priests 30

snow
(see climate)

soil 204, 310

solar
(also see Sun)
cells 381
energy 382
eruptions 242
family 41, 50, 73, 101-2
flares 269
group 50, 81, 102, 104, 117
observatory 204
satellites 381
system 20, 34, 50, 55, 61, 68,
81, 97, 101, 102, 103, 104, 106,
153, 166, 189, 193, 196, 216-17,
256-7, 274, 284
wheel 34

Solar Plexus
(see chakras) 142, 152

soul 77-9, 221, 291, 352, 357,
360, 378
earth 49, 51
human 279

sound 172, 174
celestial 199
currents 166, 173
receptacle 173
surgery 173
vorticles 173

South America 85, 91, 151,
183-4, 189, 272-3, 278, 282, 293

South Carolina 225
Charleston 262

space 194, 206, 211, 216, 243,
253, 266, 381, 383-4
age 106-7
colony 236, 370, 385

430

434

435

437

BIOGRAPHICAL SKETCH

Page Bryant is an internationally recognized psychic, teacher, lecturer and radio personality. Page has travelled and lectured internationally in the fields of metaphysics, psychic phenomena, the paranormal, and broadcasting. She has been a pioneer in radio and television in the southeastern U.S., having the first talk shows to deal exclusively with the paranormal and related subjects. She has hosted her own radio shows in Tampa and Ft. Lauderdale, Florida, before re-locating to the west. There she conducted her own talk program in Phoenix, Arizona and Los Angeles, California. She also had her own television show in St. Petersburg, Florida in 1975. She is currently a weekly feature on WTKN in Pittsburgh, Pennsylvania. Dozens of articles have been written about Page Bryant in all of the major national tabloids, as well as local newspapers nationwide. Page was the subject of a 1974 paperback entitled UNKNOWN HORIZONS: PSYCHIC IN THE DEVIL'S TRIANGLE and a 1977 paperback: ENCOUNTERS IN THE DEVIL'S TRIANGLE, both written by James Paul

Chaplin. Her latest book is entitled CRYSTALS AND THEIR USE. In 1975, Page Bryant was nominated as one of the Ten Outstanding Young Women of America.

Page Bryant is a member of The Cosmic Church of Truth in Jacksonville, Florida and the temple of the Living God in St. Petersburg, Florida, the Planetary Society, the International Halley Watch, Friends of the Earth, the Theosophical Society of America. She is a student of astronomy at Northern Arizona University in Flagstaff and is the co-founder of S.P.A.C.E.S., an amatuer astronomy club in Sedona, Arizona. Page teaches on-going classes in Sedona and there she has recently formed Earth Network, a meditation circle aimed at healing the planet with the use of mind power. Page travels extensively nationwide as a teacher, lecturer, and workshop coordinator.

Page, her husband Scott Guynup and her daughter, Mary Page Bryant currently reside in Flagstaff, Arizona. Scott, a New Age artist, is the owner of Sacred Mountain Studio, an in-home art workshop and both Page and her husband are the founders and directors of The Network for Cooperative Education, a young network designed to share Albion's teachings and related information. Page and Scott are both apprentices under Sun Bear, a Chippewa medicine man. Page is a pipe carrier and teaches Native American philosophy. Page has been a guest speaker for the Houston and Malibu Wheel Gatherings in 1981 and 1982.

OTHER SUN BOOKS TITLES

you may find of interest:

ASTROLOGY

ALAN LEO'S DICTIONARY OF ASTROLOGY by Alan Leo and Vivian E. Robson. Aaron's Rod, Casting the Horoscope, Disposition, Ecliptic, Equinoxes, Period of Sun, Objects Governed by the Planets, Mean Time.

THE ASTROLOGICAL GUIDE TO HEALTH FOR EACH OF THE TWELVE SUN SIGNS by Ariel Gordon, M.C. Information regarding the twelve signs of the Zodiac is taken from seven of the greatest authorities, past and present, on the different correspondences, as well as from personal experience, extending over many years of private practice.

ASTROLOGICAL PREDICTION by P.J. Harwood. Studing Astrology, Place and Time in Different Parts of the World, Erecting Horoscopes, Astrological Predictions, Definitions of Terms and Abbreviations, Transits and Various Directions, Life Periods, The Radical Horoscope, Marriage, Travel, Change and General Fortune, Time of Action, How Knowing Directions can Influence the Course of Life, Horoscopical Studies of Famous Individuals.

ASTROLOGY: HOW TO MAKE AND READ YOUR OWN HOROSCOPE by Sepharial. The Alphabet of the Heavens, The Construction of a Horoscope, How to Read the Horoscope, The Stars in Their Courses.

A BEGINNER'S GUIDE TO PRACTICAL ASTROLOGY by Vivian E. Robson. How to Cast a Horoscope, Planets, Signs, and Houses, How to Judge a Horoscope, How to Calculate Future Influences, etc.

THE BOWL OF HEAVEN by Evangeline Adams. My Job and How I Do It, A Grim Success, A Tale of Two Cities, "Dabbling in Heathenism", A Horrible Example, We are All Children of the Stars, Life and Death, The Money-Makers, Some Ladies of Venus, I Never Gamble, A World in Love, Astrological Marriages, My Own and Others, The New Natology, Twins and Things, Why Most People Come to Me, Am I Always Right? As I See It.

THE COSMIC KEY OF LIFE SELF-REALIZATION by A.S. Vickers. Index Charts, The Cosmic Key of Life, Helps in Selecting a Goal, Concentration, What is a Science? Key to Horoscope Blanks, Horoscopes of Noted Persons, Planetary Positions, Planetary Aspects, Sign Keywords, Appendix To Students, Astrological Smiles, Index to Astrological Attributes.

THE DIVINE LANGUAGE OF CELESTIAL CORRESPONDENCES by Coulson Turnbull. Esoteric Symbolism of the Planets, Mystical Interpretation of the Zodiac, Kabalistical Interpretation of the 12 Houses, Evolution and Involution of Soul, Character of the Planets, Hermetic Books, Nature of Signs, Etc.

THE EARTH IN THE HEAVENS - RULING DEGREES OF CITIES - HOW TO FIND AND USE THEM by L. Edward Johndro. Precession, Midheavens and Ascendants, Calculating Midheavens and Ascendants, Use of Locality Angles, Verification by World Events, Applications to Nativities.

1

ECLIPSES IN THEORY AND PRACTICE by Sepharial. The Natural Cause of an Eclipse, Eclipses of the Sun, Lunar Eclipses, Historical Eclipses, To Calculate an Eclipse of the Sun, To Calculate a Lunar Eclipse, Eclipse Signs, Eclipse Indications, The Decanates, Transits over Eclipse Points, Individuals and Eclipses, Illustrations, Conclusion.

HEBREW ASTROLOGY by Sepharial. Chaldean Astronomy, Time and Its Measures, The Great Year, The Signs of the Zodiac, How to Set a Horoscope, The Seven Times, Modern Predictions.

THE INFLUENCE OF THE ZODIAC UPON HUMAN LIFE by Eleanor Kirk. The Quickening Spirit, Questions and Answers, Disease, Development, A Warning, Marriage, The Fire, Air, Earth, and Water Triplicities, Etc. (This is an excellent book!)

THE LIGHT OF EGYPT or THE SCIENCE OF THE SOUL AND THE STARS by Thomas H. Burgoyne. Vol. 1: Realms of Spirit and Matter, Mysteries of Sex, Incarnation and Re-Incarnation, Karma, Mediumship, Soul Knowledge, Mortality and Immortality. Basic Principles of Celestial Science, Stellar Influence on Humanity, Alchemical Nature of Man, Union of Soul and Stars. Vol. II: The Zodiac and the Constellations, Spiritual Interpretation of the Zodiac, Astro-Theology and Astro-Mythology, Symbolism and Alchemy, Talismans and Ceremonial Magic, Tablets of AEth including: The Twelve Mansions, The Ten Planetary Rulers, The Ten Great Powers of the Universe, and Penetralia – The Secret of the Soul.

MANUAL OF ASTROLOGY by Sepharial. Language of the Heavens, Divisions of the Zodiac, Planets, Houses, Aspects, Calculation of the Horoscope, Reading of a Horoscope, Measure of Time, Law of Sex, Hindu Astrology, Progressive Horoscope, Etc.

MEDICAL ASTROLOGY by Henrich Däath. Basic Elements, Anatomical Sign-Rulership, Planetary Powers and Principles, Biodynamic Actions of Planets, How the Planets Crystallise in Organic and Inorganic Life, Tonicity, Atonicity and Perversion, Zodiaco-Planetary Synopsis of Typical Diseases, The Sixth and Eight Houses, The Triplicities and Quadruplicities, Planetary Sympathy and Antipathy, Guaging Planetary Strengths in the Specific Horoscope, Application, Examples, Indications of Short Life

NEW DICTIONARY OF ASTROLOGY In Which All Technical and Abstruse Terms Used In The Text Books of the Science Are Intimately Explained And Illustrated by Sepharial. Everything from Abscission to Zuriel.

THE PLANETS THROUGH THE SIGNS: Astrology for Living, by Abbe Bassett. Includes chapters on the Sun, Moon, and various planets, and how each one influences us through the different signs of the Zodiac.

PRIMARY DIRECTIONS MADE EASY by Sepharial. Principles of Directing, Polar Elevations, Illustrations, Mundane Aspects, Zodiacal Parallels, Mundane Parallels, Summary, Further Examples, Suggested Method, General Review, The Royal Horoscope, The Telescopic View, Solar and Lunar Horoscopes, Appendix.

RAPHAEL'S GUIDE TO ASTROLOGY by Raphael. The Symbols Explained, The Nature of the Aspects and Signs, The Orbits of the Planets, Persons Produced by the Signs of The Zodiac, The Form of Body Given by the Planets in the Signs, The Use of an Ephemeris, How to Erect a Map of the Heavens, How to Place the Planets in the Map, The Nature of the Planets, How to Judge a Nativity, Whether a Child Will Live or Die, Health, Mental Qualities, Money, Employment, Marriage, Travel, Etc., On the Selection of a House, Friends and Enemies, Directions or Calculating Future Events, A Short Astrological Dictionary, Etc!

RAPHAEL'S KEY TO ASTROLOGY by Raphael. Planetary Aspects and Orbs, Description of Persons Produced by the Signs, The Use of an Ephemeris, How to Erect a Map of the Heavens, The Influence of the Planets, How to Judge a Nativity, Whether a Child Will Live or Die, Health and Mental Qualities, Money Prospects and Employment, Marriage, Children and Travel, Friends and Enemies, The Kind of Death, etc.

RAPHAEL'S MEDICAL ASTROLOGY or the Effects of the Planets on the Human Body by Raphael. The Zodiac and the Human Body, Planetary Rulership and Action, Health and Constitution, Physical Condition, The Duration of Life, Examples of Early Death, Diseases, Mental Disorders, Injuries, Accidents and Deformities, Health and the Horoscope, Preventive Measures, Herbal Remedies, the Course of Disease, Astrology and Colors, etc.

RAPHAEL'S MUNDANE ASTROLOGY or The Effects of the Planets and Signs Upon the Nations and Countries of the World by Raphael. Mundane Astrology, Planetary and Zodiacal Signs and Symbols, The Twelve Mundane Houses, The Significations of the Planets,

Essential and Accidental Dignities, The Mundane Map, Concerning the Houses and the Planets, How to Judge a Mundane Map, Ellipses, Earthquakes, Comets, Planetary Conjunctions, The Parts of the World Affected by the Signs of the Zodiac. etc.

RELATION OF THE MINERAL SALTS OF THE BODY TO THE SIGNS OF THE ZODIAC by Dr. George W. Carey. Biochemistry, Esoteric Chemistry, The Ultimate of Biochemistry, The Twelve Cell-Salts of the Zodiac, Aries: The Lamb of God, Taurus: The Winged Bull, The Chemistry of Gemini, Cancer: The Chemistry of the Crab, Leo: The Heart of the Zodiac, Virgo: The Virgin Mary, Libra: The Loins, Scorpio: Influence of the Blood, The Chemistry of Sagittarius, Capricorn: The Goat of the Zodiac, The Sign of the Son of Man: Aquarius, Pisces: The Fish That Swim in the Pure Sea.

THE RISING ZODIACAL SIGN: ITS MEANING AND PROGNOSTICS by Coulson Turnbull. Aries - The Ram, Taurus - The Bull, Gemini - The Twins, Cancer - The Crab, Leo - The Lion, Virgo - The Virgin, Libra - The Balance, Scorpio - The Scorpion, Sagittarius - The Arrow, Capricorn - The Goat, Aquarius - The Waterman, Pisces - The Fishes, How To Determine the Rising Sign, Tables I, II, and III.

THE SCIENCE OF FOREKNOWLEDGE AND THE RADIX SYSTEM by Sepharial. The Science of Foreknowledge, Astrology in Shakespeare, The Great Year, Celestial Dynamics, Neptune, The Astrology of Lilith, Indian Astrology, Horoscope of Rama, Astrology of The Hebrews, Joan of Arc, The Measure of Life, Astrological Practice, Methods of Ptolemy and Benatti, The Radix System, Horoscopical Anomalies, Our Solar System, Financial Astrology.

THE SILVER KEY: A GUIDE TO SPECULATIORS by Sepharial. The Furure Method, Science of Numbers, Finding the Winner, The Lunar Key, Gravity and Evolution, Something to Come, A Warning, On Speciation, Monte Carlo and Astrology, Tables of Sidereal Times, Tables of Ascendants, Etc!

THE SOLAR EPOCH A NEW ASTROLOGICAL THESIS by Sepharial. The History of Birth, The Lunar Horoscope, The Solar Horoscope, Directional Influences, Conclusions.

THE SOLAR LOGOS OR STUDIES IN ARCANE MYSTICISM BY Coulson Turnbull. The Logos, The Kingdom of the Soul, Intuition and Motion, The Mystic Macrocosm, The Spirit of the Planets, The Mystical Sun and Moon, The Soul in Action, The Spiritual Horoscope, Health, Disease, Service, Etc.

THE STARS - HOW AND WHERE THEY INFLUENCE by L. Edward Johndro. Theory, Astronomical Fundamentals, Application of Fixed Stars to Nativities, Application of fixed Stars to Mundane Astrology, Verification by Nativities, Verification by World Events, Variable Stars, Binary Stars, Double Stars, Clusters, Nebulae and Bright Stars, General and Technical, Considerations, Conclusion.

STARS OF DESTINY – THE ANCIENT SCIENCE OF ASTROLOGY AND HOW TO MAKE USE OF IT TODAY by Katherine Taylor Craig. History and description of the Science, The Sun From Two Standpoints, The Moon and the Planets. Astrological Predictions That Have Been Verified, Practical Directions for Casting a Horoscope, Sample of General Prediction for a Year.

A STUDENTS' TEXT-BOOK OF ASTROLOGY by Vivian E. Robson. Fundamental Principles of Astrology, Casting the Horoscope, Character and Mind, Occupation and Position, Parents, Relatives and Home, Love and Marriage, Esoteric Astrology, Adoption of the New Style Calendar.

WHAT IS ASTROLOGY? by Colin Bennett. How an Astrologer Works, Sign Meanings, How Aspects Affect a Horoscope, Numerology as an Astrological Aid, Psychology In Relation to Astrology, Etc.

ATLANTIS / LEMURIA

ATLANTIS IN AMERICA by Lewis Spence. Atlantis and Antillia, Cro-Magnons of America. Quetzalcoatl the Atlantean, Atlantis in American Tradition and Religion, Ethnological Evidence, Art and Architecture, Folk-Memories of an Atlantic Continent, Analogy of Lemuria, Chronological Table, Etc.

THE PROBLEM OF LEMURIA - THE SUNKEN CONTINENT OF THE PACIFIC by Lewis Spence, Illustrated. The Legend of Lemuria, The Argument From Archaeology, The Testimony of Tradition, The Evidence from Myth and Magic, The Races of Lemuria, The Testimony of Custom, The Proof of Art, The Geology of Lemuria,

The Evidence from Biology, The Catastrophe and its Results, Life and Civilization in Lemuria, Atlantis and Lemuria, Conclusions.

WISDOM FROM ATLANTIS by Ruth B. Drown. Being, Divine Selfishness, Service, Nobility of Self-Reliance, Harmony, Divine Love, Principles of Life and Living, Man's Divine Nature, Faith, True Thinking.

AUTOSUGGESTION / HYPNOTISM

AUTO-SUGGESTION: WHAT IT IS AND HOW TO USE IT FOR HEALTH, HAPPINESS AND SUCCESS by Herbert A. Parkvn. M.D.. C.M. Auto-suggestion - What it is and how to use it, Auto-suggestion - Its effects and how to employ it to overcome physical troubles, Auto-suggestion - How to employ it to overcome mental troubles, Influences of early auto-suggestions for the forming of the character, Auto-suggestion for the formation of habits, Auto-suggestion and personal magnetism, The cultivation of optimism through auto-suggestion, Auto-suggestion for developing concentration, The achievement of success through auto-suggestion and success, Auto-suggestion and breathing exercises, Auto-suggestion: It's influence on health in the winter, The diagnosis and treatment of a typical case of chronic physical suffering, Auto-suggestion the basis of all healing, How psychic pictures are made realities by auto-suggestion.

EMILE COUÉ: THE MAN AND HIS WORK by Hugh MacNaughten Foreword and Author's Notes, Prelude, Nancy, Nancy or London, M Coué at Eton, M Coué in London, The Sub-Concious Self, On Some Stumbling Blocks, M Coué in His Relation To Christianity, On "Everything for Nothing", M. Coué, Envoi.

HOW TO PRACTICE SUGGESTION AND AUTOSUGGESTION by Emile Coué, Preface by Charles Baudouin. Interviews of Patients, Examples of the Power of Suggestion and Autosuggestion, Suggestions: General and Special, Special Suggestions for Each Ailment, Advice to Patients, Lectures Delivered by Emile Coué in America.

MY METHOD by Emile Coué. Chapters include: Autosuggestion Disconcerting in its Simplicity, Slaves of Suggestion and Masters of Ourselves, Dominance of the Imagination over the Will, The Moral Factor in all Disease, Don't Concentrate, How to Banish Pain, Psychic Culture as Necessary as Physical, Self-Mastery Means Health, Etc.

THE PRACTICE OF AUTOSUGGESTION BY THE METHOD OF EMILE COUÉ by C. Harry Brooks. The Clinic of Emile Coué, A Few of Coué's Cures, Thought is a Force, Thought and the Will, The General Formula, How to Deal With Pain, Autosuggestion and the Child, Particular Suggestions, Etc.

SELF MASTERY THROUGH CONSCIOUS AUTOSUGGESTION by Emile Coué. Self Mastery Through Autosuggestion, Thoughts and Precepts, What Autosuggestion Can Do, Education as it Ought to Be, A Survey of the "Seances", the Miracle Within, Everything for Everyone, Etc.

SUGGESTION AND AUTOSUGGESTION by Charles Baudouin. Why Do We Ignore Autosuggestion?, Representative Suggestions, Affective Suggestions, Motor Suggestions, Conditional Suggestions, The Action of Sleep, The Law of Reversed Effort, Relaxation and Collectedness, Autohypnosis, Moral Energy, Exercises, Coue's Practice, Acceptivity and Suggestibility, The Education of Children, Methods of Application,

CLAIRVOYANCE

SECOND SIGHT - A STUDY OF NATURAL AND INDUCED CLAIRVOYANCE by Sepharial. The Scientific Position, Materials and Conditions, The Faculty of Seership, Preliminaries and Practice, Kinds of Visions, Obstacles and Clairvoyance, Symbolism, Allied Psychic Phases, Experience and Use.

CONSPIRACY

THE ILLUMINOIDS – SECRET SOCIETIES AND POLITICAL PARANOIA by Neal Wilgus. Detailed picture of Weishaupt's Order of the Illuminati as well as other secret societies throughout history. Ties various far-reaching areas together including important information relating to the J.F. Kennedy assassination. "The best single reference on the Illuminati in fact and legendry" – Robert Anton Wilson in Cosmic Trigger.

CRYSTALS/MINERALS

CRYSTALS AND THEIR USE—A Study of At-One-Ment with the Mineral Kingdom by Page Bryant. Mineral Consciousness, Crystals and Their Use, Sacred Centers, Various Types of Crystals, The Amethyst, Crystal Gazing.

THE MAGIC OF MINERALS by Page Bryant. The Inner Lives of the Mineral Kingdom, Megalithic Mysteries and the Native American View, The Healing Properties of Minerals, Psychic Influences in Minerals, Stones of the Zodiac, Crystals and Their Use, General Information on Selection, Use, and Care of Minerals.

MAN, MINERALS, AND MASTERS by Charles W. Littlefield, M.D. School of the Magi, Three Masters, The Cubes, Initiation in Tibet, Hindustan, and Egypt, History, Prophecy, Numerology, Perfection. 172p. 5x8 Paperback.

PLANETARY INFLUENCES AND THERAPEUTIC USES OF PRECIOUS STONES by George Frederick Kunz. Includes various lists and illustrations, etc.

DREAMS

DREAMS AND PREMONITIONS by L.W. Rogers. Introduction, The Dreamer, The Materialistic Hypotheses Inadequate, Dreams of Discovery, Varieties of Dreams, Memories of Astral Experiences, Help from the Invisibles, Premonitory Dreams, Dreams of the Dead, How to Remember Dreams.

EARTH CHANGES (Also See Prophecy)

CHEIRO'S WORLD PREDICTIONS by Cheiro. Fate of Nations, British Empire in its World Aspect, Destiny of the United States, Future of the Jews, Coming War of Wars, Coming Aquarian Age, Precession of the Equinoxes.

THE COMING STAR-SHIFT AND MANY PROPHECIES OF BIBLE AND PYRAMID FULFILLED by O. Gordon Pickett. God Corrects His Clock in the Stars, English Alphabet as Related to Numerics, Joseph Builder of the Great Pyramid, Numerical Harmony, Prophecy, World Wars, Star-Shifts, The Flood, Astronomy, The Great Pyramids, Etc.

COMING WORLD CHANGES by H.A. and F.H.Curtiss. The Prophecies, Geological Considerations, The Philosophy of Planetary Changes, The King of the World, The Heart of the World, The Battle of Armageddon, The Remedy.

EARTH CHANGES NOW! by Page Bryant. The Earth is Changing: The Evidence, We Knew it was Coming!, The Sacred Covenant, The Externalization of the Spiritual Hierarchy, The Earth Angel: A Promise for the Future.

THE EARTH CHANGES SURVIVAL HANDBOOK by Page Bryant. The Emergence of Planetary Intelligence, Mapping the Earth, Earth Changes: Past and Future, Preparing for the Future, Walking in Balance, Etc.

NOSTRADAMUS NOW - PROPHECIES OF PERIL AND PROMISE FOR THE 1990'S AND BEYOND by Joseph Robert Jochmans Chapters include: What Were the Prophet's Secret Sources of Wisdom? What Mysterious Methods Did the Prophet Use to Make His Forecasts? Will the Prophet Return to Life? A Warning of Coming Global War For Our World Today? Is America About to Suffer Social, Political and Economic Collapse? Will Superquakes Devastate America's West and East Coasts? Is a Planetary Inter-Dimensional Doorway About to Be Opened? The Middle East Gulf War Was It Necessary, and Will It Flare Up Again? The Coming of the Man of Power From the East: Antichrist or Avatar? When Will the Downfall of the World Economic System Take Place? Could a Comet or Meteor Hit the Earth and Cause an Axis Pole Shift? Where Will be the Trouble Spots in the Middle East and Far East During the Next Ten Years? What Major Earth Cataclysms May Yet Occur? The New Russia and America Have They Changed For the Better? What Will Be Humanity's Destiny Into the Far Future? Which Future Options Will We Choose?

ORACLES OF NOSTRADAMUS by Charles A. Ward. Life of Nostradamus, Preface to Prophecies, Epistle to Henry II, Magic, Historic Fragments, Etc.

PROPHECIES OF GREAT WORLD CHANGES compiled by George B. Brownell. World-War Prophecies, Coming Changes of Great Magnitude, False Christs, The New Heaven and the New Earth, The New Order and the Old, Etc.

ROLLING THUNDER: THE COMING EARTH CHANGES by J. R. Jochmans. The Coming Famine and Earth Movements, The Destruction of California and New York, Future War, Nostradamus, Bible, Edgar Cayce. Coming Avatars, Pyramid Prophecy, Weather, Coming False Religion and the Antichrist, and much, much more! This book is currently our best selling title.

UTOPIA II: AN INVESTIGATION INTO THE KINGDOM OF GOD by John Schmidt. Why Utopia?, Mankind's Past, Present, and Future, A Sociological Look, A Political Look, An Economic Look, A Spiritual Look.

GENERAL METAPHYSICAL

THE CABALA - ITS INFLUENCE ON JUDAISM AND CHRISTIANITY by Bernard Pick. Name and Origin of the Cabala, The Development of the Cabala in the Pre-Zohar Period, The Book of Zohar or Splendor, The Cabala in the Post Zohar Period, The Most Important Doctrines of the Cabala, The Cabala in Relation to Judaism and Christianity.

THE ESSENES AND THE KABBAIAH Two Essays by Christian D. Ginsburg. Description of the Essenes, Ancient and Modern Literature, The Meaning of the Kabbalah, Kabbalistic Cosmogony, Creation of Angels and Men, The Destiny of Man and the Universe, Kabbalism, the Old Testament, and Christianity, The Books of the Kabbalah, The Schools, Indexes and Glossary.

GEMS OF MYSTICISM by H.A. and F.H. Curtiss. Spiritual Growth, Duty, Karma, Reincarnation, The Christ, Masters of Wisdom.

THE HISTORY AND POWER OF MIND by Richard Ingalese. Divine Mind; It's Nature and Manifestation, Dual Mind and its Origin, Self-Control Re-Embodiment, Colors of Thought Vibration, Meditation, Creation, and Concentration, Psychic Forces and their Dangers, Spiritual Forces and Their Uses, The Cause and Cure of Disease, The Law Of Opulance.

INFINITE POSSIBILITIES by Leilah Wendell. Chapters include: The Essence of Time, Time and Space, Inseperable Brothers, Coexistent Time, Traveling Through Time, Microcosmic Reflections, Cosmic Consciousness, The Universe in a Jar, Psychic Alchemy, Universality, The Divine Element, The Complete Whole, What Price Immortality?, Practical Infinity, Etc.

VISUALIZATION AND CONCENTRATION AND HOW TO CHOOSE A CAREER by Fenwicke L. Holmes. The Creative Power of Mind, Metaphysics and Psychology, Mental Telepathy, Visualization and Dramatization, Concentration How to Choose a Career.

GENERAL OCCULT

THE BOOK OF CHARMS AND TALISMANS by Sepharial. History and Background, Numbers and their Significance, Charms to Wear, Background of Talismans, Making Talismans.

BYGONE BELIEFS – AN EXCURSION INTO THE OCCULT AND ALCHEMICAL NATURE OF MAN by H. Stanley Redgrove. Some Characteristics of Mediaeval Thought, Pythagoras and his Philosophy, Medicine and Magic, Belief in Talismans, Ceremonial Magic in Theory and Practice, Architectural Symbolism, Philosopher's Stone, The Phallic Element in Alchemical Doctrine, Roger Bacon, Etc. (Many Illustrations).

THE COILED SERPENT by C.J. van Vliet. A Philosophy of Conservation and Transmutation of Reproductive Energy. Deadlock in Human Evolution, Spirit Versus Matter, Sex Principle and Purpose of Sex, Pleasure Principle, Unfolding of Spirit, Marriage and Soul-Mates, Love Versus Sex, Erotic Dreams, Perversion and Normalcy, Virility, Health, and Disease, Freemasonry, Rosicrucians, Alchemy, Astrology, Theosophy, Magic, Yoga, Occultism, Path of Perfection, Uncoiling the Serpent, The Future, Supermen, Immortality, Etc.

COSMIC SYMBOLISM by Sepharial. Meaning and Purpose of Occultism, Cosmic Symbology, Reading the Symbols, Law of Cycles, Time Factor in Kabalism, Involution and Evolution, Planetary Numbers, Sounds, Hours, Celestial Magnetic Polarities, Law of Vibrations, Lunar and Solar Influences, Astrology and the Law of Sex, Character and Environment, Etc.

THE ELEUSINIAN MYSTERIES AND RITES by Dudley Wright. Preface, Introduction, The Eleusinian Legend, The Ritual of the Mysteries, Program of the Greater Mysteries, The Intimate Rites, The Mystical Significance, Bibliography.

THE INNER GOVERNMENT OF THE WORLD by Annie Besant. Ishvara, The Builders of a

Cosmos, The Hierarchy of our World, The Rulers, Teachers, Forces, Method of Evolution, Races and Sub-Races, The Divine Plan, Religions and Civilizations, Etc.

THE MASCULINE CROSS AND ANCIENT SEX WORSHIP by Sha Rocco. Origin of the Cross, Emblems: Phallus, Triad, Vocabulary, Marks and Signs of the Triad, Yoni, Color of Gods, Fish and Good Friday, Tortoise, Earth Mother, Unity, Fourfold God, Meru, Religious Prostitution, Shaga, Communion Buns and Religious Cakes, Antiquity of the Cross, Crucifixion, Christna, Phallic and Sun Worship, The Phallus in California.

THE MESSAGE OF AQUARIA by Curtiss. The Mystic Life, The Sign Aquarius, Are These the Last Days?, Comets and Eclipses, Law of Growth, Birth of the New Age, Mastery and the Masters of Wisdom, Mother Earth and the Four Winds, The Spiral of Life and Life Waves, The Message of the Sphinx, Day of Judgement and Law of Sacrifice, The Spiritual Birth, The True Priesthood, Etc.

THE OCCULT ARTS by J.W. Frings. Alchemy, Astrology, Psychometry, Telepathy, Clairvoyance, Spiritualism, Hypnotism, Geomancy, Palmistry, Omens and Oracles.

THE OCCULT ARTS OF ANCIENT EGYPT by Bernard Bromage. Foreword, The Nature of the Ancient Egyptian Civilization, What the Ancient Egyptians Understood by Magic, The Destiny of the Soul According to the Egyptians, Egyptian Magic and Belief in Amulets and Talismans, The Egyptian Magicians, Black Magic in Ancient Egypt, The Astrological Implications of Egyptian Magic, Ancient Egypt and the Universal Dream Life, (Includes Various Illustrations).

OCCULTISTS & MYSTICS OF ALL AGES by Ralph Shirley. Apollonius of Tyana, Plotinus, Michael Scot, Paracelsus, Emanuel Swedenborg, Count Cagliostro, Anna Kingsford.

SEMA-KANDA: THRESHOLD MEMORIES by Coulson Turnbull. Ra-Om-Ar and Sema-Kanda, The Brotherhood, Sema-Kanda's Childhood, The Scroll, Posidona, Questioning, Ramantha's Lesson, The Great White Lodge, The Destruction of Atlantis, The Two Prisoners, The Congregation of the Inquisition, An Invitation, A Musical Evening, Two Letters, Confidences, The Horoscope, Etc.

VOICE OF ISIS by H.A. & F.A. Curtiss. Life's Duties, The Cycle of Fulfillment, Degrees and Orders, The Wisdom Religion, Concerning the Doctrine of Hell Fire, The Eleventh Commandment, Narcotics, Alcohol and Phychism, A Study of Karma, The Self, The Doctrine of Avatara, The Study of Reincarnation, Power, A Brief Outline of Evolution, The Laws, World Chains, Purity, The Origin of Man, The Symbol of the Serpent, Purification vs Deification, The Memory of Past Lives, The Cycle of Necessity, Etc!

WHAT IS OCCULTISM? by Papus. Occultism Defined, Occult Philosophical Point of View, Ethics of Occultism, Aesthetics of Occultism, Theodicy – Sociology, Practice of Occultism, The Traditions of Magic, Occultism and Philosophy.

YOUR UNSEEN GUIDE by C.J. Halsted. The Manner in Which You are Guided, How I Am Guided Consciously, Omens, The Intermediate State, Heaven, Spiritualism, The "Spirit Man" Illusion Dispelled, Evidence of My Guide's Prescience, Evolution.

GRAPHOLOGY

HOW TO READ CHARACTER IN HANDWRITING by Mary H. Booth. Principles of Analysis and Deduction, Forming Impressions from the Handwriting, The Autograph Fad, Entertaining by Graphology, Graphology as a Profession, Index.

HEALING

DIVINE REMEDIES – A TEXTBOOK ON CHRISTIAN HEALING by Theodosia DeWitt Schobert. Fuller Understanding of Spiritual Healing, Healing of Blood Troubles and Skin Diseases, Freedom from Sense Appetite, Healing of Insanity, Healing of Insomnia, Healing of Poisoning of Any Kind, General Upbuilding and Healing of the Body Temple.

THE FINER FORCES OF NATURE IN DIAGNOSIS AND THERAPY by George Starr White, M.D. The Magnetic Meridian, Vital and Unseen Forces, Polarity, Cause of Un-Health, Colors, Magnetic Energy, Sympathetic-Vagal Reflex, Actions of Finer Forces of Nature, The Human Aura, Moon-Light and Sound Treatment with Light and Color, Etc.

HEAL THYSELF: AN EXPLANATION OF THE REAL CAUSE AND CURE OF DISEASE by Edward Bach, M.B., B.S., D.P.H. by focusing on the causes rather than the results of disease and thus allowing individuals to assist in their own healing, Dr. Bach shows the vital principles which will guide medicine in the near future and are indeed guiding some of the more advanced members of the profession today.

HEALTH AND SPIRITUAL HEALING by Richard Lynch. The Key to Health, Statements for the Realization of Health, Rhythm of Life and Health, The Revelation of the Body, Realizing the Perfect Body, The Tree of Life and Health, Establishing the Incorruptible Body, Health Personified, Bringing Forth the True Body, How to Renew Your Consciousness, Individual Rebirth in Consciousness, Individual Resurrection, Ideas for Individual Ressurrection. ·

THE KEY TO MAGNETIC HEALING by J.H. Strasser. The History of Magnetic Healing, The Theory of Magnetic Healing, Proof of Its Existence, What it is, Sources of it, Are Vital Magnetism and Electricity the Same, Have all Persons Magnetic Power?, Mental Science, The Principle of Life in Man, Mind and Magnetism, The Will Power, Mind over Matter, Passivity or Hypnotism, Why is Suggestion so Effective during Passivity?, Telepathy, Experiments, Testing Susceptibility, To Find Hidden Objects, Producing the Passive State, Suggestion, Manipulation, and Passes, General Treatment by Suggestion, Producing Anaesthesia, Hypnotizing at a Distance, Suggestion during Common Sleep, Suggestion during Waking State, Telepathy or Mind—Telegraphy, The Practice of Magnetic Healing, Can Magnetic Healing be Suppressed?, Unconscious Magnetic Healing, Treatment of the Different Diseases, Nervous Diseases, Blood Diseases, caused by Congestion and Irregular Circulation, Miscellaneous Diseases, Etc!

THE PHILOSOPHY OF MENTAL HEALING – A PRACTICAL EXPOSITION OF NATURAL RESTORATIVE POWER by Leander Edmund Whipple. Metaphysical Healing, Metaphysics Versus Hypnotism, The Potency of Metaphysics in Surgery, The Progress of the Age, Intelligence and Sensation, Mental Action, The Physical Reflection of Thought.

THE PRINCIPLES OF OCCULT HEALING Edited by Mary Weeks Burnett, M.D. Occult Healing and Occultism, Healing and the Healing Intelligence. The Indestructible Self, Latent Powers of Matter, The Auras and the Ethers, Polarization, Music, Healing by Prayer, Angel or Deva Helpers, Thought Forms and Color in Healing, Magnetism – Mesmerism, Healing Miracles of the Christ, Etc

THE TWELVE HEALERS AND OTHER REMEDIES by Edward Bach. Chapters include remedies for the following: For Fear, For Uncertainty, For Insufficient Interest in Present Circumstances, For Loneliness, For Those Over-Sensitive to Influences and Ideas, For Despondency or Despair, For Over-Care for Welfare of Others.

HERBS

THE COMPLETE HERBALIST or THE PEOPLE THEIR OWN PHYSICIANS by Dr. O. Phelps Brown. By the use of Nature's Remedies great curative properties found in the Herbal Kingdom are described. A New and Plain System of Hygienic Principles Together with Comprehensive Essays on Sexual Philosophy, Marriage, Divorce, Etc.

THE TRUTH ABOUT HERBS by Mrs. C.F. Loyd. The Unbroken Tradition of Herbal Medicine, The History of Herbalism, The Birth of the Society of Herbalists, Herbs Cure-The Reason Why, The Healing Properties of Certain Herbs, The Effect of Herbs on Allergic Diseases, Herbalists' Fight for Freedom, Etc.

HISTORICAL NOVEL

CHILD OF THE SUN: A HISTORICAL NOVEL by Frank Cheavens. Alvar Nuñez Cabeza de Vaca was the first European explorer to cross the North American continent. His early 16th century wandering took him across Texas, part of New Mexico, southeastern Arizona, and down the west coast of Mexico into South America. His altruistic work and healing ministrations among the Indians of the Southwest drew to him multitudes of Indians who revered him as the Child of the Sun. Here, his story is told through the eyes of a deformed, itinerant Pueblo trader who joined him, studied with him, and witnessed the Great Spirit working through him.

HOLLOW EARTH

ETIDORHPA or THE END OF EARTH by John Uri Lloyd. Journey toward the center of the Earth thru mighty mushroom forests and across huge underground oceans with an entire series of fantastic experiences. A true occult classic! "Etidorhpa, the End of Earth, is in all respects the worthiest presentation of occult teachings under the attractive guise of fiction that has yet been written" – New York World.

BEING AND BECOMING - THE PRINCIPLES AND PRACTICES OF THE SCIENCE OF SPIRIT by Fenwicke L. Holmes. The Impersonal Mind, Becoming, Allowing Mind to Act, Unconscious Activity, The Great Law of Mind, The Law of Correspondence, Picturing our Good, Ideataion, Concentration vs. Ideation, Denials, Affirmation, Consciousness, A Healing Realization, The Personal Spirit, The Purpose of Spirit, The Motive - Love, Love Defined, Making our Unity, Love - The Healing Power, Feelings and Emotions, Why Many Fail, Mysticism, Our Power of Choice, Being, Intuition, Spirit as Formative, A Way to Escape, Identity with Spirit, Demonstrating Prosperity, The Law of Spirit, Mental Equivalents, Selling a House, Spirit as All, "I am He".

CHARACTER BUILDING THOUGHT POWER by Ralph Waldo Trine. "Have we within our power to determine at all times what types of habits shall take form in our lives? In other words, is habit-forming, character-building, a matter of mere chance, or do we have it within our control?"

CREATIVE MIND by Ernest S. Holmes. Chapters include: In the Beginning, Why and What is a Man?, The Law of Our Lives, Bondage and Freedom, The Word, The Power We Have Within Us, The Reason for the Universe, Mind in Action, Action and Reaction, Arriving at High Consciousness, The Perfect Universe, About Struggle Karma, Etc.

CRISIS IN CONSCIOUSNESS: The Source of All Conflict by Robert Powell. The Importance of Right Beginning, Zen and Liberation, The Worldly Mind and the Religious Mind, Repetition of the Pattern, Experience, Habit and Freedom, Can Illumination be Transmitted? The Equation of Unhappiness, Must We Have Religious Societies? Approach to the Immeasurable, Window on Non-Duality, Memory Without a Cause, Self or Non-Self? Common Sayings Revealing Uncommon Insights, On Contradiction, The Outer and the Inner, Etc.

THE FAITH THAT HEALS (HOW TO DEVELOP) by Fenwicke L. Holmes The New Consciousness, Cosmic Consciousness, The Law of Consciousness Outlines, Practical Use of Visions – Visualizing Prosperity and Health, the Cure of Organic Disease and "Incurables," New Healing and Prosperity Consciousness, Your Healing Word, Faith in Yourself, Developing Self-Confidence, etc.

THE FREE MIND: THE INWARD PATH TO LIBERATION by Robert Powell. Liberation and Duality, Crisis in Consciousness, Our Predicament, On Mindfulness, Living in the Essential, A Noncomparative Look at Zen and Krishnamurti, The Problem of Ambition, Only the Empty Mind is Capable of True Thoughtfulness, What Education Should Be All About, and What it Actually Is, If Awareness is Choiceless, Then Who is it That is Aware?, Free Among the Unfree, The Vicious, Vicious Circle of Self-Defense and War, Reflections on Causality: The Ultimate Failure of Metaphysics, Etc.

HEALTH AND WEALTH FROM WITHIN by William E. Towne. Health From Within, Awakening of the Soul, Will, Love and Work, The Voice of Life, Non-Attachment, The Woman – The Man, The Supreme Truth, Power of Imagination and Faith, Practical Self-Healing, The Way to Gain Results, Lengthen and Brighten Life, Etc.

ON THE OPEN ROAD - BEING SOME THOUGHTS AND A LITTLE CREED OF WHOLESOME LIVING by Ralph Waldo Trine. To realize always clearly, that thoughts are forces, that like creates like and like attracts like, and that to determine one's thinking therefore is to determine his life.

POSITIVE THOUGHTS ATTRACT SUCCESS by Mary A. Dodson and Ella E. Dodson. "Unless Your Heart Sings The Word, It Would Be Better Left Unuttered ." "Unless We Can Do The Work Better, We Have No Right To Find Fault When Another Does It." "I Am a Holy Temple, and Send Out Love and Good To All The World." "What You Accomplish is Often Determined by What You Attempt." "I Will to go on From Strength to Strength, From Character to Character, Until I Have Developed a Powerful Personality."

SO SPEAKS HIGHER POWER: A HANDBOOK FOR EMOTIONAL AND SPIRITUAL RECOVERY by Dr. Isaac Shamaya. Addiction, Stress and Recovery, Feeling, Blame, Anger, Fear and Pain, Relationships, Understanding, Love, and Higher Power.

THE SUCCESS PROCESS by Brown Landone. Five Factors Which Guarantee Success. The Process of Vivid Thinking, Tones Used in Persuading, Use of Action, Overcoming Hindrances, Developing Capacities, Securing Justice, Augmenting Your Success by Leadership, Etc.

ABOVE LIFE'S TURMOIL by James Allen. True Happiness, The Immortal Man, The Overcoming of Self, The Uses of Temptation, The Man of Integrity, Discrimination, Belief, The Basis of Action, The Belief that Saves, Thought and Action, Your Mental Attitude, Sowing and Reaping, The Reign of Law, The Supreme Justice, The Use of Reason, Self-Discipline, Resolution, The Glorious Conquest, Contentment in Activity, The Temple of Brotherhood, Pleasant Pastures of Peace.

ALL THESE THINGS ADDED by James Allen. Entering the Kingdom, The Soul's Great Need, The Competitive Laws and the Law of Love, The Finding of a Principle, At Rest in the Kingdom, The Heavenly Life, The Divine Center, The Eternal Now, "The Original Simplicity", The Unfailing Wisdom, The Might of Meekness, The Righteous Man, Perfect Love, Greatness and Goodness, and Heaven in the Heart.

AS A MAN THINKETH by James Allen. Thought and Character, Effect of Thought on Circumstances, Effect of Thought on Health and the Body, Thought and Purpose, The Thought-Factor in Achievement, Visions and Ideals, Serenity.

BYWAYS OF BLESSEDNESS by James Allen. Right Beginnings, Small Tasks and Duties, Transcending Difficulties and Perplexities, Burden-Dropping, Hidden Sacrifices, Sympathy, Forgiveness, Seeing No Evil, Abiding Joy, Silentness, Solitude, Standing Alone, Understanding the Simple Laws of Life, Happy Endings.

EIGHT PILLARS OF PROSPERITY by James Allen. Discussion on Energy, Economy, Integrity, Systems, Sympathy, Sincerity, Impartiality, Self-reliance, and the Temple of Prosperity

ENTERING THE KINGDOM by James Allen. The Soul's Great Need, The Competitive Laws and the Laws of Love, The Finding of a Principle, At Rest in the Kingdom, And All Things Added.

FROM PASSION TO PEACE by James Allen. Passion, Aspiration, Temptation, Transmutation, Transcendence, Beatitude, Peace.

FROM POVERTY TO POWER by James Allen. Two books in one: The Path to Prosperity Including World a Reflex of Mental States, The Way Out of Undesirable Conditions, Silent Power of Thought, Controlling and Directing One's Forces, The Secret of Health, Success, and Power, Etc. and The Way of Peace including Power of Meditation, The Two Masters, Self and Truth, The Acquirement of Spiritual Power, Realization of Selfless Love, Entering into the Infinite, Perfect Peace, Etc.

THE HEAVENLY LIFE by James Allen. The Divine Center, The Eternal Now, The "Original Simplicity", The Unfailing Wisdom, The Might of Meekness, The Righteous Man, Perfect Love, Perfect Freedom, Greatness and Goodness, Heaven in the Heart.

THE LIFE TRIUMPHANT by James Allen. Faith and Courage, Manliness and Sincerity, Energy and Power, Self-Control and Happiness, Simplicity and Freedom, Right-Thinking and Repose, Calmness and Resource, Insight and Nobility, Man and the Master, and Knowledge and Victory.

LIGHT ON LIFE'S DIFFICULTIES by James Allen. The Light that Leads to Perfect Peace, Light on Facts and Hypotheses, The Law of Cause and Effect in Human Life, Values - Spiritual and Material, The Sense of Proportion, Adherence to Principle, The Sacrifice of the Self, The Management of the Mind, Self-Control: The Door of Heaven, Acts and their Consequences, The Way of Wisdom, Disposition, Individual Liberty, The Blessing and Dignity of Work, Good Manner and Refinement, Diversity of Creeds, Law and Miracle, War and Peace, The Brotherhood of Man, Life's Sorrows, Life's Change, The Truth of Transitoriness, The Light that Never Goes Out.

MAN: KING OF MIND, BODY AND CIRCUMSTANCE by James Allen. The Inner World of Thoughts, The Outer World of Things, Habit: Its Slavery and Its Freedom, Bodily Conditions, Poverty, Man's Spiritual Dominion, Conquest: Not Resignation.

THE MASTERY OF DESTINY by James Allen. Deeds, Character, and Destiny, The Science of Self-Control, Cause and Effect in Human Conduct, Training of the Will, Thoroughness, Mind-Building and Life-Building, Cultivation of Concentration, Practice of Meditation, The Power of Purpose, The Joy of Accomplishment.

MEDITATIONS, A YEAR BOOK by James Allen. "James Allen may truly be called the Prophet of Meditation. In an age of strife, hurry, religious controversy, heated arguments, ritual and ceremony, he came with his message of Meditation, calling men away from the din and strife of tongues into the peaceful paths of stillness within their own souls, where 'the Light that lighteth every man that cometh into the world' ever burns steadily and surely for all who will turn their weary eyes from the strife without to the quiet within." Contains two quotes and a brief commentary for each day of the year.

MORNING AND EVENING THOUGHTS by James Allen. Contains a separate and brief paragraph for each morning and evening of the month.

OUT FROM THE HEART by James Allen. The Heart and the Life, The Nature of Power of Mind, Formation of Habit, Doing and Knowing, First Steps in the Higher Life, Mental Conditions and Their Effects, Exhortation.

THROUGH THE GATE OF GOOD by James Allen. The Gate and the Way, The Law and the Prophets, The Yoke and the Burden, The Word and the Doer, The Vine and the Branches, Salvation this Day.

THE WAY OF PEACE by James Allen. The Power of Meditation, The Two Masters: Self and Truth, The Acquirement of Spiritual Power, The Realization of Selfless Love, Entering into the Infinite, Saints, Sages, and Saviors, The Law of Service, The Realization of Perfect Peace.

PERSONALITY: ITS CULTIVATION AND POWER AND HOW TO ATTAIN by Lily L. Allen. Personality, Right Belief, Self-Knowledge, Intuition, Decision and Promptness, Self-Trust, Thoroughness, Manners, Physical Culture, Mental, Moral, and Spiritual Culture, Introspection, Emancipation, Self-Development, Self-Control and Mental Poise, Liberty, Transformation, Balance, Meditation and Concentration.

KUNDALINI

AND THE SUN IS UP: KUNDALINI RISES IN THE WEST by W. Thomas Wolfe. Chapters include: The Hindu's View, The Esoteric Christian's View, The Professional Specialist's View, The Kundalini Subject's View, Physiological Effects, Spiritual Weightlessness, Emotional and Attitudinal Changes, Changed Dream Content, Event Control, The Reason for Summoning Up the Kundalini, Christ and the Kundalini, A Modern Parallel to the Second Coming, Etc.

LIGHT

PHILOSOPHY OF LIGHT – AN INTRODUCTORY TREATISE by Floyd Irving Lorbeer. The Ocean of Light, Sight and Light, Light and Perception, Some Cosmic Considerations, Light and Health, Electrical Hypothesis, Temperament, Beauty, and Love and Light, The Problem of Space and Time, Unity and Diversity, Deity, Soul, and Immortality, Light and the New Era, Etc.

PRINCIPLES OF LIGHT AND COLOR by Edwin D. Babbitt. (Illustrated, Complete 578p. version.) The Harmonic Laws of the Universe, The Etherio-Atomic Philosophy of Force, Chromo Chemistry, Chromo Therapeutics, and the General Philosophy of Finer Forces, Together with Numerous Discoveries and Practical Applications, Etc!

LONGEVITY

FOREVER YOUNG: HOW TO ATTAIN LONGEVITY by Gladys Iris Clark. Chapter include: Ageless Symbology, Followers of Fallen Luminaries, Rejuvenation Practices, Youth in Age-Old Wisdom, Angelic Travel Guides, Longevity Begins with God Awareness, Coping with Realities, Non-Aging Techniques in Action, Musing on Transition, Cancel Out Negatives, Grecian Nostalgia, Sedona's Seven Vortices, Crystals, Etc.

MEDITATION

CONCENTRATION AND MEDITATION by Christmas Humphreys. The Importance of Right Motive, Power of Thought, Dangers and Safeguards, Particular Exercises, Time, Place, Posture, Relaxation, Breathing, Thoughts, Counting the Breaths, Visualization and Color, Stillness, Motive, Self Analogy, Higher Meditation, The Voice of Mysticism, Jhanas, Zen, Satori, Koan, Ceremonial Magic, Taoism, Occultism, Mysticism, Theosophy, Yoga, The Noble Eightfold Path, Etc.

MYTHOLOGY

A DICTIONARY OF NON-CLASSICAL MYTHOLOGY by Marian Edwardes & Lewis Spence. An exceptional work! "Not one mythology, but several, will be found concentrated within the pages of this volume..." Covers everything from Aah (Ah): An Egyptian moon-god, thru Brigit: A goddess of the Irish Celts, Excalibur: King Arthur's Sword, Hou Chi: A Chinese divine personage, ... Huitzilopochtli of the Aztecs ... Mama Cocha of Peru ... Uttu: The Sumerian ... Valkyrie (Old German): Female warriors ... Byelun: A white Russian deity, ... Meke Meke: The god-creator of Easter Island, Mwari: The Great Spirit of the Mtawara tribe of Rhodesia, Triglav (Three heads): Baltic Slav deity... and hundreds more!

NEW THOUGHT

THE GIFT OF THE SPIRIT A Selection From the Essays of Prentice Mulford With Preface and Introduction by Arthur Edward Waite. The Infinite Mind in Nature, The God in Yourself, The Doctor Within & Mental Medicine, Faith or Being Led by the Spirit, The Material Mind vs. The Spiritual Mind, What are Spintual Gifts?, Regeneration or Being Born Again, Re-Embodiment Universal in Nature, You Travel When You Sleep, Prayer In All Ages, Etc!

THE HEART OF THE NEW THOUGHT by Ella Wheeler Wilcox. Let the Past Go, The Sowing of the Seed, Thought Force, Opulence and Eternity, Morning Influences, The Philosophy of Happiness, Common Sense, Heredity and Invincibility, The Object of Life, Wisdom and Self Conquest, Concentration and Destiny, The Breath, Generosity and Balance, Etc!

THE HIDDEN POWER AND OTHER PAPERS UPON MENTAL SCIENCE by Thomas Troward. The Hidden Power, The Perversion of Truth, The "I Am", Affirmative Power, The Principle of Guidance, Desire as the Motive Power, Touching Lightly, The Spirit of Opulence, Beauty, Seperation and Unity, Entering into the Spirit of It, The Bible and New Thought, What is Higher Thought?, Etc!

THE LAW OF THE NEW THOUGHT by Willam Walker Atkinson. What is the New Thought?, Thoughts are Things, The Law of Attraction, Mind Building, The Dweller of the Threshold, Mind and Body, The Mind and its Planes, The Subconsious Plane, The Super-Conscious Faculties, The Soul's Question, The Absolute, The Oneness of All, The Immortality of the Soul, The Unfoldment, The Growth of Consciouness, The Soul's Awakening.

THOUGHT FORCES by Prentice Mulford. Chapters include: Co-operation of Thought, Some Practical Mental Recipes, The Drawing Power of Mind, Buried Talents, The Necessity of Riches, The Uses of Sickness, The Doctor Within, Mental Medicine, The Use and Necessity of Recreation, The Art of Forgetting, Cultivate Repose, Love Thyself.

THOUGHTS ARE THINGS by Prentice Mulford. The Material Mind vs. The Spiritual Mind, Who Are Our Relations?, Thought Currents, One Way to Cultivate Courage, Look Forward, God in the Trees, Some Laws of Health and Beauty, Museum and Menagerie Horrors, The God in Yourself, Healing and Renewing Force of Spring, Immorality in the Flesh, Attraction of Aspiration, The Accession of New Thought.

NUMEROLOGY

NAMES, DATES, AND NUMBERS – A SYSTEM OF NUMEROLOGY by Roy Page Walton. The Law of Numbers, The Character and influence of the Numbers, Application and Use of Numbers, Strong and Weak Names. The Number that Governs the Life, How Each Single Name Effects the Life, The Importance of Varying the Signature, How the Name Discloses the Future, Choosing a Suitable Name for a Child, Names Suitable for Marriage, How to Find Lucky Days and Months, Points to Bear in Mind.

NUMBERS: THEIR OCCULT POWER AND MYSTIC VIRTUE by W. Wynn Wescott. Pythagoras, His Tenets and His Followers, Pythagorean Views of Numbers, Kabalistic View on Numbers, Properties of the Numbers according to the Bible, the Talmuds, the Pythagoreans, the Romans, Chaldeans, Egyptians, Hindoos, Medieval Magicians, Hermetic Students, and the Rosicurcians.

NUMBER VIBRATION IN QUESTIONS AND ANSWERS by Mrs. L. Dow Balliett. Selections include: When Was Your First Birth?, The First Step in Reading a Name, Can the Name be Changed?, What Does the Birth Path Show?, The Numerical and Number Chart, Is an Esoteric Value to be Found in Gems?, Why Do We Not Add Either 22 or 11?, The Day of Reincarnation, Is Anybody Out of Place?, Are We Gods?, Of What Use is Prayer?, What Is the Soul?, Should Rooms be Furnished in our Own Colors?, What Months Are Best for Creation?, What Is Astral Music?, Where Should We Live?, Etc. Etc. Etc!

NUMERAL PHILOSOPHY by Albert Christy. A Study of Numeral Influences upon the Physical, Mental, and Spiritual Nature of Mankind.

VIBRATION: A SYSTEM OF NUMBERS AS TAUGHT BY PYTHARGORAS by Mrs. L. Dow Balliett. Chapters include: The Principles of Vibration, Numbers in Detail, What Your Name Means (broadly speaking), Business, Choosing A Husband or Wife, Pythagoras' Laws, Your Colors, Body Parts, Gems, Minerals, Flowers, Birds, Odors, Music, Guardian Angel, Symbols, Etc.

ORIENTAL (Also see "YOGA")

THE BUDDHA'S GOLDEN PATH by Dwight Goddard. Prince Siddhartha Gautama, Right Ideas, Speech, Behaviour, Right Vocation, Words, Conduct, Mindfulness, Concentration, Resolution, Environment, Intuition, Vows, Radiation, Spiritual Behaviour, Spirit, Etc.

BUSHIDO: WAY OF THE SAMURAI Translated from the classic Hagakure by Minoru Tanaka. This unique translation of a most important Japanese classic offers an explanation of the central and upright character of the Japanese people, and their indomitable inner strength. "The Way of the Samurai" is essential for businessmen, lawyers, students, or anyone who would understand the Japanese psyche.

DAO DE JING (LAO-ZI): THE OLD SAGE'S CLASSIC OF THE WAY OF VIRTUE translated by Patrick Michael Byrne. A new translation, faithful to both the letter and the poetic spirit of the original, of the ancient Chinese book of wisdom (traditionally known as the *Tao Te Ching* of Lao Tse or Lao Tsu: this version employs the new, more accurate *pinyin* transliteration). With introduction, notes and commentary.

FUSANG or THE DISCOVERY OF AMERICA BY CHINESE BUDDHIST PRIESTS IN THE FIFTH CENTURY by Charles G. Leland. Chinese Knowledge of Lands and Nations, The Road to America, The Kingdom of Fusang or Mexico, Of Writing and Civil Regulations in Fusang, Laws and Customs of the Aztecs, The Future of Eastern Asia, Travels of Other Buddhist Priests, Affinities of American and Asiatic Languages, Images of Buddha, Etc.

THE HISTORY OF BUDDHIST THOUGHT by Edward J. Thomas. The Ascetic Ideal, Early Doctrine: Yoga, Brahminism and the Upanishads, Karma, Release and Nirvana, Buddha, Popular Bodhisattva Doctrine, Buddhism and Modern Thought, Etc.

THE IMITATION OF BUDDHA - QUOTATIONS FROM BUDDHIST LITERATURE FOR EACH DAY OF THE YEAR Compiled by Ernest M. Bowden with preface by Sir Edwin Arnold. These 366 wonderful quotes are taken from a broad base of Buddhist Literature including many now hard-to-find texts.

SACRED BOOKS OF THE EAST by Epiphanius Wilson. Vedic Hymns, The Zend-Avesta, The Dhammapada, The Upanishads, Selections from the Koran, Life of Buddha, Etc.

THE WISDOM OF THE HINDUS by Brian Brown. Brahmanic Wisdom, Maha-Bharata, The Ramayana, Wisdom of the Upanishads, Vivekananda and Ramakrishna on Yoga Philosophy, Wisdom of Tuka-Ram, Paramananda, Vivekananda, Abbedananda, Etc.

PALMISTRY

INDIAN PALMISTRY by Mrs. J.B. Dale. A Summary of Judgement, Signification of Animals, Flowers, and Promiscuous Marks Found on the Hand, The Lines, The Mounts, The Line of Life, The Events, The Line of the Head and Brain, The Line of Fortune, Saturn, Venus and Mars, The Rule to Tell The Planets, The Mount of Jupiter, Apollo the Sun, The Moon, The Mount of Saturn , The Planet Mercury, Mensa: The Part of Fortune, The Fingers and Thumb, The Head and Signs of the Feet, The Arms, Etc.

PHILOSOPHY

GOETHE – WITH SPECIAL CONSIDERATION OF HIS PHILOSOPHY by Paul Carus. The Life of Goethe, His Relation to Women, Goethe's Personality, The Religion of Goethe, Goethe's Philosophy, Literature and Criticism, The Significance of "Faust", Miscellaneous Epigrams and Poems. (Heavily Illustrated).

PROPHECY (Also See Earth Changes)

THE STORY OF PROPHECY by Henry James Forman. What is Prophecy?, Oracles, The Great Pyramid Speaks, The End of the Age: Biblical Prophecy, Medieval Prophecy, Astrologers and Saints, Prophecies Concerning the Popes, Nostradamus, America In Prophecy, The Prophetic Future.

PYRAMIDOLOGY

THE GREAT PYRAMID. Two Essays plus illustrations, one from The Reminder and the other from J.F. Rowney Press. Selections include: The Pyramid's Location and Constructional Features, Some of the Pyramid's Scientific Features, other Features of the Great Pyramid, Complete History of Mankind Represented in the Pyramid, The Shortening of Time, The Symbolism of the Passages and Chambers, Etc.

THE GREAT PYRAMID - Its Construction, Symbolism, and Chronology by Basil Stewart. Construction and Astrological Features, Chart of World History, Missing Apexstone, Who Built It? Plus Various Diagrams.

REINCARNATION

LIFE AFTER LIFE: THE THEORY OF REINCARNATION by Eustace Miles. Have We Lived Before? Questions Often Asked, Does Not Oppose Christianity, Great Men Who Have Believed, etc.

THE NEW REVELATION by Sir Arthur Conan Doyle. The Search, The Revelation, The Coming Life, Problems and Limitations, The Next Phase of Life, Automatic Writing, The Cheriton Dugout.

REINCARNATION by George B. Brownell. He Knew Who He Was, Memories of Past Lives, A Remarkable Proof, Lived Many Lives, An Arabian Incarnation, Dreamed of Past Life, Great Minds and Reincarnation, The Bible and Reincarnation, Karma, Atlantis Reborn, Thought is Destiny, The Celestial Body, The Hereafter, Etc.

REINCARNATION by F. Homer Curtiss, M.D. The Doctrine, Why and How, In the New Testament, Objections Answered, Scientific Evidence and Physical Proof.

REINCARNATION by Katherine Tingley. What Reincarnation Is, Arguments for Reincarnation, Supposed Objections to Reincarnation, Reincarnation and Heredity, Reincarnation in Antiquity, Reincarnation the Master-Key to Modern Problems, Reincarnation In Modern Literature.

THE RING OF RETURN by Eva Martin. Pre-Christian Era, Early Christian and Other Writings of the First Five Centuries A.D., Miscellaneous Sources Before A.D. 1700, A.D. 1700-1900, The Twentieth Century. In this book, Miss Eva Martin has brought together a most complete and scholarly collection of references to past, present, and future life.

RELIGIONS

THE BIBLE IN INDIA - Hindoo Origin of Hebrew and Christian Revelation Translated from "La Bible Dans L'Inde" by Louis Jacolliot. India's Relation to Antiquity, Manou, Manes, Minos, Moses, What the Lessons of History are Worth, Brahminical Perversions of Primitive Vedism, Virgins of the Pagodas and Rome, Moses or Moise and Hebrew Society, Zeus - Jezeus - Isis - Jesus, Moses Founds Hebrew Society on the Model of Egypt and India, The Hindoo Genesis, Zeus and Brahma, Devas and Angels, The HindooTrinity, Adima (In Sanscrit, The First Man), Ceylon as the Garden of Paradise, The Woman of the Vedas and The Woman of the Bible, The Deluge According to the Maha-Barata, Prophecies Announcing the Coming of Christna, Birth of the Virgin Devanaguy, Massacre of all Male Children Born on the Same Night as Christna, Christna Begins to Preach the New Law, His Disciples, Parable of the Fisherman, Christna's Philosophic Teaching, Transfiguration of Christna, His Disiples Give Him The Name of Jezeus (Pure Essence), Christna and the Two Holy Women, Death of Christna, Hindoo Origin of the Christian Idea, Devanaguy and Mary, Christna and Christ, Massacre of the Innocents in India and Judea, Hindoo and Christian Transfiguration, Apocrypha of St. John, Whence the Monks and Hermits of Primitive Christianity, A Text of Manou, Etc!

NATURAL LAW IN THE SPIRITUAL WORLD by Henry Drummond. Biogenesis, Degeneration, Growth, Death, Mortification, Eternal Life, Environment, Conformity to Type, Semi-Parasitism, Parasitism, Classification.

PRINCIPAL SYMBOLS OF WORLD RELIGIONS by Swami Harshananda. Chapters include discussions of the symbols of these religions: Hinduism, Buddhism, Jainism, Sikhism, Shintoism, Islam, Christianity, Judaism, Zoroastrianism, Taoism.

THE RELIGION OF THE SIKH GURUS by Teja Singh, M.A., Teja Singh, formerly a professor of history at Khalsa College in Amritsar, outlines the foundation of history, tradition, ritual and principles which has kept disciples of the the Sikh religion strong and united into the present day.

SELF-HELP / RECOVERY (See under "Inspiration, etc.")

SOUL

THE HUMAN SOUL IN SLEEPING, DREAMING AND WAKING by F.W. Zeylmans van Emmichoven, M.D. Featured subjects include: What is the Soul?, How, by observing the phenomena of life, we can find the reality of the soul and its connections with the human organism. Man as a threefold being. Dreams. Psycho-Analysis. The awakening of the soul. Fears. Meditation, Concentration and Self Development. The counterforces that work against man's spiritual striving. Spiritual Science as a psychology of the living, developing soul, Etc.

THE INNER MAN by Hanna Hurnard. A Parable, The Inner Man, Communication with the Heavenly World, The Soul of the Inner Man, The Garments of the Soul, Soul Disease and Soul Healing, The Soul's Psychic Powers, The Mystic Way.

TAROT

THE ILLUSTRATED KEY TO THE TAROT – THE VEIL OF DIVINATION by Arthur Edward Waite. The Veil and Its Symbols, The Tarot in History, The Doctrine Behind the Veil, The Outer Method of the Oracles, The Four Suits of Tarot Cards, The Art of Tarot Divination, An Ancient Celtic Method of Divination.

THE KEY OF DESTINY by H.A. and F.H. Curtiss. The Initiate, Twelve-fold Division of the Zodiac, Reincarnation and Transmutation, The Solar System, The Letters of the Tarot, The Numbers 11 thru 22, Twelve Tribes and Twelve Disciples, The Great Work, The Labors of Hercules, Necromancy, Great Deep, Temperance, Man the Creator vs. the Devil, Celestial Hierarchies, The New Jerusalem, Etc.

THE KEY TO THE UNIVERSE by H.A. and F.H. Curtiss. Origin of the Numerical Systems, Symbols of the "O" as the Egg and the Cat, The "O" as the Aura and the Ring Pass Not, Symbol of the O, Letters of the Tarot, The Numbers 1 thru 10, The 7 Principles of Man, The 7 Pleiades and the 7 Rishis, Joy of Completion.

WESTERN MYSTICISM

ANCIENT MYSTERY AND MODERN REVELATION by W.J. Colville. Rivers of Life or Faiths of Man in All Lands, Ancient and Modern Ideas of Revelation - Its Sources and Agencies, Creation Legends - How Ancient is Humanity On this Planet? Egypt and Its Wonders: Literally and Mystically Considered, The Philosophy of Ancient Greece, The School of Pythagoras, The Delphic Mysteries, Apollonius of Tyana, Five Varieties of Yoga, Union of Eastern and Western Philosophy, Ezekiel's Wheel - What it Signifies, The Book of Exodus - Its Practical and Esoteric Teachings, The Message of Buddhism - Purity and Philanthropy, Magic in Europe in the Middle Ages, Ancient Magic and Modern Therapeutics, Bible Symbolism, The Law of Seven and the Law of Unity, The Esoteric Teachings of the Gnostics.

BROTHERHOOD OF MT. SHASTA by Eugene E. Thomas. From Clouds to Sunshine, Finding the Brotherhood, The Lake of Gold, The Initiation, Memories of the Past, In Advance of the Future, Prodigy, Trial, and Visitor, The Annihilation and the King, The Lost Lemuria.

CLOTHED WITH THE SUN - BEING THE BOOK OF THE ILLUMINATIONS OF ANNA (BONUS) KINGSFORD Edited by Edward Maitland and Samuel Hopgood Hart. Concerning the three Veils between Man and God, The Powers of the Air, The Devil and Devils, The Gods, Psyche; or the Human Soul, Dying, The Mysteries of God, The Divine Image; or the Vision of Adonai, Etc.

INNER RADIANCE by H.A. & F.A. Curtiss. The Inner Radiance, Spiritual Co-operation, Man and the Zodiac, The Soul-Language, Transmigration, Cosmic Cause of World Conditions, Planetary and Karmic Factors, The Mystic Rose, The Lords of Karma, The Great Works, The Mystery of the Elements, The Third Eye, The Round Table, The Ancient Continents, Nature's Symbology.

KALEVALA: THE LAND OF THE HEROES Translated by W. F. Kirby. The National Epic of Finland. "...the Kalevala itself could one day becomes as important for all of humanity as Homer was for the Greeks."

THE FOUR GREAT INITIATIONS, by Ellen Conroy M.A. Foreward by Leon Dabo, Initiation by Water, The Mystical Understanding of Baptism, Temptation, The Power of the Spirit, Initiation by Air, The Mystical Understanding of the Plucking of Corn on the Sabbath Day, The Sermon on the Mount, Initiation by Fire, The Transfiguration, Initiation by Earth, The Crucifiction and Ascension.

MYRIAM AND THE MYSTIC BROTHERHOOD by Maude Lesseuer Howard. A novel in the western mystic tradition.

THE WAY OF ATTAINMENT by Sydney T. Klein. The Invisible is the Real, The Power of Prayer, Spiritual Regeneration, Dogma of the Virgin Birth, Finding the Kingdom of Heaven "Within", Realizing Oneness with God, Nature of the Ascent, Reaching the Summit.

THE WAY OF MYSTICISM by Joseph James. God Turns Towards Man, The Unexpected, The Still Small Voice, His Exceeding Brightness, Man Turns Towards God, The Obstructive "Me", Where East and West Unite, Beside the Still Waters, Love's Meeting Place, Work – A Prayer, Every Pilgrim's Progress, Love's Fulfillment.

TABLOID MAGAZINE The Astral Projection. Metaphysical Tabloid Magazine from the early 1970's. Last three issues available.

YOGA (also see ORIENTAL)

YOGA PHILOSOPHY AND PRACTICE by Hari Prasad Shastri. The History and Literature of Yoga, The Epics and Bhagavad Gita, Patanjali, Shankaracharya, The Philosophy of Yoga, The Vedanta, Reason and Intuition, The Teacher (Guru), Advita (Non-Dualism), God and the World, God (Brahman) and the Individual (Jiva), The Nature of the Self, The Personal God (Ishvara), Three Views of Maya, The Three Gunas, Ethics, Action (Karma), Death and Reincarnation, Liberation, The Practice of Yoga, Subjects for Meditation, Peace of Mind, The True Self, Dream and Sleep, Vital Currents of the Body, OM, Practice in Daily Life, Austerity, Posture, Pranayama (Control of the Vital Currents), Concentration, Contemplation (Dhyana), Samadhi, Liberation in Life, Practical Program, Obstructions, Common Sense in Training, The Process in Brief, Three Yogis, Rama Tirtha, Shri Dada, Kobo Daishi, Illustrative Passages from the Literature of Yoga, Prayers from the Vedas, The Upanishads, The Bhagavad Gita, Yoga Vasishtha, The Ashtavakra Gita, Poem by Swami Rama Tirtha, Glossary, Etc!

GENERAL NON-METAPHYSICAL

BEST ENGRAVINGS by Skip Whitson. One hundred twenty three beautiful steel cut and wood cut engravings from the nineteenth century.

BUSTED IN MEXICO by Ann Palmer and Jessica Herman. One young woman's story of the devastating effects of the loss of liberty. A True Story, Introduction by Governor Jerry Apodaca.

THE LAND OF ENCHANTMENT FROM PIKE'S PEAK TO THE PACIFIC by Lilian Whiting. Chapters include: With Western Stars and Sunsets, Denver the Beautiful, The Picturesque Region of Pike's Peak, Summer Wanderings in Colorado, The Colorado Pioneers, The Surprises of New Mexico, The Story of Santa Fe, Magic and Mystery of Arizona, The Petrified Forest and the Meteorite Mountain, Los Angeles, The Spell-Binder, Grand Canyon, the Carnival of the Gods.

SUN HISTORICAL SERIES 33 titles ranging from Maine 100 years ago to Hawaii 100 years ago.

MAYDAYS AND MERMAIDS by William A. Davis. A contemporary tale of the sea. Vivid fast moving satirical yarn, spun on the paradoxical spool of tragicomedy. "Once you start this book there is a high probability that you will not put it down." - Clark Chambers, Critic.

For a PRICE LIST of all currently available Sun Books titles write: Book List, Sun Publishing Co., P.O. Box 5588, Santa Fe, NM 87502-5588

SUNSUP91.PM4